Hearsay Evidence In Criminal Proceedings

Under The Criminal Justice Act 2003

Michael Stockdale, *PhD, LL.B*

Senior Lecturer, Northumbria University

ITG, CRM

sto

std

Published in 2004 by Northumbria Law Press,

Sutherland Building, University of Northumbria at Newcastle,

Newcastle Upon Tyne, NE1 8ST

Published in 2004 by Northumbria Law Press, School of Law, Sutherland Building, Northumbria University, Newcastle upon Tyne NE1 8ST.

© Northumbria University, 2004

ISBN 187 329 8 79X

Some of the material in this book previously appeared in the fourth edition of the annual Northumbria Law Press release "Criminal and Civil Evidence".

Designed and produced by External Relations, Northumbria University

Contents

Preface   13

Table of Cases   17

Table of Statutes   31

Part One The Nature of a Hearsay Statement Under the 2003 Act   43

1.1   **Introduction to Part One**   43

1.2   **The nature of the hearsay rule**   43

1.2.1   *The position at common law*   43

1.2.2   *The position under the Criminal Justice Act 2003*   45

1.3   **Statements made orally, in documents or by conduct**   47

1.3.1   *The position at common law*   47

1.3.2   *The position under the Criminal Justice Act 2003*   47

1.4   **Statements made during other legal proceedings**   48

1.4.1   *The position at common law*   48

1.4.2   *The position under the Criminal Justice Act 2003*   48

1.5   **The purpose for which the statement is tendered**   49

1.5.1   *The position at common law*   49

1.5.2   *The position under the Criminal Justice Act 2003*   50

1.6   **Assertions implied from statements which were not intended to communicate them (implied assertions)**   51

1.6.1   *The position at common law*   51

1.6.2   *The position under the Criminal Justice Act 2003*   53

1.6.2.1   *The significance of section 115(3)(a) and the burden of proving that hearsay evidence is admissible*   55

1.6.2.2   *The significance of section 115(3)(b)*   59

1.6.2.3   *The purpose of the person making the statement*   62

1.6.2.4   *Implied statements in Criminal and Civil Proceedings*   64

1.7	**Implied assertions as real or circumstantial evidence of identification**	65
1.7.1	*The position at common law*	65
1.7.2	*The position under the Criminal Justice Act 2003*	67
1.8	**Records relied upon to prove that events not recorded did not take place**	68
1.8.1	*The position at common law*	68
1.8.2	*The position under the Criminal Justice Act 2003*	70
1.9	**Evidence produced by machines**	72
1.9.1	*The position at common law*	74
1.9.2	*The position under the Criminal Justice Act 2003*	74
1.9.2.1	*Representations of fact made by machines which do not depend for their accuracy on information supplied by a person.*	75
1.9.2.2	*Representations of fact made by machines which do depend for their accuracy on information supplied by a person.*	76
1.9.3	*The presumption preserved by section 129(2)*	78
1.9.4	*Evidence produced by machines in Civil Proceedings*	80
1.10	**Photographs, films, video recordings and tape recordings**	80
1.10.1	*The position at common law*	80
1.10.2	*The position under the Criminal Justice Act 2003*	82
1.11	**Photofits, sketches and E-fits**	83
1.11.1	*The position at common law*	83
1.11.2	*The position under the Criminal Justice Act 2003*	85

Part Two

	The Admissibility of Hearsay Evidence in Criminal Proceedings	87
2.1	**Introduction to Part Two**	87

2.2	**Statutory exceptions to the hearsay rule created by the 2003 Act (other than the exception created by section 114(1)(d))**	89
2.2.1	*Witnesses who are unavailable*	90
2.2.1.1	*Section 116 of the 2003 Act and section 23 of the 1988 Act distinguished*	91
2.2.1.2	*The operation of section 116*	96
2.2.1.2.1	Section 116(1)(a)	97
2.2.1.2.2	Section 116(1)(b)	98
2.2.1.2.3	Section 116(1)(c)	99
2.2.1.2.4	Section 116(2)(a)	100
2.2.1.2.5	Section 116(2)(b)	100
2.2.1.2.6	Section 116(2)(c)	100
2.2.1.2.7	Section 116(2)(d)	101
2.2.1.2.8	Section 116(2)(e)	102
2.2.1.2.9	Section 116(5)	110
2.2.2	*Documents created or received by persons in the course of their trades, businesses, professions or other occupations or as office holders*	113
2.2.2.1	*Section 117 of the 2003 Act and section 24 of the 1988 Act distinguished*	114
2.2.2.2	*The operation of section 117*	118
2.2.2.2.1	The nature of a "document"	119
2.2.2.2.2	Section 117(1)(a)	119
2.2.2.2.3	Section 117(1)(b) and section 117(2)	120
2.2.2.2.4	Section 117(4)-(5)	123
2.2.2.2.5	Section 117(6)-(7)	124

2.2.3	*Previous inconsistent statements*	127
2.2.3.1	*The admissibility of evidence of previous inconsistent statements*	127
2.2.3.1.1	Previous inconsistent statements made by hostile witnesses	128
2.2.3.1.2	Previous inconsistent statements made by witnesses called by other parties	130
2.2.3.1.3	Previous inconsistent statements made by the makers of hearsay statements	132
2.2.3.2	*The effect of section 119*	132
2.2.4	*Previous consistent statements*	137
2.2.4.1	*The rule against previous consistent statements*	137
2.2.4.2	*The rule's common law exceptions*	138
2.2.4.2.1	Rebuttal of suggestions of recent fabrication made during cross-examination	139
2.2.4.2.2	Identification evidence	140
2.2.4.2.3	Exculpatory statements made to the police	140
2.2.4.2.4	Voluntary sexual offence complaints made at the first reasonable opportunity	141
2.2.4.2.5	Statements which form part of the res gestae	142
2.2.4.2.6	Statements made by persons found in possession of recently stolen goods or other incriminating articles.	143
2.2.4.3	*The effects of section 120*	143
2.2.4.3.1	Suggestions of recent fabrication	147
2.2.4.3.2	Identification evidence	148
2.2.4.3.3	Recent complaints	150
2.2.5	*Documents used for memory refreshing*	153
2.2.5.1	*Memory refreshing at common law*	153

2.2.5.2	*Memory refreshing under the 2003 Act*	155
2.2.5.2.1	Section 139	156
2.2.5.2.2	Section 120(3)	160
2.2.6	**Previous statements made by witnesses who cannot** *reasonably be expected to remember the matters to which they relate well enough to give oral evidence thereof*	163
2.2.7	**Confessions as evidence for co-defendants**	169
2.2.7.1	*The position prior to the 2003 Act*	169
2.2.7.2	*The position under the 2003 Act*	171
2.2.8	**Statements upon which expert evidence is based**	175
2.2.8.1	*The position prior to the 2003 Act*	176
2.2.8.2	*The position under the 2003 Act*	177
2.2.9	**Witnesses' video recorded contemporaneous** *accounts of events witnessed thereby*	182
2.3	**Common law exceptions to the hearsay rule which will be preserved by the 2003 Act**	187
2.3.1	*Other provisions of the 2003 Act which apply to preserved common law hearsay exceptions*	188
2.3.2	*The common law exceptions which the Act will preserve*	189
2.3.2.1	*Published works dealing with matters of a public nature*	191
2.3.2.2	*Public documents*	192
2.3.2.3	*Records*	193
2.3.2.4	*Age, date or place of birth*	193
2.3.2.5	*Reputation as evidence of good or bad characte*	194
2.3.2.6	*Reputation or family tradition as evidence of pedigree etc*	195

2.3.2.7	*Statements which form part of the res gestae*	197
2.3.2.7.1	Statements made by persons emotionally overpowered by events	199
2.3.2.7.2	Statements accompanying acts	201
2.3.2.7.3	Statements relating to physical sensations or to mental states	202
2.3.2.8	*Confessions and mixed statements*	205
2.3.2.9	*Admissions made by agents*	206
2.3.2.10	*Statements made by parties to a common Enterprise*	207
2.3.2.11	*Expert witnesses and the body of expertise relevant to their field*	209
2.4	**Statutory exceptions to the hearsay rule created by statutory provisions other than the 2003 Act**	211
2.4.1	*Pre-existing statutory exceptions to the hearsay rule which the 2003 Act will repeal, replace or modify*	211
2.4.1.1	*Magistrates' Courts Act 1980, sections 5A to 5F*	212
2.4.1.2	*Criminal Procedure and Investigations Act 1996, section 68 and Schedule 2*	212
2.4.1.3	*Crime and Disorder Act 1998, paragraph 5(4) of Schedule 3*	213
2.4.1.4	*Criminal Appeal Act 1968, paragraphs 1 and 1A of Schedule 2.*	213
2.4.2	*Major examples of pre-existing statutory exceptions to the hearsay rule which the 2003 Act will retain*	214
2.4.2.1	*Statements admitted upon service of notice or by agreement under section 9 of the Criminal Justice Act 1967*	214
2.4.2.2	*Expert reports admitted under section 30 of the Criminal Justice Act 1988.*	216

2.4.2.3   *Depositions of child victims admitted under section*   217
                 43 of the Children and Young Persons Act 1933

2.4.2.4   *Copies of entries in bankers' books admitted under*   217
                 section 3 of the Bankers' Books Evidence Act 1879

2.4.2.5   *Statutory declarations admitted under section*   218
                 27(4) of the Theft Act 1968.

2.4.2.6   *Video recorded evidence in chief, cross-examination*   219
                 and re-examination admissible under Part II of
                 Youth Justice and Criminal Evidence Act 1999.

2.4.2.7   *Confessions*   219

2.4.2.7.1   The nature of a confession   220

2.4.2.7.2   The admissibility of a confession   221
                 as evidence for the prosecution

2.4.2.7.3   Oppression   223

2.4.2.7.4   Unreliability   224

2.4.2.7.5   The discretionary exclusion of confessions   227
                 tendered by the prosecution

2.4.2.7.6   The admissibility of a confession   230
                 as evidence for a co-defendant

2.4.2.7.7   Confessions made by persons whose   230
                 knowledge is derived from a hearsay source

2.4.2.7.8   Confessions and evidence of opinion   231

2.4.2.7.9   Confessions made by third parties   231

2.4.2.7.10   Confessions which implicate co-defendants   233

2.4.2.7.11   Mixed statements   234

2.4.2.7.12   The voir dire   235

2.4.2.7.13   Facts discovered in consequence of the   236
                 making of an excluded confession

2.4.2.7.14   Excluded confessions and evidence of the   238
                 accused's mode of speech, writing or expression

2.4.2.7.15	Confessions made by mentally handicapped persons and section 77 of the Police and Criminal Evidence Act 1984	238
2.4.2.7.16	The exclusion of confessions and the European Convention on Human Rights.	240
2.4.2.7.17	Admissions made by agents	241
2.5	**The admissibility of hearsay evidence by agreement of the parties**	241
2.6	**The admissibility of hearsay evidence under section 114(1)(d) of the 2003 Act**	243
2.7	**Other provisions contained in Chapter 2 of Part 11 of the 2003 Act**	248
2.7.1	*Multiple hearsay*	249
2.7.1.1	*Section 121(1)(a)*	252
2.7.1.2	*Section 121(1)(b)*	254
2.7.1.3	*Section 121(1)(c)*	254
2.7.1.4	*The "safety valve" inclusionary discretion and multiple hearsay*	256
2.7.1.5	*Statements which do not fall within the ambit of the hearsay rule and representations made by machines*	257
2.7.2	**Required capability of the maker of a statement and of those who supply or receive information or create or receive documents**	257
2.7.2.1	*Persons who cannot be identified*	259
2.7.2.2	*"Required Capability"*	259
2.7.2.3	*Section 123(4)*	259
2.7.2.4	*The ambit of section 123*	260
2.7.3	*Credibility of the maker of a hearsay statement and those who supply or receive information or create or receive documents*	261

2.7.3.1	*Statements admitted under section 117*	264
2.7.3.2	*Statements which do not fall within the ambit of the hearsay rule*	264
2.7.4	***Prosecution cases based on unconvincing Evidence***	265
2.7.4.1	*Statements which do not fall within the ambit of the hearsay rule*	269
2.7.4.2	*Representations made by machines*	270
2.7.5	***Exclusionary discretion***	270
2.7.5.1	*The new statutory exclusionary discretion*	271
2.7.5.2	*Pre-existing statutory and preserved common law exclusionary discretion*	274
2.7.6	***Proof of statements in documents***	276
2.7.6.1	*The admissibility of secondary evidence of the contents of documents at common law*	279
2.7.7	***Rules of Court***	280
2.7.7.1	*Failure to comply with prescribed requirements*	284
2.8	**The hearsay provisions of the Criminal Justice Act 2003 and the European Convention on Human Rights**	286
2.8.1	*The exclusion of defence hearsay evidence*	286
2.8.2	*The admission of hearsay evidence for the prosecution*	288
Appendix		293
	Text of those provisions of the Criminal Justice Act 2003 which are considered in this book.	
Index		321

PREFACE

As its title suggests, the purpose of this book is to examine those provisions of the Criminal Justice Act 2003 which concern the hearsay rule, the relevant provisions being contained in Chapter 2 of Part 11 of the 2003 Act. Thus, the book is not concerned with the "Evidence of Character" provisions contained in Chapter 1 of Part 11 of the 2003 Act. The "Miscellaneous and Supplemental" provisions contained in Part 3 of Chapter 11 do, however, fall within its ambit.

The Criminal Justice Act 2003 received the Royal Assent on November 20th 2003. The provisions contained in Chapters 2 and 3 of Part 11 did not come into force on the passing of the Act, and consequently were not in force at the time of writing, but, rather, provision to bring them into force is to be made by the Home Secretary by order.[1] At the time of writing, the intention, as ascertained from the Home Office, is that the Act's hearsay provisions will be brought into force during the 2005-2006 financial year. By the time of writing, however, section 132 (concerning the making of rules of court) had already been brought into force[2] and sections 139 to 141 (concerning memory refreshing) were due to come into force on 5th April 2004.[3]

The provisions contained in Chapters 2 and 3 of Part 11 of the 2003 Act will not have effect in relation to criminal proceedings begun before their commencement.[4] Moreover, in relation to the commencement of provisions of the 2003 Act, it should be noted that section 333(1)-(4) provide as follows.

(1) The Secretary of State may by order make–

    (a) any supplementary, incidental or consequential provision, and

    (b) any transitory, transitional or saving provision,

which he considers necessary or expedient for the purposes of, in consequence of, or for giving full effect to any provision of this Act.

(2) An order under subsection (1) may, in particular–

    (a) provide for any provision of this Act which comes into force before another such provision has come into force to have effect, until that other provision has come into force, with such modifications as are specified in the order, and

    (b)   amend or repeal–

    (i) any Act passed before, or in the same Session as, this Act, and

    (ii) subordinate legislation made before the passing of this Act.

(3)   Nothing in this section limits the power by virtue of section 330(4)(b) to include transitional or saving provision in an order under section 336."

(4)   The amendments that may be made under subsection (2)(b) are in addition to those made by or under any other provision of this Act."

No such provisions had been made at the time of writing.

Whilst this book only concerns a fraction of the provisions contained in the 2003 Act, many of the provisions which the book does concern are of fundamental significance in the context of English Criminal Evidence. The matters dealt with by the book's two Parts are as follows.

Part One of the book concerns the nature of a hearsay statement, contrasting the position at common law with the position as it will exist when Chapter 2 of Part 11 of the 2003 Act is in force. Particular consideration is given to the status within the new statutory hearsay regime of implied assertions, records which are relied upon to prove that events not recorded did not take place, evidence produced by machines, photographs, films, video recordings, tape recordings, photofits, sketches and e-fits.

Part Two of the book primarily concerns the nature of those exceptions to the hearsay rule which will exist when Chapter 2 of Part 11 of the 2003 Act is in force. Essentially, these will comprise a number of new hearsay exceptions which the 2003 Act creates, in particular a new inclusionary discretion to admit hearsay evidence in the interests of justice, and a variety of statutory and common law hearsay exceptions which the Act will, respectively, retain and preserve. The Act will also repeal a number of existing statutory exceptions to the hearsay rule (the main examples being sections 23 and 24 of the Criminal Justice Act 1988 (which are replaced by new provisions of the 2003 Act) and will abolish a number of common law exceptions to the hearsay rule (the best known example being the dying declaration). Further, the Act makes provision for the admission of previous inconsistent and consistent statements as evidence of the matters stated.

Part Two of the book also concerns a number of supplementary, miscellaneous and supplemental provisions contained in Chapters 2 and 3 of Part 11. These concern matters such as the admissibility of multiple hearsay, the use of exhibits, the competence and credibility of the maker of a hearsay statement, the power of the court to stop a case which is based on unconvincing evidence provided by a statement which was not made in oral evidence in the proceedings, the court's exclusionary discretion, the admissibility of expert opinion evidence, the admissibility of a confession in evidence for a co-defendant, the making of rules of court, the proof of statements in documents, the admissibility of video recorded evidence and the use of memory refreshing documents. Finally, the extent to which the admission or exclusion or hearsay evidence under the new statutory regime has the potential to produce violations of Article 6 of the European Convention on Human Rights is considered.

hroughout both Parts of the book, the author attempts to explain rule against hearsay and its major exceptions as they will exist when the provisions of Chapters 2 and 3 of Part 11 of the 2003 Act are in force. In particular, he attempts both to explain the nature and significance of the new provisions and, where they appear to exist, to identify ambiguities and potential problem areas concerning their practical application. Where rules of common law or pre-existing statutory provisions concerning the exclusion or admissibility of hearsay evidence in criminal proceedings are, respectively, preserved or retained by the 2003 Act, the relationship between the preserved or retained rules or provisions and the new provisions of the 2003 Act is fully considered. Moreover, where this is helpful in explaining the likely operation of the Act's provisions, reference is made to the Law Commission's "Evidence in Criminal Proceedings: Hearsay and Related Topics" (Law Com No.245), to the Explanatory Notes to the Criminal Justice Act, to Hansard, both Commons and Lords and to "Lord Justice Auld's Review of the Criminal Courts of England and Wales" (October 2001

Finally, the author would like to thank a number of people who have assisted in the production of this book. First, Carole and Bill Stockdale, for their continuing support throughout the period of its updating (and Carole Stockdale for proof reading). Secondly, the staff of the Legal Practice Library in Sutherland Building, Janet Hart, Margaret Howie, Catherine Probert and Ruth Downing, and Philip Judd from the University's main library, all of whom have, yet again, provided a service of excellent quality. Thirdly, Pam Beckley (of H.M.S.O.) and Heather Kelly (of Northumbria University) for their guidance in relation to copyright issues. Fourthly, Sheila Bone of Northumbria Law Press. Finally, the University Graphics Department of External Relations for their work in the production of this book.

Newcastle, March 24th 2004

---

1   *Section 336(3).*

2   *On 29th January 2004 (The Criminal Justice Act 2003 (Commencement No.2 and Saving Provisions) Order 2004).*

3   *The Criminal Justice Act 2003 (Commencement No.3 and Transitional Provisions) Order 2004.*

4   *Section 141.*

Table of Cases

Ajodha v The State [1982] AC 204 -   2.4.2.7.12

Allan v The United Kingdom The Times November 12 2002 -   2.4.2.7.16

Amys v Barton [1912] 1KB 40 -   2.3.2.7.3, 2.2.8.1

Asch v Austria (1993) 15 EHRR 597 -   2.8.2

Attorney-General v Horner (No. 2)[1913] 2 Ch 140 -   2.3.2.6

Attorney-General's Reference No 3 of -   2.2.5.1

1979 (1979) 69 Cr App R 41

Attorney General's Reference -   2.3.2.7.1, 2.8.2

(No 1 of 2003) [2003] 2 Cr App R 453

Austria v Italy ((1963) 6 YB 740 -   2.4.2.7.16

Averson v Lord Kinnaird (1805) 6 East 188 -   2.3.2.7.3

Bird v Adams [1972] Crim LR 224 -   2.4.2.7.8

Blastland v The United Kingdom App No 12045/86 -   2.8.1, 2.8.2

Brennan v The United Kingdom (2002) 34 EHRR 18 -   2.4.2.7.16

Brown v Secretary of State for Social Security The Times   2.2.2.1

7th December 1994 –

Brown v The State [2003] UKPC 10 -   2.3.2.7.1

Butler v Mountgarret (1859) 7 HL Cas 633 -   2.3.2.6

Burton v Plummer (1834) 2 A&E 341 -   2.2.5.1

C v C [2001[EWCA Civ 1625 -   2.7.2.3

Castle v Cross [1984] 1 WLR 1372 -   1.9.3

Chandrasekera v R [1937] AC 220 -   1.3.1, 1.6.2,
                                                                                          1.6.2.1

Chester-Nash v Crown Prosecution Service LTL 18/4/2000 -   1.9.1, 2.2.8.1

Comptroller of Customs v Western Lectric Co Ltd

[1966] AC 367 -   2.4.2.7.7

Cracknell v Willis [1988] 1 AC 450 -   1.9.3

Crease v Barrett (1835) 1 Cr M & R 919 -   2.3.2.6

D (A Minor) Re [1986] 2 FLR 189 -   2.2.1.1, 2.2.2.2.1

Daley v R [1994] 1 AC 117 -	2.7.4
Dillon v R [1982] AC 484 -	1.9.3
Doe d Banning v Griffin (1812) 15 East 293 -	2.3.2.6
English Exporters (London) Ltd v Eldonwall Ltd [1973] Ch 415 -	2.3.2.11
Fox v General Medical Council [1960] 1 WLR 1017 -	2.2.4.2.1
G v the United Kingdom (1983) 35 DR 75 -	2.4.2.7.16
Gilbey v Great Western Railway (1910) 102 LT 202 -	2.3.2.7.3
Greenough v Eccles (1859) 5CB NS 786 -	2.2.3.1.1
Haines v Guthrie (1884) 13 QBD 818 -	2.3.2.6
Halawa v Federation Against Copyright Theft [1995] 1 Cr App R 21-	2.4.2.7.12
Howe v Malkin (1878) 40 LT 196 -	2.3.2.7.2
Howglen Ltd, Re, [2001] 1 All ER 376 -	2.4.2.4
Huxley v Elvicta Wood Engineering Ltd LTL 19/4/2000	2.3.2.11
Imbrioscia v Switzerland 24 November 1993, Series A no.275 -	2.4.2.7.16
Jennion, Jencon v Wynne, Re [1952] CH 454 -	2.3.2.6
Johnson v Lawson (1824) 2 Bing 86 -	2.3.2.6
Jozwiak v Sadek [1954] 1 All ER 3 -	2.3.2.6
Kajala v Noble (1982) 75 Cr App R 149 -	1.10.1, 2.7.6.1
Khatibi v DPP [2004] EWHC 83 (Admin)	2.2.2.2.1, 2.2.2.2.3, 2.2.8.1
Koscot Interplanetary (UK) Ltd, Re [1972] 3 All ER 829 -	2.2.1.1
Kostovski v the Netherlands (1990) 12 EHRR 574 -	2.8.2
Lam Chi-ming v R [1991] 3 All ER 172 -	2.4.2.7.5
Li-Shi-Ling v R [1989] AC 270 -	1.10.1, 2.4.2.7.1
Lister v Quaife (1982) 75 Cr App R 313 -	2.4.2.1
Lloyd v Symonds LTL 20/3/98 -	1.10.1
Luca v Italy [2001] Crim LR 747 -	2.8.2
Lui Mei Lin v R [1989] AC 288 -	2.2.7.1
Magee v The United Kingdom (2001) 31 EHRR 35 -	2.4.2.7.16

Masquerade Music v Springsteen [2001] EMLR 654 - 2.7.6.1

Matto v Wolverhampton Crown Court [1987] RTR 337 - 2.7.5.2

Maugham v Hubbard (1828) 8 B&C 14 - 2.2.5.1

Mercer v Denne [1905] 2 Ch 538 - 2.3.2.6

Mitchell v R [1998] AC 695 - 2.4.2.7.12

Moseley v Davies (1822) 11 Price 162 - 2.3.2.6

Murdoch v Taylor [1965] AC 574 - 2.2.7.1

Neill v North Antrim Magistrates' Court [1992] 1 WLR 1221 - 2.2.1.2.3, 2.2.1.2.8, 2.3.2.7.3

G Newman (H.M. Inspector of Taxes) v FDL Hatt (2002) 04 EG 175 - 2.2.8.1

Nicholas v Penny [1950] 2 KB 466 - 1.9.1, 1.9.3

Nicholls v Parker (1805) 14 East 331n - 2.3.2.6

Nominal Defendant v Clements (1961) 104 CLR 476 - 2.2.4.2.1

Owen v Edwards (1983) 77 Cr App R 191 - 2.2.5.1, 2.2.5.2.2

Peacock v Harris (1836) 5 Ad & El 449 - 2.3.2.7.2

Post Office Counters Ltd v Tarla Mahida The Times October 31 2003 - 2.7.6.1

Prasad v R (1981) 72 Cr App R 218 - 2.4.2.7.12

Price v Manning (1889) 42 Ch D 372 - 2.2.3.1.1

Queen Caroline's Case (1820) 2 Br & B 287 - 2.2.3.1.2

R v Abadom [1983] 1 WLR 126 - 2.3.2.11

R v Acton JJ, exparte McMullen (1990) 92 Cr App R 98 - 1.6.2.1, 2.2.1.2, 2.2.1.2.9

R v Adams and Lawrence [2002] UKPC 14 - 2.4.2.7.12

R v Ali The Times November 21 2003- 2.2.4.1, 2.2.4.2.6

R v Alladice (1988) 87 Cr App R 380 - 2.4.2.7.5

R v Allen [2001] EWCA Crim 1607 - 2.2.3.2 2.4.2.7.2, 2.4.2.7.4, 2.4.2.7.5

R v Allen LTL 13/2/2001 - 2.4.2.7.10

R v Anderson (1929) 21 Cr App R 178 - 2.2.3.1.2

R v Andrews [1987] AC 281 - 1.5.1, 2.3.2.7.1, 2.7.2.4

R v Askew [1981] Crim LR 398 - 2.2.3.2

R v Aziz [1996] AC 41 - 2.4.2.7.1, 2.4.2.7.11

R v B [1997] Crim LR 220 - 2.2.4.2.4

R v Bailey [1995] 2 Cr App R 262 - 2.4.2.7.15

R v Barry (1992) 95 Cr App R 384 - 2.4.2.7.4

R v Bashir [1969] 1 WLR 1303 - 2.2.3.1.2

R v Batt & Batt [1995] Crim LR 240 - 2.2.1.2.8

R v Beales [1991] Crim LR 118 - 2.4.2.7.3

R v Beattie (1989) 89 Cr App R 302 - 2.2.3.1.2, 2.2.4.1, 2.2.4.2

R v Bedi (1992) Crim LR 299 - 2.2.2.1

R v Bellis (1911) 6 Cr App R 283 - 2.3.2.4

R v Belmarsh Magistrates' Court ex parte - 2.2.1.2.3
Gillingan [1998] 1 Cr App R 14

R v Black (1922) 16 Cr App R 118 - 2.3.2.7.3

R v Blackwell [1995] 2 Cr App R 625 - 2.4.2.7.5

R v Blastland [1986] AC 41 - 2.4.2.7.9

R v Bliss (1837) 7 A & E 550 - 2.3.2.6, 2.3.2.7.2, 2.3.2.7.3

R v Blok LTL 23/2/2000 - 2.2.1.2.8

R v Booth [1981] Crim LR 700 - 2.2.3.1.1

R v Bradshaw [1986] 82 Cr App R 79 - 2.2.8.1

R v Bray (1988) 88 Cr App R 354 - 2.2.1.2.6

R v Brophy [1982] AC 476 - 2.4.2.7.12

R v Bryant & Dickson (1946) 31 Cr App R 146 - 2.2.5.1

R v Buckley (1873) 13 Cox CC 293 - 2.3.2.7.3

R v Bullard (1992) 95 Cr App R 175 -   1.8.1

R v Burgess [1968] 2 QB 112 -   2.4.2.7.12

R v Callender [1998] Crim LR 337 -   2.3.2.7

R v Camelleri [1922] 2 KB 122 -   2.2.4.2.4

R v Canale (1990) 91 Cr App R 1 -   2.4.2.7.5

R v Carnall [1995] Crim LR 944 -   2.3.2.7.1

R v Carrington (1994) 99 Cr App R 376 -   2.2.2.2.4

R v Cash [1985] 1 QB 801 -   2.2.4.2.6

R v Castillo [1996] 1 Cr App R 438 -   2.2.1.2.6

R v Chatwood [1980] 1 All ER 467 -   2.4.2.7.8

R v Cheng (1976) 63 Cr App R 20 -   2.2.5.1

R v Chisnell [1992] Crim LR 507 -   2.2.5.1

R v Christie [1914] AC 545 -   2.2.4.3.2, 2.4.2.7.10

R v Christou [1992] 1 QB 979 -   2.2.4.2.2

R v Clarke [1995] Cr App R 425 -   1.10.1

R v Clowes [1992] 3 All ER 440 -   2.2.2.2.3

R v Cole [1990] 1 WLR 866 -   2.2.1.2.8, 2.2.2.2.5

R v Colwill [2002] EWCA Crim 1320 -   2.7.3

R v Cook [1987] 1 All ER 1049 -   1.11.1, 2.2.4.1

R v Corelli [2001] Crim LR 914 -   2.2.7.1

R v Coventry J J, ex parte Bullard (1992) 95 Cr App R 175 -   1.8.1, 1.9.1, 1.9.2.2

R v Crampton (1991) Cr App R 369 -   2.4.2.7.4

R v Croad [2001] EWCA Crim 644 -   2.2.4.2, 2.2.4.2.4

R v Cummings [1948] 1 All ER 551 -   2.2.4.2.4

R v D [2002] The Times May 21 2002 -   2.2.2.1, 2.7.2.4, 2.8.2

R v Darby [1989] Crim LR 817 -   2.2.3.1.1

R v Da Silva [1990] 1 WLR 31 -   2.2.5.1

R v Dat [1998] Crim LR 488 -	2.2.3.1.1
R v Delaney (1989) 89 Cr App R 338 -	2.4.2.7.4
R v Derby Magistrates' Court, ex parte B [1996] 1 AC 487 -	2.2.3.1.2
R v Derodra [1999] Crim LR 978 -	2.2.2.1, 2.2.2.2.2, 2.2.2.2.3,
	2.2.2.2.5
R v Devenport [1996] 1 Cr App R 221 -	2.3.2.10
R (Director of Public Prosecutions) v	1.4.2
Havering Magistrates' Court [2001] 2 All ER 997 -	
R v Donat (1985) 82 Cr App R 173 -	2.3.2.10
R v Downer (1880) 14 Cox CC 486 -	2.3.2.9
R v Dragic [1996] 2 Cr App R 232 -	2.2.1.2.8
R v Duffy [1999] QB 919 -	1.10.1, 2.2.1.1, 2.2.1.2.8,
	2.2.2.2.1,
	2.2.2.2.3
R v Edwards [2001] EWCA Crim 2185 -	2.2.8.1
R v Elleray [2003] 2 Cr App R 165 -	2.4.2.7.5
R v Elliott The Times May 15 2003 -	2.2.1.2.3
R v Everett [1988] Crim LR 826 -	2.4.2.7.4
R v Fairfax [1999] Crim LR 944 -	2.2.1.2.8
R v Fowkes The Times 8 March 1856 -	2.3.2.7.1
R v Foxley [1995] 2 Cr App R 523 -	2.2.2.2.3, 2.7.2.1
R v Fraser (1956) 40 Cr App R 160 -	2.2.3.1.1
R v French (1993) 97 Cr App R 421 -	2.2.1.2.6, 2.2.1.2.8
R v Fulling [1987] QB 426 -	2.4.2.7.3, 2.4.2.7.4
R v Funderburk [1990] 1 WLR 587 -	2.2.3.1.2
R v Galbraith [1981] 1 WLR 1039 -	2.7.4, 2.7.4.2
R v Gilfoyle [1996] 1 Cr App R 302 -	2.3.2.7.3

R v Gillard & Barrett (1991) 92 Cr App R 61 -   2.4.2.7.5

R v Gloster (1888) 16 Cox 471 -   2.3.2.7.3

R v Glover [1991] Crim LR 48 -   2.3.2.7.1

R v Gokal [1997] 2 Cr App R 266 -   2.2.1.2.8, 2.8.2

R v Goldenberg (1998) 88 Cr App R 285 -   2.4.2.7.4

R v Golder [1960] 1 WLR 1169 -   2.2.3.2

R v Golizadeh [1995] Crim LR 232 -   2.2.8.1

R v Gordon [2002] EWCA Crim 01 -   2.2.3.1.1

R v Gould (1840) 9 C & P 364   2.4.2.7.13

R v Governor of Brixton Prison,   2.2.2.2.5
ex parte Saifi [2001] 1 WLR 1134 -

R v Governor of Pentonville Prison,   2.3.2.10, 2.7.6.1
ex parte Osman [1990] 1 WLR 277 -

R v Grafton [1995] Crim LR 61 -   2.7.5.2

R v Gray [1995] 2 Cr App R 100   2.3.2.10

R v Greer [1998] Crim LR 527 -   2.2.1.2.3

R v Gregory and Mott [1995] Crim LR 506 -   2.2.1.2.8

R v Gunewardene [1951] 2 KB 600 -   2.4.2.7.10

R v H The Times 6 July 2001 -   2.2.1.2.8

R v Halpin [1975] QB 907 -   2.3.2.2

R v Hartley [2003] EWCA Crim 3027 -   2.2.4.2.4

R v Harvey (1869) 11 Cox CC 54 -   2.2.5.1

R v Harvey [1988] Crim LR 241 -   2.4.2.7.4

R v Hayter [2003] 1 WLR 1910 -   2.4.2.7.10

R v Hitchcock (1847) 16 LJ Exch 259 -   2.7.3

R v Hogan [1997] Crim LR 349 -   2.2.2.2.4

R v Honeyghon and Sales [1999] Crim LR 221 -   2.2.3.1.1

R v Hulbert (1979) 69 Cr App R 243 -   2.4.2.7.7

R v Hurst [1995] 1 Cr App R 81 -   2.2.1.2.6

R v Ilyas [1996] Crim LR 810 -   2.2.2.2.3, 2.3.2.10, 2.7.2.1

R v The Inhabitants of Eriswell (1790) 3 TR 707 -   1.4.1, 2.3.2.4

R v The Inhabitants of Rishworth (1842) 2 QB 476 -   2.3.2.4

R v Iqbal [1990] 1 WLR 756 -   2.2.1.2.8

R v Islam [1999] 1 Cr App R 22 -   2.2.4.2.4, 2.4.2.6

R v Ismail [1990] Crim LR 109 -   2.4.2.7.3

R v Izzigil [2002] EWCA Crim 925 -   2.2.1.2.6

R v Jackson [1996] 2 Cr App R 420 -   2.2.8.1

R v Jamieson [2003] EWCA Crim 193 -   2.4.2.7.2

R v Jenkins (1869) LR 1 CCR 187 -   1.6.2.1, 2.3, 2.7.2.3

R v Jenkins [2003] Crim LR 107 -   2.3.2.10

R v Jennings [1995] Crim LR 810 -   2.2.1.2.3

R v Jiminez-Paez (1994) 98 Cr App R 239 -   2.2.1.2.6

R v Jones [1997] 2 Cr App R 119 -   2.3.2.10

R v JP [1999] Crim LR 401 -   2.2.1.2, 2.2.1.2.1

R v Kearley [1992] 2 AC 228 -   1.2.1, 1.5.1, 1.6.1, 1.6.2.1, 2.3.2.7.2

R v Kelsey (1982) 74 Cr App R 213 -   2.2.5.1

R v Kennedy [1992] Crim LR 37 -   2.2.1.2.8

R v Lake (1976) 64 Cr App R 172 -   2.4.2.7.10

R v Lake Estates Watersports [2002] EWCA Crim 2067 -   2.2.2.1

R v Lillyman [1896] 2 QB 167 -   2.2.4.2.4

R v Liverpool Juvenile Court ex parte R [1988] QBI -   2.4.2.7.12

R v Lockley [1995] 2 Cr App R 554 -   2.2.1.1, 2.2.2.2.4, 2.7.5.2

R v Loosely [2001] 1 WLR 2060 -   2.7.5.2

R v Loughlin (1951) 35 Cr App R 69 -   2.2.4.2.6

R v Lovell (1923) 17 Cr App R 163 -   2.2.4.2.4

R v Lydon (1987) 85 Cr App R 221 -   1.7.1, 1.7.2

R v Lyons, Parnes, Ronson and   2.4.2.7.16
Saunders [2001] EWCA Crim 2860 -

R v M [1996] 2 Cr App R 56 -   2.8.2

R v McCay [1990] 1 WLR 645 -   2.2.4.3.2,
                                                    2.3.2.7.2

R v Mcgillivray (1993) 97 Cr App R 232 -   2.2.1.1

R v McGovern (1991) 92 Cr App R 228 -   2.4.2.7.4

R v MacKenzie (1993) 96 Cr App R 98 -   2.4.2.7.15, 2.7.4

R v Makanjuola [1995] 3 All ER 730 -   2.2.4.2.4,
                                                    2.2.4.3.3, 2.4.2.6

R v Mallory (1884) 13 QBD 33 -   2.3.2.9

R v Mann (1972) 56 Cr App R 750 -   2.2.3.1.1

R v Mansfield Justices, ex parte Sharkey [1985] QB 613 -   1.4.2

R v Martin [1996] Crim LR 589 -   2.2.1.2.8

R v Mason [1987] 3 All ER 481 -   2.4.2.7.5

R v Mason, Wood, McClelland and   2.4.2.7.3
Tierney [2002] 2 Cr App R 38 -

R v Mattey and Queeley [1995] 2 CR App R 409 -   1.6.2.1, 2.2.1.2,
                                                    2.2.1.2.9, 2.2.7.2

R v Matthews (1989) 91 Cr App R 43 -   2.4.2.7.5

R v Maw [1994] Crim LR 841 -   2.2.3.1.1, 2.2.3.2

R v Mendy (1976) 64 Cr App R 4 -   2.7.3

R v Miller [1986] 3 All ER 119 -   2.4.2.7.5

R v Miller, R v Parris, R v Abdullahi (1993) 97 Cr App R 99 -   2.4.2.7.3

R v Millett LTL 21/7/2000 -   2.2.1.2.5,
                                                    2.2.1.2.8

R v Mills [1962] 1 WLR 1152 -   2.2.5.1

R v Milner LTL 14/8/2000 -   2.2.4.2.4

R v Moghal (1977) 65 Cr App R 56 -   2.3.2.7.3

Moles, In re [1981] Crim LR 170 -   1.4.2

R v Moore [1992] Crim LR 882 -   2.2.1.2.8

R v Moss (1990) 91 Cr App R 371 -   2.4.2.7.15

R v Murray [1951] 1 KB 391 -   2.4.2.7.12

R v Murray [1997] 2 Cr App R 136 -   2.3.2.10

R v Murray (CA) 28/1/2000 -   2.4.2.7.9

R v Myers [1998] AC 124 -   2.2.7.1, 2.2.7.2,
                                                           2.4.2.7.14

R v Nathaniel [1995] 2 Cr App R 565 -   2.7.5.2

R v Nazeer [1998] Crim LR 750 -   2.2.2.2.1,
                                                           2.2.2.2.3, 2.7.6.1

R v Newport [1998] Crim LR 581 -   2.3.2.7.1

R v Nolan [2002] EWCA Crim 464 -   2.2.1.2.8

R v Nye and Loan (1977) 66 Cr App R 252 -   2.3.2.7.1

R v O'Boyle (1991) 92 Cr App R 202 -   2.2.7.1

R v O'Connor (1986) 85 Cr App R 298 -   2.7.5.2

R v Osbourne [1905] 1 KB 551 -   2.2.4.2.4

R v Osbourne and Virtue [1973] QB 678 -   2.2.4.3.2

R v Oyesiku (1971) 56 Cr App R 240 -   2.2.4.1

R v P [1998] Crim LR 663 -   2.2.3.1.2

R v Park (1994) 99 Cr App R 270 -   2.4.2.7.1

R v Parker [1995} Crim LR 233 -   2.4.2.7.3

R v Parsons LTL 17/12/99 -   2.4.2.7.9

R v Patel [1981] 3 All ER 94 -   1.8.1

R v Patel (1993) 97 Cr App R 294-   2.2.1.2.8

R v Payne [1963] 1 WLR 637 -   2.7.5.2

R v Pearce (1979) 69 Cr App R 365 -   2.2.4.2.3,
                                                           2.4.2.7.11

R v Pike (1829) 3 C & P 598 -   2.7.2.4

R v Prefas (1986) 86 Cr App R 111 -   2.2.3.1.1

Re Proulx [2001] EWCA Crim 385 -   2.4.2.7.3,
                                                           2.4.2.7.4, 2.4.2.7.5

R v Radak [1999] 1 Cr App R 187 -   2.2.1.2.6,
                                                           2.2.2.2.5, 2.8.2

R v Redgrave (1981) 74 Cr App R 10 -   2.3.2.5

R v Rice [1963] 1 QB 857 -   1.7.1, 1.7.2

R v Richardson; R v Longman [1969] 1 QB 299 -   2.7.3

R v Richardson [1971] 2 QB 484 -   2.2.5.1

R v Rigot LTL 18/2/2000 -   2.2.7.1. 2.4.2.7.9

R v Riley (1866) 4 F & F 964 -   2.2.3.1.2

R v Roberts [1942] 1 All ER 187 -   2.2.4.1, 2.2.4.2.5

R v Rock [1994] Crim LR 843 -   2.2.2.2.3

R v Rogers [1995] 1 Cr App R 374 -   2.3

R v Rowson [1986] QB 174 -   2.2.7.1

R v Rowton (1865) L & CA 520 -   2.3.2.5

R v Ruston (1786) 1 Leach 408 -   1.4.2

R v Samuel (1988) 87 Cr App R 232 -   2.4.2.7.3

R v Sang [1980] AC 425 -   2.4.2.7.5, 2.7.5.2

R v Sansui [1992] Crim LR 43 -   2.4.2.7.5

R v Sat Bhambra (1988) 88 Cr App R 55 -   2.4.2.7.1, 2.4.2.7.12, 2.7.5.2

R v Seelig [1992] 1 WLR 148 -   2.4.2.7.3

R v Sekhon (1987) 85 Cr App R 19 -   2.2.5.1

R v Setz-Dempsey (1994) 98 Cr App R 23 -   2.2.1.2.5, 2.2.2.2.5

R v Sharp [1988] 1 WLR 7 -   2.4.2.7.11

R v Shephard [1993] AC 380 -   1.9.1

R v Shone (1983) 76 Cr App R 72 -   1.8.1, 1.8.2

R v Sidney 12 June 2000   2.4.2.7.4

R v Simmonds (1967) 51 Cr App R 316 -   2.2.5.1

R v Smart [2002] EWCA Crim 772 -   2.3.2.10

R v Smurthwaite [1994] 1 All ER 898 -   2.7.5.2

R v Smythe (1980) 72 Cr App R 8 -   2.2.4.2.6

R v Somers [1963] 1 WLR 1306 -   2.3.2.11

R v Somers [1999] Crim LR 744 - 2.7.3

R v South Ribble J J, ex parte Cochrane 2.2.5.1
[1996] 2 Cr App R 544 -

R v Spiby (1990) 91 Cr App R 186 - 1.9.1, 1.9.2.1,
1.9.3, 2.2.8.1

R v Storey (1968) 52 Cr App R 334 - 2.2.4.2.3

R v Stephen Owen Sullivan The Times March 18 2003 2.8.1

R v Taylor LTL 5/6/2000 - 2.4.2.7.2,
2.4.2.7.4

R v Thomas [1998] Crim LR 887 - 2.8.2

R v Thomson [1912] 3 KB 19 - 2.3.2.7.3

R v Thompson [1976] 64 Cr App R 96 - 2.2.3.1.1

R v Thompson [1982] 1 QB 647 - 2.3

R v Tolson (1864) 4 F 7 F 103 - 1.10.1

R v Treacy [1944] 2 All ER 229 - 2.2.7.1

R v Trussler [1988] Crim LR 446 - 2.4.2.7.4

R v Turnbull [1977] QB 224 - 2.2.4.2.4,
2.2.4.3.3,
2.4.2.6, 2.7.4

R v Turner (1885) 29 Ch D 985 - 2.3.2.6

R v Turner [1975] 61 Cr App R 67 - 2.3.2.9, 2.4.2.7.9

R v Valentine [1996] 2 Cr App R 213 - 2.2.4.2.4

R v Voisin [1918] 1 KB 531 - 2.4.2.7.14

R v W [1997] Crim LR 678 - 2.2.1.2.8

R v Wahab [2003] 1 Cr App R 15 - 2.4.2.7.4,
2.4.2.7.5

R v Wainwright (1875) 13 Cox CC 171 - 2.3.2.7.3

R v Wallwork (1958) 42 Cr App R 153 - 2.2.4.2.4

R v Walsh (1989) 91 Cr App R 161 - 2.4.2.7.5

R v Warwickshall (1783) 1 Leach 263 - 2.4.2.7.13

R v Waters [1997] Crim LR 823 - 2.2.1.2.3,
2.2.1.2.7

R v Weaver (1873) LR 2 CCR 85 -   2.3.2.4

R v Webster LTL 12/1/2001 -   2.4.2.7.5

R v Westwell [1976] 2 All ER 812 -   2.2.5.1

R v Williams [1998] Crim LR 494 -   1.2.1, 1,3,1

R v Williams [2002] EWCA Crim 2208 -   2.3.2.10 1.9.2.2

R v Wood [1998] Crim LR 213 -   2.2.1.2.3

R v Wright and Ormerod (1987) 90 Cr App R 91 -   2.2.4.2.4

R v Z [2003] WLR 1489   -   2.2.4.2.3, 2.4.2.7.1, 2.4.2.7.16

Ratten v R [1972] AC 378 -   2.3.2.7.1

Read v Bishop of Lincoln [1892] AC 644 -   2.3.2.1

Rouch v Great Western Railway Co (1841) 1 QB 51 -   2.3.2.7.2

Sapporo Meru v Statue of Liberty [1968] 1 WLR 739 -   1.9.1, 1.10.1

Saunders (Ernest) v the United Kingdom   2.4.2.7.1,

(1997) 23 EHRR 313 -   2.4.2.7.16

Schenk v Switzerland (1988) 13 EHRR 242 -   2.8, 2.8.2

Sealey v The State The Times November 5 2002 -   2.2.4.2.2

Senat v Senat [1965] P 172 -   2.2.5.1

Sparks v R [1964] AC 964 -   1.2.1, 1.3.1

Sturla v Freccia (1880) 5 App Cas 623 -   2.3.2.6

Subramaniam v Public Prosecutor [1956] 1 WLR 965 -   1.2.1, 1.5.1, 2.3.2.7.3

Sugden v Lord St Leonards (1876) 1 PD 154 -   2.3

Taylor v Chief Constable of Cheshire [1987] 1 All ER 225 -   1.10.1, 1.10.2

Teper v R [1952] AC 480 -   2.3.2.7

Thomas v Connell (1838) 4 M & W 267 -   2.3.2.7.3

Thomas v Jenkins (1837) 6 A & E 525 -   2.3.2.6

Thompson v R [1998] AC 811 -   2.4.2.7.12

Tingle Jacobs & Co v Kennedy [1964] 1 WLR 638 -   1.9.3

Toohey v Metropolitan Police Commissioner [1965] AC 595 -   2.7.3

Topham v McGregor (1844) 1 C & K 320 -	2.2.5.1
Trivedi v the United Kigndom (1997) 89 D & R 136 -	2.8.2
Turner v Underwood [1948] 2 KB 286 -	2.4.2.7.2
United States v Zenni (1980) 492 F Supp 464 -	1.6.1
Unterpertinger v Austria (1991) 13 EHRR 175 -	2.8.2
Vehicle and Operator Services Agency v	2.2.2.2.3, 2.7.2.1,
George Jenkins Transport Ltd	2.8.2
The Times December 12 2003 -	
Ventouris v Mountain [1992] 3 All ER 414 -	1.10.1, 2.2.1.1, 2.2.2.2.1,
	2.2.2.2.3, 2.7.6
Vowles v Young (1806) 13 Ves 140 -	2.3.2.6
White v R [1999] 1 Cr App R 153 -	2.2.4.2.4
White v Taylor [1969] 1 Ch 150 -	2.3.2.1, 2.3.2.6
Williams v Williams [1988] QB 161 -	2.4.2.4
Woodhouse v Hall (1980) 72 Cr App R 39 -	1.5.1
Wong Kam-Ming v R [1980] AC 247 -	2.4.2.7.12
Wright v Doe d. Tatham (1837) 7 Ad & E1 313 -	1.6.1, 1.6.2.1, 2.3.2.7.2
Ymnos, The [1981] 1 Lloyds Rep 550 -	2.2.1.1, 2.4.2.7.8

Table of Statutes

Bail Act 1976
Section 7(5)   1.4.2

Bankers Books Evidence Act 1879

Section 3   2.4.2.4

Section 4   2.4.2.4

Section 5   2.4.2.4

Section 9(2)   2.4.2.4

Children and Young Persons Act 1933

Section 43   2.4.2.3

Section 107   2.4.2.3

Schedule 1   2.4.2.3

Civil Evidence Act 1968   2.3.2.4, 2.3.2.11

Section 2   2.2.1.1, 2.2.2.2.1, 2.4.2.7.7

Section 4   2.2.2.1, 2.2.2.2.1

Civil Evidence Act 1995   2.3.2.11

Section 1   1.9.1, 2.2.3, 2.2.5, 2.2.8.1, 2.3, 2.3.2.4, 2.3.2.7, 2.3.2.8, 2.3.2.9, 2.4.2.4

Section 1(2)(a)   1.9.4

Section 5(1)   2.7.2.3

Section 5(2)   2.7.3

Section 5(2)(b)   2.2.3.1

Section 6(3)   2.2.3.1

Section 6(4)   2.2.5

Section 6(5)   2.2.3, 2.2.4.2, 2.2.5

Section 7   2.3

Section 7(1)   2.3.2.8

Section 7(2)(a)   2.3.2.1

Section 7(2)(b)   2.3.2.2

Section 7(2)(c)   2.3.2.3

Section 7(3)(a)   2.3.2.5

Section 7(3)(b)   2.3.2.6

Section 7(4)   2.3.1

Section 8   2.7.6

Section 8(2)   2.7.6

Section 13   1.9.4, 2.7.6

Section 15   2.2.1.1, 2.2.2.1

Section 15(1)   2.7.6

Section 16(6)   2.2.2.2.1

Schedule 1   2.2.2.2.1

Common Law Procedure Act 1854   2.2.3.1.1

Crime and Disorder Act 1998

Section 51   2.4.1.3

Schedule 3, para 4   2.4.1.3

Schedule 3, para 5   2.4.1.3, 2.5

Schedule 3, para 5(4)   2.4.1, 2.4.1.3

Crime (International Co-operation) Act 2003

Section 7   2.2.2.1, 2.2.2.2, 2.2.2.2.4

Criminal Appeal Act 1968

Schedule 2 para 1	2.2.1.1, 2.4.1, 2.4.1.4
Schedule 2 para 1(1)	2.4.1.4
Schedule 2 para 1A	2.2.1.1, 2.4.1, 2.4.1.4

Criminal Evidence Act 1965

Section 1	2.2.2.1

Criminal Justice Act 1967

Section 9	2.2.8.2, 2.4.2.1, 2.4.2.2, 2.5
Section 9(1)	2.4.2.1
Section 9(2)	2.4.2.1
Section 9(2)(a)	2.4.2.1
Section 9(2)(b)	2.4.2.1
Section 9(2)(c)	2.4.2.1
Section 9(2)(d)	2.4.2.1
Section 9(3)(a)	2.4.2.1
9(3A)	2.4.2.1
Section 9(3)(b)	2.4.2.1
Section 9(3)(c)	2.4.2.1
Section 9(4)(a)	2.4.2.1
Section 9(4)(b)	2.4.2.1
Section 9(5)	2.4.2.1
Section 9(6)	2.4.2.1
Section 9(7)	2.4.2.1
Section 9(8)	2.4.2.1

Criminal Justice Act 1988

Section 23	1.10.1, 2.2.1.1, 2.2.1.2, 2.2.1.2.3, 2.2.1.2.8, 2.2.1.2.9, 2.2.2.1, 2.2.2.2.1, 2.2.2.2.2, 2.2.2.2.3, 2.2.3.1.3, 2.2.3.2, 2.2.4.3.2, 2.2.8.1, 2.4.1, 2.4.2.7.9, 2.7.3,
Section 23(1)	2.2.1.1, 2.2.1.2.1
Section 23(2)	2.2.1.2.3, 2.2.2.1
Section 23(2)(a)	2.2.1.2.3, 2.2.1.2.5
Section 23(2)(b)	2.2.1.2.3, 2.2.1.2.6
Section 23(2)(c)	2.2.1.1, 2.2.1.2.3
Section 23(3)	2.2.1.1, 2.2.1.2.3, 2.2.1.2.8, 2.2.2.1
Section 23(4)	2.2.1.1
Section 23(5)	2.2.1.1, 2.2.2.1
Section 24	1.8.1, 2.2.1.2.8, 2.2.2.1, 2.2.2.2.1, 2.2.2.2.2, 2.2.2.2.3, 2.2.2.2.4, 2.2.3.1.3, 2.2.4.3.2, 2.2.8.1, 2.4.1, 2.4.2.7.9, 2.7.2.1,

	2.7.3, 2.7.5, 2.7.6.1, 2.8.2
Section 24(1)	2.2.2.1
Section 24(1)(i)	2.2.2.1, 2.2.2.2.3
Section 24(1)(ii)	2.2.2.2.3, 2.7.2.1
Section 24(2)	2.2.2.2.3
Section 24(4)	2.2.2.1
Section 24(4)(iii)	2.2.2.1, 2.2.2.2.4
Section 24(5)	2.2.2.1
Section 25	2.2.1.1, 2.2.1.2.8, 2.2.2.1, 2.2.2.2.5, 2.7.5, 2.7.5.2, 2.7.6, 2.8.2
Section 26	1.10.1, 2.2.1.1, 2.2.1.2.8, 2.2.2.1, 2.2.2.2.5, 2.7.5, 2.7.5.2, 2.7.6, 2.8.2
Section 26(i)	2.2.1.2.8
Section 26(ii)	2.2.1.2.8
Section 26(iii)	2.2.1.2.8
Section 27	2.7.6
Section 27(2)	2.7.6
Section 30	2.2.2.1, 2.2.8.1, 2.2.8.2, 2.4.2.2
Section 30(1)	2.4.2.2
Section 30(2)	2.4.2.2
Section 30(3)	2.4.2.2
Section 30(4)	2.4.2.1
Section 30(4A)	2.4.2.1
Section 30(5)	2.4.2.2
Section 31	2.2.2.1
Section 32	2.4.1
Schedule 2	2.4.1
Schedule 2 para 1	2.2.3.1.3, 2.7.3
Schedule 2 para 5	2.2.1.1, 2.2.2.1, 2.2.2.2.1
Schedule 2 para 5(1)	2.2.1.1, 2.7.6
Schedule 2 para 5(2)	2.4.1
Schedule 13 para 2	2.4.1
Schedule 13 para 3	2.4.1
Schedule 13 para 4	2.4.1
Schedule 13 para 5	2.4.1
Schedule 13 para 6	2.2.2.1, 2.2.2.2, 2.2.2.2.4

Criminal Justice Act 2003

Section 41	2.4.1, 2.4.1.1
Section 99	2.3.2.5
Section 99(1)	2.7.3
Section 114	2.7.1.3, 2.7.5.1
Section 114(1)	1.2.2, 1.4.2, 1.5.2, 1.6.2, 1.6.2.1, 1.6.2.2, 1.6.2.3, 1.6.2.4, 1.7.2, 1.8.2, 1.9.2, 1.9.2.2, 1.10.2, 1.11.2, 2.1, 2.7.7, 2.7.7.1

Section	References
Section 114(1)(a)	1.2.2, 2.7.7
Section 114(1)(b)	1.2.2, 2.7.7
Section 114(1)(c)	1.2.2, 2.5, 2.7.1.2, 2.7.7
Section 114(1)(d)	1.2.2, 2.1, 2.2, 2.2.1.2.2, 2.2.3.2, 2.2.8.2, 2.3, 2.4.1.4, 2.4.2.7.7, 2.4.2.7.9, 2.2.4.3.3, 2.6, 2.7.1.4, 2.7.2.4, 2.7.5.2, 2.7.7, 2.8.1, 2.8.2
Section 114(2)	2.6
Section 114(2)(a)	2.6
Section 114(2)(b)	2.6
Section 114(2)(c)	2.6
Section 114(2)(d)	2.6
Section 114(2)(e)	2.6, 2.7.2.4
Section 114(2)(f)	2.6
Section 114(2)(g)	2.6
Section 114(2)(h)	2.6
Section 114(2)(i)	2.6
Section 114(3)	2.1
Section 115	1.2.2, 1.6.2, 2.2.8.2, 2.3.1
Section 115(1)	1.3.2, 1.6.2, 1.9.2, 1.10.2, 1.11.2
Section 115(2)	1.3.2, 1.9.2, 1.9.2.2, 1.9.4, 1.10.2, 1.11.2, 2.2.1.1, 2.2.2.1, 2.2.3.2, 2.2.4.1, 2.2.4.3.2, 2.3.1, 2.7.4.2, 2.7.5.1, 2.7.6, 2.7.6.1, 2.7.7, 2.7.7.1
Section 115(3)	1.5.2, 1.6.2, 1.6.2.1, 1.6.2.3, 1.6.2.4, 1.7.2, 1.8.2, 1.9.2.2, 2.3.1, 2.7.1.5, 2.7.3.2, 2.7.4.1, 2.7.5.1
Section 115(3)(a)	1.6.2.1, 1.6.2.2, 1.6.2.3, 1.8.2
Section 115(3)(b)	1.6.2.1, 1.6.2.2, 1.6.2.3, 1.8.2
Section 116	2.2.1, 2.2.1.1, 2.2.1.2, 2.2.1.2.1, 2.2.1.2.2, 2.2.2.1, 2.2.2.2, 2.2.2.2.2, 2.2.2.2.3, 2.2.2.2.5, 2.2.3.2, 2.2.4.3.2, 2.2.6, 2.2.8.1, 2.2.9, 2.3, 2.4.1, 2.4.1.4, 2.4.2.7.9, 2.7.1.1, 2.7.1.3, 2.7.2,

	2.7.2.2, 2.7.2.4, 2.7.5		2.2.2.1, 2.2.2.2.4, 2.7.5, 2.7.5.2
Section 116(1)(a)	2.2.1.2, 2.2.1.2.1	Section 116(4)(a)	2.2.1.2.8
Section 116(1)(b)	2.2.1.2, 2.2.1.2.2	Section 116(4)(b)	2.2.1.2.8
		Section 116(4)(c)	2.2.1.2.8
Section 116(1)(c)	2.2.1.2, 2.2.1.2.3	Section 116(4)(d)	2.2.1.2.8
Section 116(2)	2.2.1.1, 2.2.1.2, 2.2.1.2.9, 2.2.2.1, 2.2.2.2, 2.2.2.2.4, 2.4.1.4	Section 116(5)	2.2.1.1, 2.2.1.2, 2.2.1.2.3, 2.2.1.2.7, 2.2.1.2.8, 2.2.1.2.9, 2.2.2.1, 2.2.2.2, 2.2.2.2.4
Section 116(2)(a)	2.2.1.2.3, 2.2.1.2.4, 2.2.1.2.8, 2.2.1.2.9	Section 117	2.2.1.1, 2.2.1.2.8, 2.2.2, 2.2.2.1, 2.2.2.2, 2.2.2.2.1, 2.2.2.2.2, 2.2.2.2.3, 2.2.2.2.4, 2.2.2.2.5, 2.2.8.1, 2.2.8.2, 2.2.9, 2.3, 2.4.1, 2.4.2.4, 2.7.1, 2.7.1.1, 2.7.1.3, 2.7.1.4, 2.7.2, 2.7.2.2, 2.7.2.4, 2.7.3.1, 2.7.5, 2.7.6.1
Section 116(2)(b)	2.2.1.2.3, 2.2.1.2.5, 2.2.1.2.8, 2.2.1.2.9		
Section 116(2)(c)	2.2.1.2.3, 2.2.1.2.6, 2.2.1.2.8, 2.2.1.2.9		
Section 116(2)(d)	2.2.1.2.3, 2.2.1.2.7, 2.2.1.2.8, 2.2.1.2.9		
Section 116(2)(e)	2.2.1.1, 2.2.1.2.3, 2.2.1.2.8, 2.2.1.2.9, 2.2.2.1, 2.2.2.2.4, 2.7.5, 2.7.5.3, 2.8.2		
Section 116(3)	2.2.1.1, 2.2.1.2.8, 2.2.2.1, 2.2.2.2.4	Section 117(1)	2.2.2.1, 2.2.2.2, 2.2.2.2.1, 2.7.3
Section 116(4)	2.2.1.1, 2.2.1.2.8,	Section 117(1)(a)	2.2.2.2, 2.2.2.2.2

Section 117(1)(b)	2.2.2.2, 2.2.2.2.3	Section 118(1)	2.3, 2.3.1, 2.3.2
Section 117(2)	2.2.2.2.3	Section 118(1) 1 (a)	2.3.2.1
Section 117(2)(a)	2.2.2.1, 2.2.2.2, 2.2.2.2.3	Section 118(1) 1 (b)	2.3.2.2
		Section 118(1) 1 (c)	2.3.2.3
Section 117(2)(b)	2.2.2.1, 2.2.2.2, 2.2.2.2.3	Section 118(1) 1 (d)	2.3.2.4
		Section 118(1) 2	2.3.2.5
Section117(2)(c)	2.2.2.2, 2.2.2.2.3	Section 118(1) 3	2.3.2.6
Section 117(3)	2.2.2.2.3	Section 118(1) 4	2.3.1, 2.3.2.7
Section 117(4)	2.2.2.1, 2.2.2.2.4	Section 118(1) 4 (a)	2.3.2.7, 2.3.2.7.1
Section 117(5)	2.2.2.1, 2.2.2.2.4	Section 118(1) 4 (b)	2.3.2.7, 2.3.2.7.2
Section 117(5)(a)	2.2.2.1, 2.2.2.2, 2.7.5	Section 118(1) 4 (c)	2.3.2.7, 2.3.2.7.3
Section 117(5)(b)	2.2.2.2, 2.2.2.2.4	Section 118(1) 5	2.2.7.2, 2.3.2.8, 2.4.2.7, 2.4.2.7.10, 2.4.2.7.11
Section 117(6)	2.2.2.1, 2.2.2.2, 2.2.2.2.3, 2.2.2.2.5, 2.7.5.2, 2.8.2	Section 118(1) 6	2.3.1, 2.3.2.9
		Section 118(1) 6 (b)	2.3.2.9
Section 117(7)	2.2.2.1, 2.2.2.2, 2.2.2.2.3, 2.2.2.2.5, 2.7.5.2, 2.8.2	Section 118(1) 7	2.3.1, 2.3.2.10
		Section 118(1) 8	2.3.2.11
Section 117(7)(a)	2.2.2.2.5	Section 118(2)	2.3, 2.3.2
Section 117(7)(b)	2.2.2.2.5	Section 119	2.2.1.1, 2.2.3, 2.2.3.2, 2.2.7.2, 2.7, 2.7.1, 2.7.1.1, 2.7.1.3, 2.7.1.4, 2.7.2, 2.7.2.2, 2.7.2.4, 2.7.3
Section 117(7)(c)	2.2.2.2.5		
Section 117(7)(d)	2.2.2.2.5		
Section 118	2.1, 2.2.4.3.2, 2.2.9, 2.3.1, 2.3.2, 2.3.2.5, 2.7.1.1, 2.7.1.3, 2.7.2.4	Section 119(1)(a)	2.2.3.2
		Section 119(1)(b)	2.2.3.2

Section 119(2)	2.2.3.2, 2.7.3	Section 120(7)(a)	2.2.4.3.3
		Section 120(7)(b)	2.2.4.3.3
Section 120	2.2.1.1, 2.2.4, 2.2.4.2, 2.2.4.3, 2.2.4.3.2, 2.2.4.3.3, 2.2.5.2.2, 2.2.6, 2.7, 2.7.1, 2.7.1.1, 2.7.1.3, 2.7.1.4, 2.7.2, 2.7.2.2, 2.7.2.4, 2.7.3	Section 120(7)(c)	2.2.4.3.3
		Section 120(7)(d)	2.2.4.3.3
		Section 120(7)(e)	2.2.4.3.3
		Section 120(7)(f)	2.2.4.3.3
		Section 120(8)	2.2.4.3.3
		Section 121	2.2.1.1, 2.2.1.2.1, 2.2.2.2.2, 2.2.8.2, 2.4.2.7, 2.4.2.7.7, 2.6, 2.7, 2.7.1, 2.7.1.4, 2.7.1.5
Section 120(1)	2.2.4.3, 2.2.4.3.1, 2.2.4.3.2, 2.2.4.3.3, 2.2.5.2.2, 2.2.6		
		Section 121(1)	1, 2.3.1.2.2, 2.7.1.2, 2.7.1.3
Section 120(2)	2.2.4.3, 2.2.4.3.1	Section 121(1)(a)	2.2.3.2, 2.2.4.3, 2.2.6, 2.7.1.1, 2.7.1.3, 2.7.1.4
Section 120(3)	2.2.2.2.4, 2.2.4.3, 2.2.5, 2.2.5.2, 2.2.5.2.2, 2.2.6		
		Section 121(1)(b)	2.5, 2.7.1.2, 2.7.1.3, 2.7.1.3, 2.7.1.4
Section 120(4)	2.2.4.1, 2.2.4.3, 2.2.4.3.2, 2.2.4.3.3, 2.2.5.2.2, 2.2.6		
		Section 121(1)(c)	2.2.1.1, 2.4.2.7.7, 2.7.1.3, 2.7.1.4, 2.7.5.2, 2.8.2
Section 120(4)(b)	2.2.4.3.2, 2.2.4.3.3		
Section 120(5)	2.2.4.1, 2.2.4.3, 2.2.4.3.2	Section 121(2)	1.2.2, 2.7.1.5
		Section 122	2.2.3.2, 2.2.4.3, 2.2.5.2.2, 2.2.6, 2.7
Section 120(6)	2.2.4.3, 2.2.5.2.2, 2.2.6		
Section 120(7)	2.2.4.3, 2.2.4.3.3	Section 122(1)(a)	2.2.5.2.2

Section 123	2.2.1.2.1, 2.2.2.1, 2.2.2.2.2, 2.2.3.2, 2.2.4.3, 2.2.5.2.2, 2.2.6, 2.2.8.2, 2.7, 2.7.2, 2.7.2.4
Section 123(1)	2.2.1.1, 2.7.2
Section 123(2)(b)	2.7.2.1
Section 123(3)	2.7.2.2
Section 123(4)	2.7.2.3
Section 123(4)(c)	2.7.2.3
Section 124	2.2.2.2.3, 2.3.1, 2.4.2, 2.7, 2.7.3, 2.7.3.1, 2.7.3.2
Section 124(1)(b)	2.7.3.1
Section 124(2)(a)	2.7.3
Section 124(2)(c)	2.2.3.1.3, 2.2.3.2, 2.7.3
Section 124(4)	2.2.2.2.3, 2.7.3.1
Section 125	2.2.1.1, 2.2.1.2.8, 2.2.2.1, 2.2.3.2, 2.3.1, 2.4.2, 2.4.2.7, 2.4.2.7.15, 2.7, 2.7.4, 2.7.4.1
Section 125(1)	2.7.4, 2.7.4.1, 2.7.4.2
Section 125(1)(a)	2.7.4.1
Section 125(1)(b)	2.7.4
Section 125(2)	2.7.4, 2.7.4.1
Section 125(3)	2.7.4, 2.7.4.1
Section 126	2.2.1.2.8, 2.2.8.2, 2.3.1, 2.3.2.7, 2.3.2.8, 2.4.2, 2.7, 2.7.5.1
Section 126(1)	2.2.1.1, 2.2.1.2.8, 2.2.2.1, 2.2.3.2, 2.2.4.3, 2.2.5.2.2, 2.2.6, 2.4.2.7, 2.4.2.7.5, 2.6, 2.7.5, 2.7.5.1, 2.7.5.2
Section 126(1)(b)	2.7.5.1
Section 126(2)	2.1, 2.2.1.2.8, 2.2.3.2, 2.2.4.3, 2.2.5.2.2, 2.2.6, 2.7.5, 2.7.5.1, 2.7.5.2
Section 126(2)(a)	2.7.5.2
Section 126(2)(b)	2.3.2.8, 2.7.5.2
Section 127	1.9.1, 2.2.8, 2.2.8.2, 2.7.2.4
Section 127(4)	2.2.8.2, 2.7.2.4
Section 127(5)	2.2.8.2
Section 128	2.2, 2.2.7, 2.2.7.2, 2.3.2.8, 2.4.2.7, 2.4.2.7.6
Section 128(1)	2.2.3.2

Section 128(2)	2.2.1.1, 2.2.2.1, 2.2.3.2, 2.2.7.2, 2.3.2.9, 2.4.2.7, 2.4.2.7.2, 2.4.2.7.9, 2.4.2.7.10
Section 128(3)	2.3.2.9
Section 129(1)	1.9.2.2, 1.9.4, 1.10.2, 1.11.2, 2.2.4.1, 2.2.8.2, 2.7.3.2
Section 129(2)	1.9.3
Section 130	2.4.1, 2.4.1.3
Section 131	2.2.1.1, 2.2.2.1, 2.4.1, 2.4.1.4
Section 132	2.5, 2.7, 2.7.7, 2.7.7.1
Section 132(1)	2.7.7, 2.7.7.1
Section 132(2)	2.7.7, 2.7.7.1
Section 132(3)	2.7.7, 2.7.7.1
Section 132(4)	2.5, 2.7.1.2, 2.7.7
Section 132(5)	2.7.7.1
Section 132(6)	2.7.7.1
Section 132(7)	2.7.7.1
Section 132(8)	2.7.7.1
Section 132(8)(a)	2.7.7.1
Section 132(9)	2.7.7, 2.7.7.1
Section 132(10)	2.7.7.1
Section 133	2.7, 2.7.6, 2.7.6.1
Section 134(1)	1.4.2, 2.2.1.2.1, 2.2.2.2.1, 2.2.2.2.2, 2.7.6
Section 136	2.2.1.1, 2.2.2.1, 2.2.3.1.3, 2.4.1
Section 137	2.2.9
Section 137(1)(a)	2.2.9
Section 137(1)(b)	2.2.9
Section 137(1)(c)	2.2.9
Section 137(1)(d)	2.2.9
Section 137(1)(e)	2.2.9
Section 137(1)(f)	2.2.9
Section 137(2)	2.2.9
Section 137(3)	2.2.9
Section 137(3)(a)	2.2.9
Section 137(3)(b)(ii)	2.2.9
Section 137(4)	2.2.9
Section 137(5)	2.2.9
Section 137(6)	2.2.9
Section 138	2.2.9
Section 138(1)	2.2.9
Section 138(2)	2.2.9
Section 138(3)	2.2.9
Section 138(4)(a)	2.2.9
Section 138(5)	2.2.9
Section 139	2.2.5, 2.2.5.2, 2.2.5.2.1
Section 139(1)	2.2.5.2.1, 2.2.5.2.2, 2.2.6
Section 139(1)(b)	2.2.5.2.1

Section 139(2)	2.2.5.2.1
Section 140	2.2.5.2.1, 2.2.9
Section 332	2.4.1, 2.4.1.1, 2.4.1.2, 2.4.1.3
Schedule 3 Part 2	2.4.1, 2.4.1.1
Schedule 3 Part 6	2.2.1.1, 2.2.2., 2.4.1.2
Schedule 37, Part 4	2.2.1.1, 2.2.2.1, 2.4.1, 2.4.1.1, 2.4.1.2
Schedule 37, Part 6	2.4.1, 2.4.1.4

Criminal Procedure Act 1865

	2.2.7.1
Section 3	2.2.3.1.1, 2.2.3.2, 2.2.7.2
Section 4	2.2.3.1.2, 2.2.3.2, 2.2.7.2
Section 5	2.2.3.1.2, 2.2.3.2, 2.2.4.2, 2.2.7.2
Section 6	2.7.3

Criminal Procedure and Investigations Act 1996

Section 20(3)	2.2.8.2
Section 47	2.2.1.1
Section 68	2.4.1, 2.4.1.2
Schedule 1 Part II para 28	2.2.1.1
Schedule 1 para 3	2.4.1

Schedule 2	2.4.1, 2.4.1.2
Schedule 2 para 1	2.4.1.2
Schedule 2 para 2	2.4.1.2

Criminal Procedure (Insanity) Act 1964

Section 4A(2)	2.7.4

Human Rights Act 1998

Section 3(1)	2.2.1.2.8, 2.2.2.2.5, 2.4.2.7.1, 2.8.1, 2.8.2
Schedule 1	2.4.2.7.3

Indictable Offences Act 1848

	2.4.2.3

Magistrates' Court Act 1980

Section 5A	2.4.1, 2.4.1.1
Section 5B	2.4.1, 2.4.1.1
Section 5C	2.4.1, 2.4.1.1
Section 5D	2.4.1, 2.4.1.1
Section 5E	2.4.1, 2.4.1.1
Section 5F	2.4.1, 2.4.1.1

Police and Criminal Evidence Act 1984

Section 58	2.4.2.7.3
Section 68	1.8.1, 2.2.2.1
Section 69	1.9.1, 1.9.3

Section 76	2.1, 2.2.1.1, 2.2.7.1, 2.2.7.2, 2.3.2.8,		2.3.2.9, 2.4.2.7, 2.4.2.7.5, 2.4.2.7.9, 2.4.2.7.10
	2.3.2.9, 2.4.2.7,	Section 76A(1)	2.2.7.2
	2.4.2.7.2, 2.4.2.7.5,	Section 76A(2)	2.2.7.2, 2.4.2.7.5
	2.4.2.7.9, 2.4.2.7.10, 2.4.2.7.12	Section 76A(2)(a)	2.2.7.2
		Section 76A(2)(b)	2.2.7.2
Section 76(1)	2.2.7.2, 2.4.2.7.2, 2.4.2.7.10	Section 76A(3)	2.2.7.2
		Section 76A(4)	2.2.7.2
Section 76(2)	2.2.7.1, 2.2.7.2,	Section 76A(5)	2.2.7.2
	2.4.2.7.2, 2.4.2.7.3,	Section 76A(6)	2.2.7.2
	2.4.2.7.4, 2.4.2.7.5,	Section 76A(7)	2.2.7.2
	2.4.2.7.12, 2.4.2.7.13,	Section 77	2.4.2.7.15
	2.4.2.7.14, 2.4.2.7.15, 2.4.2.7.16, 2.7.4	Section 77(1)(2)	2.4.2.7.15
		Section 77(2)	2.4.2.7.15
		Section 77(3)	2.4.2.7.15
		Section 78	2.1, 2.2.1.1,
Section 76(2)(a)	2.2.7.2, 2.4.2.7.3		2.2.1.2.8, 2.2.2.1,
Section 76(2)(b)	2.2.7.2, 2.4.2.7.3, 2.4.2.7.4		2.2.2.2.5, 2.2.3.2, 2.2.4.3, 2.2.5.2.2,
Section 76(3)	2.4.2.7.2		2.2.6, 2.2.7.1,
Section 76(4)	2.4.2.7.13, 2.4.2.7.14		2.2.7.2, 2.3.2.7.1,
Section 76(4)(a)	2.4.2.7.13		2.3.2.8, 2.4.2.7.3,
Section 76(4)(b)	2.4.2.7.14		2.4.2.7.5, 2.4.2.7.12,
Section 76(5)	2.4.2.7.13		2.4.2.7.14, 2.4.2.7.15,
Section 76(6)	2.4.2.7.13		2.4.2.7.16, 2.6,
Section 76(8)	2.4.2.7.3		2.7.2.4, 2.7.5.2, 2.8.2
Section 76A	2.2, 2.2.1.1, 2.2.3.2,		
	2.2.7, 2.2.7.1, 2.2.7.2,	Section 78(1)	2.2.7.1, 2.4.2.7.5

Section 78(2)	2.2.7.1	Section 31(2)(a)	2.4.2.6
Section 81	2.2.8.2	Section 31(2)(b)	2.4.2.6
Section 82(1)	2.3.2.9, 2.4.2.7.1	Section 31(3)	2.4.2.6
		Section 53(3)	2.7.2.2
Section 82(3)	2.3.2.8, 2.4.2.7.12,	Section 54(2)	2.7.2.3
2.6		Section 60	1.9.1, 1.9.3

Theft Act 1968

Section 27(4)	2.4.2.5
Section 27(4)(a)	2.4.2.5
Section 27(4)(b)	2.4.2.5
Section 27(4A)	2.4.2.5

Youth Justice and Criminal Evidence Act 1999

Section 16(5)	2.2.1.2.8
Section 17(1)	2.2.1.2.8
Section 17(4)	2.2.1.2.8
Section 18(1)(b)	2.2.1.2.8
Section 19	2.2.1.2.8
Section 19(2)	2.2.1.2.8
Section 23	2.2.1.2.8
Section 24	2.2.1.2.8
Section 25	2.2.1.2.8
Section 26	2.2.1.2.8
Section 27	2.2.1.2.8
27(4A)	2.4.2.6
Section 27(4)(b)	2.4.2.5
Section 28	2.2.1.2.8
Section 29	1.4.2, 2.2.1.2.8
Section 30	1.4.2, 2.2.1.2.8
Section 31	1.4.2
Section 31(2)	2.4.2.6

Part One

THE NATURE OF A HEARSAY STATEMENT UNDER THE 2003 ACT

1.1 Introduction to Part One

As will be seen below, the Second Part of this book is concerned with the regime of exceptions to the rule against hearsay under which hearsay evidence will be admissible in criminal proceedings when the provisions of Chapter 2 of Part 11 of the Criminal Justice Act 2003 are in force. The provisions of Chapter 2 of Part 11 of the 2003 Act are not, however, solely concerned with reform of the statutory and common law exceptions to the hearsay rule. Rather, those provisions also both reformulate the exclusionary rules in inclusionary terms and, much more significantly, by changing the nature of that which is a hearsay statement, modify the ambit of the exclusionary rule itself. It is these latter two matters which Part One of this book concerns.

The former of the two matters which Part One concerns, namely, the reformulation of the exclusionary rule in inclusionary terms is, it is submitted, in reality, a matter of form rather than one of substance. In consequence, this matter is dealt with summarily, at 1.2.2 below. Conversely, the statutory modification of the ambit of the hearsay rule by changing the nature of that which is a hearsay statement is a matter of real practical significance. This is so because, once Chapter 2 of Part 11 of the 2003 Act is in force, certain statements which fall within the ambit of the hearsay rule at common law will no longer amount to hearsay statements and, conversely, certain statements which do not fall within the ambit of the hearsay rule at common law will henceforth amount to hearsay statements for the purposes of the new statutory hearsay regime.

Only when a hearsay statement has been identified does it become necessary or indeed relevant to consider whether the statement falls within the ambit of a hearsay exception. Thus, it is with the nature of a hearsay statement as such statements will exist when Chapter 2 of Part 11 is in force with which Part One of this book is almost exclusively concerned. In relation to each aspect of the hearsay rule's operation, the existing common law position will first be examined, and this will be followed by consideration of the extent to which the common law position will be altered by provisions of the 2003 Act.

1.2 The nature of the hearsay rule

1.2.1 The position at common law

Basically, in its common law manifestation, the hearsay rule is the rule that, subject to various common law and statutory exceptions, a statement is not admissible in legal proceedings as evidence of the truth of the facts stated unless the statement was made in the course of those proceedings.[1] The hearsay rule is applicable both to a statement made by a person who is not called to give evidence in the proceedings[2] and to a statement made, other than in the course of the proceedings, by a person who is called to give evidence in the proceedings.[3]

An example of the application of the hearsay rule to a statement made out of court by a person who was not called to give evidence in the proceedings is provided by the facts of *Sparks v R*.[4] The appellant, who was a white man, was charged with the indecent assault of a young girl. At the appellant's trial, the girl did not testify and the evidence of the girl's mother, that the girl had told her that "it was a coloured boy", was held to be inadmissible. The appellant was convicted. The Privy Council held that the evidence had properly been excluded because it was hearsay evidence which did not fall within the ambit of an exception to the hearsay rule.

An example of the application of the hearsay rule to a statement made out of court by a person who was called to give evidence in the proceedings is provided by *R v Williams*.[5] The appellant was charged with handling stolen goods. He claimed that he had purchased the goods from Mr McGrath, their owner, who had died by the time of the appellant's trial. At his trial, the appellant tendered a page from the proof of evidence which his solicitor had taken from him in which the appellant gave details of a visit to Mr McGrath's's house, of the interior of the house and of Mr McGrath's life and lifestyle. The trial judge held that the evidence was inadmissible. The appellant was convicted. On appeal, the appellant asserted that the page was not caught by the hearsay rule but, rather, was admissible to prove his knowledge at the time when the proof was taken. The Court of Appeal held that the appellant's knowledge was not an issue in the proceedings and was not relevant to such an issue. What was relevant was how the appellant had obtained his knowledge. The page was only relevant if relied upon to prove that the appellant had acquired his knowledge by visiting Mr McGrath. The page thus fell within the ambit of the hearsay rule and was not admissible because the hearsay exception upon which the appellant relied (concerning the admissibility of a statement as evidence of its makers' state of mind[6]) did not apply.

---

1   See, for example, Lord Oliver of Aylmerton in *R v Kearley [1992] 2 AC 228 at p.259* and Mr De Silva (delivering the opinion of the Privy Council) in *Subramaniam v Public Prosecutor [1956] 1 WLR 965 at p. 969*.

2   See, for example, *Sparks v R [1964] AC 964*.

3   See, for example, *R v Williams [1998] Crim LR 494*. Evidence of statements made out of court by a witness may also infringe the rule against previous consistent statements, the operation of which under the 2003 Act is considered at 2.2.4 below.

4   [1964] AC 964.

5   [1998] Crim LR 494.

6   The admissibility of such statements is considered at 2.3.2.7.3, below.

1.2.2 The position under the Criminal Justice Act 2003

When it comes into force, section 114(1) of the 2003 Act will govern the admissibility of hearsay evidence in criminal proceedings. Section 114(1) provides that:

> "(1) In criminal proceedings a statement not made in oral evidence in the proceedings is admissible as evidence of any matter stated if, but only if–
>
> (a) any provision of this Chapter or any other statutory provision makes it admissible,
>
> (b) any rule of law preserved by section 118 makes it admissible,
>
> (c) all parties to the proceedings agree to it being admissible, or
>
> (d) the court is satisfied that it is in the interests of justice for it to be admissible."

As can patently be seen upon examination of the text of section 114(1), the new statutory formulation of the hearsay rule is expressed in inclusionary terms (though subject to the requirements of one or more of section 114(1)(a)-(d) being satisfied) rather than in terms of the inadmissibility of hearsay evidence subject to exceptions. That the rule is stated in inclusionary rather than in exclusionary terms is a reflection of Government policy in this context.[7] As Mr Michael Wills (the Parliamentary Under-Secretary of State for the Home Department) stated in Standing Committee B in the House of Commons on Tuesday 28 January 2003,

> "We have cast the primary rule in inclusionary terms because that better reflects the principle that cogent and reliable evidence should be capable of being put before fact finders, subject to the important safeguards in the Bill."[8]

> "Practitioners should be encouraged to focus on the principle that all relevant hearsay is potentially admissible as evidence–I stress "relevant" and "potentially".[9]

> "Our general approach is that there should be automatic categories of admissibility, and judicial discretion elsewhere."[10]

> "The categories of admissibility are specifically designed to cover cases where direct evidence is unavailable, as well as hearsay evidence of a kind that is likely to be reliable."[11]

---

7   *The Law Commission had, more traditionally, formulated their primary rule, in clause 1 of their draft Bill, in exclusionary terms (see "Evidence in Criminal Proceedings: Hearsay and Related Topics", Law Com No 245).*

8   *See Hansard (Commons) 28 January 2003 Column 600.*

9   *See Hansard (Commons) 28 January 2003 Column 601.*

10   *See Hansard (Commons) 28 January 2003 Column 602.*

11   *See Hansard (Commons) 28 January 2003 Column 606.*

"Reliable statements that do not fall within one of the recognised categories or in a preserved common law rule will remain potentially admissible under clause 98(1)(d)."[12]

Whilst the hearsay rule is expressed by section 114(1) in inclusionary terms, it is submitted that the practical effect of the subsection appears to be that statements which were not made in oral evidence in the proceedings and are tendered as evidence of matters stated therein are only admissible in criminal proceedings if they fall within the ambit of one or more of the exceptions to the hearsay rule which are recognised by section 114(1)(a)-(d). Consequently, whilst the reformulation of the hearsay rule in inclusionary terms may have the effect of encouraging practitioners to recognise the potential admissibility of hearsay evidence under the new statutory regime, it is suggested that, in reality, this aspect of the 2003 Act's hearsay reforms neither modifies the nature of that which will or will not be admissible in criminal proceedings nor changes the nature of the rule against hearsay from that of an exclusionary rule to that of an inclusionary rule. Perhaps it is arguable, however, that, once Chapter 2 of Part 11 of the 2003 Act is in force, the hearsay rule should, at least technically, no longer be termed the "exclusionary rule". The validity of this proposition is doubted by the present author as, it is submitted that (unlike the position in civil proceedings), when Chapter 2 of Part 11 of the 2003 Act is in force, the practical position in criminal proceedings will continue to be that some, perhaps many, hearsay statements will still be rendered inadmissible or otherwise excluded in consequence of their hearsay nature. Even so, in acknowledgment of the spirit of this aspect of the common law exclusionary rule's statutory reformulation, the use of the term "exclusionary rule" as a description of the hearsay rule will be avoided throughout the remainder of the present book.

Thus, at face value, section 114(1) of the 2003 Act, whilst patently both reformulating the new statutory manifestation of the hearsay rule in terms of admissibility rather than in terms of inadmissibility and (under section 114(1)(c)-(d)) creating new exceptions to the hearsay rule[13], does not appear to change the nature of those statements which, when the hearsay provisions of the 2003 Act are in force, will properly be classified as hearsay statements.[14]

---

12 *See Hansard (Commons) 28 January 2003 Column 619. Note, that clause 98(1)(d) was subsequently enacted in slightly modified form as section 114(1)(d) of the 2003 Act. Section 114(1)(d) is considered at 2.6 below.*

13 *The nature of which is considered, respectively, at 2.5 and 2.6 below.*

14 *The only definition of "hearsay statement" which the 2003 Act provides is that contained in section 121(2) which applies only for the purposes of section 121(1) but which, it is submitted, equates with that which is inherent within the hearsay regime which the 2003 Act creates. Section 121(2) defines a hearsay statement as "…a statement, not made in oral evidence, that is relied on as evidence of a matter stated in it." Section 121, which deals with multiple hearsay, is considered at 2.7.1 below.*

In reality, however, as is demonstrated below[15], the effect of section 114(1) when read in conjunction with the section 115 definitions of "statement" and "matter stated", is that certain evidence which falls within the ambit of the common law hearsay rule will not fall within the ambit of the hearsay rule as that rule will exist under the 2003 Act and, conversely, that certain evidence which does not fall within the ambit of the common law hearsay rule will fall within the ambit of its statutory successor.

1.3 Statements made orally, in documents or by conduct

1.3.1 The position at common law

At common law, the hearsay rule is applicable to oral statements[16], to statements made by conduct[17] and to documentary statements.[18] Examples of the application of the hearsay rule to statements made orally and in documents were considered at 1.2 above. An example of the application of the hearsay rule to a statement made by conduct is provided by *Chandrasekera v R*.[19] In *Chandrasekera*, the victim of a murder, whose throat had been cut, was asked, before she died, whether her injuries had been caused by the appellant. The victim responded by nodding her head. At the trial of the appellant for murder, witnesses testified as to the putting of the question to the victim and as to her nodding in response. The Privy Council held that the statement had properly been admitted because it fell within the ambit of a hearsay exception.[20] Had this not been the case, however, it appears that the statement would not have been admissible because it was not made in the course of the trial and was relied on by the prosecution as evidence of the truth of the facts stated (i.e. to prove that the victim's throat had been cut by the appellant).

1.3.2 The position under the Criminal Justice Act 2003

Section 115(1)-(2) of the 2003 Act provides that:

> "(1) In this Chapter references to a statement or to a matter stated are to be read as follows.
>
> (2) A statement is any representation of fact or opinion made by a person by whatever means; and it includes a representation made in a sketch, photofit or other pictorial form."

This statutory definition of a "statement" is clearly wide enough to encompass oral statements, statements made by conduct and documentary statements. Thus it appears that the examples of hearsay statements which were considered at 1.2 and at 1.3.1 above remain valid examples of hearsay statements under the 2003 Act.

---

15 *See, in particular, 1.6.2, 1.8.2, 1.9.2.2 and 1.11.2, below.*

16 *See for example Sparks v R [1964] AC 964, considered at 1.1.2 above.*

17 *See, for example, Chandrasekera v R [1937] AC 220.*

18 *See, for example, R v Williams [1998] Crim LR 494, considered at 1.2 above.*

19 *[1937] AC 220.*

20 *Namely, section 32 of the Ceylon Evidence Ordinance of 1895.*

The significance of the reference in the statutory definition to a "sketch, photofit or other pictorial form" is considered at 1.11, below.

1.4 Statements made during other legal proceedings

1.4.1 The position at common law

As the definition of the hearsay rule at common law which was relied upon at 1.2 above makes clear, the hearsay rule does not merely apply to statements made out of court but also (and, as usual, subject to common law and statutory exceptions) applies to statements made during other legal proceedings. A venerable example is provided by *R v The Inhabitants of Eriswell*[21]. John Sharpe, a pauper, was examined on oath before two Justices of the Peace in order to determine the place of his last legal settlement. Several years later, the examination, which John Sharpe had signed, was admitted in evidence in the course of distinct legal proceedings as proof of the place of John Sharpe's last legal settlement. The Court of King's Bench held that the examination should not have been admitted as proof of the place of John Sharpe's last legal settlement because it was a hearsay statement which did not fall within an exception to the hearsay rule.

1.4.2 The position under the Criminal Justice Act 2003

As was seen at 1.2.2 above, section 114(1) of the 2003 Act provides that:

> "(1) In criminal proceedings a statement not made in oral evidence in the proceedings is admissible as evidence of any matter stated if, but only if—
>
> (a) any provision of this Chapter or any other statutory provision makes it admissible,
>
> (b) any rule of law preserved by section 118 makes it admissible,
>
> (c) all parties to the proceedings agree to it being admissible, or
>
> (d) the court is satisfied that it is in the interests of justice for it to be admissible."

For the purposes of Chapter 2 of the 2003 Act, "oral evidence" is defined[22] as including,

> "...evidence which, by reason of any disability, disorder or other impairment, a person called as a witness gives in writing or by signs or by way of any device..."

and "criminal proceedings" are defined[23] as:

> "...criminal proceedings in relation to which the strict rules of evidence apply"...

---

21 *(1790) 3 TR 707.*
22 *By section 134(1).*
23 *By section 134(1).*

Section 114(1) only applies to "a statement not made in oral evidence in the proceedings". Thus it appears that, as is presently the case at common law (see 1.4.1 above), the new statutory formulation of the hearsay rule will not merely apply to statements made out of court but will also (subject to any applicable common law or statutory exceptions) apply to statements made in the course of other legal proceedings.

The statutory definition of "oral evidence" makes clear that a witness may potentially give oral evidence in the proceedings in a variety of ways (e.g. via a sign language interpreter). This has long been the case at common law[24], and, moreover, the examination of a witness through an intermediary or the use of aids to communication may already form the subject matter of a special measures direction under the Youth Justice and Criminal Evidence Act 1999.[25]

Further, it should be noted that under the special measures regime created by the 1999 Act, where a witness does not give direct oral testimony in court but a statement made by the witness (i.e. a video recorded statement) forms part of the witness' evidence in the proceedings, the statement is to be treated as if the witness had made it by direct oral testimony in court.[26] In such circumstances, however, unlike those in which a witness actually does give direct "oral (i.e. non-hearsay) evidence" via, for example, a sign language interpreter, the video recorded statement is hearsay evidence admitted under a hearsay exception, the effect of the hearsay exception being that the statement is "treated" as if it had been made by the witness' direct oral evidence in court.

Finally, the effect of the statutory definition of "criminal proceedings" is that, as is currently the position at common law, the hearsay rule as it will exist when the relevant provisions of the 2003 Act are in force will not apply in the context of criminal proceedings in relation to which the strict rules of evidence do not apply. Examples of such proceedings are provided by applications for bail and by proceedings under section 7(5) of the Bail Act 1976.[27]

1.5 The purpose for which the statement is tendered

1.5.1 The position at common law

The hearsay rule does not prevent the admission of a statement for a purpose other than that of proving the truth of the facts stated.[28] Thus, if evidence of the making of a statement is tendered not to prove that facts stated are true or false but to prove that the statement was made, the statement will not, for that purpose,

---

24 *See for example, R v Ruston (1786) 1 Leach 408.*

25 *See Youth Justice and Criminal Evidence Act 1999, sections 29 and 30.*

26 *Youth Justice and Criminal Evidence Act 1999, section 31.*

27 *See In re Moles [1981] Crim LR 170, R v Mansfield Justices, Ex p Sharkey [1985] QB 613 and R (Director of Public Prosecutions) v Havering Magistrates' Court [2001] 2 ALL ER 997.*

28 *See Subramaniam v Public Prosecutor [1956] 1 W.L.R. 965.*

fall within the ambit of the hearsay rule.[29] A statement which is relied upon for some purpose other than that of proving the truth of the facts stated is sometimes described as "original evidence" in order to distinguish it from hearsay evidence.[30]

An example of the practical application of this distinction is provided by the decision of the Privy Council in *Subramaniam v Public Prosecutor*[31], in which evidence of statements made to the appellant was admissible not as proof of the truth of the facts stated but as evidence of the appellant's state of mind. The facts of *Subramanian* were as follows. The appellant was charged with an offence concerning the unlawful possession of ammunition. He raised the defence of duress, asserting that he had acted as he had, in consequence of threats made to him by terrorists. The trial judge, classifying them as hearsay statements, refused to allow the appellant to give evidence of statements made to him by the terrorists and the appellant was convicted. The Privy Council held that the statements did not fall within the ambit of the hearsay rule, and thus should have been admitted as evidence of duress, because whether they were true or false they might have been believed by the accused.

A second example of the practical application of the distinction between hearsay evidence and original evidence is provided by the decision of the Divisional Court in *Woodhouse v Hall*.[32] In *Woodhouse v Hall*, the manageress of a sauna, was charged with managing a brothel. Magistrates held that the evidence of police officers concerning offers of "hand relief" made to them by women employed at the sauna fell within the ambit of the hearsay rule and, consequently, was inadmissible. The Divisional Court held, however, that the evidence did not fall within the ambit of the hearsay rule. This was so because the issue before the court was whether the women had made the offers[33], not the truth or falsehood of what they had said.

1.5.2 The position under the Criminal Justice Act 2003

As was seen at 1.2.2 above, Section 114(1) of the 2003 Act provides that:

"(1)   In criminal proceedings a statement not made in oral evidence in the proceedings is admissible as evidence of any matter stated if, but only if–

(a)   any provision of this Chapter or any other statutory provision makes it admissible,

(b)   any rule of law preserved by section 118 makes it admissible,

(c)   all parties to the proceedings agree to it being admissible, or

(d)   the court is satisfied that it is in the interests of justice for it to be admissible."

---

29   See *Subramaniam v Public Prosecutor [1956] 1 W.L.R. 965 and see, also, Lord Oliver of Aylmerton in R v Kearley [1992] 2 AC 228 at p. 261.*

30   See *Lord Ackner in R v Andrews [1987] AC 281 at p.295.*

31   *[1956] 1 W.L.R. 965.*

32   *(1980) 72 Cr App R 39.*

33   *If two or more women had made such offers then the sauna was a brothel.*

Section 114(1) only concerns the admissibility of a statement "as evidence of any matter stated". Thus, viewing section 114(1) at face value, it seems that where the purpose for which a statement is tendered would presently infringe the common law hearsay rule its admission for that purpose will, in future, infringe the common law rule's statutory successor. As is demonstrated below[34], however, in consequence of the new statutory definition of "matter stated"[35], certain evidence which falls within the ambit of the common law hearsay rule will not fall within the ambit of its statutory successor because it will not be tendered as evidence of a "matter stated".

1.6 Assertions implied from statements which were not intended to communicate them (implied assertions)

1.6.1 The position at common law

At common law the hearsay rule does not merely apply to statements which were intended to communicate the facts which the statements are tendered to prove but, rather, is also applicable to statements which were not intended to communicate the facts which they are tendered to prove but from which the existence of the relevant fact may be implied.[36] Thus, it may be said that the hearsay rule applies both to express and implied assertions though, as the Law Commission recognised[37], the term "implied assertions":

> "2.4   is a rather misleading shorthand term for utterances or behaviour from which a fact (including a state of mind or an intention) may be inferred, although they are not intended to communicate that fact.[7]
>
> [7] See paras 7.5 – 7.9 below."

> "7.7   This is a somewhat unfortunate expression, for two reasons. First, it begs the question of whether the words or conduct in question are an assertion of the fact that they are adduced to prove. It is at least arguable that they are not assertive at all, but directly probative – in which case it would follow that they should not be caught by the hearsay rule.

> 7.8   Second, the word "implied" is here used in an unusual sense. Normally it refers to a statement which is not expressly spoken or written but is intended to be understood from what is said or done. But where there is an assertion of the fact to be proved, it is immaterial whether that assertion is express or (in the ordinary sense) implied. An assertion of a fact is no less of an assertion because it is implicit in an express assertion of a different fact, or because it takes the form of nonverbal

---

34   *See, in particular, 1.6.2, 1.8.2 and 1.9.2.2, below.*
35   *See section 115(3).*
36   *R v Kearley [1992] 2 AC 228.*

37   *In their Report "Evidence in Criminal Proceedings: Hearsay and Related Topics", Law Com No 245, at paragraphs 2.4 and 7.7-7.8.*

as a gesture. An assertion can therefore be implied (in the ordinary sense) without being what is described in the context of hearsay as an "implied assertion."[11]"

"[11] Conversely, it may sometimes be arguable that even an express assertion of a fact should not be treated as being truly assertive in view of the purpose with which it is made. See para 7.27 below."

An example of the application of the common law hearsay rule to statements which were not intended to communicate the facts which they are tendered to prove but from which the existence of the relevant facts may be implied is provided by *R v Kearley*.[38] In *Kearley*, the appellant was charged with possession of a controlled drug with intent to supply. In order to prove that the appellant was a supplier, the prosecution wished to adduce evidence of police officers who, whilst searching the appellant's house, had received telephone calls and requests from visitors asking for the appellant and asking for drugs. When the matter reached the House of Lords, it was not clear whether the requests had been relevant to an issue before the court.[39] Their Lordships indicated, however, that, upon the assumption that the telephone requests did amount to implied assertions to the effect that the accused was a supplier of drugs, the hearsay rule applied to them just as it applied to express assertions.[40].

Whilst the decision of the House of Lords in *Kearley* appears to have conclusively established that the common law hearsay rule is applicable to statements which were not intended to communicate the facts which they are tendered to prove but from which the existence of the relevant facts may be implied, it remains unclear whether assertions implied from conduct which was not intended to amount to a communication fall within the ambit of the that rule. In *Wright v Doe d Tatham*[41], more than one hundred and fifty years prior to the decision in *Kearley*, Parke B had assumed that they did. His Lordship[42], considering various examples, was of the view that, inter alia, if a sea captain embarked on a ship with his family after conducting a thorough examination of it, his conduct would amount to an example of hearsay evidence if tendered in relation to an issue of seaworthiness.

In *R v Kearley*, their Lordships, whilst applying *Wright's* case in determining that assertions implied from oral statements may, at common law, fall within the ambit of the hearsay rule, did not refer to Parke B's obiter "sea captain" example and did not expressly deal with the issue of the evidential status of assertions which may be implied from conduct which was not intended to amount to a communication of information. Lord Bridge[43] did, however (by reference to the judgment of District Judge Bertelsman in the American case of *United States v Zenni*[44]), appear to

---

38 [1992] 2 AC 228.
39 See Lord Ackner at p. 253.
40 See Lord Ackner at p. 254.
41 (1837) 7 Ad & El 313.

42 At p.388.
43 At p. 248.
44 (1980) 492 F Supp 464.

recognise that Wright's case did establish such a principle. Thus, it may be that the better view is that assertions which may be implied from conduct which was not intended to amount to a communication of information are properly to be regarded at common law as falling within the ambit of the hearsay rule, but the position has never been conclusively determined.

1.6.2 The position under the Criminal Justice Act 2003

Section 115(1) and (3) of the 2003 Act provides as follows:

> "(1) In this Chapter references to a statement or to a matter stated are to be read as follows…
>
> (3) A matter stated is one to which this Chapter applies if (and only if) the purpose, or one of the purposes, of the person making the statement appears to the court to have been—
>
> (a) to cause another person to believe the matter, or
>
> (b) to cause another person to act or a machine to operate on the basis that the matter is as stated."

The purpose of section 115 of the 2003 Act is stated at paragraph 400 of the Explanatory Notes to the Criminal Justice Act to be as follows.

> "Its purpose is to overturn the ruling in Kearley [1992] 2 AC 228 that "implied assertions" are covered by the hearsay rule and therefore prima facie inadmissible."

Thus, whilst section 114(1) of the 2003 Act does not patently redefine the hearsay rule, it appears, as is demonstrated at 1.6.2.1 below, that an "implied assertion" in the sense of an assertion which may be implied from a statement which was not intended to communicate the facts which the statement is tendered to prove[45] will not amount to a "matter stated" for the purposes of section 114(1). Consequently, it appears that, when section 114(1) of the 2003 Act is in force, an "implied assertion" of this type will no longer fall within the ambit of the hearsay rule. This, it appears, will equally be true in relation to assertions implied from conduct which was not intended to amount to a communication[46], if indeed, such assertions ever fell within the ambit of the hearsay rule's common law manifestation.

It should be noted, however that, as is demonstrated at 1.6.2.1 below, the provisions of the 2003 Act will only remove from the ambit of the hearsay rule "implied assertions" in the sense of:

> "…utterances or behaviour from which a fact (including a state of mind or an intention) may be inferred, although they are not intended to communicate that fact."[47]

45   *Considered at 1.6.1 above.*
46   *Considered at 1.6.1 above.*

47   *"Evidence in Criminal Proceedings: Hearsay and Related Topics", Law Com No 245, paragraph 2.4.*

Thus, it seems that the new provision will not remove from the ambit of the hearsay rule a:

> "...statement which is not expressly spoken or written but is intended to be understood from what is said or done." [48]

Thus, for example, as was recognised at 1.3.2 above and is demonstrated at 1.6.2.1 below, it appears that an implied statement of the type which *Chandrasekera v R*[49] concerned will continue to fall within the ambit of the hearsay rule when the new statutory hearsay regime is in force in the criminal context.

The best explanation of the rationale for the removal of the former type of "implied assertions" from the ambit of the hearsay rule was provided by the Law Commission.[50]

> "7.18 If it is known that a person spoke or acted in such a way as to cause someone else to infer the truth of a particular proposition, two inferences may be drawn: first that that person at that time believed that proposition to be true, and second that that belief was correct. Neither inference is inevitable: the person may have been seeking to mislead, or may have been mistaken. The hearsay rule recognises that if *both* these risks are present then, in the absence of an opportunity to cross-examine the person in question, there is good reason to exclude evidence of his or her words or conduct.
>
> 7.19 If, however, the risk of deliberate fabrication can be discounted, the possibility of a mistake is not necessarily sufficient reason to exclude evidence of the words or conduct. An example of this is the principle of res gestae, which, as preserved by our draft Bill,[21] permits evidence of a statement which "was made by a person so emotionally overpowered by an event that the possibility of concoction or distortion can be disregarded".
>
> 7.20 Where there is a substantial risk that an out-of-court assertion may have been deliberately fabricated, therefore, we think it right that the assertion should fall within the hearsay rule – whether it is express or implied. It follows that the rule should extend to any conduct which is intended to give the impression that a particular fact is true, and is adduced as evidence of that fact. But where that risk is not present – in other words, where the person from whose conduct a fact is to be inferred can safely be assumed to have believed that fact to be true – we do not think a court should be precluded from inferring that fact merely because that person may have been mistaken in believing it

---

48 *"Evidence in Criminal Proceedings: Hearsay and Related Topics", Law Com No 245, paragraph 7.8.*

49 *[1937] AC 220.*

50 *In their Report "Evidence in Criminal Proceedings: Hearsay and Related Topics", Law Com No 245, at paragraphs 7.18-7.20.*

And if that person did not intend anyone to infer it, it follows that that person cannot have been seeking to mislead anyone about it."

"21 Clause 6(5)(a)."

1.6.2.1 The significance of Section 115(3)(a) and the burden of proving that hearsay evidence is admissible

Section 115(3)(a) provides that:

"(3) A matter stated is one to which this Chapter applies if (and only if) the purpose, or one of the purposes, of the person making the statement appears to the court to have been—

(a)   to cause another person to believe the matter, or..."

In the course of explaining the basis of their recommendations which resulted in what is now section 115(3)(a) of the 2003 Act, the Law Commission51 indicated that:

"The crucial question, we have argued, is whether the person whose words or conduct are in question intended to convey the impression that the fact which it is now sought to infer from those words or that conduct was true. Only if that person did not intend to convey that impression can it safely be assumed that he or she was not deliberately seeking to mislead. It follows that what is crucial is not the way in which that person happened to express himself or herself, but the impression that his or her words or conduct were intended to convey."

7.26   Thus evidence that a caller said "Can I have my usual stuff?" would be admissible to prove that the accused did habitually supply unlawful drugs; but this is not because the caller's words do not amount to an assertion. It is because the caller's intention is not to give anyone the impression that the person addressed is a drug dealer, but simply to request drugs. The caller intends the words to be heard only by a person whom the caller believes to be a drug-dealer: obviously the caller has no wish to convince that person, or anyone else, that that person is a drug-dealer.

7.27   From this point of view it makes no difference that the caller says "The stuff you sold me last week was bad". The inference to be drawn from these words is essentially the same as in the case of the words "Can I have my usual stuff?" – namely that the person whom the caller intends to address is in the habit of supplying drugs to the caller. On its face, admittedly, this is an express assertion that the person addressed sold drugs to the caller last week; and, since the caller obviously

---

51   In their Report *"Evidence in Criminal Proceedings: Hearsay and Related Topics"*, *Law Com No 245*, at paragraphs 7.25-7.32.

intends to say exactly what he or she does say, in one sense the caller intends to assert that fact. But it is not the caller's intention to cause the person addressed to infer that that fact is true, since he or she already knows it. In that sense there is no intention to assert.

7.28 The point may be further illustrated by reference to *Teper*.[26] The defendant was charged with arson of his own shop. A woman had been heard to shout to a passing motorist "Your place burning and you going away from the fire". If the woman's intention were to draw the attention of bystanders to the fact that Teper was leaving the scene, her words would be hearsay, since she might have been trying to mislead the bystanders. If, however, she was intending only to indicate to the motorist that she knew he was Teper, she could not be seeking to mislead anyone about who he was. If he was Teper, he knew he was; and if he was not, she could not hope to convince him that he was. She might still be asserting that he was Teper, but she would not be intending to persuade anyone of this.

7.29 We recognise that it may sometimes be difficult to ascertain what impression, if any, the words or conduct in question were intended to convey, and legal argument may result.[27] But a party seeking to adduce evidence must always show, to the appropriate standard of proof, that the facts are such as to render the evidence admissible; and it will usually be possible to infer from the circumstances the intentions of the person in question.

7.30 It may be difficult in some cases for the prosecution to prove beyond reasonable doubt that that person did not intend to convey to an observer the fact that it is now sought to prove; but, in view of the risk of fabricated evidence being admitted without the opportunity for cross-examination, we think it is right that there should be this safeguard.

7.31 In the case of defence evidence the point will have to be proved only on the balance of probabilities; but, if it appears more likely that the relevant intention did not exist than that it did, we think it right that the defence should be permitted to adduce the evidence. The possibility that it may have been fabricated can be taken into account in assessing the weight that it should be given.

7.32 This reasoning suggests that the crucial question should be, not whether the maker of the statement appears to have intended to assert the fact which the statement is adduced to prove, but whether he or she appears to have intended to cause another person to believe that fact."

"[26] [1952] AC 480.

[27] This problem was anticipated by the Crown Prosecution Service, the Society of Public Teachers of Law, Mr Justice Curtis, Alan Suckling QC, Professor John Jackson, Peter Mirfield and David Ormerod."

Under section 115(3)(a), the crucial issue is the purpose or purposes for which the statement appears to have been made. Where a person who made a statement, whether by words or by conduct, appears to have done so for the purpose of causing another person to believe a matter which he stated, the relevant words or conduct will fall within the ambit of the hearsay rule as that rule will exist under the 2003 Act provided that, adopting the wording of section 114(1), the statement was "not made in oral evidence in the proceedings" and is tendered "as evidence of [the] matter stated". The statement will fall within the ambit of the hearsay rule both if the abovementioned purpose appears to have been the sole purpose for which the statement was made and where it merely appears to have been one of several purposes for which the statement was made. Conversely, where a person who made a statement, whether by words or by conduct, neither appears to have done so for the purpose of causing another person to believe a matter which he stated nor (see the discussion of section 115(3)(b) at 1.6.2.2 below) for the purpose of causing another person to act or a machine to operate on the basis that the matter was as stated, the relevant words or conduct will not fall within the ambit of the hearsay rule as that rule will exist under the 2003 Act. This will be so because, under section 115(3), the matter stated will not be a "matter stated" for the purposes of Chapter 2 of Part 11 of the 2003 Act and, consequently, will not be a "matter stated" for the purposes of the section 114(1) hearsay rule.

Thus, whilst the statement made by conduct in *Chandrasekera v R.*[52] was an implied statement within the normal meaning of that expression, such a statement would appear to be a hearsay statement under the provisions of the 2003 Act because it appears that the victim, when she made the statement, did so for the purpose of causing another person/other persons to believe that the appellant had caused her injuries. Conversely, applying the provisions of the 2003 Act to the facts of *R v Kearley*,[53] it appears that the requests which that case concerned would not fall within the ambit of the section 114(1) hearsay rule if, as seems to have been the case, the persons making them neither did so for the purpose of causing another person to believe that the appellant was a supplier of drugs nor (see the discussion of section 115(3)(b) at 1.6.2.2 below) did so for the purpose of causing another person to act or a machine to operate on the basis that he was.

If facts similar to those of *Kearley* arise when the hearsay provisions of the 2003 Act are in force, the burden of proving to the requisite standard of proof that the relevant evidence does not fall within the ambit of the hearsay rule because the persons who made the requests neither did so for the purpose of causing another person to believe that the appellant was a supplier of drugs nor (see the discussion of section 115(3)(b) at 1.6.2.2 below) did so for the purpose of causing another person to act or a machine to operate on the basis that he was, will be borne by the party tendering the relevant evidence. That this will be so is not a consequence of

---

52 *[1937] AC 220 (considered at 1.3.1 above).*
53 *[1992] 2 AC 228 (considered at 1.6.1 above).*

any provision of the 2003 Act itself. Rather, it is a consequence of the principle of common law, which the 2003 Act has not modified, that where it is necessary to resolve a question of fact in order to determine whether evidence is admissible, the burden of proving the relevant fact lies on the party tendering the relevant evidence.[54] Similarly, again in consequence of a principle of common law which the 2003 Act has not modified, if the relevant evidence is tendered by the prosecution, the requisite standard of proof will be proof beyond reasonable doubt[55], whereas if the relevant evidence is tendered by the defence, the requisite standard of proof will merely be proof on the balance of probabilities[56].

With reference to facts such as those of Kearley, the Law Commission[57] appears to have been of the view that, the burden of proving that the relevant evidence did not fall within the ambit of their reformulated hearsay rule was one which the prosecution would not find it difficult to satisfy to the criminal standard of proof.

> "7.41 In the borderline cases we described above, we believe that the difficulty of applying the law would be reduced by our recommended formulation of the hearsay rule. In a case such as *Kearley*...for example, we think a court would normally have little difficulty in concluding that it was not the callers' purpose to cause anyone to believe that anyone was (or was not) selling drugs."

What, however, of assertions implied from conduct which was not intended to amount to a communication? Applying the provisions of the 2003 Act to Parke B's sea captain example from *Wright v Doe d Tatham*[58] upon the assumption that those facts arose in a criminal context, it appears that, again, it would not be difficult for the party tendering the evidence to satisfy the burden of proving to the requisite standard of proof that the conduct of the sea captain did not fall within the ambit of the hearsay rule. This, it seems, would be so as the sea captain would, presumably, neither have acted as he did for the purpose of causing another person to believe that the ship was seaworthy nor (see the discussion of section 115(3)(b) at 1.6.2.2 below) would have done so for the purpose of causing another person to act or a machine to operate on the basis that that was so.

---

54 *See, for example, R v Acton JJ, ex parte McMullen (1990) 92 Cr App R 98; R v Mattey and Queeley [1995] 2 Cr App R 409; R v Jenkins (1869) LR 1 CCR 187.*

55 *See R v Acton JJ, ex parte McMullen (1990) 92 Cr App R 98; R v Jenkins (1869) LR 1 CCR 187.*

56 *See R v Mattey and Queeley [1995] 2 Cr App R 409.*

57 *In their Report "Evidence in Criminal Proceedings: Hearsay and Related Topics", Law Com No 245, at paragraph 7.4.1.*

58 *(1837) 7 Ad & El 313 (considered at 1.3.1 above).*

1.6.2.2 The significance of Section 115(3)(b)

Section 115(3)(b) provides that:

"(3) A matter stated is one to which this Chapter applies if (and only if) the purpose, or one of the purposes, of the person making the statement appears to the court to have been...

(b) to cause another person to act or a machine to operate on the basis that the matter is as stated."

The Law Commission[59] explained the basis of what is now section 115(3)(b) as follows.

"... we think it would be going too far to say that a statement should *never* fall within the hearsay rule unless it appears to have been intended to cause another to believe the fact stated. We have argued that a statement should be regarded as hearsay if it seems possible that it may have been deliberately fabricated; and there may be cases where a statement is deliberately fabricated although it is not intended that another person should believe it to be true. This may be so if it is intended that another person, while not necessarily believing the fact stated, should *act on the basis that it is true.*

7.34 Suppose, for example, that A's job involves reimbursing his colleagues for their travelling expenses. It is sought to prove that his colleague B travelled to Glasgow on a particular date, by adducing her claim form in which she stated that she had done so. We believe that that evidence should fall within the hearsay rule, because the claim might be fabricated. But if it were necessary, in order to bring a statement within the hearsay rule, to show that it was made with the intention of causing a person to *believe* it, it might be argued that B's claim is made with no such intention. It may be that, when a claim is submitted to A, all he is required to do is to check that it complies with the rules laid down for such claims; and if it does, he automatically pays it. If B tells him she has been to Glasgow on business, he will pay for that journey. He will not consider whether he *believes* that B has been to Glasgow, and it is probably of no concern to B whether he believes it or not.[28] But she does intend that he should act on the basis that it is true; and we believe that this should be sufficient to bring her statement within the hearsay rule."

"28 There is a similar difficulty in the law of deception: where a person assumes that everything is as it should be, and the defendant dishonestly takes advantage of that assumption, is the defendant obtaining by deception? See A T H Smith, "The Idea of Criminal Deception" [1982] Crim LR 721."

---

59 *In their Report "Evidence in Criminal Proceedings: Hearsay and Related Topics", Law Com No 245, at paragraphs 7.33-7.34.*

The effect of section 115(3)(b) is that even where a statement was not made for the purpose of causing another person to believe a matter stated, the matter stated will still be a "matter stated" for the purposes of Chapter 2 of Part 11 of the 2003 Act if it appears that either the sole or at least one of the purposes of its maker was, adopting the wording of section 115(b), "to cause another person to act or a machine to operate on the basis that the matter is as stated." In such circumstances, the statement will fall within the ambit of the section 114(1) hearsay rule provided that, adopting the wording of section 114(1), the statement was "not made in oral evidence in the proceedings" and is tendered "as evidence of [the] matter stated".

Consider the Law Commission's example, reproduced above. Presumably B's claim form would fall within the ambit of the hearsay rule at common law because it takes the form of an assertion that B had travelled to Glasgow on the relevant day, it being an assertion which is made other than in the course of the proceedings and which is tendered to prove that B did travel to Glasgow on the relevant day.

In relation to the application of the section 114(1) hearsay rule in such circumstances, it is submitted that at least one of B's purposes in completing the claim form may be to cause A to believe that the journey had taken place because, for example, if A does not believe this to be so the result may be that (in consequence of inquiries being raised by or at the instigation of A) internal disciplinary or even criminal proceedings might be instigated against B. Thus, it is submitted that the matter stated in the claim form might well be a "matter stated" in the section 115(3)(a) sense, in which case the claim form will fall within the ambit of the section 114(1) hearsay rule. The significance of section 115(3)(b) would be that even if B does not make the statement for the purpose of causing any person to believe the relevant matter (in which case section 115(3)(a) will be inapplicable) the matter stated in the claim form will still be a "matter stated" for the purposes of Chapter 2 of Part 11 of the 2003 Act provided that B makes the statement for the purpose of causing a person to act on the basis that the matter was as stated. If this is so the claim form will still fall within the ambit of the section 114(1) hearsay rule. Thus, the existence of section 115(3)(b) defeats an argument that might otherwise be raised at B's trial, namely, that the claim form is not a hearsay statement because B did not complete it for the purpose of making A believe that the journey had taken place.

Now, as a variation of the Law Commission's example, suppose that A agrees to process B's fraudulent expenses claims on the basis that A and B will split the proceeds. In those circumstances the argument that B does not complete the form for the purpose of causing A to believe that B had travelled to Glasgow on the relevant day would, on its face, seem to be conclusive, and section 115(3)(b) would, thus, appear be required in order for the statement to fall within the ambit of the section 114(1) hearsay rule. Even in this latter situation, however, it is arguable that section 115(3)(a) might at times be applicable in such circumstances in that whilst B will not complete the claim form for the purpose of causing A to believe that B had travelled to Glasgow on the relevant day, B may do so for the purpose of causing others in the organisation employing both A and B (through whose hands the claim form or information derived therefrom might at some stage pass, for example, for auditing purposes) to believe that B had travelled to Glasgow on the relevant day. This is to assume, of course, that section 115(3)(a) is applicable where a person makes a written statement not knowing whether it will fall into the hands of some other unascertained person but intending that if it does do so, the unascertained person will believe that the matters stated are true. In this context it is necessary to consider the distinction drawn by the Law Commission between "purpose" and "intention", which is considered at 1.6.2.3, below. What is again clear, however, is that, as was indicated above, the existence of section 115(3)(b) will defeat the otherwise tenable argument that the claim form is not a hearsay statement because B did not complete it for the purpose of making A believe that the journey had taken place.

The Law Commission[60] explained what is now section 115(3)(b) as it concerns the operation of machines in the following way.

> "...we believe that a statement should fall within the hearsay rule in any case where it is made with the intention that some action should be taken on the basis that the fact stated is true – even if the taking of that action involves no human intervention, but only the operation of a machine. Suppose, for example, that the processing of B's expenses claim is carried out not by A but by a computer system, which has been programmed to print a cheque for the appropriate amount if the information provided by the claimant appears to meet the specified criteria. Clearly the risk of fabrication is just as great as if the information were given to a human, and it would be arbitrary to apply different rules to the two cases."

As was indicated immediately above, it appears that B's claim form falls within the ambit of the hearsay rule at common law and, it is submitted, the fact that B intends to submit the form to a machine rather than to another person does not take it outside of the ambit of the common law rule. So far as the 2003 Act is concerned, if the information is to be typed into the machine by a human operator, it is arguable that B might make the statement for the purpose, even if only one of several purposes, of causing the operator to believe that she had travelled to Glasgow on the relevant day, in which case the matter stated will be a "matter stated" within the meaning of section 115(3)(a). If this is not the case, and the machine will "read" the information from the claim form without it first being "processed" by the mind of a human operator, it is still arguable that B might intend to cause others in the organisation employing B through whose hand the claim form or information derived therefrom may at some stage pass (e.g. an auditor) to believe that B had travelled to Glasgow on the relevant day. Again, in this context, it is necessary to consider the distinction drawn by the Law

---

60 *In their Report "Evidence in Criminal Proceedings: Hearsay and Related Topics", Law Com No 245, at paragraph 7.35.*

Commission between "purpose" and "intention", which is considered at 1.6.2.3, below. What is once again clear, however, is that the existence of section 115(3)(b) will defeat the otherwise tenable argument that the claim form is not a hearsay statement because B did not complete it for the purpose of making A believe that the journey had taken place. Thus, even if B does not make the statement for the purpose of making any person believe the relevant matter, the statement will still fall within the ambit of the section 114(1) hearsay rule if at least one of B's purposes is to make a machine operate on the basis that the matter was as stated.

1.6.2.3 The purpose of the person making the statement

Section 115(3) refers to the "purpose", rather than the intention, of the person making the statement. Again, the reason why this is so was explained by the Law Commission.[61]

"7.36 We have so far been referring to the *intention* with which the statement in question is made. But the word "intention" is ambiguous. In some contexts it refers only to the *purpose* with which a person acts – the objective that that person hopes to achieve by acting as he or she does. In others, it includes not only purpose but also what is sometimes called "oblique" intention. In this wider sense, a person "intends" not only the consequences that he or she *wishes* to bring about, but also those that he or she knows to be an inevitable side-effect of the consequences that he or she desires. In our recent reports we have used the word in the latter sense, reserving the word "purpose" for the former.[29]

7.37 The point is perhaps unlikely to be of great practical importance, but we have considered whether the applicability of the hearsay rule to a particular statement should depend on the *intention* (in our wider sense) or only on the *purpose* with which the statement is made. Should a person's words or conduct count as a hearsay statement of a fact if that person does not positively desire that another should thereby be caused to believe that fact (or that another should be caused to act, or a machine to operate, on the basis that it is true), but knows that this will inevitably occur?

7.38 Our reason for focusing on the "intention" of the putative declarant is that, if that person is not seeking to convey a particular impression, it follows that he or she cannot be seeking to convey a *misleading* impression: the possibility of deliberate fabrication is thus ruled out.[30] But this argument seems equally applicable where, although he or she knows that a particular inference will inevitably be drawn, that is not

---

61 *In their Report "Evidence in Criminal Proceedings: Hearsay and Related Topics", Law Com No 245, at paragraph 7.36-7.3.8.*

his or her purpose. Moreover, if we were to include within the hearsay rule the case where he or she knows that a particular inference *will* be drawn, it is hard to see any rational basis for excluding the case where he or she knows that it *may* be drawn. We believe that the most defensible place to draw the line is between those consequences that it is the putative declarant's purpose to bring about, and those that it is not."

"[29] See Legislating the Criminal Code: Offences Against the Person and General Principles (1993) Law Com No 218, paras 7.1 – 7.14, and cl 1(a) of the Criminal Law Bill annexed to that report.

[30] See paras 7.20 – 7.21 above."

It is necessary at this point to return to the Law Commission's example concerning B's claim form, which was considered at 1.6.2.2 above. When B completes the form for submission to A it is clearly possible that she may do so without the purpose of causing A to believe that she had travelled to Glasgow on the relevant day whilst possessing "oblique intention" in that regard. In other words it is clearly possible that B's purpose may solely be to cause A to act upon the basis that the matter is as stated in the claim form and that, whilst realising that A may well believe that the matter is as stated therein, B does not desire to bring this latter consequence about. In such circumstances, whilst section 115(3)(a) would be inapplicable, the claim form would still fall within the ambit of the section 114(1) hearsay rule due to the operation of section 115(3)(b).

Equally, it is submitted, if B does not make the statement for the purpose of making A believe that the matters are as stated in the claim form (or, as in the Law Commission's second example, if B makes the statement for processing by a computer system), it is submitted that if B desires those who might subsequently come into contact with the claim form (e.g. for auditing purposes) to believe that the trip to Glasgow did take place, then both 115(3)(a) and , consequently, the section 114(1) hearsay rule itself will be applicable. If, however, B does not desire to bring this consequence about, it is submitted that the fact that B realises that such persons, if they were to read the claim form, might well believe that the trip to Glasgow had taken place, would not activate section 115(3)(a) as it would not be B's purpose to cause the relevant persons to believe the relevant matter. In such circumstances, however, it appears that the effect of section 115(3)(b) would be that, provided that B intends to cause a person to act or a machine to operate upon the basis that the matter is as stated in the claim form, the claim form will still fall within the ambit of the section 114(1) hearsay rule.

Finally, it should be noted that section 115(3) does not require that the section 115(3)(a) or (b) purpose is the sole purpose for which the statement was made. Rather, it appears that provided that the section 115(3)(a) or (b) purpose was at least one of the purposes (not even the dominant purpose) for which the statement was made, the "matter stated" is still one to which Chapter 2 of Part 11 of the 2003

Act applies. Thus, in such circumstances, the section 114(1) hearsay rule will still be applicable to the relevant statement provided that, again adopting the wording of section 114(1), the statement was "not made in oral evidence in the proceedings" and is tendered "as evidence of [the] matter stated".

The Law Commission explained the position in relation to statements which are made for more than one purpose as follows.[62]

> "...we see no reason to confine the hearsay rule to statements which are made *solely*, or even primarily, for one of the specified purposes. Where a person has more than one purpose for what he or she says or does, we believe it should be sufficient that at least one of those purposes falls within the categories we have identified."

Thus, to return on one final occasion to the Law Commission's example of B's claim form, if B completes the claim form both for the purpose of causing A (or some other person in the organisation) to believe that B had travelled to Glasgow on the relevant day and for the purpose of causing A to act on the basis that B had travelled to Glasgow on the relevant day, it appears that the requirements of section 115(3) will still be satisfied. Indeed, it appears that this will be so even if B has some third purpose for making the statement and even if this third purpose is the dominant purpose for which the claim form is made.

1.6.2.4 Implied assertions in Criminal and Civil Proceedings

It is submitted that the operation of section 115(3) of the 2003 Act adds unnecessary complexity to the application of the hearsay rule. This unnecessary complexity might, it is submitted, have been avoided by creating a new hearsay exception to encompass implied assertions in the sense of assertions which may be implied from statements which were not intended to communicate the facts which the statements are tendered to prove, rather than by modifying concepts integral to the nature of the hearsay rule itself. Under the 2003 Act as enacted, however, it will not only be necessary for the court to consider when a statement is or is not tendered as evidence of the truth of the facts stated, itself often a vexed question in practice, but, rather, the court will also be required to consider to consider whether the purpose of its maker fell within one of the three categories of purpose specified by section 115(3). The case law concerning the nature of a hearsay statement is, it is suggested, already sufficiently complex without adding what appears to be an additional level of complexity to it.

It is submitted that a further disadvantage of section 115(3) of the 2003 Act is that once sections 114(1) and 115 of the Criminal Justice Act 2003 are in force, the nature of that which is a hearsay statement will differ between Criminal and Civil contexts. This is so as whilst the definition of "hearsay" contained in section 1 of

---

62 *In their Report "Evidence in Criminal Proceedings: Hearsay and Related Topics", Law Com No 245, at paragraph 7.39.*

the Civil Evidence Act 1995 effectively equates both with the common law definition of the hearsay rule and with that which is implicit within section 114(1) of the Criminal Justice Act 2003, the 1995 Act does not contain any provisions of equivalent effect to section 115(3) of the 2003 Act. Thus, in relation to the classification as hearsay of "implied assertions" in the sense of assertions which may be implied from statements which were not intended to communicate the facts which the statements are tendered to prove, it is submitted that the approach of the Civil Courts will presumably equate with that adopted at common law by the House of Lords in *R v Kearley*. Whilst, in the civil context, this will not result in the exclusion of evidence, because, under section 1 of the 1995 Act, the hearsay nature of evidence no longer results in its exclusion in civil proceedings, the classification of such "implied statements" as hearsay will bring sections 2-6 of the 1995 Act into play. This would not be the case if such statements did not fall within the ambit of the hearsay rule in the civil context.

1.7 Implied assertions as real or circumstantial evidence of identification.

1.7.1 The position at common law

In *R v Rice* [63], the Court of Criminal Appeal held that a used air ticket in the name of two of the appellants was properly admitted for the prosecution to prove that one of them, namely Rice, had flown to Manchester on the relevant day because, for that purpose, it was real evidence, not hearsay evidence. The basis of their Lordships' decision was essentially that the ticket was relevant and was admissible as "real evidence" because, as a matter of common sense, it had probably been used by a man bearing the name which was on it. Their Lordships indicated, however, that the operation of the hearsay rule would prevent the ticket from being relied on as evidence that it had been issued to the person whose name was on it and, for the same reason, doubted whether the ticket would have been admissible to prove that the named person had made the booking.

In relation to the distinction drawn in *Rice* between the use of the ticket to prove that a person called Rice had made the booking and the use of the ticket to prove that a person called Rice had used the ticket, the Law Commission[64] expressed the view that:

> "The distinction between these two uses of the ticket seems artificial: it was no more likely that the ticket had been used by someone called Rice than that it had been issued to someone of that name... In our view it would have been better to treat the ticket as direct evidence, and admissible, on the latter issue as well as the former."

---

63 [1963] 1 QB 857.
64 *In their Report "Evidence in Criminal Proceedings: Hearsay and Related Topics", Law Com No 245, at paragraphs 7.17-7.21.*

It is submitted that, in *Rice*, the true relevance of the used air ticket was that of an implied assertion to the effect that the accused had taken the relevant flight. Since the "assertion" was used as evidence of his having taken the flight, it is thus submitted that the "assertion" should properly have been classified as amounting to a hearsay statement.

In *R v Lydon*[65], The appellant, Sean Lydon, was charged with robbery and taking a conveyance without authority. His co-accused had pleaded guilty. Evidence of the discovery of a gun and two notes on the grass verge of a road which the getaway car would have used was admitted in support of identification evidence. One note read "Sean rules" and the other read "Sean rules 85". Ink stains on the gun could have come from the same ink which had been used to write the notes. The appellant was convicted. The Court of Appeal held that the evidence had properly been admitted as circumstantial evidence of identification because there had been no reliance upon the truth of the contents of the notes, the jury being entitled to infer that the person who had written the note had either been called Sean or had been associated with a person called Sean.

In relation to the admission of the evidence in Lydon, the Law Commission[66] asserted that:

> "It would have made no difference to the evidence's admissibility, but only to its weight, if the pieces of paper had borne the appellant's name in full. They were not so much an assertion by the writer (that his name was Sean) as something that a person not named Sean (and not associated with such a person) would be unlikely to write."

The evidence in *Lydon* was admitted for the purpose of identifying Sean Lydon as the robber. It is submitted that to the extent to which the evidence in *Lydon* is properly regarded as amounting to implied assertions to the effect that the notes had been written by Sean Lydon or by an associate thereof then the evidence should properly have been regarded, at common law, as falling within the ambit of the hearsay rule.

---

65 *(1987) 85 Cr App R 221.*
66 *In their Report "Evidence in Criminal Proceedings: Hearsay and Related Topics", Law Com No 245, at paragraph 7.16.*

1.7.2 The position under the Criminal Justice Act 2003

The nature and significance of section 115(3) of the 2003 Act was considered at 1.6.2 above. Applying section 115(3) of the 2003 Act to the facts of *R v Rice*[67], it appears that the ticket would not fall within the ambit of the section 114(1) hearsay rule if relied upon by the prosecution to prove that it had been used by a person called Rice, provided that the person who made the statement which the ticket contained neither made the statement that it contained for the purpose of causing another person to believe that the ticket had been used by a person called Rice nor did so for the purpose of causing another person to act or a machine to operate upon that basis. Moreover, it seems that the even if the person who made the statement which the ticket contained had realised that this would cause another person to believe or to act upon the basis, or would cause a machine to operate upon the basis, that the ticket had been used by a person called Rice, the ticket would not fall within the ambit of the section 114(1) hearsay rule provided that the person who made the statement had not made it for the purpose of bringing about one or more of those consequences.[68]

Because the ticket was tendered by the prosecution, the burden of proving that the ticket did not fall within the ambit of the section 114(1) hearsay rule (i.e. of persuading the court that the maker of the statement did not make it for one of the abovementioned purposes) would be borne by the prosecution to the criminal standard of proof.[69] Thus, if the judge was not satisfied beyond reasonable doubt that that maker of the statement did not make it for one of the abovementioned purposes, it appears that the ticket would fall within the ambit of the section 114(1) hearsay rule if tendered to prove that it was used by a person called Rice. Whether or not the prosecution were able to discharge this burden to the standard required by law would presumably depend upon whether the maker of the statement might have had any reason to achieve the result of causing another to believe or to act upon the basis, or a machine to operate upon the basis, that the ticket had been used by a person called Rice. In practice, it might well be that in circumstances such as those of Rice's case, the obvious inference for the court to draw from the facts before it would be that the maker of the statement had no such purpose in mind[70], in which case the ticket would not fall within the ambit of the section 114(1) hearsay rule.

Applying section 115(3) of the 2003 Act to the facts of *R v Lydon*[71], it appears that the notes would not fall within the ambit of the hearsay rule if relied upon by the

---

67   *[1963] 1 QB 857 (considered at 1.7.1 above).*

68   *See 1.6.2.3 above.*

69   *See 1.6.2.1 above.*

70   *In their Report "Evidence in Criminal Proceedings: Hearsay and Related Topics", Law Com No 245, at paragraph 7.2.9, recognised that*
>   *"...it will usually be possible to infer from the circumstances the intentions of the person in question."*

71   *(1987) 85 Cr App R 221 (considered at 1.7.1 above)..*

prosecution as identification evidence provided that the prosecution could satisfy the court to the criminal standard of proof that the writer had neither made the statements for the purpose of causing another person to believe that he was or was associating with a person called Sean nor had done so for the purpose of causing another person to act or a machine to operate upon that basis. It is submitted that, upon the facts of *Lydon*, it is difficult to see how the court could do otherwise than conclude that the writer of the notes did not make the statements for either of these purposes and, consequently, applying section 115(3) to those facts, it is submitted that the notes would not appear to fall within the ambit of the section 114(1) hearsay rule.

1.8 Records relied upon to prove that events not recorded did not take place

1.8.1 The position at common law

In *R v Patel*[72], the Court of Appeal considered the applicability of the hearsay rule where records are adduced as evidence of the non-existence of facts not recorded in them. An issue at the trial to which the appeal related had been whether a Mr Ashraf was an illegal entrant into the U.K. The prosecution had adduced the evidence of an immigration officer to prove that Mr Ashraf's name did not appear in certain Home Office records, thus proving that he was an illegal entrant. The Court of Appeal, obiter, suggested, in relation to the admissibility of the records, that the prosecution should have called an officer who was responsible for the compilation and custody of the records to testify that they had been compiled and kept in such a way that if Mr Ashraf's name was not recorded therein then he must have been an illegal entrant. Upon the facts of *Patel's* case, however, no such officer had been called for this purpose and, consequently, the Court of Appeal held that the immigration officer's evidence was inadmissible due to the operation of the hearsay rule.

In *R v Shone*[73], the appellant was charged with handling stolen goods, namely, vehicle springs. In order to prove that the goods had neither been sold nor used in a repair by their lawful owner, the prosecution called the owner's stock clerk and part sales manager to testify that if the springs had been sold or used in a repair then the record cards which they kept would have been marked accordingly, which they were not. The appellant was convicted. The Court of Appeal, applying the approach which, it appears, the Court of Appeal in *Patel* would have applied to such evidence, held that the evidence of the stock clerk, Mrs Morpeth, and the parts sales manager, Mr Brock, was direct evidence from which the jury were entitled to infer that the goods had been stolen. Thus, the Court of Appeal held that the evidence was not hearsay evidence and had properly been admitted.

---

72   *[1981] 3 All ER 94.*
73   *(1983) 76 Cr App R 72.*

In relation to evidence of this type, the Law Commission[74] recognised that:

> "7.10 Closely connected to the problem of "implied assertions" is that of negative assertions. For the purposes of the hearsay rule it is obviously immaterial whether the fact to be proved is positive or negative, provided that an assertion of the fact is adduced as evidence of its truth. The difficulty arises where it is debatable whether the evidence of a negative fact is an assertion of it, or a fact suggesting in some other way that it is true."

> 7.11 Suppose, for example, that the fact to be proved is the fact that a particular event did not occur. The fact-finders may be invited to reason that, if it had occurred, its occurrence would have been recorded; and that, since its occurrence was not recorded, it did not occur. But is the non-recording of the event an assertion that it did not occur, or is it directly probative? In *Shone*[12] the evidence of a stock clerk and a sales manager that workers would have made entries on record cards if certain items had been lawfully disposed of, that there were no such entries, and that those items must therefore have been stolen, was held not to be hearsay but direct evidence of that fact. It seems that, if an inference is drawn from what a document says, the document is hearsay; but if an inference is drawn from what it does not say (or from the fact that no document exists), that is direct evidence."

> "[12] (1983) 76 Cr App 72."

It is submitted that the evidence which was admitted in *Shone* should have been regarded as falling within ambit of the common law exclusionary hearsay rule because there is no logical reason either for distinguishing a positive inference from a negative one for the purposes of the hearsay rule or for regarding the calling of witnesses to testify as to the method of compilation and custody of a record as being of relevance in determining its hearsay status. Rather, it is submitted that such evidence should properly have been regarded as hearsay evidence, though as evidence which potentially fell within the ambit of one of the hearsay rule's statutory exceptions.[75] That the case has been the subject of criticism was subsequently recognised by the Divisional Court.[76]

---

74 *In their Report "Evidence in Criminal Proceedings: Hearsay and Related Topics", Law Com No 245, at paragraphs 7.10-7.11.*

75 *At the time when Shone was decided, the relevant statute would have been the Criminal Evidence Act 1965. Subsequently such evidence, if classified as hearsay, might have been admissible under section 68*

of the Police and Criminal Evidence Act 1984 and, most recently, under section 24 of the Criminal Justice Act 1988. For the position under the Criminal Justice Act 2003 see 2.2.2, below.

76 *In R v Bullard (1992) 95 Cr App R 175.*

1.8.2 The position under the Criminal Justice Act 2003

The nature and significance of section 115(3) of the 2003 Act was considered at 1.6.2 above. In relation to the application of section 115(3) in the context of the failure to record a fact, the position is stated thus by paragraph 401 of the Explanatory Notes to the Criminal Justice Act.

> "...where the assertion relates to a failure to record an event, sometimes known as negative hearsay, it will not be covered by Chapter 2 if it was not the purpose of the person who failed to record the event to cause anyone to believe that the event did not occur."

Applying section 115(3) to the facts of *R v Shone*[77], it appears that the evidence of the stock clerk and part sales manager that the record cards did not record the sale or use of the springs would not be likely to fall within the ambit of the section 114(1) hearsay rule. It seems that the evidence would not fall within the ambit of the section 114(1) hearsay rule, even though it was relied upon by the prosecution to prove that the springs had not been sold or used, provided that the prosecution persuaded the court to the criminal standard of proof that the person who failed to record the sale or use of the springs neither did so for the purpose of causing another person to believe that the springs had not been sold or used nor did so for the purpose of causing another person to act or a machine to operate on the basis that the springs had not been sold or used.[78] Presumably, upon facts such as those of *Shone's* case, there will often be little difficulty in persuading the court to the criminal standard of proof that the persons responsible for the compilation of the relevant records would have had no such purpose in failing to record matters which did not occur. That this is likely to be so was recognised by the Law Commission.[79]

> "...where a person has failed to record an event,[33] it will often be clear that that failure was not intended to give the impression that the event had not occurred. Either the event did not occur, or that person did not realise that it had: in either case, it will not have been his or her purpose to cause anyone to believe that it had not happened, because it will not have crossed his or her mind that anyone might think it had. And therefore the record will be direct evidence that the event did not occur."
>
> "[33] As in Shone, para 7.11 above."

It is submitted that, in such circumstances, any purpose which the persons responsible for the compilation of the relevant records may have in relation to the compilation thereof will normally relate to the recording of positive events, such as the receipt and sale of items. The use of such records to prove that a positive

---

77 (1983) 76 Cr App R 72 (considered at 1.8.1 above).

78 *In relation to the incidence of the legal burden or proof and the nature of the requisite standard of proof in such circumstances, see 1.6.2 above.*

79 *In their Report "Evidence in Criminal Proceedings: Hearsay and Related Topics", Law Com No 245, at paragraphs 7.41.*

recorded event did take place will, it appears, normally fall within the ambit of the hearsay rule as it will exist under the 2003 Act, as, it is suggested, a purpose of recording the occurrence of the event will, presumably, normally be to cause other persons to believe or to act upon the basis, or to cause a machine to operate upon the basis, that that the event took place. Thus, the purpose of recording the receipt of an item might well be to cause other employees to believe or to act upon the basis, or a machine to operate on the basis, that the item is in stock. Equally, the purpose or recording the sale of an item may well be to cause other employees to believe or to act upon the basis, or a machine to operate on the basis, that the item is no longer in stock. Conversely, it seems that the use of such records to prove that an event which was not recorded therein did not take place will not normally be likely to fall within the ambit of the hearsay rule as it will exist under the 2003 Act, because failing to record an event which did not take place will not normally be a conscious act (or indeed any form of act at all) to which any purpose at all may be ascribed.

What would be the position, however, where an employee who intended to steal an item which had been delivered to his employer failed to record the receipt of the item in his employer's stock records so as to cause the employer and the supplier to believe that the item had never been delivered to the employer's premises? Suppose that the lorry driver who had been responsible for delivering the item from the supplier to the employer's premises was charged with its theft and that, at the trial, the employee (i.e. the real thief) was called by the prosecution to produce the stock record, the prosecution relying upon the stock record to prove that the item had never been delivered to the employer's premises by the lorry driver. Presumably the lorry driver would, in his defence, assert that he had delivered the item. In such circumstance, would the court necessarily infer that the employee might have had a section 115(3)(a) or (b) purpose in failing to record the delivery of the item? Since the burden of proving the admissibility of the evidence (i.e. that it did not fall within the ambit of the section 114(1) hearsay rule) would be borne by the prosecution[80], it is submitted that the defence would merely need to put a reasonable doubt in the court's mind concerning the possibility that the item might have been stolen after rather than prior to delivery in order to persuade the court that the stock records did indeed fall within the ambit of the section 114(1) hearsay rule. This, it is submitted, would be so because if there was a reasonable doubt that the goods might have been stolen after rather than prior to delivery then it is unlikely that the court would be satisfied beyond reasonable doubt that the employee who failed to record their delivery had no section 115(3)(a) or (b) purpose in failing to do so.

What, however, if, upon the above facts, the employee himself was charged with the theft of the item? It is submitted that in those circumstances there must be a

---

80   *In relation to the incidence of the legal burden or proof and the nature of the requisite standard of proof in such circumstances, see 1.6.2 above.*

distinct likelihood that the court would infer that the employee would have a section 115(3)(a) or (b) purpose in failing to record the delivery of the item. Certainly, if the employee wished to rely upon the stock records in his defence he would presumably have a difficult task in persuading the court on the balance of probabilities that he had no such purpose.[81] Thus, it appears likely that, in such circumstances, the stock records would fall within the ambit of the section 114(1) hearsay rule. Consequently, it would appear to be necessary in such circumstances for the defence to have recourse to one or more of the exceptions to the rule against hearsay which are examined in the second part of this book.

1.9 Evidence produced by machines

1.9.1 The position at common law

At common law, the hearsay rule does not apply to a printout produced by a machine or to information which was displayed on a machine's visual display unit or even to words which were "spoken" by the machine (for example, "speak your weight scales") provided that the machine produced the printout or displayed or otherwise expressed the information without relying upon data which had passed through a human mind.[82] Rather, at common law, such evidence, is classified as "real evidence", and this is so whether the machine takes the form of a simple machine, such as a car speedometer[83], or takes the form of a more complex machine, such as a computer.[84] The hearsay rule is, however, applicable at common law to a machine's printout or to information which was displayed on its visual display unit (and, presumably, to words which were "spoken" by a machine) which is tendered as evidence of the truth of the facts "stated" by the machine if, in producing the printout or displaying or otherwise expressing the relevant information, the machine relied upon data which had passed through a human mind.[85] In this latter situation it appears that a printout produced by a machine or information displayed or otherwise expressed thereby will not fall within the ambit of the hearsay rule, however, if admissible evidence of the data that was fed into the machine (i.e. of the data which had passed through a human mind) is adduced.[86]

In *R v Spiby*[87], the appellant had been convicted of being knowingly concerned in the fraudulent evasion of the prohibition on importation of a controlled drug. At the appellant's trial, the prosecution adduced in evidence printouts produced by a computerised machine (a "Norex machine") which had operated at a hotel at which a Mr Zoabir had been staying. The function of the Norex machine was to

---

81 *In relation to the incidence of the legal burden or proof and the nature of the requisite standard of proof in such circumstances, see 1.6.2 above.*

82 *See, for example, R v Spiby (1990) 91 Cr App Rep 186 and see, also, Sapporo Meru v Statue of Liberty [1968] 1 W.L.R. 739 and R v Wood (1982) 76 Cr App R 23.*

83 *See, for example, Nicholas v Penny [1950] 2 KB 466.*

84 *See, for example, R v Spiby (1990) 91 Cr App R 186.*

85 *See, for example, R v Coventry JJ, Ex Parte Bullard (1992) 95 Cr App R 175.*

86 *See R v Wood (1982) 76 Cr App R 23.*

87 *(1990) 91 Cr App R 186.*

record details of telephone calls for billing purposes. The printouts, inter alia, showed that several telephone calls had been made to the appellant's home and to his club from two rooms at the hotel which Mr Zoabir had occupied and from a public telephone in the hotel. The Court of Appeal held that the printouts did not fall within the ambit of the hearsay rule but, rather, were real evidence because their content did not depend upon anything which had passed through a human mind.[88]

In *R v Coventry Justices, ex parte Bullard and another*[89], upon the application of the City of Coventry District Council, liability orders had been made against the two applicants for judicial review in respect of their alleged failure to pay the community charge (poll tax). It appeared that the Council had relied upon a computer printout to prove the amounts which the applicants were liable to pay and the amounts that were unpaid. The Divisional Court, upon the assumption that the information that the printout contained amounted to or was derived from information implanted into the computer by a human, held that the printout was hearsay and was inadmissible either to prove the amounts that the applicants were liable to pay or to prove the amounts that were unpaid.[90]

In *R v Wood*[91], the accused had been convicted of handling stolen metal. At the appellant's trial, in order to prove that the metal found at his company's premises came from the stolen consignment, the prosecution relied upon chemical analysis of the metal found at the accused's premises and of retained samples of the metal in the stolen consignment. The scientists who had analysed the samples had used x-ray spectrometry and a neuron transmission monitor and had fed the results produced by these tests into a computer which had then calculated the percentages of various metals in the sample. The relevant scientists had all been called to give evidence at the trial. The Court of Appeal regarded the computer as a mere tool which had not contributed any knowledge but which had merely performed calculations which could have been performed manually. Their Lordships' held that the figures produced by the computer did not fall within the ambit of the hearsay rule but, rather, that the computer printout was real evidence the proof and relevance of which depended upon the testimony of the relevant witnesses.

---

88 The decision of the Court of Appeal in *R v Spiby* was overruled by the House of Lords in *R v Shephard* [1993] AC 380 in relation to the operation of section 69 of the Police and Criminal Evidence Act 1984 (which concerned the admissibility of documents produced by computers). The decision in *Spiby* remained good law, however, in relation to the classification of the printouts produced by the Norex machine as real evidence. Moreover, subsequent to the decision of the House of Lords in *Shepard*, section 69 of the 1984 was repealed by section 60 of the Youth Justice and Criminal Evidence Act 1999 (see the Youth Justice and Criminal Evidence Act 1999 (Commencement No. 2) Order 2000 (SI 2000 No. 1034 (C.27)).

89 (1992) 95 Cr App R 175.

90 It should be noted that if the facts of *Bullard* arose today, the printouts would be admissible under section 1 of the Civil Evidence Act 1995 (see also the Magistrates' Courts (Hearsay Evidence in Civil Proceedings) Rules 1999).

91 (1982) 76 Cr App R 23.

The Law Commission[92] effectively explained the distinction at common law between the decisions in *Bullard and Wood* upon the basis that, in the former case, the data that had been fed into the machine had not been proved by admissible evidence whereas in the latter case it had been so proved.

> "7.46 By contrast, the present law does sometimes exclude evidence of a statement generated by a machine, where the statement is based on information fed into the machine by a human being. In such a case, it seems, the statement by the machine is admissible only if the facts on which it is based are themselves proved.
>
> 7.47 In *Wood*,[39] for example, it was sought to prove that certain metal found in the appellant's possession was of the same type as a stolen consignment, by adducing evidence of figures produced by a computer which had analysed the results of X-rays and other tests carried out by chemists. It was held that this was not hearsay because the chemists had given oral evidence of the results of the tests. In the absence of admissible evidence of those results, the computer's analysis of the results would not have been admissible either. In *R v Coventry Justices, ex p Bullard*,[40] on the other hand, a computer printout stating that a person was in arrears with his poll tax was held to be inadmissible hearsay because it must have been based on information "implanted" into the computer by a human, which had not been properly proved."

> "[39] (1982) 76 Cr App R 23.
>
> [40] (1992) 95 Cr App R 175."

The position, it is submitted, equates with the "evidential gap"[93] which can exist in criminal proceedings where expert opinion evidence is based on hearsay evidence of the primary facts to which the expert's opinion relates. In such circumstances if the evidential gap is not closed by admissible evidence of the primary facts the operation of the hearsay rule renders the expert opinion inadmissible.[94]

1.9.2 The position under the Criminal Justice Act 2003

Under the 2003 Act, the admissibility of representations of fact made by machines which, respectively, do and do not depend for their accuracy on information provided by persons are governed by distinct principles.

---

92 In their Report *"Evidence in Criminal Proceedings: Hearsay and Related Topics"*, Law Com No 245, at paragraphs 7.46-7.47.

93 Considered at 2.2.8 below.

94 See, for example, *Chester-Nash v Crown Prosecution Service* LTL 18/4/2000. It should be noted that section 127 of the Criminal Justice Act 2003, which is considered at 2.2.8 below, makes specific provision concerning the closure of this evidential gap.

1.9.2.1 Representations of fact made by machines which do not depend for their accuracy on information supplied by a person.

Section 115(1)-(2) of the 2003 Act provide that:

"(1)   In this Chapter references to a statement or to a matter stated are to be read as follows.

(2)   A statement is any representation of fact or opinion made by a person by whatever means; and it includes a representation made in a sketch, photofit or other pictorial form."

The position, under the 2003 Act, of sketches and photofits is considered at 1.10, below. In relation to evidence produced by machines without reliance upon data which has passed through a human mind, the position is stated by paragraph 402 of the Explanatory Notes to the Criminal Justice Act as follows.

"Subsection (2) preserves the present position whereby statements which are not based on human input fall outside the ambit of the hearsay rule...documents produced by machines which automatically record a process or event or perform calculations will not therefore be covered by Chapter 2."

The Law Commission[95] explained the position under the equivalent clause of their draft Bill as follows.

"7.44   The hearsay rule does not apply to...documents produced by machines which automatically record an event or circumstance (such as the making of a telephone call from a particular number,[36] or the level of alcohol in a person's breath).[37] In such a case the court is not being asked to accept the truth of an assertion made by any person. The evidence is not hearsay but real evidence.

7.45   Our draft Bill preserves this rule by confining the word "statement" to a representation made by a person.[38] The conclusions printed out (or "spoken") by a machine are not a statement for the purposes of the Bill, and therefore the hearsay rule does not apply to them."

[36] Eg Neville [1991] Crim LR 288; Spiby (1990) 91 Cr App R 186.

[37] Castle v Cross [1984] 1 WLR 1372. In that case, the disputed statement from the machine was not a blood-alcohol reading, but a statement that the defendant had failed to provide a sample of his breath large enough for it to analyse. See also Owens v Chesters (1985) 149 JP 295.

[38] See cl 2(2) of the draft Bill."

---

95   *In their Report "Evidence in Criminal Proceedings: Hearsay and Related Topics", Law Com No 245, at paragraphs 7.44-7.45.*

Thus, applying section 115(2) to the facts of R v Spiby[96], it appears that the printouts would not fall within the ambit of the section 114(1) hearsay rule because the printouts did not amount to a representation of fact or opinion made by a person.

1.9.2.2 Representations of fact made by machines which do depend for their accuracy on information supplied by a person.

Section 129(1) of the 2003 Act provides that:

"(1) Where a representation of any fact–

(a) is made otherwise than by a person, but

(b) depends for its accuracy on information supplied (directly or indirectly) by a person,

the representation is not admissible in criminal proceedings as evidence of the fact unless it is proved that the information was accurate."

The operation of what is now section 129(1) of the 2003 Act is explained by paragraph 432 of the Explanatory Notes to the Criminal Justice Act as follows.

"This section provides where a statement generated by a machine is based on information implanted into the machine by a human, the output of the device will only be admissible where it is proved that the information was accurate."

The Law Commission[97], with reference to the distinction between those circumstances in which evidence produced by machines was admissible as real evidence at common law and those in which such evidence was treated at common law as falling within the ambit of the hearsay rule, explained the position under what is now section 129(1) of the 2003 Act in the following way.

"7.48 We believe that this distinction is well-founded and should clearly be preserved. In a case such as ex p Bullard it would be absurd to admit the printout without requiring proof of the input on which it was based. The question is, on what basis should such evidence be excluded? One view is that it is hearsay, because it is tantamount to a statement made by the person who fed the data into the machine.[41] An alternative view is that the statement by the machine, properly understood, is conditional on the accuracy of the data on which it is based; and that, if those data are not proved to have been accurate, the statement therefore has no probative value at all. The question of hearsay does not arise, because the statement is simply irrelevant.

---

96 *(1990) 91 Cr App R 186 (considered at 1.9.1 above).*

97 *In their Report "Evidence in Criminal Proceedings: Hearsay and Related Topics", Law Com No 245, at paragraphs 7.48-7.50.*

7.49   We believe that the latter view is closer to the truth, and that it is therefore unnecessary to complicate our hearsay rule by extending it to statements made by machines on the basis of human input. On the other hand we do not think it would be safe to assume that everyone will share this view. We must anticipate the argument that, if such statements are inadmissible at present, that is because they are hearsay; that, under our recommendations, they would no longer be hearsay, because our formulation of the rule would apply only to representations made by people; and that they would therefore cease to be inadmissible.

7.50   We have therefore concluded that a separate provision is necessary, independent of the hearsay rule."

"41 This is how the matter appears to have been regarded in ex p Bullard."

Thus, the Law Commission's intention appears to have been that the combined effect of what are now sections 115(2) and 129(1) of the 2003 Act would be that evidence produced by machines which relied upon data which had passed through a human mind would not fall within the ambit of the hearsay rule (because, under section 115(2) the evidence would not amount to a representation of fact or opinion made by a person) but that such evidence would be subject to the admissibility requirement imposed by section 129(1). Applying these principles to the facts of *R v Coventry Justices, ex parte Bullard and another*[98], it appears that, under the 2003 Act, the printouts would not fall within the ambit of the hearsay rule but that they would only be admissible if the prosecution proved to the criminal standard of proof that they were accurate. It is submitted that the facts of *R v Wood*[99] provide an example of how this burden of proof may be satisfied (i.e. by calling both those persons who were responsible for conducting the tests the results of which were fed into the machine and those who actually fed the relevant data therein), though there is presumably no reason why the accuracy of the relevant data could not be proved by the hearsay evidence of such persons provided that such evidence was admissible under an exception to the hearsay rule.

What would the position be under the 2003 Act in relation to a word-processed document, typed into a personal computer by its maker and printed out at a later date? Such a document should, it is submitted, be regarded as a representation of fact made by a person and, consequently, should fall within the ambit of section 115(2), rather than within that of section 129(1). Thus, it is submitted, if such a document is relied upon as evidence of a matter stated it should, under the 2003 Act, be regarded as falling within the ambit of the section 114(1) hearsay rule. If such a document is properly so regarded, however, then to what extent does data typed in to a database by a human operator logically differ from it? Is the data

---

98   *(1992) 95 Cr App R 175 (considered at 1.9.2.1 above).*
99   *(1982) 76 Cr App R 23 (considered at 1.9.2.1 above).*

embodied in the printouts in *Bullard* properly to be regarded as a representation of fact made otherwise than by a person or are the *Bullard* printouts, like, it is submitted, a word processed document, merely the document in which a representation of fact made by a person is embodied? Conversely, if the printout in *Bullard* is properly regarded as a representation of fact which was made otherwise than by a person then should the word-processed document also be so regarded? To what extent does a word-processed letter, typed by a council officer, which states that Mr A owes the council £x, logically differ from entries in a database to the same effect typed by the same officer? To what extent would the position differ if the letter were a standard letter into which the officer had typed the amount owed and into which Mr A's address and/or the amount, which he allegedly owed, had been inserted from the council's database by mean of the use of mail-merge technology? It is submitted that the precise nature of the distinction between those representations of fact which are made by a person and those which are made by a machine but which depend for their accuracy upon information supplied by a person is unclear. Indeed, in *R v Wood*[100], Lord Lane CJ, delivering the judgment of the Court of Appeal, recognised that their Lordships' decision related only to the particular computer and to the particular programme which the case concerned and that there are many types of computer, many different types of programme and many types of use to which they may be put.

Perhaps the provisions of section 115(2) and 129(1) of the 2003 Act are too simplistic to effectively encompass the wide variety of potentially evidence producing machines which already exist and which may well come into existence in the foreseeable future. It will, of course, be for the courts to apply these statutory provisions to the evidential realities of the computer age.

1.9.3 The presumption preserved by section 129(2)

Section 129(2) of the 2003 Act provides that:

> "(2)   Subsection (1) does not affect the operation of the presumption that a mechanical device has been properly set or calibrated."

Paragraph 432 of the Explanatory Notes to the Criminal Justice Act explains the effect of what is now section 129(2) as follows.

> "Subsection (2) preserves the common law presumption that a mechanical device has been properly set or calibrated.

It is assumed that the presumption to which section 129(2) refers is that which the Law Commission referred to in Part 16 of their report.[101] This is the presumption

---

100 *(1982) 76 Cr App R 23 at p. 26.*

101 *In their Report "Evidence in Criminal Proceedings: Hearsay and Related Topics", Law Com No 245, at paragraphs 13.13-13.21. In Part 13 of the report the Law Commission recommended the repeal of section 69 of the Police and Criminal Act 1984, which* concerned the admissibility of statements in documents produced by computers. Section 69 was subsequently repealed by section 60 of the Youth Justice and Criminal Evidence Act 1999 (see the Youth Justice and Criminal Evidence Act 1999 (Commencement No. 2) Order 2000 (SI 2000 No. 1034 (C.27)).

that, unless there is evidence to the contrary, machines (such as breath test machines[102], traffic lights[103], speedometers[104] and computers[105]) were working properly at any given time. Thus, Lord Denning MR, with reference to the operation of the presumption in the context of the operation of traffic lights106, recognised that the presumption, in the absence of evidence in rebuttal, is that such devices are in proper working order.

Whilst it is stated in some academic works that the presumption only applies to machines of a type which normally work properly[107], it is submitted that the authorities footnoted in the preceding paragraph do not appear to impose such a requirement.[108] Moreover, whilst the presumption is sometimes classified as an aspect of the presumption of regularity it is submitted that it is better regarded as a distinct, if related, presumption.[109] Thus, whilst in the context of the presumption of regularity the Privy Council[110] has held both that where a fact is central to an offence and where an offence touches and concerns the accused's liberty the courts will not presume a fact's existence in the prosecution's favour, the authorities concerning the drawing of the presumption that machines were in proper working order at a given time[111] do not appear to treat the operation of the presumption as being limited in this way.

An example of the operation of the presumption in the context of criminal proceedings is provided by R v Spiby[112], their Lordships holding that the presumption was applicable to the Norex machine which the case concerned. This aspect of the Court of Appeal's decision in Spiby was subsequently overruled by the House of Lords in R v Shephard [1993] AC 380 upon the basis that the operation of section 69 of the Police and Criminal Evidence Act 1984 (which concerned the admissibility of statements in documents produced by computers) left no room on the facts of the case for the operation of the presumption. Section 69 of the 1984 Act has since been repealed, however[113] and, consequently, it appears that the approach of the Court of Appeal in Spiby is now good law.

---

102 See *Castle v Cross [1985] 1 All ER 87; Cracknell v Willis [1988] 1 AC 450.*

103 See *Tingle Jacobs & Co v Kennedy [1964] 1 WLR 638.*

104 See *Nicholas v Penny [1950] 2 KB 466.*

105 See *R v Spiby (1990) 91 Cr App R 186.*

106 In *Tingle Jacobs & Co v Kennedy [1964] 1 WLR 638 at p. 639.*

107 See, for example, *Cross and Tapper on Evidence,* 9th ed, Butterworths, 1999, at p.33. Similarly, Murphy, in *Murphy on Evidence,* 8th ed, Blackstone Press, 2003, at 694, is of the view that the presumption arises upon proof of the primary fact that the machine normally works properly. In contrast, Keane, in the *Modern Law of Evidence,* 5th ed, Butterworths, 2000, at p 639, regards the presumption as one which has no primary fact (i.e. as one which the court must draw in relation to machines of a type which are normally in working order unless it is rebutted).

108 See, in particular, *Simon Brown LJ Castle v Cross [1985] 1 All ER 87 at p. 89.* See, also, *Law Com No 245, Evidence in Criminal Proceedings: Hearsay and Related Topics* para 13.13 and *Phipson on Evidence,* 14th ed, Sweet and Maxwell, 1990 at 23-14.

109 See *Castle v Cross [1985] 1 All ER 87 at p.89* (reproduced below). See also *Law Com No 245, Evidence in Criminal Proceedings: Hearsay and Related Topics* para's 13.16-13.17.

110 See *Lord Fraser of Tullybelton delivering the judgment of the Privy Council in Dillon v R [1982] AC 484 at p.487.*

111 See, for example: *Nicholas v Penny [1950] 2 KB 466; Castle v Cross [1985] 1 All ER 87; R v Spiby (1990) 91 Cr App R 186.*

112 (1990) 91 Cr App R 186 (considered at 1.9.1 above).

113 By section 60 of the Youth Justice and Criminal Evidence Act 1999 (see the Youth Justice and Criminal Evidence Act 1999 (Commencement No. 2) Order 2000 (SI 2000 No. 1034 (C.27)).

1.9.4 Evidence produced by machines in Civil Proceedings

It should be noted that the Civil Evidence Act 1995, which governs the admissibility of hearsay evidence in civil proceedings, does not contain provisions equivalent to sections 115(2) and 129(1) of the 2003 Act. Consequently, it is submitted that under the statutory definitions of "hearsay" and "statement" contained, respectively, in sections 1(2)(a) and 13 of the 1995 Act, the approach that the civil courts will take when determining whether or not evidence produced by a machine falls within the ambit of the hearsay rule is likely to equate to that taken by the criminal and civil courts at common law.[114]

1.10 Photographs, films, video recordings and tape recordings

1.10.1 The position at common law

At common law the hearsay rule does not apply to photographs, video recordings or films of persons, events, objects, or locations which do not contain, or are not tendered as evidence of, statements made orally, in writing or by conduct, such evidence being classified as "real evidence".[115] Thus, for example, the common law hearsay rule does not apply to a video recording of the commission of an offence (provided of course that the video recording is not tendered as evidence of the truth of facts stated on tape by persons whose statements were video recorded).[116] Equally, at common law, the hearsay rule does not apply to photographs, video recordings or films of information displayed by the visual display units of machines which produce the information which they display without relying upon data which has passed through a human mind, such evidence again being classified as "real evidence".[117] Thus, for example, the common law hearsay rule did not apply to photographs of echoes of vessels on the screen of a radar set.[118] Moreover, the common law, hearsay rule is not applicable to tape recordings of mere sounds (for example, the sound of dogs barking)[119] or, it is submitted, to recordings of words "spoken" by machines which do not rely upon information which has passed through a human mind in producing their "spoken" output[120], such evidence, once again, being classified not as hearsay evidence but as real evidence.[121]

At common law, the hearsay rule is applicable to photographs, video recordings or films which contain oral or written statements or statements made by conduct (for example, to microfilm of written documents[122], to video recordings of the making

---

114 *Considered at 1.9.1 above.*

115 *See: R v Tolson (1864) 4 F & F 103; Kajala v Noble (1982) 75 Cr App R 149; Taylor v Chief Constable of Cheshire [1987] 1 All ER 225; R v Clarke [1995] Cr App R 425.*

116 *See, for example, Taylor v Chief Constable of Cheshire [1987] 1 All ER 225.*

117 *See 9.1 above.*

118 *See Sapparo Meru v Statue of Liberty [1968] 1 WLR 739.*

119 *An example of the admission of such evidence is provided by Lloyd v Symonds LTL 20/3/98.*

120 *See 9.1 above.*

121 *See Sapparo Meru v Statue of Liberty [1968] 1 WLR 739 and see R v Clarke [1995] Cr App R 425.*

122 *See Myers v DPP [1965] AC 1001.*

of witness statements orally[123] or to video recordings of the making of confessions by re-enactment[124]) which are tendered as evidence of the facts stated. Equally, at common law, the hearsay rule is applicable to tape recordings of oral statements (for example, covert tape recordings of conversations[125]) which are relied on as evidence of the truth of the facts stated. Presumably, where they are relied upon as evidence of the truth of the facts stated, the common law hearsay rule also applies to photographs, video recordings or films of the visual display units of machines which rely upon data which has passed through a human mind in producing the information which they display and to tape recordings of words "spoken" by machines which rely upon such data in producing their "spoken" output.[126]

An example of the treatment of a video recording which did not contain a statement as real evidence is provided by the facts of *Taylor v Chief Constable of Cheshire*.[127] The appellant was convicted of theft. Prior to the trial, police officers had viewed a videotape taken by a shop's C.C.T.V. system of the alleged commission of the alleged offence by the appellant, but the tape had been erased by the time of the trial. At the trial, the magistrates had permitted the police officers to give evidence of the contents of the video recording. The Divisional Court held that the evidence did not fall within the ambit of the hearsay rule and had properly been admitted, the evidence amounting to direct evidence of what had happened at the relevant place at the relevant time and effectively equating with a direct view of the relevant events by an eye-witness and/or with a witness viewing the relevant events live via a visual display unit.

An example of the treatment of a video recording which did contain an oral statement as hearsay evidence is provided by the facts of *R v Duffy*.[128] The appellant was convicted of robbery and manslaughter. At her trial, the judge, in the exercise of his discretion under section 26 of the Criminal Justice Act 1988, excluded a video recording of an interview of an eyewitness, Martin Coyne junior, who had severe speech difficulties and who was, in consequence of his disabilities, unfit to attend as a witness. The words spoken by Mr Coyne were virtually incomprehensible to anyone other than Mr Evans, a social worker who knew Mr Coyne and who had conducted the relevant part of the interview. The Court of Appeal, like the trial judge, treated the video recording as hearsay evidence but, taking into account the fact that Mr Evans had been available to give evidence of a kind which was similar to that given by a foreign language interpreter, held that the judge should have exercised his discretion so as to admit the evidence under the hearsay exception created by section 23 of the 1988 Act.

---

123 See *R v Duffy [1999] QB 919.*
124 See *Li Shu-Ling v R [1989] AC 270.*
125 See *Ventouris v Mountain [1992] 3 All ER 414.*

126 See *9.1 above.*
127 *[1987] 1 All ER 225.*
128 *[1999] QB 919.*

1.10.2 The position under the Criminal Justice Act 2003

As has already been seen, section 115(1),(2) provide as follows:

> "(1)   In this Chapter references to a statement or to a matter stated are to be read as follows.
>
> (2)   A statement is any representation of fact or opinion made by a person by whatever means; and it includes a representation made in a sketch, photofit or other pictorial form."

The nature and significance of section 115(2) of the 2003 Act was considered at 1.9.2 above. In relation to the operation of what is now section 115(2) in the context of tapes, films or photographs, paragraph 402 of the Explanatory Notes to the Criminal Justice Act states that:

> "Subsection (2) preserves the present position whereby statements which are not based on human input fall outside the ambit of the hearsay rule. Tapes, films or photographs which directly record the commission of an offence...will not therefore be covered by Chapter 2."

The Law Commission[129] described the position as follows.

> "7.44   The hearsay rule does not apply to tapes, films or photographs which record a disputed incident actually taking place,[35]...In such a case the court is not being asked to accept the truth of an assertion made by any person. The evidence is not hearsay but real evidence.
>
> 7.45   Our draft Bill preserves this rule by confining the word "statement" to a representation made by a person.[38]"

> [35] Eg Dodson (1984) 79 Cr App R 220, in which the two accused were photographed by security cameras during their attempted robbery of a building society.

> [38] See cl 2(2) of the draft Bill."

Applying the section 115(2) definition of "statement" to the facts of *Taylor v Chief Constable of Cheshire*[130], it is submitted that the video recording showing the alleged commission of an offence by the accused would not fall within the ambit of the hearsay rule as it will exist under the provisions of the 2003 Act because the video recording did not contain a "representation of fact or opinion made by a person". In contrast, applying the section 115(2) definition to the facts of *R v Duffy*[131], it appears that, because the video recording which *R v Duffy* concerned did contain a "representation of fact or opinion made by a person", the *Duffy* video recording would fall within the ambit of the section 114(1) hearsay rule.

---

129 *In their Report "Evidence in Criminal Proceedings: Hearsay and Related Topics", Law Com No 245, at paragraphs 7.44-7.45.*

130 *[1987] 1 All ER 225 (considered at 1.10.1 above).*

131 *[1999] QB 919 (considered at 1.10.1 above).*

What would be the position under the 2003 Act, however, if the sound quality of videotaped evidence, such as that which *Duffy* concerned, had been subjected to digital computer enhancement? When the sounds made by the witness were enhanced by the computer operator using his software in a way which might have involved him in the making of subjective judgments concerning matters such as which technique he should apply to the digitised sounds and to what extent he should apply it, would the product of the enhancement still be a representation of fact made by the witness or would it be a representation of fact made by the computer which depended for its accuracy upon information supplied by the witness? In other words, would the product of the enhancement process amount to hearsay evidence for the purposes of the 2003 Act or would it, for the purposes of that Act fall outside the ambit of the section 114(1) hearsay rule but be subject to the admissibility requirement imposed by section 129(1) of the 2003 Act?[132] To what extent does a video recorded interview the sound quality of which has been subjected to digital enhancement by a human computer operator differ from a printout from a database which has processed words typed into it by a council officer? Once again, for the reasons stated at 1.9.2.2 above, it is submitted that the nature of the distinction between representations of fact which are made by a person and those which are made by a machine, but which depend for their accuracy upon information supplied by a person, is not entirely clear.

1.11 Photofits, sketches and E-fits.

1.11.1 The position at common law

At common law it has been held that photofits and sketches of an offender, prepared from descriptions of the offender given by witnesses, do not fall within the ambit of the hearsay rule.[133] In *R v Cook*[134], the appellant was convicted of robbery and indecent assault. At his trial a photofit, which a police officer had produced prior to the appellant's arrest from a description of the offender which the victim had given, had been admitted in evidence for the prosecution. The appellant argued before the Court of Appeal that the photofit should have been excluded both because it was a hearsay statement and because it was a previous consistent statement. The Court of Appeal held that the photofit had properly been admitted because its production amounted to an imperfect form of the operation of a camera, a photofit not amounting to or resembling a written statement and neither falling within the ambit of the hearsay rule nor within that of the rule against previous consistent statements.

---

132 *Considered at 1.9.2.2 above.*
133 *See R v Cook [1987] QB 417.*
134 *[1987] QB 417.*

It is submitted that, logically, photofits and sketches of offenders do not equate with photographs of offenders, because, unlike a photograph of an offender, a photofit or a sketch of an offender is a document which records, if in a non verbal form, a witness' out of court description thereof. Viewed in another way, a photograph of an offender may be distinguished from a photofit or a sketch thereof because, unlike the photograph, the photofit and the sketch are not images produced by machines which do not rely upon data which has passed through a human mind.[135] Thus, it is submitted that photofits and sketches do not equate with photographs but, rather, equate with written statements, photofits and sketches merely amounting to alternative methods of recording the witness' out of court description of the offender. Thus, it is submitted that photofits and sketches should properly be regarded at common law as falling within the ambit of the hearsay rule if tendered as evidence of the truth of the facts stated (i.e. as evidence of the appearance of the offender). Certainly, the common law status of photofits and sketches gives rise to the anomaly, recognised by the Law Commission[136], that whilst the photofit or sketch derived from the witness' description of the accused is admissible at common law, the effect of the hearsay rule is that:

> "...the court is not permitted to receive evidence of the words the witness used to describe what the attacker looked like, evidence which the hearsay rule would certainly exclude..."

Another potential problem, related to the admissibility of photofits and sketches at common law, in relation to which there does not appear to be any direct authority, is the position of E-fits. Essentially, an E-fit is a photofit produced by a machine relying upon data which has been processed by a human brain. Applying the common law principle that photofits, like photographs, are real evidence[137], E-fit evidence would not appear to fall within the ambit of the hearsay rule at common law. Conversely, applying the common law principle that the output of machines which rely upon data which has passed through a human mind does fall within the ambit of the hearsay rule if relied upon as evidence of the truth of the facts stated[138], E-fit evidence would appear to be hearsay evidence at common law if so relied upon. The common law status of E-fits remains unclear though, it is suspected that a court considering the position of E-fit evidence at common law would be more likely to adopt the solution of classifying such evidence as real evidence, and thus of treating it as admissible, rather than that of classifying it as hearsay evidence, and thus as inadmissible subject to the operation of a hearsay exception.

---

135 *See 1.9 above.*

136 *In their Report "Evidence in Criminal Proceedings: Hearsay and Related Topics", Law Com No 245, at paragraph 10.6.*

137 *See 1.10.1 above.*

138 *See 1.9.1 above.*

1.11.2 The position under the Criminal Justice Act 2003

Section 115(1)-(2) of the 2003 Act provide that:

"(1)   In this Chapter references to a statement or to a matter stated are to be read as follows.

(2)   A statement is any representation of fact or opinion made by a person by whatever means; and it includes a representation made in a sketch, photofit or other pictorial form."

It appears that the effect of section 115(2) in relation to the status under the 2003 Act of sketches and photofits of offenders produced from descriptions given by witnesses is that, because representations of fact made in sketches and photofits are classified as "statements", sketches of offenders and photofits will fall within the ambit of the section 114(1) hearsay rule if they are tendered as evidence of a matter "stated".[139] The status of E-fit evidence under the 2003 Act appears, however, to be less clear. On the one hand it might be argued that the E-fit, like the photofit and the sketch, will fall within the ambit of the section 114(1) hearsay rule, the E-fit being, for the purposes of section 115(2):

"...a representation made in...other pictorial form".

On the other hand it might be argued that, for the purposes of section 115(2), the representation which the E-fit contains is not

"made by a person".

If this is the case, the E-fit evidence will not fall within the ambit of the hearsay rule as that rule will exist under the 2003 Act. Rather, if E-fit evidence does not fall within the ambit of the section 114(1) hearsay rule it would appear to be subject to the admissibility requirement imposed by section 129(1) of the 2003 Act concerning representations which are made "other than by a person".[140] It is submitted that the status of such evidence under the 2003 Act remains to be determined by the courts.

---

139 *In relation to the admissibility of such evidence under a hearsay exception created by the 2003 Act see 2.2.4.3.2, below.*

140 *See 1.9.2.2 above.*

Part Two

THE ADMISSIBILITY OF HEARSAY EVIDENCE IN CRIMINAL PROCEEDINGS

2.1 Introduction to Part Two

Part One of this book, above, was primarily concerned with the nature of those statements which will amount to hearsay statements when Chapter 2 of Part 11 of the Criminal Justice Act 2003 is brought into force. Part Two of this book is primarily concerned with the nature of those exceptions to the hearsay rule under which hearsay evidence will be admissible in criminal proceedings when Chapter 2 of Part 11 of the 2003 Act is in force. Part Two of this book also concerns a number of supplementary provisions which are contained in Chapter 2 of Part 11 (concerning multiple hearsay, exhibits, competence, credibility, unconvincing hearsay evidence, exclusionary discretion, expert evidence, representations not made by persons, depositions, retrials, rules of court and the proof of statements in documents) and the miscellaneous and supplemental evidential provisions which are contained in Chapter 3 of Part 11 (concerning video evidence and memory refreshing).

Once Chapter 2 of Part 11 of the 2003 Act is in force, hearsay evidence will be admissible in criminal proceedings[1] in accordance with section 114(1) of the Act, which provides as follows:

"(1)   In criminal proceedings a statement not made in oral evidence in the proceedings is admissible as evidence of any matter stated if, but only if—

(a)   any provision of this Chapter or any other statutory provision makes it admissible,

(b)   any rule of law preserved by section 118 makes it admissible,

(c)   all parties to the proceedings agree to it being admissible, or

(d)   the court is satisfied that it is in the interests of justice for it to be admissible."

Thus, when Chapter 2 of Part 11 of the 2003 Act is in force, hearsay evidence will be admissible in criminal proceedings if it falls within the ambit of any of the four categories of hearsay exceptions recognised by section 114(1) of that Act. First, hearsay evidence may be admissible under a statutory exception to the hearsay rule

---

1   *In relation to the meaning of "criminal proceedings" for the purposes of Chapter 2 of Part 11 of the 2003 Act see 2.2.2 above.*

(other than the exception created by section 114(1)(d)) whether the statutory exception is one which the 2003 Act itself will create or is one which was (or will be) created by some other statutory provision. Secondly, hearsay evidence may be admissible under a common law exception to the hearsay rule which is preserved by section 118 of the 2003 Act. Thirdly, hearsay evidence may be admissible by agreement of the parties. Finally, hearsay evidence may be admissible in accordance with section 114(1)(d) of the 2003 Act, which will create a new, discretionary, statutory exception to the hearsay rule, the purpose of which, according to paragraph 396 of the Explanatory Notes to the Criminal Justice Act:

> "...is that the court should be able to admit an out-of-court statement which does not fall within any of the other categories of admissibility, where it is cogent and reliable."

Whilst, as Parts One and Two of this book demonstrate, Chapter 2 of Part 11 of the 2003 Act will significantly modify both the nature of those statements which fall within the ambit of the hearsay rule and the nature of the exceptions to that rule, it should be noted that section 114(3) of the 2003 Act provides that:

> "(3)Nothing in this Chapter affects the exclusion of evidence of a statement on grounds other than the fact that it is a statement not made in oral evidence in the proceedings."

Thus, for example, it appears the provisions of the 2003 Act will not prevent the exclusion of hearsay evidence which falls within the ambit of one of the hearsay exceptions recognised by the 2003 Act on the basis that the evidence is irrelevant, is inadmissible evidence of opinion or in the exercise of the trial judge's exclusionary discretion (either his common law exclusionary discretion or that conferred upon him by section 78 of the Police and Criminal Evidence Act 1984[2]). Similarly, as Mr Michael Wills (the Parliamentary Under-Secretary of State for the Home Department) stated in Standing Committee B in the House of Commons on Tuesday 28 January 2003:

> "...neither Chapter 2 nor anything else in the Bill is intended to affect the common law rule in criminal trials that prevents witnesses from expressing their opinions on what might have happened in the case. ...if an out-of-court statement contains opinion evidence, that part of the statement will not be admissible unless it falls within one of the exceptions to the general rule against opinion."[3]

---

2   *Note, that the section 78 and common law exclusionary discretions are expressly preserved by section 126(2) of the 2003 Act, which is considered at 2.7.5.2, below.*

3   *See Hansard (Commons) 28 January 2003 Column 621.*

Equally, as paragraph 399 of the Explanatory Notes to the Criminal Justice Act recognises in relation to the operation of section 114(3):

> *"Subsection (3)* provides that out of court statements may still be excluded even if they fulfil the requirements in this Chapter. For example, confessions must meet the additional requirements of sections 76 and 78 of the Police and Criminal Evidence Act 1984 before admission."

The admissibility of hearsay evidence in criminal proceedings under each of the four categories of hearsay exceptions which are recognised by section 114(1) of the 2003 Act will be considered in the course of the present Part of this book. Following the present introductory section, Part Two's second and third sections concern, respectively, those statutory exceptions to the hearsay rule (other than the exception created by section 114(1)(d) of the 2003 Act) which will be created by the 2003 Act itself and the most significant pre-existing examples of statutory exceptions to the hearsay rule (i.e. hearsay exceptions created, by statutory provisions other than the 2003 Act) which will be retained when the 2003 Act's hearsay regime is in force. The next three sections of Part Two concern, respectively, those common law exceptions to the hearsay rule which will be preserved by the 2003 Act, the admissibility of hearsay evidence under the 2003 Act by agreement of the parties and the admissibility of hearsay evidence in the exercise of the court's inclusionary discretion under section 114(1)(d) of the 2003 Act. The final section of Part Two, and thus of this book, concerns a variety of other provisions contained in Chapter 2 of Part 1 of the 2003 Act, which mainly concern the admissibility, credibility and use of hearsay evidence in criminal proceedings.

2.2 Statutory exceptions to the hearsay rule created by the 2003 Act (other than the exception created by section 114(1)(d))

Chapter 2 of part 11 of the Criminal Justice Act 2003 will both create a number of new statutory exceptions to the hearsay rule and will repeal several existing exceptions thereto. Other than the new "safety valve"[4] discretionary hearsay exception created by section 114(1)(d) of the Criminal Justice Act 2003, which is considered at 2.6 below, the new hearsay exceptions which the 2003 Act creates are considered in sections 2.2.1 to 2.2.9, below. The nature of the statutory exceptions to the hearsay rule which the 2003 Act will repeal is considered at 2.4.1, below.

---

4   *The "safety valve" terminology was used by the Law Commission to describe the inclusionary discretion created by Clause 9 of their draft Bill of which section 114(1)(d) of the 2003 Act appears to be a descendant (see "Evidence in Criminal Proceedings: Hearsay and Related Topics", Law Com No 245, at paragraphs 1.39 and 8.133 and following).*

2.2.1 Witnesses who are unavailable

Section 116 of the 2003 Act provides as follows.

"(1) In criminal proceedings a statement not made in oral evidence in the proceedings is admissible as evidence of any matter stated if–

    (a) oral evidence given in the proceedings by the person who made the statement would be admissible as evidence of that matter,

    (b) the person who made the statement (the relevant person) is identified to the court's satisfaction, and

    (c) any of the five conditions mentioned in subsection (2) is satisfied.

(2) The conditions are–

    (a) that the relevant person is dead;

    (b) that the relevant person is unfit to be a witness because of his bodily or mental condition;

    (c) that the relevant person is outside the United Kingdom and it is not reasonably practicable to secure his attendance;

    (d) that the relevant person cannot be found although such steps as it is reasonably practicable to take to find him have been taken;

    (e) that through fear the relevant person does not give (or does not continue to give) oral evidence in the proceedings, either at all or in connection with the subject matter of the statement, and the court gives leave for the statement to be given in evidence.

(3) For the purposes of subsection (2)(e) "fear" is to be widely construed and (for example) includes fear of the death or injury of another person or of financial loss.

(4) Leave may be given under subsection (2)(e) only if the court considers that the statement ought to be admitted in the interests of justice, having regard–

    (a) to the statement's contents,

    (b) to any risk that its admission or exclusion will result in unfairness to any party to the proceedings (and in particular to how difficult it will be to challenge the statement if the relevant person does not give oral evidence),

    (c) in appropriate cases, to the fact that a direction under section 19 of the Youth Justice and Criminal Evidence Act 1999 (c. 23) (special measures for the giving of evidence by fearful witnesses etc) could be made in relation to the relevant person, and

    (d) to any other relevant circumstances.

(5) A condition set out in any paragraph of subsection (2) which is in fact satisfied is to be treated as not satisfied if it is shown that the circumstances described in that paragraph are caused–

(a) by the person in support of whose case it is sought to give the statement in evidence, or

(b) by a person acting on his behalf,

in order to prevent the relevant person giving oral evidence in the proceedings (whether at all or in connection with the subject matter of the statement)."

2.2.1.1 Section 116 of the 2003 Act and section 23 of the 1988 Act distinguished

Section 116 of the 2003 Act may essentially be regarded as a descendant of section 23 of the Criminal Justice Act 1988, a provision which the 2003 Act will repeal.[5] There are, however, a number of differences between section 23 of the 1988 Act and section 116 of the 2003 Act.

(a) A major difference between section 23 of the 1988 Act and section 116 of the 2003 Act is that whereas section 23 was limited in its application to statements which were made in documents, section 116 will not be limited to documentary statements but, rather, will apply to "statements" in the sense in which they are defined by section 115(2) of the 2003 Act.

Section 115(2) defines a statement as follows.

"A statement is any representation of fact or opinion made by a person by whatever means; and it includes a representation made in a sketch, photofit or other pictorial form."

Thus, unlike section 23 of the 1988 Act, it appears that section 116 of the 2003 Act will encompass not only statements which were made in documents but also statements which were made orally or by conduct. What is not quite so clear, however, is whether, where A makes his statement orally and B writes it down without giving A an opportunity to check and sign or otherwise verify it, A's statement may be proved only by calling B to prove it or whether, in the absence of B, A's statement may be proved by producing B's written version thereof. The written statement would not be admissible under section 23 of the 1988 Act because, it not having been written or checked and verified by A, it was not "made in a document" by A.[6] Similarly, it may be that for the purposes of the 2003 Act the written statement, not having been checked and verified by A, should not be regarded as a statement made by A but rather should be regarded as a statement

---

5   *See section 136.*
6   *See R v Mcgillivray (1993) 97 Cr App R 232 and Re D (A Minor) [1986] 2 FLR 189 (a case* *under section 2 of the Civil Evidence Act 1968, which has since been repealed).*

made by B. If this is correct, then it appears that whether or not A's statement may be proved by means of the production of B's written statement will depend upon the operation of the rules concerning multiple hearsay, which are contained in section 121 of the 2003 Act and are examined at 2.7.1, below.

Essentially, the effect of these rules in the present context would appear to be that if the written statement is properly regarded as B's statement, the written statement will not be admissible to prove A's oral statement unless one of the statements (i.e. either A's oral statement or B's written statement) is admissible under section 117, section 119 or section 120 of the 2003 Act[7], the parties agree to the admission of the statement for this purpose or the court exercises its discretion under section 121(1)(c) to admit the written statement for this purpose. It may be, however, that if the document has been "received"[8] by a police officer it will fall within the ambit of the section 117 hearsay exception (which is considered at 2.2.2 below), in which case the multiple hearsay problem (if this problem indeed exists), would appear to be solved.

What of a covert tape recording of A's statement made by B? Certainly, it appears that such a tape recording, as opposed to a tape recording which A intentionally made, would not have fallen within the ambit of section 23 of the 1988 Act, A not having made his statement in a document.[9] It is submitted, however, that a tape recording of A's statement may be distinguished from B's written but unverified version of A's statement. The basis of this submission is that the tape recording can hardly be regarded as a statement made by B, and that, under the 2003 Act, the court, even if it regarded the written but unverified statement as a statement made by B, would still be justified in regarding the covert tape recording as a statement made by A.

(b) A second distinction between section 23 of the 1988 Act and section 116 of the 2003 Act is that section 116(1)(b) will require that:

> "(b) the person who made the statement (the relevant person) is identified to the court's satisfaction…"

Section 23 of the 1988 Act contains no such provision.10 The Law Commission regarded the version of this provision in their draft Bill as necessary both in order that the court could be satisfied of the existence of the maker of the hearsay statement and in order that the other party could make enquiries concerning the maker and could, in appropriate circumstances, adduce evidence for the purpose

---

7   Which are, respectively, considered at 2.2.2, 2.2.3 and 2.2.4, below.

8   See 2.2.2.2.3, below.

9   In relation to the admissibility of tape recordings under section 23 of the 1988 Act see *R v Duffy* [1999] QB 919, *R v Lockley* [1995] 2 Cr App R 554 and *Ventouris v Mountain (Italia Express) (Ship)* [1992] 3 All ER 414 (a case under section 2 of the Civil Evidence Act 1968, which has since been repealed).

10   Though it may be that section 23(2)(c) of the 1988 Act, where the statutory ground which it concerns is relied upon, implicitly requires the party relying upon it to prove the identity of the unavailable maker of the hearsay statement (see Keane, *The Modern Law of Evidence*, 5th ed, Butterworths, 2000).

of discrediting him.[11] Moreover, the Law Commission recognised that in the absence of such a provision the admissibility of the evidence of the hearsay evidence of an unavailable witness in criminal proceedings could give rise to a violation of Article 6(3)(d) of the European Convention on Human Rights.[12]

(c) Thirdly, section 23 of the 1988 Act expressly provides that its operation is subject to paragraph 1A of schedule 2 to the Criminal Appeal Act 1968 (requiring that evidence which was given orally at the original trial is normally to be given orally at the retrial)13, that section 23 does not render admissible a confession made by a defendant which is inadmissible under section 76 of the Police and Criminal Evidence Act 1984[14] and that section 23 does not apply to committal proceedings.[15]

So far as section 116 of the 2003 Act is concerned, section 128(2) of that Act provides that,

> "Subject to subsection (1), nothing in this Chapter makes a confession by a defendant admissible if it would not be admissible under section 76 of the Police and Criminal Evidence Act 1984...",

It appears that the effect of section 128(2) will be that a confession made by a defendant which is not admissible under section 76 of the 1984 Act will not be admissible under any of the other exceptions to the hearsay rule which the 2003 Act will create, preserve or retain except, potentially, under section 76A of the 1984 Act.[16]

In relation to evidence at retrial, section 131 of the 2003 Act will substitute a new provision for paragraphs 1 and 1A of Schedule 2 to the 1968 Act which, inter alia, will permit the admission at a retrial (under section 116 of the 2003 Act), of the hearsay evidence of a person who gave oral evidence at the original trial.[17]

Concerning the issue of the admissibility of hearsay evidence at committal proceedings, section 23(5) of the 1988 Act was not included in section 23 as originally enacted but was inserted into section 23 by the Criminal Procedure and Investigations Act 1996.[18] It is submitted that the failure to reprise section 23(5) within the context of the 2003 Act is in line with the raft of amendments and repeals concerning the allocation of cases triable either way and the sending of cases to the Crown Court which will come into effect when the relevant provisions of the 2003 Act are brought into force.[19]

---

11 See *"Evidence in Criminal Proceedings: Hearsay and Related Topics"*, *Law Com No 245*, at paragraph 8.6.
12 See *"Evidence in Criminal Proceedings: Hearsay and Related Topics"*, *Law Com No 245*, at paragraph 8.8. The significance of Article 6(3)(d) in the context of the admission or exclusion of hearsay evidence in criminal proceedings is considered at 2.8 below.
13 Section 23(1).
14 Section 23(4).
15 Section 23(5).
16 Section 76 of the 1984 Act is examined at 2.4.2.9.2 below and 76A of that Act is examined at 2.2.7.2 below.
17 See 2.4.1 below.
18 Section 47, Schedule 1, Part II, paragraph 28.
19 The provisions of the 2003 Act which concern these matters, namely, Part 6 of Schedule 3 and Part 4 of Schedule 37, fall outside the scope of this book and are thus not reproduced in its appendix.

(d) A fourth distinction between section 23 of the 1988 Act and section 116 of the 2003 Act is that the provisions of section 116 which concern the unavailability of a witness through fear[20] are both more comprehensive and more complex than those of section 23(3), which they will replace. The new provisions equate with those contained in the Law Commission's draft Bill and result from criticisms of section 23(3) of the 1988 Act which the Law Commission regarded as cogent.[21] The nature and effect of the new provisions is considered at 2.2.1.2, below.

(e) Fifthly, section 116(5) of the 2003 Act provides that any of the statutory conditions of admissibility imposed by section 116(2) of that Act, which concern the reason for the witness' unavailability, will not be treated as satisfied if it is shown that the relevant circumstances were caused (either by the person in support of whose case the hearsay statement is tendered or by a person acting on behalf thereof) for the purpose of preventing the witness from giving oral evidence. Section 23 of the 1988 Act contains no equivalent provision to section 116(5). The Law Commission[22] regarded this new provision as necessary because under the provisions of their draft Bill, the admissibility of hearsay evidence which satisfied the requirements of the clauses which equate with section 116 of the 2003 Act would be automatic[23], whereas the admissibility of hearsay evidence under section 23 of the 1988 Act is subject both to the exclusionary discretion conferred by section 25 of the 1988 Act and, potentially, to the leave requirements imposed by section 26 of that Act. The nature and effect of section 116(5) is considered at 2.2.1.2 below.

(f) A sixth distinction between section 23 and section 116 concerns the extent to which section 23 does, and section 23 will, apply to multiple (i.e. "second hand") hearsay. The Law Commission[24] was of the view that section 23 of the Criminal Justice Act 1988 does not extend to encompass multiple hearsay. The Law Commission[25] recognised, however, that the view that section 23 of the 1988 Act does not encompass multiple hearsay is not necessarily correct.

Whilst, as the Law Commission recognised, the authorities concerning the operation of section 23 of the 1988 Act do not make the position clear, reference to the authorities concerning the now repealed section 2 of the Civil Evidence Act 1968, suggests that whilst second hand hearsay evidence is not generally admissible under section 23 of the 1988 Act [26], such evidence may be admissible under section 23 where the maker of the hearsay statement could have given direct oral evidence

---

20 *I.e. section 116(2)(e), (3) and (4).*

21 *See "Evidence in Criminal Proceedings: Hearsay and Related Topics", Law Com No 245, at paragraphs 8.48 to 8.70.*

22 *See "Evidence in Criminal Proceedings: Hearsay and Related Topics", Law Com No 245, at paragraph 8..27.*

23 *It should be noted, however, that where evidence is admissible under section 116 its admissibility will still be subject to the exercise of the court's exclusionary discretion (see 2.7.5 below).*

24 *See "Evidence in Criminal Proceedings: Hearsay and Related Topics", Law Com No 245, at paragraph 8.25.*

25 *At paragraph 8.26.*

26 *See Re Koscot Interplanetary (UK) Ltd [1972] 3 All ER 829.*

of the relevant facts (even though he had no personal knowledge of them) in accordance with some other exception to the hearsay rule.[27] Whilst the position in relation to section 23 of the 1988 Act is not totally clear, what does appear to be clear is that, in consequence of the operation of section 121 of the 2003 Act[28], some second hand hearsay evidence will be potentially admissible under section 116 of the 2003 Act.

(g) Seventhly, the definition of "statement" for the purposes of Chapter 2 of Part 11 of the 2003 Act differs from that of "statement" for the purposes of Part II of the 1988 Act. For the purposes of the 1988 Act "statement" is defined[29] as:

> "any representation of fact, however made".

In contrast, for the purposes of the 2003 Act[30]:

> "A statement is any representation of fact or opinion made by a person by whatever means; and it includes a representation made in a sketch, photofit or other pictorial form."

The major significance of the new definition of "statement" is that, as was seen in Part One of this book, above, certain evidence which falls within the ambit of the hearsay rule at common law (and which would thus potentially fall within the ambit of the hearsay exception created by section 23 of the 1988 Act under the definition of statement contained therein) will not fall within the ambit of the hearsay rule as that rule will exist in the context of criminal proceedings once Chapter 2 of Part 11 of the 2003 Act is in force. Equally, evidence of this type, namely, evidence which is at common law but will not under the 2003 Act be hearsay evidence, will, in consequence of the new definition of "statement", not fall within the ambit of the hearsay exception created by section 116. Since such evidence does not fall within the ambit of the hearsay rule itself, the fact that it does not fall within the ambit of the section 116 hearsay exception will, of course, be of no practical significance.

A second consequence of the new section 115(2) definition of "statement", reproduced immediately above, will be that the hearsay exception created by section 116 of the 2003 Act, unlike that created by section 23 of the 1988 Act, will encompass not merely representations of fact but also representations of opinion (i.e. hearsay opinion evidence) The hearsay exception created by section 23 of the 1988 Act does not encompass opinion evidence because, as was seen immediately above, for the purposes of the hearsay provisions of the 1988 Act a "statement is defined[31] as meaning "any representation of fact, however made".

---

27 See *The Ymnos [1981] 1 Lloyd's rep 550*.

28 *Which is considered at 2.7.1 below.*

29 *By Schedule 2, para 5 (as inserted by section 15 of the Civil Evidence Act 1995).*

30 *Section 115(2).*

31 *By paragraph 5(1) of Schedule 2 to the 1988 Act.*

(h) An eight distinction between section 23 and section 116 is that whereas the admissibility of evidence under section 23 of the 1988 Act is subject to the exclusionary discretion conferred by section 25 of that Act and may be subject to the section 26 leave requirement, no provisions equivalent to section 25 and section 26 of the 1988 Act exist within the statutory framework created by Chapter 2 of Part 11 of the 2003 Act. Thus, in circumstances in which the conditions of admissibility which section 116 lays down are satisfied, the position under section 116 of the 2003 Act, unlike that under section 23 of the 1988 Act, will, to adopt the expression used by the Law Commission[32], be one of "automatic admissibility".

This "automatic admissibility" is subject to one exception, namely, that, as is seen at 2.2.1.2.8 below, section 116(2)(e) of the 2003 Act will confer a specific exclusionary discretion in the context of section 116 itself. Moreover, the court will continue to possess both its common law discretion to exclude evidence tendered by the prosecution and its discretion under section 78 of the Police and Criminal Evidence Act 1984 to exclude such evidence. Additionally, section 126(1) of the 2003 Act will confer upon the Court discretion to exclude admissible hearsay evidence for the purpose of preventing undue waste of time. The nature of the section 126(1) discretion, the role of exclusionary discretion in relation to the admission of hearsay evidence under the 2003 Act, and the reasons why the Law Commission recommended the repeal of sections 25 and 26 of the 1988 Act without their replacement by corresponding provisions of the new legislation are considered at 2.7.5 below. In this context the reader is also directed to section 125 of the 2003 Act (stopping the case where evidence is unconvincing) which is considered at 2.7.4, below.

(i) Finally, section 123(1) of the 2003 Act imposes express requirements concerning the "required capability" (i.e. the competence) of the maker of a hearsay statement for the purposes of, inter alia, section 116 thereof. In contrast, the provisions of the 1988 Act do not impose any such requirements (though it appears that the competence of the maker of the hearsay statement is a matter which the court should take into account in the exercise of its discretion under section 26 of the 1988 Act).[33] The operation of section 123(1) is considered at 2.7.2, below.

2.2.1.2 The operation of section 116

Essentially, a hearsay statement will be admissible under section 116 of the 2003 Act as evidence of matter stated if its maker's oral evidence would be admissible as evidence of the relevant matter[34], its maker is identified to the satisfaction of the court[35] and any one of the conditions specified by section 116(2) is satisfied.[36] In relation to these three requirements it is submitted that the general principle that

---

32 See, generally, Part 8 of "Evidence in Criminal Proceedings: Hearsay and Related Topics", Law Com No 245.

33 See R v D The Times May 21 2002.

34 See section 116(1)(a).
35 See section 116(1)(b).
36 See section 116(1)(c).

the party who tenders evidence bears the burden of proving the facts upon which the admissibility of the relevant evidence depends to the standard required by law will, subject to one exception, be applicable. Thus, it is submitted that where hearsay evidence is tendered under section 116 by the prosecution, the prosecution will bear the burden of proving beyond reasonable doubt the existence of any facts the existence of which forms an essential prerequisite to the admissibility of evidence under section 116.[37] Conversely, it is submitted that where hearsay evidence is tendered under section 116 by the defence, the defence will bear the burden of proving on the balance of probabilities the existence of any facts the existence of which forms an essential prerequisite to the admissibility of evidence under section 116.[38] The exception, referred to above, concerns the operation of section 116(5), considered at 2.2.1.2.9 below, in relation to which it appears that the burden of proving that a section 116(2) condition is not satisfied due to the operation of section 116(5) will be borne not by the party tendering the hearsay evidence but, rather, by the party who asserts that the relevant condition is not satisfied.

2.2.1.2.1 Section 116(1)(a)

In relation to the requirement, imposed by section 116(1)(a), that "oral evidence given in the proceedings by the person who made the statement would be admissible as evidence of" the matter stated, it should be noted that section 134(1) of the 2003 Act provides that:

> ""oral evidence" includes evidence which, by reason of any disability, disorder or other impairment, a person called as a witness gives in writing or by signs or by way of any device"

The effect of the section 116(1)(a) requirement, which effectively reprises a requirement of section 23 of the Criminal Justice Act 1988[39], will be that if the operation of a principle of the law of evidence would have rendered inadmissible the maker's oral evidence in relation to the matter stated, then his hearsay evidence in relation to that matter will not be rendered admissible by section 116 of the 2003 Act. The Law Commission[40] regarded the equivalent provision of their draft Bill as excluding:

> "...hearsay evidence of (1) facts which are not admissible at all, whoever gives evidence of them; and (2) facts which are admissible, but of which the declarant could not have given oral evidence."

---

37 See, for example, R v Acton JJ, ex parte McMullen (1990) 92 Cr App R 98 (a case concerning section 23 of the Criminal Justice Act 1988).

38 See, for example, R v Mattey and Queeley [1995] 2 Cr App R 409 (a case concerning section 23 of the Criminal Justice Act 1988).

39 See R v JP [1999] Crim LR 401.

40 See "Evidence in Criminal Proceedings: Hearsay and Related Topics", Law Com No 245, at paragraph 8.10.

Thus, if the maker's oral evidence in relation to the matter would, for example, be inadmissible because it is irrelevant, because it is inadmissible evidence of opinion or under the provisions of Chapter 1 of Part 11 of the 2003 Act concerning evidence of bad character, it appears that section 116 of the 2003 Act will not make his hearsay evidence admissible. Similarly, if the maker did not have the "required capability" to make the statement (i.e. was not competent to make it) at the time when he made it, the effect of section 123 of the 2003 Act (considered at 2.7.2, below) is that the statement will not be admissible. Finally, if the maker's oral evidence of the matter would itself infringe the hearsay rule (i.e. if the maker's hearsay statement is itself being tendered to prove or is based upon a "second hand" hearsay statement contained therein), section 116 will not automatically make this multiple hearsay admissible[41]; rather, the admissibility of the multiple hearsay will be dependent upon the operation of section 121 of the 2003 Act, which is considered at 2.7.1 below.

2.2.1.2.2 Section 116(1)(b)

The reasons why the Law Commission recommended the imposition of the requirement, now imposed by section 116(1)(b) of the 2003 Act, that "the person who made the statement (the relevant person) is identified to the court's satisfaction" were considered at 2.2.1.1 above. The example given by the Law Commission[42] was that of:

> "...the defence calling a witness to say that when he was on a train in a particular foreign city he heard two men he did not know talking about how they carried out a murder for which the defendant was being charged and saying that the defendant had not been there."

The effect of section 116(1)(b) in the context of this example will be that the witness' evidence will only be admissible in evidence for the defence if the two men are identified to the court's satisfaction. Presumably, if only one of the two men can be identified to the court's satisfaction, the witness' evidence will be admissible under section 116 to the extent to which it relates to the evidence of the identified man, but will only be admissible in relation to the evidence of the unidentified man if some other exception to the hearsay rule (such as that created by section 114(1)(d) of the 2003 Act[43]) is applicable.[44]

---

41 For an example of the exclusion of hearsay evidence tendered under section 23 of the Criminal Justice Act 1988 on this basis see *R v JP [1999] Crim LR 401*.

42 See *"Evidence in Criminal Proceedings: Hearsay and Related Topics", Law Com No 245, at paragraph 8.6.*

43 Which is considered at 2.6 below.

44 In relation to the admissibility of third party confessions when the hearsay provisions of the 2003 Act are in force see, also, 2.4.2.7.9, below.

2.2.1.2.3 Section 116(1)(c)

Concerning the requirement imposed by section 116(1)(c), namely, the requirement that "any of the five conditions mentioned in subsection (2) is satisfied", the wording of section 116(1)(c) makes clear that it will only be necessary to satisfy any one of these conditions in order to satisfy the section 116(1)(c) requirement. In relation to the first four conditions, whilst the wording of section 116(2)(a)-(d) is not identical to that of section 23(2)(a)-(c) of the 1988 Act, the conditions appear, subject to the operation of section 116(5) (which is considered below), to effectively equate with those imposed by section 23(2) of the 1988 Act. The condition imposed by section 116(2)(e) is, however, significantly different to that imposed by section 23(3) of the 1988 Act.

It appears that in order for hearsay evidence to be admissible under section 23 of the 1988 Act the court must be satisfied by admissible evidence that one or more of the conditions laid down by section 23(2),(3) is/are satisfied.[45] [It should be noted that all but one of the authorities relied upon below in support of this proposition concerned the condition imposed by section 23(3) of the 1988 Act (i.e. that the maker of the statement does not give oral evidence through fear). The most recent authority[46], in which the Court of Appeal had regard to several of the earlier authorities, concerned, however, the condition imposed by section 23(2)(a) (i.e. that the maker of the statement is unfit to attend by reason of his bodily or mental condition).]

The authorities concerning section 23(3) appear to establish that the fact that the section 23(3) condition is satisfied may not be proved via inadmissible hearsay evidence[47] and that where a witness is called to prove that a condition has been satisfied the witness must be sworn[48] and the other party will be entitled to cross-examine the witness.[49] Indeed, there is authority for the proposition that oral evidence may be required in order to satisfy the court that the section 23(3) (or, it seems, the section 23(2)(a)[50]) condition has been satisfied[51], though there is also authority for the proposition that, in appropriate circumstances, the court may decide that the section 23(3) condition has been satisfied upon the basis of hearsay evidence which is admissible under an exception to the hearsay rule.[52] Where evidence is received to prove that the section 23(3) condition has been satisfied it may be that of the maker of the hearsay statement himself (the court being entitled to take into account the demeanour of the witness in this regard[53]) or that of some

---

45 See, for example, Neill v North Antrim Magistrates' Court [1992] 1 WLR 1221 and R v Belmarsh Magistrates' Court ex parte Gilligan [1998] 1 Cr App R 14.

46 R v Elliott The Times May 15 2003.

47 See, for example, Neill v North Antrim Magistrates' Court [1992] 1 WLR 1221 (a case concerning article 3(3)(b) of the Criminal Justice (Evidence Etc) (Northern Ireland) Order 1988)

48 See R v Jennings [1995] Crim LR 810 though see also R v Greer [1998] Crim LR 527.

49 See R v Wood [1998] Crim LR 213; R v Elliott The Times May 15 2003.

50 See R v Elliott The Times May 15 2003.

51 See R v Belmarsh Magistrates' Court ex parte Gilligan [1998] 1 Cr App R 14.

52 See Neill v North Antrim Magistrates' Court [1992] 1 WLR 1221 and R v Rutherford [1998] Crim LR 490.

53 See R v Waters [1997] Crim LR 823.

other witness, such as a doctor or a police officer.[54]

It is submitted that the approach of the courts in relation to the admissibility of hearsay evidence under section 116 of the 2003 Act, particularly in relation to section 116(2)(e) and 116(2)(b), is likely to equate with that encountered in relation to section 23(2)(a),(3) of the 1988 Act.

2.2.1.2.4 Section 116(2)(a)

It is submitted that the section 116(2)(a) condition, "that the relevant person is dead is self explanatory and that, in the present context, nothing further need to be said in relation to it.

2.2.1.2.5 Section 116(2)(b)

In relation to the section 116(2)(b) condition "that the relevant person is unfit to be a witness because of his bodily or mental condition", it should be noted that under section 23(2)(a) of the 1988 Act it has been held that a person is "unfit to attend as a witness" not merely where he is unable to attend court but also where (for example, due to mental disorder) he is unable to give evidence in accordance with the relevant hearsay statement if he was called as a witness.[55] Equally, again under section 23(2)(a), it has been held that a judge is entitled to find that a person is unfit to attend as a witness if attending court to give evidence would expose the person to a risk (even to a modest risk) of serious permanent consequences (such as the risk that the witness might have a stroke).[56]

It is submitted that in either of the abovementioned situations a person would equally be unfit to be a witness within the meaning of section 116(2)(b) of the 2003 Act.

2.2.1.2.6 Section 116(2)(c)

Concerning the section 116(2)(c) condition "that the relevant person is outside the United Kingdom and it is not reasonably practicable to secure his attendance", the courts have held in relation to the operation of section 23(2)(b) of the 1988 Act that in determining whether it is not reasonably practicable to secure the attendance of the maker of a hearsay statement who is outside the United Kingdom, the question is whether, taking into account the background of the case as a whole, this is not reasonably practicable on the date when the application to admit the hearsay statement is made, the judge (if the application is made during the course of the trial itself[57]) not being required to consider whether it might

---

54 See, respectively: R v Waters [1997] Crim LR 823; R v Elliott The Times May 15 2003; Neill v North Antrim Magistrates' Court [1992] 1 WLR 1221.

55 See R v Setz-Dempsey (1994) 98 Cr App R 23.

56 R v Millett LTL 21/7/2000

57 If the application is made prior to the trial the judge will be required to consider whether it would be reasonably practicable to secure the witness' attendance at the trial (R v Hurst [1995] 1 Cr App R 81).

become reasonably practicable on some future occasion.[58] This does not mean, however, that where the prosecution fail to take steps to secure the attendance of the maker of a hearsay statement because they are unaware that he was living abroad, the fact that it is impossible to secure his attendance on the day of the trial will satisfy the requirements of section 23(2)(b).[59]

In determining whether the section 23(2)(b) condition is satisfied, the judge (with whose exercise of discretion the Court of Appeal will not readily interfere) should consider the importance of the hearsay evidence (including the degree of prejudice to the defence, if any, if the evidence is not admitted), the expense and inconvenience of securing the attendance of the person who made the hearsay statement (though this will not necessarily be a major consideration in relation to a prosecution witness) and the reasons given by the party tendering the hearsay evidence as to why it is not reasonably practicable for the person who made the hearsay statement to attend court.[60] Attendance, for the purposes of section 23(2)(b), includes not only attendance in court itself but also the giving of evidence from outside the UK by live link.[61] Moreover, the fact that an official of an embassy located in the United Kingdom is immune from process does not render the official's hearsay statement admissible under section 23(2)(b) because, whilst it is not reasonably practicable to secure the official's attendance, the official is not outside the United Kingdom.[62]

It is submitted that the courts are likely to apply section 23(2)(b) authorities when interpreting the equivalent words of section 116(2)(c) of the 2003 Act.

2.2.1.2.7 Section 116(2)(d)

With regard to the section 116(2)(d) condition "that the relevant person cannot be found although such steps as it is reasonably practicable to take to find him have been taken", the Law Commission recognised that where the party tendering the hearsay evidence relies upon section 116(2)(d) and the other party asserts that the section 116(2)(d) condition is not satisfied due to the operation of section 116(5) (which is considered at 2.2.1.2.9 below), the burden of proving that all reasonably practicable steps have been taken and the person cannot be found is borne by the party tendering that evidence and only if that burden is discharged will the other party be required to prove, for the purposes of section 116(5), that the former party was responsible for the person's unavailability.63 The Law Commission64 recognised, however, that "recommendation 9" (which resulted in section 116(5) of the 2003 Act) was unlikely to be of significance in the context of the section 116(2)(d) condition for the following reason.

---

58 *R v French (1993) 97 Cr App R 421; R v Bray (1989) 88 Cr App R 354; R v Izzigil [2002] EWCA Crim 925.*

59 *R v Bray (1988) 88 Cr App R 354.*

60 *R v Castillo [1996] 1 Cr App R 438.*

61 *R v Radak [1999] 1 Cr App R 187.*

62 *R v Jiminez-Paez (1994) 98 Cr App R 239.*

63 *See "Evidence in Criminal Proceedings: Hearsay and Related Topics", Law Com No 245, at paragraph 8.42.*

64 *See "Evidence in Criminal Proceedings: Hearsay and Related Topics", Law Com No 245, at paragraph 8.42.*

"If a party tenders a statement on the ground that all reasonable steps have been taken to find the declarant, but without success, that party must prove, to the appropriate standard of proof, that all reasonable steps have been taken. If it is suggested that, on the contrary, that party has taken steps to ensure that the declarant does not come to court, that party would have to disprove that suggestion in order to show that he or she had taken reasonable steps to produce the declarant. It is true that in this situation there may be no room for the operation of recommendation 9, but only because there is no need for it."

2.2.1.2.8 Section 116(2)(e)

When considering the section 116(2)(e) condition, "that through fear the relevant person does not give (or does not continue to give) oral evidence in the proceedings, either at all or in connection with the subject matter of the statement, and the court gives leave for the statement to be given in evidence", it is necessary to have regard also to section 116(3)-(4). Section 116(3)-(4) provide that:

"(3) For the purposes of subsection (2)(e) "fear" is to be widely construed and (for example) includes fear of the death or injury of another person or of financial loss.

(4) Leave may be given under subsection (2)(e) only if the court considers that the statement ought to be admitted in the interests of justice, having regard—

   (a) to the statement's contents,

   (b) to any risk that its admission or exclusion will result in unfairness to any party to the proceedings (and in particular to how difficult it will be to challenge the statement if the relevant person does not give oral evidence),

   (c) in appropriate cases, to the fact that a direction under section 19 of the Youth Justice and Criminal Evidence Act 1999 (c. 23) (special measures for the giving of evidence by fearful witnesses etc) could be made in relation to the relevant person, and

   (d) to any other relevant circumstances."

Section 116(2)(e) itself differs from section 23(3) of the 1988 Act in several respects. First, unlike section 23(3), section 116(2)(e) will not require, in the words of section 23(3), "that the statement was made to a police officer or some other person charged with the duty of investigating offences or charging offenders". The rationale underlying this change was expressed as follows by Mr Michael Wills (the Parliamentary Under Secretary of State for the Home Department) during the Criminal Justice Bill's time before Standing Committee B in the House of Commons.[65]

"...on balance the Law Commission concluded that this was an unnecessary hurdle for the defence to overcome. We pursued that approach because we believed that it could put the defence at a distinct disadvantage if a defence witness had to be interviewed by a police officer or an equivalent person charged with a duty to investigate offences before the statement could be admitted."

Secondly, unlike section 23(3), section 116(2)(e) will only apply where the person does not give evidence through fear and will not apply where, again in the words of section 23(3), the person "is kept out of the way". Thirdly, section 116(2)(e), unlike section 23(3), expressly provides that the section 116(2)(e) condition will be satisfied not only where the person does not give oral evidence in the proceedings through fear but will also be satisfied where the person, "does not continue to give" evidence (though, as judicially interpreted, section 23(3) is, in practice, of the same effect).[66] Fourthly, it appears that section 116(2)(e), unlike section 23(3), will apply where the person does give oral evidence in the proceedings but, out of fear, does not give oral evidence "in connection with the subject matter of the statement". Finally, unlike section 23(3), the section 116(2)(e) condition will only be satisfied where the court gives leave for the hearsay statement to be given in evidence.[67]

Section 116(3) of the 2003 Act provides that, "fear" is to be widely construed and (for example) includes fear of the death or injury of another person or of financial loss". During the criminal Justice Bill's Committee Stage in the House of Lords[68], Baroness Scotland of Asthal (the Minister of State for the Criminal Justice System and Law Reform) indicated (with reference to the then clause 109, now section 117), that:

"The list outlining the species of issues capable of causing fear...are simply examples rather than an exhaustive list.

Clause 109 does not attempt to provide an exhaustive definition of what may constitute a sufficient basis of fear. Indeed,...Clause 109(3) states that fear should be interpreted widely. That is the reason. It is drafted in the terms used in the Law Commission's draft Bill and seeks to achieve a compromise between, on the one hand, the difficulty of setting in legislation a comprehensive list of the circumstances in which fear justifies the reception of a hearsay statement and, on the other hand, the danger that in the absence of any definition, a court might hold that a particular kind of fear is not what Parliament meant."

65 See *Hansard (Commons) 28 January 2003* Column 630.
66 *R v Waters [1997] Crim LR 823.*
67 *Though it should be remembered that the operation of section 23 as a whole, unlike that of section 116, is subject to the section 25 exclusionary* discretion and may be subject to the section 26 leave requirement.
68 See *Hansard (Lords) 18 september 2003 Columns 1128 and 1129.*

In relation to the operation of section 23(3) of the 1988 Act, the courts have held that fear need not be based upon reasonable grounds.[69] Indeed, fear need not necessarily be related to the offence in question.[70] Fear must, however, be current fear, i.e., under section 23(3), the question for the court is whether the maker of the hearsay statement is in fear at the time when he would be expected to testify and evidence that he was in fear several months before the trial may not be sufficient to justify a finding by the judge that he is in fear at the time when he is due to testify.[71] It is submitted that these section 23(3) authorities reflect the approach which the courts are likely to take when determining whether, for the purposes of section 116(2)(e), a person does not give oral evidence through fear.

The section 116(2)(e) leave requirement, in the more limited context of the person who does not give oral evidence through fear, reprises the leave requirement imposed by section 26 of the 1988 Act to the extent that it will impose an "interests of justice" test, though the specific matters to which section 116(4)

---

69 *R v Waters [1997] Crim LR 823.*
70 *R v Martin [1996] Crim LR 589.*
71 *R v H [2001] Crim LR 815.*
72 *Essentially, a witness may be eligible for assistance under section 17 of the 1999 Act if the court is satisfied that the quality of the witness' evidence is likely to be diminished by reason of the witness' fear or distress in connection with testifying in the proceedings (section 17(1)). In determining whether a witness is eligible for assistance under section 17, section 19(2) provides that:*

> *"...the court must take into account, in particular—*
>> *(a) the nature and alleged circumstances of the offence to which the proceedings relate;*
>> *(b) the age of the witness;*
>> *(c) such of the following matters as appear to the court to be relevant, namely-*
>>> *(i) the social and cultural background and ethnic origins of the witness,*
>>> *(ii) the domestic and employment circumstances of the witness, and*
>>> *(iii) any religious beliefs or political opinions of the witness;*
>> *(d) any behaviour towards the witness on the part of-*
>>> *(i) the accused,*
>>> *(ii) members of the family or the associates of the accused, or*
>>> *(iii) any other person who is likely to be an accused or a witness in the proceedings."*

A sexual offence complainant is automatically eligible for assistance under section 17 unless the complainant informs the court that the complainant does not wish to be so eligible (section 17(4)).

Where a witness is eligible for assistance the court must determine whether any or any combination of the available special measures would in its opinion be likely to improve the quality of the witness' evidence and, if so, determine which would in its opinion be likely to maximise so far as practicable the quality of the evidence and give a direction providing for the relevant measure or measures to apply to the witness' evidence (section 19(2)). Moreover, section 19(3) provides that:

> *"In determining for the purposes of this Chapter whether any special measure or measures would or would not be likely to improve, or to maximise so far as practicable, the quality of evidence given by the witness, the court must consider all of the circumstances of the case, including in particular—*
>> *(a) any views expressed by the witness; and*
>> *(b) whether the measure or measures might tend to inhibit such evidence being effectively tested by a party to the proceedings."*

The full range of special measures is not available in relation to a witness who is eligible in consequence of fear or distress about testifying (section 18(1)(b)), the potentially available measures being screening of the witness so that the witness cannot see the accused (section 23), live link (section 24), evidence in private (section 25), removal of wigs and gowns (section 26), the admission of video recorded evidence in chief (section 27)and the admission of video recorded cross-examination and re-examination (section 28). Two additional measures (namely intermediaries (section 29) and aids to communication (section 30)) are potentially available where a witness is eligible for assistance in consequence of age or incapacity.

directs the court to have regard are not identical to those contained in section 26 of the earlier Act. First, as is the case under section 26(i) of the 1988 Act, the court is directed by section 116(4)(a) to have regard "to the statement's contents". Secondly, the section 116(4)(b) requirement that the court have regard "to any risk that its admission or exclusion will result in unfairness to any party to the proceedings (and in particular to how difficult it will be to challenge the statement if the relevant person does not give oral evidence"), differs from the section 26(ii) requirement in that it, unlike section 26(ii), will expressly require the court to consider the risk of unfairness to all parties and not merely to consider the risk of unfairness to the accused. Thirdly, section 116(4)(c) is a totally new provision which will require the court to have regard, "in appropriate cases, to the fact that a direction under section 19 of the Youth Justice and Criminal Evidence Act 1999 (c. 23) (special measures for the giving of evidence by fearful witnesses etc) could be made in relation to the relevant person".[72] Finally, section 116(4)(d), which will require the court to have regard, "to any other relevant circumstances", effectively equates with section 26(iii) of the 1988 Act.

The Law Commission[73] explained the rationale behind what is now the section 116(2)(e) discretion as follows.

> "8.58 Our starting point is to favour automatic admissibility for all first-hand hearsay where the declarant is identifiable but unavailable; but the issue of frightened witnesses is unique. Unlike death or illness, fear is a state of mind, and it can be difficult to tell whether a witness is genuinely frightened or merely reluctant. We were repeatedly told, especially at Judicial Studies Board seminars attended by the Commissioner with special responsibility for criminal law,[85] that there is a very genuine risk that, if the statements of frightened witnesses were automatically admissible, prospective witnesses could give statements to the police in the knowledge that they could at a later stage falsely claim to be frightened, with the result that they could avoid having to go to court and be cross-examined. The general thrust of these responses was therefore that it would be undesirable to have an automatic exception to the hearsay rule for frightened witnesses. We agree, and believe that the leave of the court should continue to be required."

> "[85] See para 1.23 above."

The Law Commission[74] considered the way in which the discretion, now embodied in section 116(2)(e),(4), should be exercised by the criminal courts

> "8.59 In view of this conclusion, we must consider how the court should decide whether to give leave. We believe that a statement should readily

---

73 See "Evidence in Criminal Proceedings: Hearsay and Related Topics", Law Com No 245, at paragraph 8.58.
74 See "Evidence in Criminal Proceedings: Hearsay and Related Topics", Law Com No 245, at paragraphs 8.59-8.62.
75 Section 116(5) is considered at 2.2.1.2.9, below.

be admitted where the witness is in fear, provided that the interests of justice do not dictate otherwise. In deciding whether the admission of such a statement is in the interests of justice, the court should have regard to what was said in the statement; to any risk of unfairness, whether to the defendant, to a co-defendant or to the prosecution; where appropriate, to the fact that the evidence could be received otherwise than from the witness in person in the courtroom;[86] and to any other relevant circumstances.

8.60 Any part played by a party to the proceedings in intimidating the witness would obviously be a factor taken into account by the court in the exercise of its discretion. If, for example, a prosecution witness has been intimidated by the accused, or persons acting on behalf of the accused, it is likely that the statement would be admitted. Conversely, if the witness's fear has no connection with the accused, it may not be fair to allow the statement to be admitted without the accused having a chance to cross-examine.

8.61 If it transpires that it is the party seeking to adduce the statement that has intimidated the witness, the question of discretion may not arise at all. This is because we have recommended that a party who deliberately ensures that a witness is not available to testify should not be able to rely on that witness's statement.[87] Similarly, if the party seeking to adduce the statement of a frightened witness were shown[88] to have caused the witness's fear in order to deter him or her from giving evidence, the exception for frightened witnesses would not apply.

8.62 Different people fear different things; and our view is that a court should look at matters through the eyes of the witness, bearing in mind his or her personal weaknesses, and assess whether that witness's failure to testify is reasonable in all the circumstances.89 The characteristics and circumstances of the witness clearly fall within the phrase "other relevant circumstances"."

[86] Eg, a video-recording of the witness's testimony may be available; or he or she could testify from behind a screen, or via a television link under s 32 of the 1988 Act. We suggest that consideration should be given to extending these latter powers. At present, they are confined to offences against the person, cruelty to children and sexual offences, but it is difficult to see why this should be so. The Recorder of London advocated the wider use of television links. Our view is that evidence by television link is clearly better than hearsay, and we believe the matter should be looked into further. We considered making some suggestions for reform but we have not consulted fully on this issue as it does not involve the use of hearsay, and so we do not think it appropriate to this project. It is no doubt the sort of issue that will be considered by the inter-departmental group (consisting of officials from the Home Office, the Lord Chancellor's Department, the Legal Secretariat to the Law

Officers, the Crown Prosecution Service, the Department of Health and the Scottish Office) which, the Home Office announced on 23 January 1997, has been asked to reviewcourt procedures for people with learning disabilities.

[87] See paras 8.27 – 8.30 above.

[88] The burden of proof would be on the party opposing the admission of the statement: see paras 8.31 – 8.32 above.

[89] A similar approach can be found in the case of the defence of self-defence, where factfinders have to assess whether the threatened individual acted reasonably, taking into account his or her personal circumstances."

It should be noted that the reference by the Law Commission at note 86 (reproduced immediately above) to video recording etc was made prior to the introduction of the special measures regime under the Youth Justice and criminal Evidence Act 1999 and that the Law Commission's references at notes 87 and 88 (again reproduced immediately above) to parties who ensure that a witness is not available or put a witness in fear to deter the witness from giving evidence relate to what is now section 116(5) of the 2003 Act.[75] The Law Commission[76] also specifically considered the possibility of a witness who was in fear of prosecution for perjury.

> "8.66 Conversely, the draft Bill does not provide that any particular kind of fear will not suffice. We considered the possibility of a provision to the effect that the fear of prosecution for perjury is not enough. The exception for a witness who is "in fear" is designed to facilitate the reception of evidence from intimidated witnesses and from those who are just scared of the process of giving evidence; it would be quite wrong for it to be used where the witness was only afraid of being prosecuted. But we decided that it was unnecessary to make express provision for this situation, since no court would think it "in the interests of justice" to allow a witness's statement to be read on this basis."

During the Criminal Justice Bill's time before Standing Committee B in the House of Commons[77], Mr Michael Wills (the Parliamentary Under Secretary of State for the Home Department) recognised that:

> "Leave can be granted only where it is in the interests of justice that the evidence be admitted. If, therefore, the witness's fears could be satisfactorily addressed, thus enabling him or her to give oral evidence, the interests of justice would not be served by admitting the out-of-court statement. The clause also makes specific reference, in subsection (4)(c), to the possibility of fear being addressed by a special measures direction under section 19 of the Youth Justice and Criminal Evidence At 1999, which includes the use of measures such as the giving of evidence behind a screen, or the use of live video link."

---

76 See *"Evidence in Criminal Proceedings: Hearsay and Related Topics"*, Law Com No 245, at paragraph 8.66.

77 See *Hansard (Commons) 28 January 2003* Column 629.

During the Criminal Justice Bill's Committee Stage in the House of Lords[78], Baroness Scotland of Asthal (the Minister of State for the Criminal Justice System and Law Reform) considered the nature of those circumstances in which the fear of financial loss might justify a witness' not attending court to give oral evidence.

> "This is a question of quantum and nature. One would have to balance the fear of financial loss against the interests of justice. If, for example, someone said, "I don't want to come to court because I shall lose an hour or two's worth of extra money", that is one thing, However, if the witness is out of the jurisdiction and would lose all forms of gainful employment because he happened to operate in a narrow sphere, and if he were able to convince all concerned that his work was something that he would be incapable of replacing and would be bound to bring about a form of nervous psychosis, that is quite another matter.

> We have a very broad spectrum. It is for the court to exercise good sense and judgment and to consider whether the reasons given by the witness are such that it believes that the interests of justice demand that the evidence should properly be admitted."

It is submitted that in the context of her Ladyship's example, section 116(2)(e) would, in practice, appear to be otiose in that if the witness was outside the jurisdiction and was unwilling to return because this would cause him to lose merely one hour's worth of remuneration, the admissibility of his hearsay evidence might well be justified under section 116(2)(c), which was considered at 2.2.1.2.6 above, upon the basis that he was outside the U.K. and it was not reasonably practicable to secure his attendance, in which case the section 116(4) interests of justice test would, of course, be inapplicable.

During the Criminal Justice Bill's time before Standing Committee B in the House of Commons[79], Mr Michael Wills (the Parliamentary Under Secretary of State for the Home Department) also considered an example of circumstances in which the fear of financial loss might justify a witness' not attending court to give oral evidence.

> "...imagine a local corner shop in a troublesome estate....The owners of the shop might have a well founded fear that by coming forward to give evidence they will lose customers. The matter is not just about pounds and pence. Although it could be construed as financial loss, the problem goes right to the heart of the corner shop owner's livelihood and way of life."

---

78 *See Hansard (Lords) 18 september 2003 Column 1130.*

79 *See Hansard (Commons) 28 January 2003 Column 634.*

Further guidance as to the nature of those factors which might influence the courts in the exercise of the section 116(2)(e) discretion may be provided by reference to authorities concerning the exercise under the Criminal Justice Act 1988 of the section 25 exclusionary discretion and the section 26 leave requirement, both of which require the application of an interests of justice test. Thus, the following matters concerning the exercise of judicial discretion under sections 25 and 26, of the 1988 Act are worthy of note in the present context. First, the interests of justice include both the interests of the accused and the interests of the prosecution.[80] Secondly, the court is more likely to admit hearsay evidence that is of good quality and to exclude hearsay evidence which is of poor quality.[81] Thirdly, in considering the possibility of controverting the hearsay evidence, the court should, inter alia, take into account the possibility of so doing by calling witnesses (including the accused himself[82]), by cross-examining witnesses and by attacking the credibility of the maker of the relevant hearsay statement.[83] Fourthly, where the party who opposes the admission of the hearsay evidence has had an adequate opportunity to consider the hearsay evidence pre-trial, or where an adjournment can provide him with such an opportunity, this may render the admission of the hearsay evidence more likely.[84] Fifthly, where hearsay evidence forms an important part of the prosecution's case, its importance will not, in itself, necessarily require the court to exclude the evidence[85] (and may indeed persuade the court that the hearsay evidence should be admitted in the interests of justice[86]) though, in appropriate circumstances, (for example, where the hearsay evidence would be difficult to controvert[87] or where, had the prosecution acted differently, the trial could have taken place on an earlier occasion with the maker of the hearsay statement present to testify[88]), its importance may increase the likelihood that the court will refuse to admit it. Sixthly, where identification evidence forms the main ingredient of the prosecution's case, it appears that the courts should exercise caution before admitting it in hearsay form[89] (though, in appropriate circumstances, it appears that hearsay identification evidence may properly be admitted under section 23 or 24 of the 1988 Act).[90] Seventhly, the court may, in the exercise of its discretion, exclude some parts of the statement but admit other parts thereof.[91] Eighthly (whether the hearsay evidence is tendered by the prosecution or by a former co-defendant), when the court is deciding whether hearsay evidence which favours

---

80 *R v Cole [1990] 1 WLR 866; R v W [1997] Crim LR 678; R v Gokal [1997] 2 Cr App R 266.*

81 *R v Cole [1990] 1 WLR 866; R v Patel (1993) 97 Cr App R 294; R v Fairfax [1995] Crim LR 949..*

82 *See, in particular, R v Gokal [1997] 2 Cr App R 266 and see also, R v Millett LTL 21/7/2000 and R v Nolan [2002] EWCA Crim 464.*

83 *R v Cole [1990] 1 WLR 866; R v Gokal [1997] 2 Cr App R 266; R v Radak [1999] 1 Cr App R 187; R v Nolan [2002] EWCA Crim 464.*

84 *R v Iqbal [1990] 1 WLR 756; O'Sullivan v DPP LTL 27/3/2000.*

85 *R v Moore [1992] Crim LR 882.*

86 *R v Batt and Batt [1995] Crim LR 240.*

87 *See R v Radak [1999] 1 Cr App R 187.*

88 *See R v French (1993) 97 Cr App R 421.*

89 *See Neill v North Antrim Magistrates [1992] 1 WLR 1221.*

90 *See R v Fairfax [1995] Crim LR 949; R v Dragic [1996] 2 Cr App R 232.*

91 *R v Blok LTL 23/2/2000.*

one co-defendant but prejudices the interests of another co-defendant should be admitted under section 23 or section 24, it appears to be necessary to take into account the conflicting interests of the two co-defendants.[92] Ninthly, the giving of proper directions to the jury concerning the weight of hearsay evidence and the fact that its maker is not available for cross-examination may, in appropriate circumstances, counter-balance the prima-facie unfairness of its admission.[93]

Further, under section 3(1) of the Human Rights Act 1998, the court will, if possible, be required to exercise its section 116(2)(e) discretion so as not to result in a violation of Article 6 of the European Convention on Human Rights. The extent to which the admission or exclusion of hearsay evidence is potentially capable of resulting in a violation of Article 6 of the Convention (including the approach of the courts in this context to the admission of hearsay evidence under sections 23 or 24 of the 1988 Act) is considered at 2.8 below.

Finally, it must be remembered that regardless of the section 116(2)(e) discretion (which will not apply where the section 116(2)(a)-(d) conditions are relied upon), the court will possess discretion to exclude hearsay evidence in criminal proceedings (see section 126, which is considered at 2.7.5 below) and may be required to stop the case where a prosecution case that is based on hearsay evidence is unconvincing (see section 125, which is considered at 2.7.4 below). It should be noted, however, that unlike the court's common law exclusionary discretion and its exclusionary discretion under section 78 of the Police and Criminal Evidence Act 1984 (both preserved by section 126(2)), the section 116(2)(e) discretion will encompass not only evidence tendered by the prosecution but also evidence tendered by the defence. Moreover, as is seen at 2.7.5.1 below, the new discretion to exclude hearsay evidence tendered by prosecution or defence which will be conferred upon the criminal courts by section 126(1) of the 2003 Act will be concerned with exclusion for the purpose of preventing undue waste of time and not with exclusion for the purpose of preserving the fairness of the proceedings or in the interests of justice.

2.2.1.2.9 Section 116(5)

Section 116(5) relates to the statutory conditions imposed by section 116(2) (which were considered at 2.2.1.2.4 to 2.2.1.2.8 above). Section 116(5) provides as follows:

> "(5) A condition set out in any paragraph of subsection (2) which is in fact satisfied is to be treated as not satisfied if it is shown that the circumstances described in that paragraph are caused—
>
> (a) by the person in support of whose case it is sought to give the statement in evidence, or

---

92 *R v Duffy* [1999] 1 Cr App R 307; *R v Gregory and Mott* [1995] Crim LR 507.

93 *R v Cole* [1990] 1 WLR 866; *R v Kennedy* [1992] Crim LR 37.

(b) by a person acting on his behalf,
in order to prevent the relevant person giving oral evidence in the
proceedings (whether at all or in connection with the subject matter of
the statement)."

The Law Commission's rationale for the making of the recommendation now
embodied in section 116(5) was summarised at 2.2.1.1, above.

It appears that section 116(5) will be potentially applicable in circumstances in
which the party tendering hearsay evidence under section 116 of the 2003 Act
proves to the standard required by law[94] that the section 116(2) condition upon
which he relies is satisfied.[95] In such circumstances, if a party who is opposed to the
admission of the hearsay evidence proves to the standard required by law[96] that the
requirements of section 116(5) are satisfied then the effect of section 116(5) will be
that the court must treat the relevant section 116(2) condition as not satisfied.[97]

Essentially, the requirements of section 116(5) will be satisfied if it is proved by the
party opposed to the admission of the hearsay evidence that the circumstances
which must be shown to exist in order for the relevant section 116(2) condition to
be satisfied were caused, either by the party tendering the hearsay evidence or by
someone acting on his behalf, "in order to prevent the relevant person giving oral
evidence in the proceedings (whether at all or in connection with the subject
matter of the statement)". The Law Commission[98] recognised that the imposition
of the burden of proof under section 116(5) upon the party who was opposed to
the admission of the evidence amounted to an exception to the general rule that
the party who tenders evidence bears the burden of proving facts upon which the
admissibility of the relevant evidence depends to the standard required by law, but
regarded the exception as justified for the following reason.

"The justification for reversing the burden of proof is that, if the general rule
were applied, the party seeking to adduce the evidence would have to prove a
negative, namely that he or she was *not* responsible; and we consider this
undesirable."

---

94 I.e. the criminal standard of proof if that party is
the prosecution, the balance of probabilities if party is
a defendant (see, for example, R v Acton JJ, ex parte
McMullen (1990) 92 Cr App R 98 and R v Mattey
and Queeley [1995] 2 Cr App R 409 (both cases
concerning section 23 of the Criminal Justice Act
1988).
95 See "Evidence in Criminal Proceedings: Hearsay
and Related Topics", Law Com No 245, at paragraph
8.42.
96 I.e. the criminal standard of proof if that party is
the prosecution, the balance of probabilities if that party
is a defendant (see, for example, R v Acton JJ, ex parte
McMullen (1990) 92 Cr App R 98 and R v Mattey
and Queeley [1995] 2 Cr App R 409 (both cases
concerning section 23 of the Criminal Justice Act 1988).

97 See "Evidence in Criminal Proceedings: Hearsay
and Related Topics", Law Com No 245, at paragraph
8.42 and see, also, paragraph 407 of the Explanatory
Notes to the Criminal Justice Act.
98 See "Evidence in Criminal Proceedings: Hearsay
and Related Topics", Law Com No 245, at paragraph
8.31.

Further, section 116(5) (and the Law Commission's recommendation which resulted in section 116(5)) appears to resolve two problems which the Law Commission[99] had considered.

> "8.28 On consultation, the respondents who dealt with this point were unanimously in favour, but we were warned of two outstanding problems. First, a person should not be regarded as responsible for the fact that the declarant cannot or will not give oral evidence where the unavailability arises out of the alleged offence. For example, where the defendant has in fact killed the victim, but before he died the victim was heard to say that he provoked the defendant so that the defendant is not to blame, the defendant should surely be allowed to rely upon this statement in answer to a charge of murder even though he may strictly speaking be "responsible" for the absence of the victim.

> 8.29 The second problem is that it might be contended that a defendant is "responsible" for the absence of a declarant although the defendant has not done anything to the declarant. For example, a defence declarant may have gone abroad and refused to come back because he is terrified that if he is cross-examined, he may say something (although he does not know what) which might upset or antagonise the defendant, even though he has no grounds for that fear. Professor Sir John Smith helpfully suggested that a person should be regarded as being responsible for the unavailability of a declarant only if he or she deliberately prevents the declarant from attending. The crucial point, it seems to us, is that if a party acts with the intention of preventing a witness from giving evidence, that party should not be able to rely on the hearsay statement of that witness. If the matter is put like this, the defendant in the previous paragraph would be able to adduce the statement of the dead victim, because although he is responsible for the victim's unavailability, he did not cause it in order to stop the victim testifying."

Finally, it should be remembered that, as was explained at 2.2.1.2.7 above, it may be that there will be no room for the operation of section 116(5) in the context of the section 116(2)(d) condition. There does, however, appear to be ample scope for the operation of section 116(5) in the context of the other statutory conditions, contained in section 116(2)(a)-(c), (e).

---

99 See *"Evidence in Criminal Proceedings: Hearsay and Related Topics", Law Com No 245, at paragraphs 8.28-8.29.*

2.2.2 Documents created or received by persons in the course of their trades, businesses, professions or other occupations or as office holders

Section 117 of the 2003 Act provides as follows.

"(1) In criminal proceedings a statement contained in a document is admissible as evidence of any matter stated if—

   (a) oral evidence given in the proceedings would be admissible as evidence of that matter,

   (b) the requirements of subsection (2) are satisfied, and

   (c) the requirements of subsection (5) are satisfied, in a case where subsection (4) requires them to be.

(2) The requirements of this subsection are satisfied if—

   (a) the document or the part containing the statement was created or received by a person in the course of a trade, business, profession or other occupation, or as the holder of a paid or unpaid office,

   (b) the person who supplied the information contained in the statement (the relevant person) had or may reasonably be supposed to have had personal knowledge of the matters dealt with, and

   (c) each person (if any) through whom the information was supplied from the relevant person to the person mentioned in paragraph (a) received the information in the course of a trade, business, profession or other occupation, or as the holder of a paid or unpaid office.

(3) The persons mentioned in paragraphs (a) and (b) of subsection (2) may be the same person.

(4) The additional requirements of subsection (5) must be satisfied if the statement—

   (a) was prepared for the purposes of pending or contemplated criminal proceedings, or for a criminal investigation, but

   (b) was not obtained pursuant to a request under section 7 of the Crime (International Co-operation) Act 2003 (c. 32) or an order under paragraph 6 of Schedule 13 to the Criminal Justice Act 1988 (c. 33) (which relate to overseas evidence).

(5) The requirements of this subsection are satisfied if—

   (a) any of the five conditions mentioned in section 116(2) is satisfied (absence of relevant person etc), or

(b) the relevant person cannot reasonably be expected to have any recollection of the matters dealt with in the statement (having regard to the length of time since he supplied the information and all other circumstances).

(6) A statement is not admissible under this section if the court makes a direction to that effect under subsection (7).

(7) The court may make a direction under this subsection if satisfied that the statement's reliability as evidence for the purpose for which it is tendered is doubtful in view of—

(a) its contents,

(b) the source of the information contained in it,

(c) the way in which or the circumstances in which the information was supplied or received, or

(d) the way in which or the circumstances in which the document concerned was created or received."

2.2.2.1 Section 117 of the 2003 Act and section 24 of the 1988 Act distinguished

Section 117 of the 2003 Act may essentially be regarded as a descendant of section 24 of the Criminal Justice Act 1988, a provision which the 2003 Act will repeal.[100] The distinctions which exist between section 117 of the 2003 Act and section 24 of the 1988 Act are much less significant than those which exist between section 116 of the 2003 Act and section 23 of the 1988 Act, which were considered at 2.2.1.1, above. This is so because, unlike section 116 of the 2003 Act, the operation of section 117 of that Act will, like section 24 of the 1988 Act, be limited to the domain of documentary hearsay. Moreover, several of the distinctions which do exist between section 117 of the 2003 Act and section 24 of the 1988 Act duplicate distinctions which exist between section 116 of the 2003 Act and section 23 of the 1988 Act.

The nature of those distinctions between section 117 and section 24 which duplicate distinctions between section 116 and section 23 may be dealt with briefly.

(a) First, the provisions of section 116 which concern the unavailability of a witness through fear[101] (which appear to apply in the context of section 117 via section 117(4)-(5)[102]), are both more comprehensive and more complex than those of section 23(3).[103]

(b) Secondly, neither section 23 nor section 24 of the 1988 Act contains a provision equivalent to section 116(5) of the 2003 Act[104] (which appears to apply in the context of section 117 via section 117(4)-(5)[105]).

---

100 *See section 136.*
101 *I.e. section 116(2)(e), (3) and (4).*
102 *See 2.2.2.2.4 below.*

103 *See 2.2.2.1 and 2.1.2.8 above.*
104 *See 2.2.2.1 and 2.1.2.9 above.*
105 *See 2.2.2.2.4 below.*

(c) Thirdly, as has already been seen[106], the effects of the statutory definition of "statement" for the purposes of the 2003 Act[107] will be to exclude certain evidence from the ambit of the hearsay rule which would have fallen within the ambit of that rule at common law[108], to exclude this evidence from the ambit of sections 116 and 117 of the 2003 Act[109] (which would potentially have fallen within the ambit of sections 23 and 24 of the 1988[110]) and to include hearsay evidence of admissible opinion (which would not have fallen within the ambit of section 23 of the 1988 Act) within the ambit of sections 116 and 117 of the 2003 Act.

(d) Fourthly, like section 116 of the 2003 Act[111], section 117 makes no express provision concerning the use of hearsay evidence at retrials, the admissibility of confessions made by defendants or the admissibility of evidence at committal proceedings. Like section 116, section 117 will, however, be subject to section 128(2) of the 2003 Act concerning the admissibility of confessions made by defendants.[112] Equally, it is submitted that the failure to reprise section 24(5) of the 1988 Act in the context of the section 117 of 2003 Act (like the failure to reprise section 23(5) in the context of section 116), is in line with the raft of amendments and repeals concerning the allocation of cases triable either way and the sending of cases to the Crown Court which will come into effect when the relevant provisions of the 2003 Act are brought into force.[113].Unlike the position encountered in relation to section 116, however, section 131 of the 2003 Act does not provide that evidence which was given orally at the original trial may be given under section 117 thereof at a retrial.

(e) Finally, the 2003 Act (via section 123 thereof[114]), unlike the 1988 Act, imposes express "required capability" (i.e. competence) requirements concerning those persons who create or receive documents, supply information etc. So far as section 24 of the 1988 Act is concerned, it is submitted that the competence of the person who supplies or receives information or creates a document and that of any intermediaries is, like that of the maker of a hearsay statement for the purposes of section 23[115], a matter which the court should take into account in the exercise of its discretion under section 26 of the 1988 Act.[116] The "required capability" of the various persons whom section 117 will potentially concern is considered at 2.7.2, below.

There are several other distinctions which may be drawn between section 117 of the 2003 Act and section 24 of the 1988 Act.

---

106 At 2.1 above.
107 See Section 115(2).
108 See Part One of this book, above.
109 See 2.2.2.1 above.
110 See paragraph 5 of Schedule 2 to the 1988 Act (as inserted by section 15 of the Civil Evidence Act 1995).
111 See 2.2.2.1 above.
112 See 2.2.1.1 above.

113 See 2.2.1.1 above. The provisions of the 2003 which concern these matters, namely, Part 6, Schedule 3 and Part 4 of Schedule 37, fall outside the scope of this book and are thus not reproduced in its appendix.
114 Which is considered at 2.7.2 below.
115 See 2.2.1.1 above.
116 See R v D The Times May 21 2002.

(a) First, whereas section 24 applies to a statement "in a document"[117], section 117 will apply to a statement "contained in a document"[118]. It is submitted, however, that this is a distinction without a practical difference in that a statement which is "contained in a document" will also be "in a document" and a statement which is "in a document" will also be "contained in a document".[119]

(b) Secondly, whereas section 24 of the 1988 Act applies where "the document was created or received" by a person in the course of a trade or business etc[120], section 117 of the 2003 Act will apply where "the document or the part containing the statement was created or received" by such a person[121]. Thus, it is clear that section 117 will be potentially applicable to documents which were not created or received by the person who created or received them solely in the course of his trade or business etc, provided that the part containing the statement which is tendered under section 117 was so created or received. This might, it is submitted, be the case where the relevant document contains several parts, some of which are of relevance to the trade, business etc of the person who created or received the document and some of which are not so relevant.

(c) Thirdly, section 24(4) of the 1988 Act provides that the requirements imposed by section 23(2),(3) concerning the unavailability of the maker of the statement and an additional requirement imposed by section 24(4)(iii) do not apply to statements which were obtained pursuant to a request under section 7 of the Crime (International Co-operation) Act 2003 (overseas evidence for use in the U.K.), pursuant to an order under Schedule 13, paragraph 6, of the 1988 Act itself (letters of request) or under section 30 or 31 of the 1988 Act itself (expert reports and glossaries etc). Section 117(4) of the 2003 Act provides that the requirements imposed by section 117(5) will not apply in the former two cases, but makes no reference to sections 30 and 31 of the 1988 Act. It is submitted, however, that the effect of sections 30 and 31 of the 1988 Act will be to make the evidence to which they relate admissible in criminal proceedings regardless of the operation of section 117 of the 2003 Act and, consequently, that it will not be necessary to comply with the requirements imposed by section 117(5) in order for evidence to be admissible under section 30 or section 31 of the 1988 Act.

(d) Fourthly, the wording of section 24 of the 1988 Act does not make clear whether the requirements imposed by section 24(4) apply to the person who created or received the document or to the supplier of the information which the document contains. There is authority in favour of the adoption of both interpretations of section 24, but the most recent (and most satisfactory) favours

---

117 *Section 24(1).*
118 *Section 117(1).*
119 *The expression "contained in a document" had previously appeared in section 1 of the Criminal Evidence Act 1965 (which was repealed by the Police and Criminal Evidence Act 1984) and in section 4 of the Civil Evidence Act 1968 (which was repealed by*

the Civil Evidence Act 1995) whilst the expression "in a document" had appeared in section 68 of the Police and Criminal Evidence Act 1984 (which was repealed by the Criminal Justice Act 1988).
120 *Section 24(1)(i).*
121 *Section 117(2)(a).*

the latter interpretation, under which it is the unavailability of the person with personal knowledge of the facts which would potentially satisfy the requirements of section 24.[122]

Under section 117 of the 2003 Act, the requirements imposed by section 117(5) of that Act will apply to "the relevant person", the relevant person being defined in section 117(2)(b) as "the person who supplied the information contained in the statement". Whilst section 117(5) will feed into section 116(2) and the "relevant person" for the purposes of section 116 is defined (in section 116(1)) as "the person who made the statement", it is submitted that, for the purposes of section 116(2) as it will operate in the context of section 117(5)(a), it is the section 117(2)(b) definition of "relevant person" which should be adopted. Certainly, the Law Commission, having recognised that section 24 was ambiguous in this respect, intended that the requirements which are now embodied in what is now section 117(5) would apply to the supplier of information[123] and the wording of their draft Bill[124], unlike that of sections 116 and 117 of the 2003 Act, was not ambiguous in this respect. Moreover, the Explanatory Notes to the Criminal Justice Act also assume[125] that it is the supplier of information to whom the relevant statutory conditions will be applicable in the context of section 117.

(e) Finally, whereas the admissibility of evidence under section 24 of the 1988 Act is subject to the exclusionary discretion conferred by section 25 of that Act and may be subject to the section 26 leave requirement, no provisions equivalent to section 25 and section 26 exist within the statutory regime created by Chapter 2 of Part 11 of the 2003 Act. Unlike the position in relation to section 116 of the 2003 Act (considered at 2.2.1.1 above), however, the position under section 117 is not one of "automatic admissibility". Rather, section 117(6) and (7) will confer upon the court discretion to exclude evidence tendered under section 117 upon the basis that its reliability as evidence for the purpose for which it is tendered is doubtful. Further, it appears that where a party tendering hearsay evidence under section 117 attempts to satisfy the requirements of section 117(5) by relying upon the condition mentioned in section 116(2)(e), the section 116(4) discretion (considered at 2.2.1.2.8 above), will be applicable. Moreover, the court will continue to possess both its common law discretion to exclude evidence tendered by the prosecution and its discretion under section 78 of the Police and Criminal Evidence Act 1984 to exclude such evidence. Additionally, section 126(1) of the 2003 Act will confer upon the court discretion to exclude admissible hearsay for the purpose of preventing undue waste of time.

---

122 See *R v Bedi (1992) Crim LR 299; Brown v Secretary of State for Social Security The Times December 7 1994; R v Derodra [1999] Crim LR 978 (the Court of Appeal in Derodra adopting the interpretation which appears to implement the underlying policy of the statutory provision); R v Lake Estates Watersports [2002] EWCA Crim 2067.*

123 See *"Evidence in Criminal Proceedings: Hearsay and Related Topics", Law Com No 245, at paragraph 8.83.*

124 *Clauses 3 and 4.*

125 *At para 409.*

The nature of the section 126(1) discretion, the role of exclusionary discretion in relation to the admission of hearsay evidence under the 2003 Act, and the reasons why the Law Commission recommended the repeal of sections 25 and 26 of the 1988 Act without their replacement by corresponding provisions of the new legislation are considered at 2.7.5, below. In this context the reader is also directed to section 125 of the 2003 Act (stopping the case where evidence is unconvincing) which is considered at 2.7.4, below. The operation of the section 117(6)-(7) discretion itself is considered at 2.2.2.2.5 below.

2.2.2.2 The operation of section 117

Essentially, a hearsay statement will be admissible under section 117 of the 2003 Act as evidence of a matter stated if oral evidence would be admissible as evidence of the relevant matter[126], the document or the relevant part thereof was created or received by a person in the course of a trade, business, profession or other occupation or an office holder[127], the information which the statement contains was provided by a person who had or may reasonably be supposed to have had personal knowledge of the relevant matters[128] and any intermediaries through whom the information passed between the latter person and the former person (if, indeed, they are different persons) received the information in the course of a trade, business, profession or other occupation or as an office holder.[129] Additionally, if the statement which the document contains was prepared for the purposes of criminal proceedings or for a criminal investigation (and was not obtained pursuant to a request under section 7 of the Crime (International Co-operation) Act 2003 or an order under paragraph 6 of Schedule 13 to the Criminal Justice Act 1988), it will also be necessary either to satisfy one of the conditions imposed by section 116(2)[130] or the additional condition imposed by section 117(5)(b).[131] Moreover, unlike section 116 of the 2003 Act, section 117 is not an "automatic admissibility" provision but, rather, the admissibility of hearsay evidence under section 117 will be subject to the operation of the section 117(6)-(7) exclusionary discretion, concerning the reliability of the hearsay evidence for the purpose for which it is tendered. The nature of this new exclusionary discretion is considered at 2.2.2.2.5, below.

In relation to the burden and standard of proof concerning the admissibility of evidence under section 117, it is submitted that the comments made at 2.2.1.2 in relation to the burden of proving that evidence is admissible under section 116 of the 2003 Act are equally applicable in relation to the requirements imposed by section 117(1). Again, these comments are subject to the exception concerning the operation of section 116(5)[132] (section 116(5) appears to be applicable in the context of section 117 in circumstances in which a section 116(2) condition is

---

126 *See section 117(1)(a).*
127 *Section 117(1)(b), (2)(a).*
128 *Section 117(1)(b), (2)(b).*
129 *Section 117(1)(b), (2)(c).*

130 *See 2.2.1.2.4-2.2.1.2.8, above.*
131 *See 2.2.2.2.4 below*
132 *See 2.2.1.2 above.*

relied upon in order to satisfy the section 117(5)(a) requirement). The position in relation to the onus of proof in relation to the exercise of the exclusionary discretion conferred by section 117(6)-(7) of the 2003 Act is considered at 2.2.2.2.5, below.

2.2.2.2.1 The nature of a "document"

For the purposes of section 117(1), the statement must be "contained in a document". Section 134(1) of the 2003 Act defines a document as:

> "anything in which information of any description is recorded".

This definition of document is identical to the extremely wide definition which was inserted into the 1988 Act by the Civil Evidence Act 1995.[133] Thus, a document within the section 134(1) meaning of that term may, for example, encompass anything from a video tape[134] to the hard disc of a computer[135] to a label on a blood sample.[136]

Unlike section 23 of the 1988 Act, section 117 of the 2003 Act does not require that the statement was "made" in a document but merely requires that it is "contained" therein. Consequently, it appears that, like section 24 of the 1988 Act, section 117 of the 2003 Act will be potentially applicable to a statement contained in a document even though the statement was written down by B from information supplied by A and was not checked and signed or otherwise verified by A.[137] Equally, it appears that, like section 24, section 117 will be potentially applicable to a tape recording of A's oral statement made by B even though A did not know that his statement was being tape recorded by B.[138]

2.2.2.2.2 Section 117(1)(a)

In relation to the requirement, imposed by section 117(1)(a), that "oral evidence given in the proceedings would be admissible as evidence of" the matter stated, it should be noted that section 134(1) of the 2003 Act provides that:

> ""oral evidence" includes evidence which, by reason of any disability, disorder or other impairment, a person called as a witness gives in writing or by signs or by way of any device"

133 *See paragraph 5 of Schedule 2 to the 1988 Act and section 16(6) of and Schedule 1 to the 1995 Act.*

134 *See, for example, R v Duffy [1999] QB 919.*

135 *See, for example, R v Nazeer [1998] Crim LR 750.*

136 *Khatibi v DPP [2004] EWHC 83 (Admin).*

137 *See, for example, Re D (A Minor) [1986] 2 FLR 189 (a case under section 2 of the Civil Evidence Act 1968, which has since been repealed).*

138 *In Ventouris v Mountain (Italia Express) (Ship) [1992] 3 All ER 414, such tape recordings were held to be inadmissible under section 4 of the Civil Evidence Act 1968 (which has since been repealed). It is submitted, however, that if similar facts arose in a criminal case, the relevant evidence would be admissible under section 117 of the 2003 Act. Section 117 (like section 24 of the 1988 Act) differs from section 4 of the 1968 Act, inter alia, both in that section 117, unlike section 4, does not require the relevant document to form part of a record and in that the requirements of section 117 are satisfied where the person acting in the course of the trade or business etc receives the relevant document in the course thereof whereas section 4 only applied where a person compiled a record whilst acting in the course of a duty.*

The effect of the section 117(1)(a) requirement, which effectively reprises a requirement of section 24 of the Criminal Justice Act 1988, is that section 117 will not apply to a hearsay statement unless oral evidence of the fact as evidence of which the hearsay statement is tendered would be admissible. Unlike section 116 of the 2003 Act and section 23 of the 1988 Act, however, section 117 of the 2003 Act, like section 24 of the 1988 Act, does not require that the oral evidence of the maker of the relevant statement would have been admissible. Thus, it appears that section 117, like section 24, will be potentially applicable to a statement even though the oral evidence of the person who created or received the document would itself be hearsay evidence[139] (i.e. the section has the potential to render "second hand hearsay" admissible).[140] It appears, however, that the section 117 hearsay exception will not apply to a statement if oral evidence of the relevant facts would be excluded under some rule of evidence other than the hearsay rule, for example, because the evidence is irrelevant or because it amounts to inadmissible evidence of opinion or of bad character. Moreover, evidence will not be admissible under section 117 where the person who created or received the document, the supplier of information or any intermediary through whom the information passed on its way from the supplier of information to the creator/receiver of the document either did not have the "required capability" to make it (i.e. was not competent to make it) at the relevant time or, if the relevant person cannot be identified, where that person cannot reasonably be assumed to have had the "required capability" to make it at the relevant time.[141]

2.2.2.2.3 Section 117(1)(b) and section 117(2)

Section 117(1)(b) directs the court to the requirements of section 117(2), section 117(2) requiring that:

> "(a) the document or the part containing the statement was created or received by a person in the course of a trade, business, profession or other occupation, or as the holder of a paid or unpaid office,
>
> (b) the person who supplied the information contained in the statement (the relevant person) had or may reasonably be supposed to have had personal knowledge of the matters dealt with, and
>
> (c) each person (if any) through whom the information was supplied from the relevant person to the person mentioned in paragraph (a) received the information in the course of a trade, business, profession or other occupation, or as the holder of a paid or unpaid office."

---

139 *See, for example, R v Derodra [1999] Crim LR 978.*

140 *In relation to the role of section 117 in the context of multiple hearsay see section 121 (considered at 2.7.1 below).*

141 *See section 123 (considered at 2.7.2 below).*

Essentially, these requirements reprise those of section 24(1)(i)-(ii), (2) of the 1988 Act, (though, as was noted at 2.2.2.1 above, the wording of section 117, unlike that of section 24, makes clear that the section 117 hearsay exception will be applicable even though only the part of the document in which the statement is contained was created or received in the course of the trade, business etc). The effect of the requirements imposed by section 117(1)(b) and 117(2) appears to be as follows.

Section 117 will not apply to a hearsay statement unless the person who created or received the document or the relevant part thereof did so in the course of a trade, business, profession or other occupation or as the holder of a paid or unpaid office.[142] It is submitted that, as in the case of section 24(1)(i), in determining whether the requirement that the person who created or received the document did so in the course of a trade, business, profession or other occupation, or as the holder of a paid or unpaid office, the court will, in appropriate circumstances, be entitled to infer, from matters such as the nature and source of the document, that this was so without receiving evidence from the person who created or kept the document.[143]

It appears that a document is created by a person whether the relevant person writes it, types it, word processes it, enters it into a computer database[144] or, it is submitted, switches on the tape recorder or video recorder which records it.[145] An example of the receipt of a document by a person is provided by *R v Clowes*[146], which concerned the receipt by liquidators of transcripts of interviews. Whilst the rationale for the admissibility of "business documents" under section 117 appears to be that, in general, such documents are reliable[147], it may be that this "safeguard" is less obviously applicable to documents which are received in the course of a business than to documents which are created in the course thereof[148], and that the

---

142 See section 117(2)(a).

143 *R v Foxley [1995] 2 Cr App R 523; R v Ilyas [1996] Crim LR 810; Vehicle and Operator Services Agency v George Jenkins Transport Ltd The Times December 5 2003; Khatibi v DPP [2004] EWHC 83 (Admin).*

144 *See, for example, R v Derodra [1999] Crim LR 978.*

145 *Thus, for example, it is submitted that the person who switched on the video recorder in the criminal case of R v Duffy [1999] QB 919 (concerning section 23 of the 1988 Act) or switched on the tape recorder in the civil case of Ventouris v Mountain (Italia Express) (Ship) [1992] 3 All ER 414 (concerning provisions of the Civil Evidence Act 1968 which have since been repealed) was creating a document within the meaning of section 117(2)(a) of the 2003 Act (and within that of section 24(1)(i) of the 1988 Act).*

146 *[1992] 3 All ER 440.*

147 *See "Evidence in Criminal Proceedings: Hearsay and Related Topics", Law Com No 245, at paragraph 8.74.*

148 *See Murphy, "A Practical Approach to Evidence" 8th ed, Blackstone Press, 2003 at p.351. Moreover, in the context of sections 23 and 24 of*

the 1988 Act it has been cogently argued that since all documents which are admitted in evidence in criminal proceedings will at some stage be received by a person acting in the course of an office etc, this essentially rendered section 23 of the 1988 Act otiose as any document which fell within its ambit would also fall within that of section 24 (see Ockleton "Documentary Hearsay in Criminal Cases" [1992] Crim LR 15 and see Keane "The Modern Law of Evidence" 5th ed, Butterworths, 2000 at p. 325). This, it is submitted, is no longer absolutely true following the decision of the Court of Appeal in R v Nazeer [1988] Crim LR 750 as, it is submitted, there may be circumstances in which the contents of a lost document containing a hearsay statement which is proved by oral secondary evidence is admissible under section 23 even though it has never been received by a person acting in the course of an office etc. In relation to the respective ambits of sections 116 and 117, of course, the applicability of section 116, unlike section 117, to oral evidence clearly means that the ambit of the former section is of potentially significantly greater ambit than that of the latter.

discretion which section 117(6),(7) will confer will thus be of particular significance in relation to documents of the latter type.[149]

Section 117, again like section 24 of the 1988 Act, will not apply to a hearsay statement unless the supplier of information had or may reasonably be supposed to have had personal knowledge of the matters dealt with by the hearsay statement.[150] Section 117(3) provides that:

> "(3) The persons mentioned in paragraphs (a) and (b) of subsection (2) may be the same person."

Thus, section 117(3) makes clear that, as is currently the case in relation to section 24(1)(ii)[151], the person who supplies the information and the person who creates the document may, but need not be, one and the same. It is submitted that, as in the case of section 24(1)(ii), in determining whether the supplier of information had or may reasonably be supposed to have had personal knowledge of the matters dealt with, the court will, in appropriate circumstances, be entitled to infer, from matters such as the nature and source of the document, that this was so without receiving evidence from the person who created or kept the document.[152]

Further, in relation to the requirement imposed by section 117(2)(c), the effect of that provision, like that of section 24(2) of the 1988 Act, will be that if the information which is contained in the document passed between the supplier of information and the creator/receiver of the document via one or more intermediaries (i.e. if it did not pass directly from the supplier of information and the creator/receiver of the document but, rather, passed between them via a third party or third parties), the section will only apply if the intermediary(ies) received the information in the course of a trade, business, profession or other occupation or as the holder of a paid or unpaid office. Presumably if the information passed through the hand of the intermediary in documentary form or if the intermediary reduced the information into documentary form before passing it on to the person who created or received the document which is tendered in evidence, the intermediary will, as well as satisfying the requirements of section 117(2)(c), also be a person who received or created a document in the course of a trade or business etc for the purposes of section 117(2)(a) if the document which he created or received is tendered in evidence.

Finally, in relation to the operation of section 124, which concerns the credibility of the maker of a hearsay statement who is not called, it should be noted that, under section124(4), the court, for the purposes of section 117, will be required to treat the persons specified by section 117(2)(a),(b) and (c) as the maker of the statement. Section 124(4) is considered at 2.7.3.1, below.

---

149 *The nature of this discretion is considered at 2.2.2.2.5 below.*

150 *Section 117(2)(b).*

151 *See R v Rock [1994] Crim LR 843.*

152 *R v Foxley [1995] 2 Cr App R 523; R v Ilyas [1996] Crim LR 810; Vehicle and Operator Services Agency v George Jenkins Transport Ltd The Times December 5 2003; Khatibi v DPP*

2.2.2.2.4 Section 117(4)-(5)

Section 117(4)-(5) of the 2003 Act provide as follows.

"(4) The additional requirements of subsection (5) must be satisfied if the statement—

(a) was prepared for the purposes of pending or contemplated criminal proceedings, or for a criminal investigation, but

(b) was not obtained pursuant to a request under section 7 of the Crime (International Co-operation) Act 2003 (c. 32) or an order under paragraph 6 of Schedule 13 to the Criminal Justice Act 1988 (c. 33) (which relate to overseas evidence).

(5) The requirements of this subsection are satisfied if—

(a) any of the five conditions mentioned in section 116(2) is satisfied (absence of relevant person etc), or

(b) the relevant person cannot reasonably be expected to have any recollection of the matters dealt with in the statement (having regard to the length of time since he supplied the information and all other circumstances)."

Essentially, the effect of these provisions will be that if the statement which the document contains was prepared for the purposes of criminal proceedings or for a criminal investigation (and was not prepared pursuant to a request under section 7 of the Crime (International Co-operation) Act 2003 or an order under paragraph 6 of Schedule 13 to the Criminal Justice Act 1988), it will either be necessary to satisfy one of the conditions imposed by section 116(2) or to satisfy the additional condition imposed by section 117(5)(b). An example of a statement prepared for the purposes of contemplated criminal proceedings is provided by a statement made by a witness during a previous trial, the statement being contained in a transcript.[153] An example of a statement prepared for the purposes of a criminal investigation is provided by a custody record.[154]

The conditions imposed by section 116(2) were considered at 2.2.1.2.4-2.2.1.2.8, above. It was submitted at 2.2.2.1 above that in relation to the operation of the section 116(2) conditions in the context of hearsay evidence tendered under section 117, the "relevant person" will be the supplier of the information which the hearsay statement contains. It is additionally submitted that where a party tendering hearsay evidence under section 117 relies upon a section 116(2) condition, section 116(5)[155] will be applicable and that where the condition relied upon is that contained in section 116(2)(e), section 116(3)-(4)[156] will be applicable.

---

153 *R v Lockley [1995] 2 Cr App R 554.*
154 *R v Hogan [1997] Crim LR 349.*

155 2.2.1.2.8
156 2.2.1.2.9

Unlike the section 116(2) conditions, the additional condition contained in section 117(5)(b) does not concern the unavailability of a witness and thus, quite properly, section 116(5) (which concerns the cause of the witness' unavailability) will not be applicable in the context of the section 117(5)(b) condition. In relation to the operation of the condition imposed by section 24(4)(iii) of the 1988 Act (which equates with the section 117(5)(b) condition), it has been held that the maker of the hearsay statement cannot reasonably be expected to have any recollection of the matters dealt with therein in circumstances in which he could reasonably be expected to remember some parts thereof but could not reasonably be expected to remember other parts thereof, the latter parts being treated as independent statements for the purposes of admissibility under section 24.[157] Presumably the courts are likely to adopt a similar approach in relation to the admissibility of hearsay statements under section 117. There is also authority to the effect, however, that where a memory refreshing document is available, the court should take its existence into account when determining what the maker can reasonably be expected to recollect for the purposes of section 24(4)(iii).[158] If the courts adopt this approach when the provisions of the 2003 Act are in force and, consequently, a court, finding that the section 117(5)(b) condition is not satisfied, declines to admit a hearsay statement which may be used for memory refreshing, it should be noted that the memory refreshing document may, in any event, become admissible in evidence under section 120(3) of the 2003 Act.[159]

2.2.2.2.5 Section 117(6)-(7)

Section 117(6)-(7) provide as follows.

"(6) A statement is not admissible under this section if the court makes a direction to that effect under subsection (7).

(7) The court may make a direction under this subsection if satisfied that the statement's reliability as evidence for the purpose for which it is tendered is doubtful in view of–

(a) its contents,

(b) the source of the information contained in it,

(c) the way in which or the circumstances in which the information was supplied or received, or

(d) the way in which or the circumstances in which the document concerned was created or received."

The nature of those provisions under which the courts will possess discretion to exclude evidence tendered under section 117 of the 2003 Act was considered at

---

157 *R v Carrington (1994) 99 Cr App R 376.*
158 *See R v Derodra [1999] Crim LR 978, though see also R v Setz-Dempsey (1994) 98 Cr App R 23.*

159 *Section 120(3) is considered at 2.2.5.2.2 below.*

2.2.2.1 above. In relation to the nature of the section 117(6)-(7) discretion itself, it appears that the discretion will only exist only when the court is satisfied for one or more of the reasons specified by section 117(7)(a)-(d) that a hearsay statement which is tendered under section 117 is of doubtful reliability as evidence for the purpose for which it is tendered. Where this is the case the subsections do not appear to require the court to exclude the relevant hearsay evidence (i.e. they appear to confer a discretion rather than imposing a duty). It is submitted, however, that the subsections do not make clear whether, once the doubtful reliability of the statement as evidence for the relevant purpose is established, the court will only be entitled to take the unreliability of the statement into account when deciding whether to admit or exclude it under section 117(7) or whether at that stage the court will also be entitled to take additional factors into account other than the matters specified by section 117(7)(a)-(d). Moreover, the section does not appear to make clear where the onus of proof lies in relation to the operation of the section 117(7) discretion. Is it a discretion, like the inclusionary discretion created by section 26 of the 1988 Act[160], in relation to the exercise of which a party will bear the burden of persuading the court in favour of its exercise or is it a discretion, like the exclusionary discretion conferred by section 78 of the Police and Criminal Evidence Act 1984[161], the operation of which will not impose a burden of proof on any party?

The Law Commission[162] explained the rationale and operation of the recommended power which finally manifested itself in the form of the section 117(6)-(7) exclusionary discretion as follows.

> "8.74 ...although business documents can be assumed in the main to be reliable, this assumption may not be true for each and every document; and, where it is apparent that a particular document is not or may not be reliable, it would be undesirable for it to be automatically admissible as a business document. For example, a letter would qualify as a business document as soon as it was posted, but there may be reason in the particular case to suspect that the contents are not to be relied upon. Or consider the case where a neighbour tells a social worker that she heard the couple next door beating their children on the previous night. The social worker makes a note in the official file. That note is a business document and automatically admissible; but if there were a provision along the suggested lines, the court could take into account information which led it to suspect that the account was at least exaggerated, and direct that it was not a business document.

---

160 *See R v Radak [1999] 1 Cr App R 187.*
161 *See R v Governor of Brixton Prison, ex parte Safi The Times Wednesday January 24 2001.*
162 *See "Evidence in Criminal Proceedings: Hearsay and Related Topics", Law Com No 245, at paragraphs 8.74-8.76.*

8.75   Thus, where a statement is tendered in evidence and the court has cause to doubt its reliability, the court needs to be given an additional power to direct that the statement shall not be admissible as a business document. The court would take into account the purpose for which the statement is tendered[101], the contents of the statement, the source of the information, and the way in which or the circumstances in which the information was supplied or received or the document was created or received. Where there is no particular reason to doubt the reliability of the statement, this power would not be available.

"8.76   The party opposing the admission of the evidence would make a representation to the court, based on facts to which it could point, but without having to call evidence, and invite the court to consider whether a direction should be given that the document in question is not to be admitted as a business document. If it were necessary for the party tendering the document to call evidence to prove that the document was reliable, a voir dire would be held, in the same way as if that party had to call evidence to prove that the document was received in the course of a business."

    [101] There may be things about the document (such as the date) which are known to be unreliable, but which are not material to the use which the party wants to make of the statement."

It is submitted that the wording of section 117(7) does not make clear whether, in the context of exercising the section 117(6),(7) discretion, the court will be required to adopt the approach outlined by the Law Commission at 8.76 above. Thus, whether in practice the court will require the party tendering the hearsay evidence to establish its reliability when the section 117(6),(7) discretion comes into play appears at present to be unclear. Moreover, in circumstances in which the court is satisfied that a hearsay statement tendered under section 117 is of doubtful reliability as evidence for the relevant purpose, will it then be for the party tendering the hearsay evidence to persuade the court not to exercise its exclusionary discretion or (as is the case under section 25 of the 1988 Act[163]), will it be for the party objecting to the admission of the evidence to persuade the court to exercise that discretion so as to exclude the relevant evidence?

Further, under section 3(1) of the Human Rights Act 1998, the court will, if possible, be required to exercise its section 117(6),(7) discretion so as not to result in a violation of Article 6 of the European Convention on Human Rights. The extent to which the admission or exclusion of hearsay evidence is potentially capable of resulting in a violation of Article 6 of the Convention (including the approach of the courts in this context to the admission of hearsay evidence under sections 23 or 24 of the 1988 Act) is considered at 2.8 below.

---

163 *R v Cole [1990] 1 WLR 866.*

Finally, it must be remembered that, regardless of the precise nature and ambit of the section 117(6),(7) discretion, when Chapter 2 of Part 11 of the 2003 Act is in force, the court will still possess discretion, both at common law and under other statutory provisions, to exclude hearsay evidence tendered under section 117. It should be noted, however, that one important characteristic which the section 117(6)-(7) discretion will share with the discretion presently conferred by section 25 of the 1988 Act, but which is not possessed by the court's common law exclusionary discretion or by that conferred by section 78 of the Police and Criminal Evidence Act 1984 (both of which only encompass evidence tendered by the prosecution), is that the section 117(6)-(7) discretion (like the section 25 discretion) may be exercised so as to exclude both prosecution and defence evidence.

2.2.3 Previous inconsistent statements

Section 119 of the 2003 Act will not change the nature of those circumstances in which the previous inconsistent statements of witnesses who give oral evidence in criminal proceedings are admissible in evidence. The section will, however, create two new hearsay exceptions which, whilst they will only apply in circumstances in which previous inconsistent statements are admissible in criminal proceedings, will result in such statements being admitted not merely as evidence of their makers' credibility but, rather, as evidence of the matters stated.[164]

Since section 119 will only be applicable in circumstances in which a previous inconsistent statement is admissible in evidence in criminal proceedings, it is necessary, before considering section 119 itself, to first consider the nature of those circumstances in which previous consistent statements are admissible in evidence in criminal proceedings.

2.2.3.1 The admissibility of evidence of previous inconsistent statements

Evidence of previous inconsistent statements may be admissible in criminal proceedings in any of three situations. The three situations referred to are where a hostile witness is being cross-examined by or on behalf of the party who called him, where a witness called by one party is being cross-examined by or on behalf of another party and where it is sought to discredit the maker of a hearsay statement who has not given oral evidence in the proceedings in relation to the subject matter of the hearsay statement.[165]

---

164 *Previous consistent statements may be admissible in civil proceedings as evidence of matters stated under section 1 of the Civil Evidence Act 1995 (see Civil Evidence Act 1995, section 6(5)).*

165 *The same principles govern the admissibility of previous inconsistent statements in civil proceedings (see Civil Evidence Act 1995, section 6(3) and section 5(2)(b)).*

2.2.3.1.1 Previous inconsistent statements made by hostile witnesses

Section 3 of the Criminal Procedure Act 1865 (which applies to both criminal and civil proceedings), provides as follows.

> "A party producing a witness shall not be allowed to impeach his credit by general evidence of bad character; but he may, in case the witness shall in the opinion of the judge prove adverse, contradict him by other evidence, or, by leave of the judge, prove that he has made at other times a statement inconsistent with his present testimony; but before such last mentioned proof can be given the circumstances of the supposed statement, sufficient to designate the particular occasion, must be mentioned to the witness, and he must be asked whether or not he has made such a statement".

For the purposes of section 3 of the 1865 Act, it is necessary to distinguish between an unfavourable witness and a hostile witness (i.e. a witness who, in the words of section 3, "proves adverse"[166]).

Essentially, an unfavourable witness is a witness who is not hostile to the party who called him but whose evidence proves unfavourable to that party's case. This might be so where, for example, it is expected that a witness will give evidence in line with a statement which he had previously made out of court but, by the time when he testifies, perhaps due to age or incapacity, he has either forgotten the facts to which his earlier statement related or even gives evidence which is inconsistent with his earlier statement.

In contrast, a witness is a hostile or "adverse" witness if it appears that he does not want to tell the truth to the court on behalf of the party who called him.[167] Such hostility may either take the form of the giving of inconsistent testimony or that of "forgetting" the facts to which the previous inconsistent statement related.[168]

A party must obtain the leave of the court to treat his witness as hostile.[169] The question whether a witness is hostile is one which falls within the ambit of the trial judge's discretion[170] and the determination of this question by the trial judge will depend upon the judge's view of the witness' testimony, of his demeanour and of his responsiveness to questions.[171] Before the judge gives a party leave to treat his witness as hostile, it may be appropriate for counsel and the judge to suggest to the witness that the witness might like to memory refresh from an out of court statement and, only then, if this offer is refused and the witness does not adequately explain why his testimony differs from the statement, for the judge to

---

166 *For the purposes of section 3, "adverse" means hostile (Greenough v Eccles (1859) 5 CB NS 786 (a case concerning an equivalent provision contained in the Common Law Procedure Act 1854)).*
167 *See R v Prefas (1986) 86 Cr App R 111.*
168 *R v Honeyghon and Sales [1999] Crim LR 221.*

169 *See, for example, R v Gordon [2002] EWCA Crim 01.*
170 *See: Price v Manning (1889) 42 Ch D 372; R v Gordon [2002] EWCA Crim 01.*
171 *R v Gordon [2002] EWCA Crim 01.*

consider giving leave to treat the witness as hostile.[172] If the witness refuses to memory refresh in such circumstances, however, this does not mean that the judge is required to treat the witness as a hostile witness.[173]

The jury should normally be present when a witness is examined in order to determine whether he is hostile but, exceptionally (i.e. where it might be necessary to exclude the evidence of a hostile prosecution witness on the basis that the probative value of his evidence is outweighed by its prejudicial effect), it may be appropriate to determine this issue on the voir dire.[174]

Where a party applies to the court for leave to treat his witness as hostile and the judge gives leave this has two consequences. Both of these consequences concern the use of previous inconsistent statements by the party who called the witness, a previous inconsistent statement being a statement made by the witness on a previous occasion which, in the words of section 3 of the 1865 Act, is "inconsistent with his present testimony". The first consequence of the giving of leave to treat a witness as hostile is that, at common law, the trial judge may, in the exercise of his discretion, permit the party who called the hostile witness to cross-examine the witness to the extent that the witness may be asked leading questions and his previous inconsistent statement may be put to him[175] (though, in accordance with section 3 of the 1865 Act, his bad character, bias and previous convictions cannot not be raised). Where a prosecution witness is not prepared to admit the truth of a previous inconsistent statement, the Court may find it necessary to limit the extent of cross-examination by counsel for the prosecution, or even to exclude the evidence of the hostile witness altogether, in order to protect the accused from the potential prejudice which might result from detailed cross-examination on the previous inconsistent statement.[176]

The second consequence of the giving of leave to treat a witness as hostile is that, where it applies, section 3 of the 1865 Act appears to supplement the common law by permitting a party (if the leave of the court is granted[177]) to prove the previous inconsistent statement (whether written or oral[178]) of a hostile witness.[179] Before the previous inconsistent statement is proved however, in the words of section 3:

---

172 *R v Maw [1994] Crim LR 841 (though, it appears that where a prosecution witness during trial (though not during committal proceedings (R v Mann (1972) 56 Cr App R 750)) gives evidence which is inconsistent with his out of court statements, counsel for the prosecution is under a duty to apply to the judge to have him declared hostile (R v Fraser (1956) 40 Cr App R 160)). Whether such memory refreshing is necessary and, if so, by what method it should take place are both matters of judicial discretion (R v Gordon [2002] EWCA Crim 01).*

173 *R v Gordon [2002] EWCA Crim 01.*
174 *R v Darby [1989] Crim LR 817; R v Honeyghon [1999] Crim LR 221.*
175 *R v Thompson (1976) 64 Cr App R 96.*
176 *R v Dat [1998] Crim LR 488; R v Honeyghon [1999] Crim LR 221.*
177 *See R v Booth [1981] Crim LR 700.*
178 *See R v Prefas (1986) 86 Cr App R 111.*
179 *See Greenough v Eccles (1859) 5 CB NS 786.*

"...the circumstances of the supposed statement, sufficient to designate the particular occasion, must be mentioned to the witness, and he must be asked whether or not he has made such a statement".

It is arguable that section 3 of the 1865 Act does not apply to a hostile witness who refuses to testify because in such circumstances there is no "present testimony" for the witness' previous statement to be inconsistent with, though the position is not clear.[180] If this is indeed the case, it appears that even though the previous inconsistent statement may not be proved under section 3, the hostile witness may still, at common law, be cross-examined on the previous inconsistent statement.[181]

2.2.3.1.2 Previous inconsistent statements made by witnesses called by other parties

Sections 4 and 5 of the Criminal Procedure Act 1865 (which apply to both criminal and civil proceedings) concern the cross-examination of a witness by a party other than the party who called the witness. Section 4 of the 1865 Act provides as follows.

"If a witness, upon cross-examination as to a former statement made by him relative to the subject-matter of the indictment or proceeding, and inconsistent with his present testimony, does not distinctly admit that he made such statement, proof may be given that he did in fact make it; but before such proof can be given the circumstances of the supposed statement, sufficient to designate the particular occasion, must be mentioned to the witness, and he must be asked whether or not he has made such statement."

The inconsistent statement to which section 4 relates may be an oral statement or a written statement.[182] If the witness admits having made the previous inconsistent statement, no further evidence of the statement is admissible.[183] If the witness does not admit having made the statement, however, the statement may be proved under section 4, provided that the other requirements of the section have been satisfied (i.e. the statement must be "relative to the subject-matter of the indictment or proceeding", the circumstances of its making must have been mentioned to the witness and he must have been asked whether he made it). In determining whether the other requirements of section 4 have been satisfied, the main problem would appear to be that of determining whether the previous inconsistent statement is "relative to the subject-matter of the indictment or proceeding". In practice, however, this appears to be a matter which is within the ambit of the trial judge's discretion.[184] Where cross-examination in relation to a previous inconsistent statement is not "relative to the subject-matter of the

---

180 *R v Thompson (1976) 64 Cr App R 96 left this point open.*
181 *See R v Thompson (1976) 64 Cr App R 96.*
182 *R v Derby Magistrates' Court, ex parte B [1996] AC 487.*
183 *R v P [1998] Crim LR 663.*
184 *R v Bashir [1969] 1 WLR 1303.*

indictment or proceeding" but, rather, merely relates to the credibility of the witness, it appears that such cross-examination is permissible at common law but section 4 of the 1865 Act will not apply and, consequently, if the witness denies having made the previous consistent statement in such circumstances, it appears that the statement cannot be proved under section 4.[185]

Section 5 of the 1865 Act provides as follows.

> "A witness may be cross-examined as to previous statements made by him in writing, or reduced into writing, relative to the subject-matter of the indictment or proceeding, without such writing being shown to him; but if it is intended to contradict such witness by the writing, his attention must, before such contradictory proof can be given, be called to those parts of the writing which are to be used for the purpose of so contradicting him: Provided always that it shall be competent for the judge, at any time during the trial, to require the production of the writing for his inspection, and he may thereupon make such use of it for the purposes of the trial as he may think fit."

Under section 5, a witness may be cross-examined in relation to a previous inconsistent statement in writing which is "relative to the subject-matter of the indictment or proceeding" without showing the written statement to the witness.[186] Prior to section 5 of the 1865 Act coming into force, it was necessary, in order to cross-examine a witness in relation to an inconsistent statement at common law, to first show the witness the written statement and to put it in evidence (i.e. prove it and read it out).[187] Whilst section 5, when it applies, removes this common law requirement, the section does not prevent counsel from permitting the witness to see the written statement without putting it in evidence, provided that the statement is not used to contradict the witness.[188]

Where cross-examining counsel does not intend to put the written statement in evidence, counsel must still be able to produce the document as, under section 5, the judge may require its production.[189] Moreover, once the judge has inspected the document, section 5 provides that the judge may make such use of it for the purposes of the trial as he thinks fit. Consequently, whilst the judge is entitled to permit the entire statement to go before the jury he may, alternatively, decide to exercise his discretion so as only to permit those parts of the statement to which cross-examination related to go before them.[190]

If the witness does not admit the truth of the written statement, the written statement must be put in evidence if it is to be used to contradict him.[191] If the written statement is to be put in evidence to contradict the witness, the relevant

---

185 *R v Funderburk [1990] 1 WLR 587.*
186 *R v Derby Magistrates' Court, ex parte B [1996] AC 487.*
187 *Queen Caroline's Case (1820) 2 Br &B 287.*
188 *See R v Riley (1866) 4 F&F 964.*
189 *R v Anderson (1929) 21 Cr App R 178.*
190 *R v Beattie (1989) 89 Cr App R 302.*
191 *R v Riley (1866) 4 F&F 964.*
192 *R v Riley (1866) 4 F&F 964.*

If the witness does not admit making the written statement, it may be proved under section 4 of the 1865 Act.[193] If the witness does admit making the written statement, the judge may still, under section 5, direct that the written statement, or a part thereof, is put before the jury.[194]

2.2.3.1.3 Previous inconsistent statements made by the makers of hearsay statements

Essentially, section 124(2)(c) of the 2003 Act (which is considered at 2.7.3 below), will permit the admission in evidence of an inconsistent statement made by the maker of a hearsay statement who does not give oral evidence in relation to the subject matter of the hearsay statement. At the time of writing, such evidence is admissible (in the context of the hearsay exceptions created by sections 23 and 24 of the Criminal Justice Act 1988) under paragraph 1 of Schedule 2 to the Criminal Justice Act 1988 (which will be repealed when the hearsay provisions of the 2003 Act are brought into force[195]).

2.2.3.2 The effect of section 119

Until section 119 of the 2003 Act comes into force, if, in the context of criminal proceedings, a witness does not admit the truth of a previous inconsistent statement and the previous inconsistent statement, whether written, oral or made in some other way[196], is proved under section 3, 4 or 5 of the Criminal Procedure Act 1865, the statement is not admitted as evidence of the truth of the facts stated but is admitted merely for the purpose of discrediting its maker's testimony, and the jury should be directed to this effect.[197] In contrast, if the witness does admit that the previous consistent statement is true, then it appears that the jury is entitled to rely upon the readopted version of his evidence.[198] Clearly, where a witness does confirm his inconsistent statement during cross-examination, the witness' credibility may be adversely affected.[199]

Section 119 of the 2003 Act provides as follows.

> "(1) If in criminal proceedings a person gives oral evidence and—
>
>   (a)   he admits making a previous inconsistent statement, or
>
>   (b)   a previous inconsistent statement made by him is proved by virtue of section 3, 4 or 5 of the Criminal Procedure Act 1865 (c. 18), the statement is admissible as evidence of any matter stated of which oral evidence by him would be admissible.

193 *R v Derby Magistrates' Court, ex parte B [1996] AC 487.*

194 *R v Derby Magistrates' Court, ex parte B [1996] AC 487; R v Beattie (1989) 89 Cr App R 302.*

195 *See section 136.*

196 *See the definition of "statement" in section 115(2).*

197 *R v Golder [1960] 1 WLR 1169; R v Askew [1981] Crim LR 398.*

198 *R v Maw [1984] Crim LR 841; R v Allen LTL 13/2/2001.*

199 *R v Allen LTL 13/2/2001.*

(2) If in criminal proceedings evidence of an inconsistent statement by any person is given under section 124(2)(c), the statement is admissible as evidence of any matter stated in it of which oral evidence by that person would be admissible."

Once section 119 of the 2003 Act is in force, the effect of section 119(1)(a) will be that where, in the context of criminal proceedings, a witness admits making a previous inconsistent statement (even though the witness does not admit that the statement is true), the inconsistent statement will become admissible evidence of any matter stated of which the witness' oral evidence would be admissible. Equally, the effect of section 119(1)(b) will be that where, in the context of criminal proceedings, a previous inconsistent statement is proved under section 3, section 4 or section 5 of the Criminal Procedure Act 1865 (even though the witness does not admit that the statement is true), the inconsistent statement will become admissible evidence of any matter stated of which the witness' oral evidence would be admissible. Again, the effect of section 119(2) will be that where evidence of an inconsistent statement made by the maker of a hearsay statement who is not called as a witness is admitted under section 124(2)(c) of the 2003 Act, the inconsistent statement will be admitted as evidence of any matter stated of which the witness' oral evidence would be admissible.

Paragraph 414 of the Explanatory Notes to the Criminal Justice Act provides the following example of the operation of section 119, specifically of section 119(2), in the context of the admission of evidence of an inconsistent statement under section 124(2)(c) of the 2003 Act.

"445 *Subsection (2)* envisages the following type of situation. A makes a statement to the police that she saw B 'outside the jewellers' at midday on Monday'. A does not testify at trial but her statement is admitted under *Section 116*. As explained below, *Section 124* provides that evidence can be admitted in this type of situation in relation to the credibility of A. Subsection (2)(c) of *Section 124* provides that evidence can be admitted to prove that A had made another statement inconsistent with this statement (for example, A had said earlier that she did not see B on Monday at all). *Section 119(2)* provides that if there is such an inconsistent statement, it not only goes to the credibility of A, but it is also admissible as to the truth of its contents (that A did not see B on Monday)."

The Law Commission intended that their recommendation which eventually resulted in section 119 would, inter alia, remove the anomaly that the out of court statement of a witness who did not testify through fear was potentially admissible as hearsay evidence under section 23 of the Criminal Justice Act 1988 (which, as was seen at 2.2.1 above, is to be replaced by section 116 of the 2003 Act) but that where a witness did attend but turned hostile through fear his out of court statement would not be admissible as evidence of a matter stated.[200] The Law

Commission[201] provided the following two examples of the operation of what is now section 119 in the context of the hostile witness.

> "10.99 To illustrate the effect of our recommended reform in relation to hostile witnesses, we now consider two commonplace examples, the alleged assault victim and the accomplice who turns prosecution witness. In each case the witness fails to come up to proof.
>
> 10.100 In the former case, the alleged victim, having been deemed hostile by the court on application by the prosecution, denies the truth of the complaint made to the police on the night of the alleged assault. He or she now says it was all made up. On cross-examination by the prosecution the witness has difficulty explaining the injuries received, of which there is independent evidence. Under our recommendation the fact-finders would be able to convict if, despite the witness's repudiation of the incriminating statement, they were sure that the accused committed the assault charged. But if there were no other evidence, the court might be persuaded that a conviction would be unsafe, in which case it would direct an acquittal or dismiss the information.
>
> 10.101 In the latter case, suppose that W has already pleaded guilty and is now a witness for the prosecution. W has been deemed hostile and claims that he did not make the confession attributed to him in which he implicated D. That confession is admissible against D, as if W were a testifying co-accused."[202]

In relation to cross-examination of a co-defendant concerning an inconsistent statement which incriminates another co-defendant, the Law Commission[203] recognised that the effect of their recommendation would be that the previous inconsistent statement would be potentially admissible as evidence of a matter stated against the latter co-defendant. Thus, once section 119 is in force, it appears that it will no longer be the case that evidence which a co-defendant gave orally in court incriminating a co-defendant will be admissible evidence of the latter's guilt whereas a statement made out of court by a co-defendant incriminating his co-defendant and inconsistent with his testimony in court will not be admissible as evidence of the latter's guilt. The Law Commission justified the admissibility of

---

200 See *"Evidence in Criminal Proceedings: Hearsay and Related Topics"*, *Law Com No 245*, at paragraph 10.90.

201 See *"Evidence in Criminal Proceedings: Hearsay and Related Topics"*, *Law Com No 245*, at paragraphs 10.99-10.101.

202 Mr Michael Wills, the Parliamentary Under Secretary of State for the Home Department, gave Standing Committee B an example of the operation of what is now section 119 in the context of a domestic violence scenario which was similar in nature to the Law Commission's assault scenario (see Hansard (Commons) 28 January 2003 Column 643).

203 See *"Evidence in Criminal Proceedings: Hearsay and Related Topics"*, *Law Com No 245*, at

the former co-accused's previous inconsistent statement against the latter co-accused upon the basis that the former co-accused will be available for cross-examination by the latter co-accused and the inconsistency of the former co-accused will be obvious to the tribunal of fact.[204] The Law Commission[205] also recognised that their recommendation would at times operate in favour of the accused, i.e. when the testimony of a witness is adverse to the accused but the witness' previous inconsistent statement is in his favour.

The Law Commission[206] outlined the practical consequences of their recommendation as follows. [It should be noted that paragraph (4) of the extract, immediately below, appears to relate to the duty of the court under what is now section 125 of the 2003 Act. Section 125 is considered at 2.7.4, below.]

"(1) A defendant could be convicted even where the complainant does not come up to proof, because the fact-finders could accept the complainant's out-of-court statement as true (even though he or she does not confirm it in the witness box).[120]

(2) When considering a submission of no case to answer, the court would have to take account of the contents of a previous inconsistent statement admitted in evidence.

(3) Where the previous statement was relied on by the prosecution, section 78 of PACE would apply.

(4) If the quality of the out-of-court statement were such that a conviction would be unsafe, the court would be under a duty to direct an acquittal (or, on summary trial, to dismiss the information).

(5) The judge would have to treat the previous statement as evidence in the summing up.

(6) Where a previous inconsistent statement was admitted in evidence although the witness maintained that it was untrue, a careful direction might be needed. Although the weight to be attached to the oral testimony and the out-of-court statement would be a matter for the fact-finders, it might help a jury if they were told that they are not obliged to accept either version of events as true, and if their attention were drawn to other items of evidence which might help them decide which parts of the evidence to believe and which to reject."

"[120] But see (4) below."

---

204 See *"Evidence in Criminal Proceedings: Hearsay and Related Topics"*, *Law Com No 245*, at paragraph 10.96.

205 See *"Evidence in Criminal Proceedings: Hearsay and Related Topics"*, *Law Com No 245*, at paragraph 10.97.

206 See *"Evidence in Criminal Proceedings: Hearsay and Related Topics"*, *Law Com No 245*, at paragraph 10.98

It should be noted that section 119 of the 2003 Act will not make an inconsistent statement admissible as evidence of a fact if the oral evidence of the statement's maker would not be admissible as evidence of the relevant fact. This, it is submitted, will be the case where, for example, the evidence is irrelevant, amounts to inadmissible evidence of opinion or to inadmissible evidence of bad character. Similarly, where the maker of an inconsistent statement did not have the "required capability" to make it (i.e. was not competent to make it) at the time when he made it, the effect of section 123 of the 2003 Act (considered at 2.7.2, below) will be that the inconsistent statement will not be admissible under section 119 as evidence of matters stated (though, it appears, the operation of section 123 will neither prevent the cross-examination of the witness in relation to the inconsistent statement not its proof under section 3, 4 or 5 of the 1865 Act). It also appears, however, that, in consequence of the operation of section 121(1)(a) of the 2003 Act, which is considered at 2.7.1 below, the fact that an inconsistent statement itself contains or is based upon a hearsay statement will not prevent the admission of the inconsistent statement under section 119 to prove that the latter statement was made (though, presumably, the latter statement will only be admissible if it, also, falls within the ambit of an exception to the rule against hearsay). Equally, it appears that, again in consequence of the operation of section 121(1)(a) of the 2003 Act, an inconsistent statement which is admissible under section 119 may be proved by a hearsay statement which is admissible under some other exception to the rule against hearsay.

Where an inconsistent statement does fall within the ambit of one of the hearsay exceptions created by section 119, it must not be forgotten, that its admissibility will still be subject to the exercise of the court's exclusionary discretion.[207]

It is submitted that when section 119 of the 2003 Act is in force, there may still be circumstances in which, for the purpose of discrediting its maker, a party may be permitted to prove an inconsistent statement which does not fall within the ambit of section 119 even though the inconsistent statement does not fall within the ambit of some other hearsay exception which the 2003 Act will create, preserve or retain. In such circumstances the inconsistent statement will not, of course, be admissible as evidence of a matter stated. As has already been demonstrated, this might be the case where, under section 123 of the 2003 Act, the maker of the inconsistent statement did not have the "required capability" to make it at the time when he made it. This might equally be so, it is submitted, in circumstances in which a confession made by the accused is inadmissible for his co-accused under section 76A of the Police and Criminal Evidence Act 1984 (which is to be inserted into the 1984 Act by section 128(1) of the 2003 Act)[208]. Where the accused's confession is not admissible for his co-accused under section 76A, the effect of section 128(2) of the 2002 Act appears to be that the confession will not be

---

207 *Perhaps at common law or under section 78 of the Police and Criminal Evidence Act 1984 (see section 126(2) of the Criminal Justice Act 2003)* *or under section 126(1) of the 2003 Act (see, generally, 2.7.5 below).*

208 *See 2.2.7.2 below.*

admissible under any other hearsay exception. It is submitted, however, that in the context of cross-examination of the accused on behalf of the co-accused, the fact that no hearsay exception is applicable will not prevent the confession, if inconsistent with its maker's testimony, from being proved under section 4 or section 5 of the 1865 Act and relied upon as evidence of its maker's credibility, provided that this is relevant to the co-accused's defence.[209]

It should also be noted that where an inconsistent statement is not admissible under section 119, this will not necessarily mean that the statement will not be admissible as evidence of a matter stated under some other exception to the hearsay rule, such as that created by section 114(1)(d) of the 2003 Act.[210]

Finally, it should be noted that where a documentary statement is admitted under section 119 of the 2003 Act and the document or a copy thereof is exhibited, the effect of section 122 of the 2003 Act will be that the jury cannot take the document with them when they retire unless either the court considers this appropriate or all the parties agree that the jury should take it with them.

2.2.4 Previous consistent statements

Section 120 of the Criminal Justice Act 2003 will create a number of statutory exceptions to the hearsay rule concerning the admission of evidence of previous consistent statements made by witnesses who are called to give oral evidence. Section 120 will not, however, abolish the common law rule against previous consistent statements. Rather, subject to certain modifications which are examined below, the section will essentially adopt as hearsay exceptions three of the existing common law exceptions to the rule against previous consistent statements.

Before considering the effects of section 120 in relation to the admissibility and evidential significance of previous consistent statements, it is first necessary to consider the nature of the common law exclusionary rule itself and that of its common law exceptions.

2.2.4.1 The rule against previous consistent statements

A previous consistent (or self-serving) statement is a previous oral or written statement made by a witness which is consistent with the witness's testimony in court.[211] Essentially, the rule against previous consistent statements is the common law rule that, subject to exceptions, evidence of a witness' previous consistent statements is inadmissible as evidence of the witness' consistency (i.e. credibility).[212] Moreover, subject to its exceptions, the operation of the hearsay rule prevents a previous consistent statement from being admissible as evidence of the facts stated. Thus, in the absence either of an exception to the rule against previous consistent statements or of an exception to the hearsay rule, a witness cannot be

---

209 *See 2.2.7.2 below.*
210 *The hearsay exception created by section 114(1)(d) is considered at 2.6 below.*

211 *R v Roberts [1942] 1 All ER 187.*
212 *R v Beattie (1989) 89 Cr App R 302.*

asked in chief whether he has made a previous consistent statement and other witnesses cannot be called to give evidence of the previous consistent statement.[213] The rule applies in the contexts of examination in chief, cross-examination and re-examination.[214]

Like the common law hearsay rule[215], it has been held that the rule against previous consistent statements does not apply to a sketch or a photofit.[216] It is submitted that the criticism of the common law classification of such evidence as falling outside the ambit of the hearsay rule (see 1.11.1 above) is equally applicable to the common law classification of such evidence as not falling within the ambit of the rule against previous consistent statements. Moreover, whereas once the 2003 Act comes into force, photofits and sketches will potentially fall within the ambit of the hearsay rule[217], the Act does not appear to make any equivalent provision so far as previous consistent statements are concerned. Consequently, when the 2003 Act is in force, it is submitted that sketches and photofits will technically remain outside the ambit of the rule against previous consistent statements. In practice, however, it appears that the fact that photofits and sketches will continue to fall outside the ambit of the rule against previous consistent statements will be of no significance as, it is submitted, in consequence of the definition of "statement" in section 115(2), the sketch or photofit is likely to fall within the ambit of the hearsay exception created by section 120(4)-(5) of the 2003 Act (which is considered at 2.2.4.3, below). Whether an e-fit will be admissible under section 120(4)-(5) or, conversely, will be subject to the admissibility requirement imposed by section 129(1) of the 2003 Act, appears, however (for the reasons outlined at 1.11.2 above), to remain open to doubt.

2.2.4.2 The rule's common law exceptions

The rule against previous consistent statements, like the common law hearsay rule, has its common law exceptions. If a statement falls within the ambit of a common law exception to the rule against previous consistent statements but not within the ambit of an exception to the hearsay rule, the statement is only admissible as evidence of consistency (i.e. credibility) and not as evidence of the truth of the facts stated.[218] Thus, where evidence of a previous consistent statement is admitted in a criminal trial prior to section 120 of the 2003 Act coming into force, it is important that (unless the statement falls within the ambit of an exception to the hearsay rule) the judge directs the jury as to the limited purpose for which they are entitled to make use of such evidence.[219]

---

213 *R v Roberts [1942] 1 All ER 187; R v Oyesiku (1971) 56 Cr App R 240.*

214 *R v Ali The Times November 11 2003.*

215 *See 1.11.1 above.*

216 *R v Cook [1987] 1 All E.R. 1049.*

217 *See the definition of "statement" in section 115(2).*

218 *R v Beattie (1989) 89 Cr App R 302.*

219 *R v Croad [2001] EWCA Crim 644. In the context of civil proceedings, where a statement falls within the ambit of an exception to the rule against previous consistent statements, it appears that the statement may be relied upon as evidence of matters stated (see Civil Evidence Act 1995, section 6(5). For the exceptions to the rule in civil proceedings see section 6(2) of the 1995 Act.*

At common law (i.e. in criminal proceedings before section 120 of the 2003 Act comes into force), it appears that a previous inconsistent statement may be admissible in the absence of an exception to the hearsay rule in any of the following situations. First, for the purpose of rebutting a suggestion made during cross-examination that the witness has recently fabricated his evidence. Secondly, where it takes the form of evidence of a previous identification of the accused by an identification witness. Thirdly, where it takes the form of a wholly exculpatory statement made by the accused to the police. Fourthly, where it takes the form of evidence of a voluntary sexual offence complaint made at the first reasonable opportunity. Fifthly, where the statement forms part of the res gestae. Finally, where it takes the form of a statement made by a person found in possession of recently stolen goods or other incriminating articles explaining his possession thereof.[220]

It should be noted that there is no general exception to the rule against previous consistent statements permitting the re-examination of a witness in relation to a previous statement made thereby where the witness has been cross-examined concerning inconsistencies in his testimony.[221] It appears, however, that the court does possess a residual discretion to permit such re-examination to take place in the interests of justice in circumstances in which, in consequence of cross-examination, the jury would be misled either as to a material fact or as to the terms of a previous statement made by the witness.[222]

2.2.4.2.1 Rebuttal of suggestions of recent fabrication made during cross-examination

The first of the six common law exceptions to the rule against previous consistent statements, identified immediately above, applies where it is suggested to a witness during cross-examination not merely that his evidence is untrue but, more specifically, that he has recently fabricated it. In such circumstances, the witness' previous consistent statements, if made either contemporaneously or sufficiently early to be capable of rebutting the suggestion of recent fabrication, are admissible, as evidence of credibility, in rebuttal of the allegation of recent fabrication.[223] This exception to the rule against previous consistent statements may apply even though the cross-examining party does not expressly suggest that the witness' evidence is a recent fabrication if the judge is satisfied that the challenge made by the cross-examining party either amounts to an allegation of recent fabrication or might be regarded by the jury as amounting to such an allegation.[224] The judge must also be satisfied both that the statement is consistent with his testimony and,

---

220 See *R v Ali The Times* November 11 2003.
221 See: *R v Beattie (1989) 89 Cr App R 302; R v Ali The Times* November 11 2003.
222 See *R v Ali The Times* November 11 2003. *Where applicable, the same result may be achieved by virtue of the operation of section 5 of the Criminal Procedure Act 1865 (The Times November 11 2003). Section 5 of the 1865 Act was considered at 2.2.3.1.2 above.*
223 *R v Oyesiku (1971) 56 Cr App R 240.*
224 See: *R v Ali The Times* November 11 2003; *R v Oyesiku (1971) 56 Cr App R 240; Nominal Defendant v Clements (1961) 104 CLR 476.*

in the context of the time when the statement was made and the circumstances of its making, that the statement does tend to rebut the allegation of recent fabrication.[225]

At common law such evidence, where admissible, is not admitted as evidence of the truth of the facts stated but, rather, is merely admitted as evidence of credibility.[226]

2.2.4.2.2 Identification evidence

Under the second of the six common law exceptions to the rule against previous consistent statements referred to above, an identification witness may testify that he identified the accused on a previous occasion (for example, at an identification parade).[227] Such evidence may, alternatively, be given by a person who witnessed the making of the identification by the identification witness.[228] Where such evidence is admitted at common law, it is admitted to prove that the witness was able to make an identification at the relevant time (i.e. as evidence of consistency).[229]

2.2.4.2.3 Exculpatory statements made to the police

Under the third of the common law exceptions to the rule against previous consistent statements, which were identified above, statements made by the accused to the police which are wholly exculpatory (i.e. which are wholly in the accused's favour), whilst not admissible as evidence of the truth of the facts stated, are routinely tendered by the prosecution and are admitted for the limited purpose of providing evidence of the accused's attitude at the time when they were made.[230] The court will not admit such a statement, however, if the accused specifically and carefully prepared it for the purpose of its becoming prosecution evidence.[231] Where such a statement is admitted, the greater the time gap between the making of the initial allegation by the police to the accused and the making of the statement by the accused, the less the weight the accused's statement will carry.[232]

It should be noted that there is now authority for the proposition that even where a statement was wholly exculpatory at the time when the accused made it, it may

---

225 See: *R v Ali The Times November 11 2003; R v Oyesiku (1971) 56 Cr App R 240; Nominal Defendant v Clements (1961) 104 CLR 476.*

226 See *Fox v General Medical Council [1960] 1 WLR 1017.*

227 *R v Christie [1914] AC 545; Sealey v The State [2002] UKPC 52.*

228 *R v Christie [1914] AC 545 ; Sealey v The State [2002] UKPC 52*

229 *R v Christie [1914] AC 545 ; Sealey v The State [2002] UKPC 52*

230 See *R v Pearce (1979) 69 Cr App R 365; R v Storey (1968) 52 Cr App R 334. A related issue*

is that of the admissibility of statements made by the accused when incriminating objects were discovered in his possession (see *"Evidence in Criminal Proceedings: Hearsay and Related Topics"*, Law Com No 245, at paragraph 8.89, see Colin Tapper, *"Cross on Evidence"* 9th ed, Butterworths, 1999 at p. 283 and see *R N Gooderson, "Previous Consistent Statements"* in [1968] CLJ 64, 70–74).

231 See *R v Pearce (1979) 69 Cr App R 365.*

232 *R v Pearce (1979) 69 Cr App R 365.*

---

be adverse to the accused (and thus a confession) by the time when it is tendered by the prosecution in criminal proceedings.[233]

2.2.4.2.4 Voluntary sexual offence complaints made at the first reasonable opportunity

The fourth of the common law exceptions to the rule against previous consistent statements, referred to above, applies where a sexual offence[234] complainant of either sex[235] made a voluntary complaint at the first reasonable opportunity following commission of the alleged offence. In such circumstances, evidence of the details of the complaint is admissible for the prosecution.[236] Such evidence may take the form of the complainant's oral evidence[237], that of the oral evidence of the person to whom the complaint was made[238], that of a written complaint "given" (it appears, even by mistake) by the complainant to the person to whom the complaint was "made[239] or even that of a written complaint which was never sent to its intended recipient.[240] Where evidence of a complaint is admissible at common law under this exception to the rule against previous consistent statements, the complaint is not admitted as evidence of the truth of the facts stated[241] but, rather, is admitted both as evidence of the complainant's consistency[242] (i.e. credibility[243]) and, where consent is an issue (either legally, in the sense that absence of consent is an element of the offence, or factually, in the sense that the complainant denies that she consented244),as evidence of the absence of consent.[245] Evidence of the making of such a complaint cannot corroborate the complainant's testimony[246] (because it is not independent of the complainant) and, equally (again because it is not independent of the complainant) cannot (in, for example, the context of a Turnbull[247]or Makanjuola[248] warning) support the complainant's unreliable testimony.[249] The trial judge should clearly direct the jury as to the limited purpose for which such evidence is admitted[250] and should do so even where the evidence was not relied upon as a previous consistent statement by the prosecution.[251]

It appears that evidence of a recent complaint is not admissible at common law where the complainant does not give evidence[252], because, in such circumstances,

---

233 See *R v Z* [2003] 1 WLR 1489 and see 2.4.2.7.1 below.
234 E.g. *rape or indecent assault (see R v Osbourne [1905] 1 KB 551).*
235 *R v Camelleri [1922] 2 KB 122.*
236 *R v Lillyman [1896] 2 QB 167.*
237 *R v Lillyman [1896] 2 QB 167.*
238 *R v Lillyman [1896] 2 QB 167.*
239 *R v B [1997] Crim LR 220.*
240 *R v Milner LTL 14/8/2000.*
241 *R v Lillyman [1896] 2 QB 167.*
242 *R v Osbourne [1905] 1 KB 551.*
243 *R v Lovell (1923) 17 Cr App R 163).*
244 *See R v Osbourne [1905] 1 KB 551.*

245 *R v Lillyman [1896] 2 QB 167.*
246 *R v Lovell (1923) 17 Cr App R 163.*
247 *R v Turnbull [1977] QB 224.*
248 *R v Makanjuola [1995] 3 All ER 730.*
249 *R v Islam [1999] 1 Cr App R 22.*
250 *R v Osbourne [1905] 1 KB 551; R v Islam [1999] Cr App R 22.*
251 *R v Croad [2001] EWCA Crim 644.*
252 *Though it has been suggested that, in such circumstances, evidence of the fact of the complaint, as opposed to its details, may be admissible (R v Walkwork (1958) 42 Cr App R 153 (but see also R v Wright and Ormerod (1987) 90 Cr App R 91)).*

there is no issue of consistency.[253] Further, it appears that such evidence should not be admitted where it is inconsistent with the complainant's evidence in court because, in such circumstances, it does not provide evidence of consistency.[254] Moreover, where the person to whom the complaint was made does not give evidence, the testimony of the complainant concerning the making of the complaint is of no evidential value.[255]

A complaint is not voluntary if, in the circumstances, it probably would not have been made had the complainant not been questioned.[256] Questions which merely anticipate a complaint do not, however, prevent a complaint from being voluntary.[257]

Whether a complaint was made at the first reasonable opportunity does not merely depend upon the time gap between the time when the alleged offence was allegedly committed and the time when the complaint was made but, rather, also depends upon factors such as the personal characteristics of the complainant and the availability of persons in whom the complainant could reasonably be expected to confide.[258] Where complaints were made to more than one person, the fact that the witness who is called to give evidence of the making of a complaint was not the first person to whom a complaint was made by the complainant does not necessarily mean that the complaint to the witness was not made at the first reasonable opportunity (though this does not mean that the judge will be prepared to admit evidence of the making of several complaints where this might lead the jury to believe that they were evidence of the truth of the facts stated).[259] Where there is conflicting evidence concerning the time when a complaint was made, the judge should give the jury a careful direction concerning the conflicting evidence and clearly direct the jury to the effect that that they must first be sure that the victim made a complaint close to the relevant event and, only if this is so, then go on to consider whether the complaint is consistent with the complainant's testimony.[260]

2.2.4.2.5 Statements which form part of the res gestae

Statements which form part of the res gestae are admissible under an exception to the rule against previous consistent statements.[261] As is seen below[262], such statements also fall within the ambit of an exception to the hearsay rule

---

253 *R v Wallwork (1958) 42 Cr App R 153.*
254 *R v Wright and Ormerod (1987) 90 Cr App R 91; R v Milner LTL 14/8/2000.*
255 *White v R [1999] 1 Cr App R 153.*
256 *R v Osbourne [1905] 1 KB 551.*
257 *R v Osbourne [1905] 1 KB 551.*

258 *R v Cummings [1948] 1 All ER 551; R v Valentine [1996] 2 Cr App R 213).*
259 *R v Valentine [1996] 2 Cr App R 213.*
260 *R v Hartley [2003] EWCA Crim 3027.*
261 *R v Roberts [1942] 1 All ER 187.*
262 *At 2.3.2.7.*

2.2.4.2.6 Statements made by persons found in possession of recently stolen goods or other incriminating articles.

It appears that statements made by persons found in possession of recently stolen goods or other incriminating articles explaining their possession of the goods or articles are admissible under an exception to the rule against previous consistent statements.[263] In the absence of such an explanation, the court, in the context of a charge of theft, handling stolen goods or burglary, may be entitled to draw an inference of guilt under the "doctrine of recent possession".[264]

2.2.4.3 The effects of section 120

As it relates to the operation of the rule against previous consistent statements[265], section 120 of the 2003 Act provides as follows. [Note: section 120(3) and 120(6) are not reproduced here as they are, respectively, considered at 2.2.5.2.2 and 2.2.6, below.]

"(1) This section applies where a person (the witness) is called to give evidence in criminal proceedings.

(2) If a previous statement by the witness is admitted as evidence to rebut a suggestion that his oral evidence has been fabricated, that statement is admissible as evidence of any matter stated of which oral evidence by the witness would be admissible....

(4) A previous statement by the witness is admissible as evidence of any matter stated of which oral evidence by him would be admissible, if–

(a) any of the following three conditions is satisfied, and

(b) while giving evidence the witness indicates that to the best of his belief he made the statement, and that to the best of his belief it states the truth.

(5) The first condition is that the statement identifies or describes a person, object or place....

(7) The third condition is that–

(a) the witness claims to be a person against whom an offence has been committed,

(b) the offence is one to which the proceedings relate,

---

263 See *R v Ali The Times* November 11 2003.
264 See *R v Aves (1950) 34 Cr App R 159; R v Loughlin (1951) 35 Cr App R 69; R v Smythe (1980) 72 Cr App R 8; R v Cash [1985] 1 QB 801.*
265 Note that section 120(3) (concerning memory refreshing documents) and section 120(6)

(concerning statements relating to matters which a witness cannot reasonably be expected to remember well enough to give oral evidence in relation thereto) are reproduced and considered at, respectively, 2.2.5.2.2 and 2.2.6 below.

    (c)   the statement consists of a complaint made by the witness (whether to a person in authority or not) about conduct which would, if proved, constitute the offence or part of the offence,

    (d)   the complaint was made as soon as could reasonably be expected after the alleged conduct,

    (e)   the complaint was not made as a result of a threat or a promise, and

    (f)   before the statement is adduced the witness gives oral evidence in connection with its subject matter.

(8)   For the purposes of subsection (7) the fact that the complaint was elicited (for example, by a leading question) is irrelevant unless a threat or a promise was involved."

Before Standing Committee B, Mr Michael Wills (the Parliamentary Under Secretary of State for the Home Department) expressed the rationale underlying what is now section 120 of the 2003 Act in the following way.[266]

"In proposing the reforms, we are endeavouring to strike a balance between maintaining an exclusive emphasis on oral evidence and preventing relevant evidence from being kept from the fact finders. The reforms reflect the fact that it is wrong in principle for evidence to be kept from the court when it is of better quality than the oral evidence available at the time of the trial. The proposals would allow the court to see the full picture, and in so doing would reduce the risk of injustice. "

The Criminal Justice Act 2003 will not abolish the common law rule against previous consistent statements. Indeed, the Law Commission, recognising that long arguments concerning the relevance of specific statements might ensue at trial if the rule were abolished[267], did not recommend the rule's abolition. Section 120 of the 2003 Act will, however, create several new exceptions to the hearsay rule, three of which (subject to certain modifications which are examined below) will essentially encompass three of the six common law exceptions to the rule against previous consistent statements, which were considered above.

The relevant exceptions are that which concerns the rebuttal of suggestions of recent fabrication[268], that which concerns statements made by identification witnesses[269] and that which concerns recent complaints made by sexual offence complainants.[270] In each of these three cases, the effect of section 120 will be that, where the exception applies, the statement (unlike the position at common law) will be admissible as evidence of matters stated (the Law Commission[271] having

---

266 *Hansard (Commons) 28 January 2003 Column 648.*
267 *See "Evidence in Criminal Proceedings: Hearsay and Related Topics", Law Com No 245, at paragraph 10.33.*

268 *See section 120(2).*
269 *See section 120(4),(5).*
270 *See section 120(4),(7).*
271 *See "Evidence in Criminal Proceedings: Hearsay and Related Topics", Law Com No 245, at paragraph 10.39.*

recognised that directing juries concerning the distinction between evidence which is merely relevant to credibility and evidence which is relevant to an issue in the proceedings is likely to cause confusion). The exceptions will apply whether the statement was made orally, in writing or in some other way.[272] It should be noted, however, that where a documentary statement is admitted under section 120 of the 2003 Act and the document or a copy thereof is exhibited, the effect of section 122 of the 2003 Act will be that the jury cannot take the document with them when they retire unless either the court considers this appropriate or all the parties agree that the jury should take it with them.

Section 120 will not convert the remaining three exceptions to the rule against previous consistent statements into hearsay exceptions; the relevant exceptions being those relating to statements which form part of the res gesate, wholly exculpatory statements made to the police by the accused and statements made by persons found in possession of recently stolen goods or other incriminating articles.

So far as statements which form part of the res gestae are concerned, it is submitted that the creation of a new hearsay exception to encompass such statements is unnecessary as such statements already fall within the ambit of the common law exceptions to the hearsay rule which section 118 of the 2003 Act will preserve.[273]

In relation to wholly exculpatory statements made by the accused to the police, the Law Commission[274] recommended that the existing law be retained in relation to such evidence.[275] Thus, such statements will remain potentially admissible (though not as evidence of matters stated) under the common law exception to the rule against previous consistent statements which concerns them, but not under a specific hearsay exception. Whilst exculpatory statements made by the accused will not possess their own specific hearsay exception, this does not mean, however, that, in appropriate circumstances, they will not be potentially admissible as evidence of matters stated under one or more of the other exceptions to the hearsay rule which the 2003 will create, retain or preserve.

The Law Commission do not appear to have considered the position in relation to statements made by persons found in possession of recently stolen goods or other incriminating articles. It is submitted that, as in relation to exculpatory statements made by the accused to the police, the effect of the hearsay provisions of the 2003 Act will be that such statements will continue to be admissible under an exception to the rule against previous consistent statements but, not falling within the ambit of their own specific hearsay exception, will only be admissible as evidence of the matters stated therein if one or more of the other exceptions to the hearsay rule which the 2003 Act will create, retain or preserves is applicable thereto.

---

272 *See the wide definition of "statement" in section 115(2).*
273 *See 2.3.2.7 below.*
274 *See "Evidence in Criminal Proceedings: Hearsay and Related Topics", Law Com No 245, at paragraph 8.92.*

275 *And, it appears, in relation to evidence of the accused's response when incriminating objects were found in his possession.*

In relation to the three common law exceptions, to the rule against previous consistent statements which the 2003 Act will promote to the status of statutory hearsay exceptions, it is necessary to consider the extent to which their nature will be altered by the provisions of section 120. Prior to considering the ambit of each of the three exceptions individually, however, it is first necessary to consider two matters which relate to the operation of the three new statutory hearsay exceptions in general.

First, it should be noted that the effect of section 120(1) will be that the hearsay exceptions created by section 120 will only apply if the maker of the consistent statement is called to give evidence in the proceedings. It should be remembered, however, that if the maker of the consistent statement is not called, the statement may be potentially admissible under one or more of the other exceptions to the hearsay rule which will exist when the 2003 Act is in force.

Secondly, the hearsay exceptions created by section 120 of the 2003 Act will not apply if the witness' oral evidence would not be admissible as evidence of the relevant matter.[276] This, it is submitted, will be the case where, for example, the evidence is irrelevant, amounts to inadmissible evidence of opinion or to inadmissible evidence of bad character. Similarly, where the maker of a consistent statement did not have the "required capability" to make it (i.e. was not competent to make it) at the time when he made it, the effect of section 123 of the 2003 Act (considered at 2.7.2, below) will be that the consistent statement will not be admissible under section 120 as evidence of matters stated (though, it is submitted, the statement might still be technically admissible under one of the common law exceptions to the rule against previous consistent statements as evidence of its maker's credibility).

It appears, however, that, in consequence of the operation of section 121(1)(a) of the 2003 Act (which is considered at 2.7.1 below), the fact that a consistent statement itself contains or is based upon a hearsay statement will not prevent the admission of the consistent statement under section 120 to prove that the latter statement was made (though, presumably, the latter statement will only be admissible if it, also, falls within the ambit of an exception to the rule against hearsay). Equally, it appears that, again in consequence of the operation of section 121(1)(a) of the 2003 Act, a consistent statement which is admissible under section 120 may be proved by a hearsay statement which is admissible under some other exception to the rule against hearsay.

Where a consistent statement does fall within the ambit of one of the hearsay exceptions created by section 120, it must not be forgotten, however, that its admissibility will still be subject to the exercise of the court's exclusionary discretion.[277]

---

276 *See section 120(2)-(4).*

277 *Perhaps at common law or under section 78 of the Police and Criminal Evidence Act 1984 (see section 126(2) of the Criminal Justice Act 2003) or under section 126(1) of the 2003 Act (see, generally, 2.7.5 below).*

Finally, it is submitted that the 2003 Act will not abolish any of the common law exceptions to the rule against previous statements (including those which it promotes to the status of statutory hearsay exceptions). The ambit of the common law exceptions and that of the new statutory variants will not, however, be identical (for example, the former will not be subject to the "required capability" provisions imposed by section 123). Consequently, it is submitted that in circumstances in which the provisions of section 120 are inapplicable to a consistent statement (for example, where, under section 123 of the 2003 Act, the maker of the consistent statement does not have the "required capability" to make it at the time when he made it) the statement may still be potentially admissible as evidence of its maker's credibility (though not as evidence of matters stated) under one or more of those common law exceptions to the previous consistent statements rule. Of course, in circumstances in which the requirements of section 120 are not satisfied, a previous consistent statement may still be admissible as evidence of matters stated under one or more of the other exceptions to the rule against hearsay which the 2003 Act will create, retain or preserve.

2.2.4.3.1 Suggestions of recent fabrication

The Law Commission did not recommend any modification of the ambit of the exception to the rule against previous consistent statements which concerns suggestions of recent fabrication but did recommend that when previous consistent statements are admissible for this purpose they be admitted as evidence of matters stated.278 Consequently, section 120(1),(2) provide as follows.

> "(1) This section applies where a person (the witness) is called to give evidence in criminal proceedings.
>
> (2) If a previous statement by the witness is admitted as evidence to rebut a suggestion that his oral evidence has been fabricated, that statement is admissible as evidence of any matter stated of which oral evidence by the witness would be admissible."

It is submitted that the ambit of the hearsay exception, created by section 120(1)-(2), concerning suggestions of recent fabrication, will effectively equate with that of the common law exception to the rule against previous consistent statements which it will replace. Thus, it appears that the only consequence of the coming into force of section 120(1)-(2) will be that where a statement is admitted under the recent fabrication exception, the statement will be admitted not merely as evidence of its maker's credibility but, rather, will be admitted as evidence of matters stated of which the witness' oral evidence would be admissible.

2.2.4.3.2 Identification evidence

Essentially, the Law Commission's rationale for the creation of the hearsay exception embodied in section 120(1),(4)-(5) of the 2003 Act was that the identification of the offender by the witness in court is really a formality and that what is significant in reality is the witness' earlier identification of the accused, it being a fiction that the earlier identification merely supports the evidence which the witness gives in court.[279] In defining the limits of their new hearsay exception, the Law Commission also sought to remove certain anomalies which exist at common law, namely, that the identification exception to the rule against previous consistent statements does not extend to identification of objects (such as car number plates)[280] and that sketches and photofits produced from information given by the witness are admissible whilst the witness' written statement describing the offender is not.[281]

Section 120(1),(4)-(5) provide as follows.

"(1)   This section applies where a person (the witness) is called to give evidence in criminal proceedings...

(4)   A previous statement by the witness is admissible as evidence of any matter stated of which oral evidence by him would be admissible, if–

    (a)   any of the following three conditions is satisfied, and

    (b)   while giving evidence the witness indicates that to the best of his belief he made the statement, and that to the best of his belief it states the truth.

(5)   The first condition is that the statement identifies or describes a person, object or place...."

In relation to the admissibility of identification evidence under section 120(1), (4)-(5), it appears that the new hearsay exception created by those provisions will be wider in scope than the common law exception to the rule against previous consistent statements which it will replace. This, it seems, will be so because the new statutory hearsay exception will not merely encompass previous statements identifying persons but, rather, will also encompass previous statements describing persons and previous statements identifying or describing objects or places. Thus, for example, it appears that the new hearsay exception will encompass a "statement", describing an offender, which an identification witness made to the police and will do so whether the statement was taken down in writing or

---

278 See *"Evidence in Criminal Proceedings: Hearsay and Related Topics"*, Law Com No 245, at paragraphs 10.41-10.45.

279 See *"Evidence in Criminal Proceedings: Hearsay and Related Topics"*, Law Com No 245, at paragraph 10.19 and 10.46.

280 See *"Evidence in Criminal Proceedings: Hearsay and Related Topics"*, Law Com No 245, at paragraph 10.21 and 10.48-10.50.

281 See *"Evidence in Criminal Proceedings: Hearsay and Related Topics"*, Law Com No 245, at paragraphs 10.46 and 10.51.

(pursuant to the section 115(2) definition of "statement") was documented in the form of a sketch or in that of a photifit. Equally, the new hearsay exception will, it appears, encompass an out of court statement in which a witness identified an object, such as a car registration number.[282]

It appears, however, that the new statutory hearsay exception, created by section 120(1),(4)-(5), will not encompass all of the situations in which evidence in the form of statements identifying or describing persons, objects or places may potentially be tendered by the prosecution in criminal proceedings. It may be, for example, that the identification witness is dead by the time of the trial or is otherwise unavailable, perhaps in consequence of ill health. In such circumstances, it is submitted that a statement made by the witness to the police may still be potentially admissible under one or more of the other hearsay exceptions which the 2003 Act will create, retain or preserve, for example, under section 116 of the 2003 Act (which was considered at 2.2.1 above).

Similarly, it may that, by the time of the trial, the identification witness is unable to remember the details of the identification that he made at the police station (perhaps the number of the person whom he identified) or even cannot remember making an identification at all. In such circumstances, if the witness is not prepared, when testifying, to indicate both that to the best of his belief he made the statement identifying the accused and that to the best of his belief the statement is true[283], it seems that the section 120(1),(4)-(5) hearsay exception will not apply. It is submitted, however, that, in circumstances such as these, the court would still be entitled to permit the prosecution to call a witness who witnessed the making of the identification by the identification witness to prove that the identification witness did identify the accused. It may well be that such evidence would be admissible (under section 118 of the 2003 Act) under a preserved common law exception to the hearsay rule, i.e. as forming part of the res gestae.[284]

---

282 See *"Evidence in Criminal Proceedings: Hearsay and Related Topics"*, Law Com No 245, at paragraphs 10.6 and 10.48-10.50.

283 See section 120(4)(b).

284 See *R v McCay [1990] 1 WLR 645* (concerning circumstances in which the identification witness could remember making the identification but could not remember its details and a police officer was permitted to repeat the witness' statement at the identification parade, "It is number 8"). The decision of the Court of Appeal in *R v McCay*, that this evidence was admissible as forming part of the res gestae, has been criticised upon the basis that it improperly extended the ambit of the common law res gestae doctrine (which will be preserved by section 118 of the 2003 Act) in that the statement which it concerned cannot truly said to be one which explained why the witness performed the relevant act (see, for example, *Blackstone's Criminal Practice 2003*, Oxford, at F18.1). The relevant limb of the res gestae doctrine is considered at 2.3.2.7.2 below. See, also, *R v Osbourne [1973] QB 678* (concerning circumstances in which an identification witness could not even remember that she had made an identification and a police officer was permitted to testify that she had identified the accused). Academic views differ as to the proper evidential status and admissibility of such evidence. For example, in *Phipson on Evidence*, 15th ed, Sweet and Maxwell, 2000, it is suggested at 14-05 that such evidence falls within the ambit of the hearsay rule and is inadmissible unless one or other of the hearsay exceptions created by sections 23 and 24 of the Criminal Justice Act 1988 (which the 2003 Act will repeal) are applicable whereas at 25-14 of the same work it is suggested, placing reliance upon the decision of the House of Lords in *R v Christie [1914] AC 545*, that such evidence is either admissible under a specific common law exception to the hearsay rule or as original evidence and that the decision of the Court of Appeal in *R v Osbourne [1973] QB 678* was correctly decided.

Alternatively, the identification evidence would appear to be potentially admissible under some other exception to the hearsay rule which the 2003 Act will create, preserve or retain, perhaps under the section 114(1) (d) "safety valve" inclusionary discretion, which is considered at 2.6 below.

2.2.4.3.3 Recent complaints

The Law Commission's recommendations which resulted in the hearsay exception which will be created by section 120(1),(4),(7)-(8) of the 2003 Act sought to deal with three problems which exist at common law. First, the anomaly that the common law "recent complaints" exception to the rule against previous consistent statement only relates to recent complaints of sexual offences and not to complaints of other offences.[285] Secondly, that at common law the judge is required to give the jury a direction concerning the relevance of the evidence which is difficult for the jury to understand.[286] Thirdly, the fact that if the complainant was "assisted" in making the complaint then the complaint is not admissible at common law.[287] A fourth problem, namely that the requirement that the complaint be made at the first reasonable opportunity was too restrictive, had already been resolved by the courts themselves by the time when the Law Commission made their recommendations and, consequently, no change was recommended in relation to that requirement.[288]

Section 120(1),(4),(7)-(8) of the 2003 Act provide as follows.

> "(1) This section applies where a person (the witness) is called to give evidence in criminal proceedings...
>
> (4) A previous statement by the witness is admissible as evidence of any matter stated of which oral evidence by him would be admissible, if–
>
>   (a) any of the following three conditions is satisfied, and
>
>   (b) while giving evidence the witness indicates that to the best of his belief he made the statement, and that to the best of his belief it states the truth...
>
> (7) The third condition is that–
>
>   (a) the witness claims to be a person against whom an offence has been committed,
>
>   (b) the offence is one to which the proceedings relate,

---

285 See *"Evidence in Criminal Proceedings: Hearsay and Related Topics", Law Com No 245*, at paragraphs 10.22, 10.54-10.56.

286 See *"Evidence in Criminal Proceedings: Hearsay and Related Topics", Law Com No 245*, at paragraphs 10.23, 10.54 and 10.57.

287 See *"Evidence in Criminal Proceedings: Hearsay and Related Topics", Law Com No 245*, at paragraphs 10.25, 10.54 and 10.59.

288 See *"Evidence in Criminal Proceedings: Hearsay and Related Topics", Law Com No 245*, at paragraphs 10.24 and 10.58.

(c)   the statement consists of a complaint made by the witness (whether to a person in authority or not) about conduct which would, if proved, constitute the offence or part of the offence,

(d)   the complaint was made as soon as could reasonably be expected after the alleged conduct,

(e)   the complaint was not made as a result of a threat or a promise, and

(f)   before the statement is adduced the witness gives oral evidence in connection with its subject matter.

(8)   For the purposes of subsection (7) the fact that the complaint was elicited (for example, by a leading question) is irrelevant unless a threat or a promise was involved."

In relation to the first problem referred to above, section 120(7) makes clear that, under the 2003 Act, the complaint need not relate to a sexual offence but, rather, may relate to any conduct which, if proved, would constitute part or all of an offence to which the proceedings relate. Thus, the section will produce a fundamental increase in the ambit of the former common law "recent complaints" exception to the rule against previous consistent statements, under which the complaint will in future be potentially admissible regardless of the nature of the offence complained of. The rationale underlying this fundamental increase in the ambit of the former common law exception was expressed by Mr Michael Wills (the Parliamentary Under Secretary of State for the Home Department) who stated that [289]:

"The restriction of the exception to sexual offences is difficult to justify because evidence of a recent complaint may be of value in any case."

The second problem, identified above, will be dealt with under the section 120 regime by rendering recent complaints admissible as evidence of matters stated of which the witness' oral evidence would be admissible (i.e. by converting the recent complaint's exception into a hearsay exception).

As regards the third problem, referred to above, section 120(7) will not require that the complaint be a voluntary complaint, but section 120(7)(e) will require that the complaint was not made in consequence of a threat or a promise. Indeed, section 120(8) makes clear that, in the absence of a threat or a promise, the fact that the complaint was obtained by questioning will not affect its admissibility under section 120. Thus, as the Law Commission anticipated [290], it appears that the fact that the complaint was drawn out of the complainant by questioning will largely be relegated to the status of a matter which is merely of relevance in determining its evidential weight. It is submitted, however, that whether the complaint was or

---

289 *Hansard (Commons) 28 January 2003 Column 640.*

290 *See "Evidence in Criminal Proceedings: Hearsay and Related Topics", Law Com No 245, at paragraphs 10.26 and 10.59.*

was not a voluntary complaint may still be a factor which at times is capable of persuading the court to exclude evidence of a recent complaint in the exercise of its exclusionary discretion.[291]

Concerning the fourth problem, identified above, the requirement that the complaint be made at the first reasonable opportunity is retained by section 120(7)(d). It is submitted that, as the Law Commission appears to have envisaged[292], the courts are likely to follow the established common law authorities, considered at 2.2.4.2.3 above, when determining the effect of this requirement.

Other than those that have already been considered immediately above, section 120 imposes a number of other requirements which will form essential prerequisites to the operation of the new "recent complaints" hearsay exception. First, there is the requirement which will be imposed by section 120(4)(b), namely, that the witness must indicate in court both that to the best of his belief he made the statement and that to the best of his belief the statement is true. It is submitted that this requirement is unlikely to cause any problems in practice in that if the witness is unable to do this (or indeed is hostile) the statement will remain potentially admissible under one or more of the other hearsay exceptions which are preserved, created or retained by the 2003 Act.

The requirements which will be imposed by section 120(7)(a)-(c) (namely, that the witness claims to be the victim of an offence, that the relevant offence be one with which a party is charged in the proceedings and that the statement comprise a complaint, whether or not to a person in authority, of conduct which, in part or in whole, constitutes the relevant offence), do not appear to be problematic and simply appear to reflect the nature of the exception as it currently exists at common law, but transposed from the context of the sexual offence alone to that of criminal offences in general. Similarly, the requirement which will be imposed by section 120(7)(f) (i.e. that the witness must give oral evidence concerning the subject matter of the complaint prior to its admission in evidence under section 120) appears to reflect the common law requirement that the complaint is not admissible under the exception if the complainant does not testify.

It should be noted that even if one or more of the abovementioned requirements of section 120(7) are not satisfied in relation to a complaint (and thus evidence of the complaint is not admissible under section 120), the complaint may still be potentially admissible under another exception to the hearsay rule which the 2003 Act will preserve, create or retain (for example, under the section 114(1)(d) "safety valve" inclusionary discretion.

---

291 *The nature of the court's exclusionary discretion is considered at 2.7.5 below.*

292 *See "Evidence in Criminal Proceedings: Hearsay and Related Topics", Law Com No 245, at paragraph 10.58.*

Finally, one matter which section 120 does not appear to make clear is whether, in line with the common law authorities considered above, evidence of a recent complaint, admitted under section 120 will be capable of corroborating or supporting its maker's oral testimony. It is submitted that the better view is that when, for example in the context of a *Turnbull*[293] direction, the judge is directing the jury concerning the nature of that evidence which is capable of corroborating or supporting the evidence of a complainant, they should be directed to the effect that the witness' complaint, admitted under section 120, is not independent and, consequently, is not capable of providing such support.

2.2.5 Documents used for memory refreshing

Memory refreshing forms the subject of two provisions of the Criminal Justice Act 2003. First, section 120(3) (found in Chapter 2 of Part 11 of the 2003 Act) concerns the nature of those circumstances in which a memory refreshing document is admissible in criminal proceedings as evidence of matters stated. Secondly, section 139 (found in Chapter 3 of Part 11 of the 2003 Act) concerns the nature of those circumstances in which memory refreshing may take place in criminal proceedings. Prior to considering these two provisions, however, it is first necessary to consider the common law principles which currently govern the use and admissibility of memory refreshing documents in criminal proceedings.[294]

2.2.5.1 Memory refreshing at common law

Before going into the witness box it is normally permissible for a witness who so desires to read through a statement that he made reasonably close to the time when the events which it documents took place, it not being necessary for the statement to be a contemporaneous statement.[295] It seems, however, that, in some circumstances, such prior reading of his statement may affect the weight of the witness' evidence and, consequently, it appears to be desirable, certainly in the case of prosecution witnesses, to inform the other parties that the witness has read through his statement.[296]

Essentially, once a witness is in the witness box, the common law position is that the witness may only refresh his memory by reference to a document if two requirements are satisfied. First, the court must be satisfied that the document was made contemporaneously with the occurrence of the events which it documents (i.e. it was either made at the time when the events took place or sufficiently shortly thereafter that those events were still fresh in his memory).[297] Secondly, the

---

293 *See R v Turnbull [[1977] QB 224.*

294 *In relation to the position in civil proceedings, it should be noted that the nature of those circumstances in which a memory refreshing document may be made evidence in the proceedings remains governed by the common law (Civil Evidence Act 1995, section 6(4)), but it*

appears that such a document may be admissible under section 1 of the Civil Evidence Act 1995 Act as evidence of the matters stated (Civil Evidence Act 1995, section 6(5)).

295 *R v Richardson [1971] 2 QB 484.*

296 *R v Westwell [1976] 2 All ER 812.*

297 *R v Richardson [1971] 2 QB 484.*

court must be satisfied that the document was either made by the witness himself or, if it was not made by him, that the witness verified both that it had been made and that it was accurate whilst the events which it documents were still fresh in his memory.[298]

Whether a document was made contemporaneously with the occurrence of an event is a question of fact and degree.[299] In the context of memory refreshing it appears that the concept of contemporaneity should be applied not rigidly but with a degree of elasticity.[300]

Where the witness does not make the document himself, verification may take the form of the witness reading the statement and confirming it or, alternatively, may take the form of the statement being read back to the witness who then confirms it.[301]

It appears that where the original document has been lost, the court may permit memory refreshing to take place from a copy provided that the court is satisfied as to its authenticity.[302] Moreover, it appears that the court may permit memory refreshing to take place in such circumstances even though the latter document is not a precise copy of the former, provided that they are substantially the same.[303] Further, it seems that where a document was compiled from earlier contemporaneous notes whilst the facts were still fresh in the witness' memory, the court may permit the use both of the original notes and of the subsequent document for the purpose of memory refreshing.[304] Indeed, it appears that where a witness writes a note from a tape recording of a conversation which he overheard, the witness may be permitted to rely upon the note as a memory refreshing document.[305]

The fact that a witness who is permitted to use a memory refreshing document cannot remember the facts which it contains even after she has referred to it does not prevent her giving evidence of those facts with the assistance of the document (i.e. by testifying that she made the record, that it was accurate and, consequently, that she can testify that the recorded events took place).[306] In such circumstances, however, it appears that the memory refreshing document must normally be the original, not a copy.[307]

---

298 *R v Kelsey (1982) 74 Cr App R 213.*

299 *R v Simmonds (1967) 51 Cr App R 316; R v South Ribble JJ, ex parte Cochrane [1996] 2 Cr App R 544.*

300 *R v Richardson [1971] 2 QB 484.*

301 *R v Kelsey (1982) 74 Cr App R 213.*

302 *See, for example, R v Chisnell [1992] Crim LR 507.*

303 *See R v Cheng (1976) 63 Cr App R 20.*

304 *Attorney-General's Reference (No.3 of 1979) (1979) 68 Cr App R 41.*

305 *See R v Mills [1962] 1 WLR 1152.*

306 *R v Bryant and Dickson (1946) 31 Cr App R 146; Maugham v Hubbard (1828) 8 B&C 14.*

307 *See, for example R v Harvey (1869) 11 Cox CC 54 (though the use of a copy which can be proved to be accurate may be permissible (see, for example, Burton v Plummer (1834) 2 A&E 341; Topham v McGregor (1844) 1 C&K 320).*

Further, the court possesses discretion to permit a witness who has started to give his evidence but who cannot recollect relevant facts to temporarily cease giving evidence in order to memory refresh from non-contemporaneous document.[308] It seems that the court may permit the witness to do so even though the witness had already read the relevant statement prior to going into the witness box.[309] Where the court permits a witness to read such a statement, the witness may either read the statement in the witness box or may leave the witness box in order to read it.[310] Moreover, it appears that the court possesses discretion to permit the witness to keep the non-contemporaneous document when the witness starts to give evidence again.[311]

Normally, a memory refreshing document is not admissible in evidence (the admissible evidence being the witness' oral testimony), though the other party is entitled to inspect the memory refreshing document and to cross-examine the witness in relation to it provided that such cross-examination is relevant.[312] A memory refreshing document is, however, admissible in evidence in a number of situations. First, where the witness is cross-examined on parts of the document which were not used for memory refreshing and the party who called the witness desires its admission in evidence.[313] Secondly, where it is expressly or impliedly suggested during cross-examination that the document was fabricated.[314] Thirdly, where the witness' evidence and the memory refreshing document are inconsistent.[315] Finally, where it is difficult for the jury to follow cross-examination unless they are given copies of the memory refreshing document to look at.[316]

At common law, if a memory refreshing document is admitted in evidence, it is normally only admitted as evidence of the witness' credibility.[317] Where the issue of fabrication is raised, however, the document may be admitted as evidence of the truth of the facts stated for the limited purpose of determining whether it is authentic.[318]

2.2.5.2 Memory refreshing under the 2003 Act

Sections 139 and 120(3) of the 2003 Act concern, respectively, the nature of those circumstances in which memory refreshing may take place in the witness box in criminal proceedings and the creation of a new statutory hearsay exception

---

308 *R v Da Silva [1990] 1 WLR 31; R v South Ribble JJ, ex parte Cochrane [1996] 2 Cr App R 544.*

309 *R v South Ribble JJ, ex parte Cochrane [1996] 2 Cr App R 544.*

310 *If the witness leaves the witness box to read the statement it appears that there must be no communication with him other than to ensure that he can read it in peace (R v Da Silva [1990] 1 WLR 31).*

311 *See R v South Ribble JJ, ex parte Cochrane [1996] 2 Cr App R 544.*

312 *R v Sekhon (1987) 85 Cr App R 19. The same is true of a document used by the witness to refresh his memory before he went into the witness box (Owen v Edwards (1983) 77 Cr App R 191).*

313 *Senat v Senat [1965] P 172. Cross-examination on those parts which were used for memory refreshing does not have this effect.*

314 *R v Sekhon (1987) 85 Cr App R 19.*

315 *R v Sekhon (1987) 85 Cr App R 19.*

316 *R v Sekhon (1987) 85 Cr App R 19.*

317 *R v Sekhon (1987) 85 Cr App R 19.*

318 *R v Sekhon (1987) 85 Cr App R 19.*

applicable where memory refreshing documents are admissible in evidence. It should be noted, however, that the provisions of the 2003 Act will not regulate the nature of those circumstances in which memory refreshing documents are admissible in evidence in criminal proceedings. Rather, it appears that, even when Chapters 2 and 3 of Part 11 of the 2003 Act are in force, this is a matter which will continued to be governed by the common law principles which were considered at 2.2.5.1, above. [Note: as was indicated in the Preface to this book, sections 139-141 of the 2003 Act will come into force in April 2004 and thus will be in force prior to the coming into force of the 2003 Act's hearsay provisions.]

2.2.5.2.1 Section 139

Section 139(1) of the 2003 Act provides as follows.

> "(1) A person giving oral evidence in criminal proceedings about any matter may, at any stage in the course of doing so, refresh his memory of it from a document made or verified by him at an earlier time if–
>
> (a) he states in his oral evidence that the document records his recollection of the matter at that earlier time, and
>
> (b) his recollection of the matter is likely to have been significantly better at that time than it is at the time of his oral evidence."

The rationale underlying what is now section 139 of the 2003 Act (and was then clause 123 of the Criminal Justice Bill) was expressed in Standing Committee B by Mr Michael Wills, the Parliamentary Under-Secretary of State for the Home Department, as follows.[319]

> "We want to rebalance the system in the interests of victims and witnesses, and the provisions are key to helping witnesses give the best evidence. It is crucial to ensure that rules of evidence do not artificially prevent the true and full story from being presented in court, and the provisions in chapter 3 will make it much easier for witnesses to give their evidence.
>
> ...clause 123 will give witnesses wider access to their statements so that they can refer to them when they give evidence. The main objectives of the reforms are to improve the position of witnesses giving evidence and to ensure that courts have the best evidence available to them and that rules of evidence assist in providing full and accurate accounts."

It appears that, in the context of criminal proceedings, Section 139 of the 2003 Act will have three effects. First, it will replace with a new statutory test the common law test of contemporaneity (considered at 2.2.5.1 above), the application of which determines whether a witness can make use of a memory refreshing document whilst testifying. Secondly, it will render otiose the court's common law discretion

---

319 *Hansard (Commons) 28 January 2003, Column 672.*

(referred to at 2.2.5.1 above) to permit a witness who has started to give his evidence but who cannot recollect relevant facts to temporarily cease giving evidence in order to read a non-contemporaneous document. Finally, it will prevent the use of an audio or video recording as a memory refreshing document, but will not prevent the use of a transcript of a sound recording of a witness' statement for memory refreshing purposes.

In relation to the first two of these three effects, Lord Justice Auld[320], who had recommended the adoption of the test now embodied in section 139(1)[321], regarded the new test as recognising the reality of the approach of the courts at common law in those cases in which the court is prepared to exercise its discretion so as to permit a witness who cannot recollect relevant facts to read a non-contemporaneous document. The reality of this approach was that the basis of a witnesses testimony in court:

"...should be an exercise in truthfulness rather than a test of long or short term memory." [322]

According to his Lordship, the implementation of this new test will:

"...permit most witness statements made much nearer the time to be used as memory refreshers." [323]

His Lordship also regarded section 139(1) as finally removing the common law anomaly relating to those non-contemporaneous documents which, at common law (and subject to the exercise of the discretion referred to immediately above), a witness may read prior to going into the witness box but may not take with him into the witness box.[324]

Thus, section 139(1)(b) will replace the common law test of contemporaneity with a new statutory test requiring merely that the witness' "...recollection of the matter is likely to have been significantly better at that time than it is at the time of his oral evidence." Consequently, it appears that, when section 139 of the 2003 Act is in force, a witness will be able to memory refresh from a document even though the facts were not fresh in the witness' memory when the relevant document was made, provided that the witness' recollection of the relevant events is likely to have been significantly better at the time when he made or verified the relevant document than it is at the time when he testifies in the proceedings. The witness will, of course, in accordance with section 139(1)(b), be required to testify that the

---

320 See Chapter 11 of Lord Justice Auld's Review of the Criminal Courts of England and Wales" (October 2001) at paragraph 84.

321 A test the adoption of which had been advocated by the editors of Archbold 2001 (see See Chapter 11 of Lord Justice Auld's Review of the Criminal Courts of England and Wales" (October 2001) at paragraph 83 of Chapter 11).

322 See Chapter 11 of Lord Justice Auld's Review of the Criminal Courts of England and Wales" (October 2001) at paragraph 84.

323 See Chapter 11 of Lord Justice Auld's Review of the Criminal Courts of England and Wales" (October 2001) at paragraph 84.

324 See Chapter 11 of Lord Justice Auld's Review of the Criminal Courts of England and Wales" (October 2001) at paragraph 84.

document records his recollection of the relevant matter at the time when he made or verified the document.

In relation to the operation of what is now section 139 of the 2003 Act, Mr Michael Wills, the Parliamentary Under-Secretary of State for the Home Department, provided the following guidance.[325]

> "As to the refreshing of memory, clause 123 is intended to create a presumption that witnesses in criminal proceedings may refresh their memory from their statement. They may do so if they say that the document represents their recollection at the time when they made it, and their recollection was likely to have been significantly better at the time the statement was made. That presumption reflects, as I said at the beginning of my remarks, the Government's manifesto commitment to give witnesses access to their statements while they give evidence. It also reflects the fact that witnesses have unfettered access to their statements outside the courtroom."

Finally, so far as section 139(1) is concerned, in relation to the requirement that the document must have been made or verified by the witness, it is assumed that the approach of the courts, when determining whether, for the purpose of section 139(1), a document was so made or verified, will equate with that which they presently adopt at common law in relation to this issue (outlined at 2.2.5.1 above).

In relation to the third of the three effect which, it appears, section 139 of the 2003 Act will have, which were referred to above (namely, that of section 139(2)), paragraph 444 of the Explanatory Notes to the Criminal Justice Act indicates that:

> "In view of the practical difficulties associated with memory refreshing in the witness box from an audio or video recording, *subsection* (2) makes provision for a witness to refresh his memory from a transcript of such recording."

Section 139(2) of the 2003 Act provides as follows.

> "(2) Where–
>
> (a) a person giving oral evidence in criminal proceedings about any matter has previously given an oral account, of which a sound recording was made, and he states in that evidence that the account represented his recollection of the matter at that time,
>
> (b) his recollection of the matter is likely to have been significantly better at the time of the previous account than it is at the time of his oral evidence, and
>
> (c) a transcript has been made of the sound recording,
>
> he may, at any stage in the course of giving his evidence, refresh his memory of the matter from that transcript."

---

325 *Hansard (Commons) 28 January 2003, Column 673.*

The explanation provided by the Explanatory Notes as to the effect of section 139(2) must be considered in the context of section 140, which, inter alia, provides that:

"In this Chapter—...

"document" means anything in which information of any description is recorded, but not including any recording of sounds or moving images;..."

Thus, an audio or video recording will not be a "document" for the purposes of section 139(1) and, consequently, section 139(1) will not authorise memory refreshing in criminal proceedings from such a document. It, thus, appears that when section 139 is in force, a witness will not be able to rely upon an audio recording of an oral statement as a memory refreshing document but that a witness will be able to rely upon transcript of an audio recording for memory refreshing purposes provided that the requirements of section 139(2) are satisfied. With regard to video recordings in relation to which the video camera's microphone has recorded the sound of an oral statement, the position would appear to equate with that of an audio recording. Where, however, a video camera has visually recorded a statement which a witness made by sign language, it is submitted that, under section 139, the witness will neither be entitled to rely upon the video recording itself as a memory refreshing document (as it will not be a "document" within the meaning of section 140) nor upon a transcript thereof (as the video recording would not be a "sound recording" for the purposes of section 139(2)).

Moreover, it should be noted that section 139(2) only applies to a recording of a statement made by the witness who is giving oral evidence. Consequently, section 139(2) does not appear to apply when a witness seeks to rely for memory refreshing purposes upon a transcript, or notes made from, a sound recording of a conversation which the witness both overheard and also tape recorded. It is submitted, however, that, in such circumstances, whilst the sound recording does not fall within the ambit of section 139(2) and whilst it is not a document for the purposes of section 139(1), if the witness had himself made or verified the transcript or notes prior to the trial, the court might be prepared to regard the transcript as a memory refreshing document for section 139(1) purposes. Consequently, it is submitted that, in such circumstances, the witness might be entitled to use the transcript for memory refreshing purposes under section 139(1), provided that the other requirements of that subsection were satisfied.

Further, it is submitted that problems may ensue under section 139 of the 2003 Act where a witness used a sound recording of his oral statement (which, perhaps, no longer exists) to assist him in producing written notes which do not amount to a transcript of the recording and which, thus, do not fall within the ambit of section 139(1). In such circumstances it is submitted that the court might, again, be prepared to treat the notes as the memory refreshing document, made by the witness, for the purposes of section 139(1) and thus permit their use for memory refreshing purposes under that subsection. If such a result would seem to stretch the relationship between section 139(1) and 139(2) almost to breaking point, it might be argued that the notes could legitimately be distinguished from a transcript in that they were a product of the witness' memory assisted by his use of the audio recording in compiling them rather than a mere transcription of the oral statement which the machine had recorded.

Finally, whilst it appears that the operation of section 139 of the 2003 Act will remove the possibility that an audio or video recording may itself be used for memory refreshing, it should be noted that, when Chapter 2 of Part 11 of the 2003 Act is in force, an audio or video recording may, in any event, be admissible in its own right under one or more of the other hearsay exceptions which the 2003 Act will create, preserve or retain. The same might be true of notes compiled by a witness from a lost audio recording of his audio recorded statement, even if such notes do not fall within the ambit of section 139(1), and of a transcript of a video recording of a statement made by sign language, even if such a statement does not fall within the ambit of section 139.

2.2.5.2.2 Section 120(3)

Section 120(1),(3) of the 2003 Act provide as follows.

"(1) This section applies where a person (the witness) is called to give evidence in criminal proceedings...

(3) A statement made by the witness in a document—

(a) which is used by him to refresh his memory while giving evidence,

(b) on which he is cross-examined, and

(c) which as a consequence is received in evidence in the proceedings,

is admissible as evidence of any matter stated of which oral evidence by him would be admissible."

The Law Commission[326] did not recommend the abolition of the rules concerning the use of memory refreshing documents because they accepted that whilst the process of memory refreshing is often a fiction (i.e. in circumstances in which the witness never actually remembers the facts to which the statement in the document relates), at times the witness' memory is indeed refreshed by the document. The Law Commission[327] also recognised, however, that if memory refreshing documents continued to be admitted merely as evidence of the witness' consistency in the context of their proposed reforms, this would create the anomaly that if a document was not used for memory refreshing but was admitted under their recommended hearsay exception which now takes the form of section 120(1),(4),(6) (examined at 2.2.6 below) the document would be admitted as

---

326 See "*Evidence in Criminal Proceedings: Hearsay and Related Topics*", *Law Com No 245*, at paragraph 10.81.

327 See "*Evidence in Criminal Proceedings: Hearsay and Related Topics*", *Law Com No 245*, at paragraph 10.82.

evidence of matter stated therein but that if the document was used for memory refreshing and was admitted following cross-examination of the witness on it, the document would not be admissible as evidence of the relevant matters. Thus, the Law Commission[328] recommended that such documents should be admissible as evidence of matters stated of which the witness' oral evidence would be admissible whether tendered as hearsay evidence or whether relied on as memory refreshing documents and admitted, following cross-examination, under the common law rules which govern the admission of memory refreshing documents.

The Law Commission does not have appear to have intended that the provisions which now take the form of section 120(1),(3) of the 2003 Act would render a non-contemporaneous memory refreshing document admissible in evidence, but, reading section 120(1),(3) in conjunction with section 139(1) of the 2003 Act (which was considered at 2.2.5.2.1 above), this does appear to be the potential effect of these provisions, operating in tandem. It is submitted that the Law Commission cannot have anticipated this result because section 139(1) is not a product of their recommendations but, rather, appears to be a consequence of Lord Justice Auld's subsequent Review of the Criminal Courts of England and Wales.[329]

It should be noted that that the fact that a witness is permitted to memory refresh from a document under section 139(1) will not automatically mean that the document will be admissible, under section 120(1),(3) of the 2003 Act, as evidence of a matter stated therein. Rather, it is submitted that the effect of section 120(1),(3) will be that where a witness memory refreshes in the witness box and, in accordance with the common law principles outlined at 2.2.5.1 above, the memory refreshing document, exceptionally, becomes admissible in evidence, the document will only be admissible as evidence of a matter stated in it if the witness' oral evidence of the relevant matter would be admissible.

Thus, it is submitted, the hearsay exception created by section 120(1),(3) will not apply where for example, the evidence is irrelevant, amounts to inadmissible evidence of opinion or to inadmissible evidence of bad character. Similarly, it seems that where the maker of a memory refreshing document did not have the "required capability" to make the statement which it contains (i.e. was not competent to make it) at the time when he made it, the effect of section 123 of the 2003 Act (considered at 2.7.2, below) will be that the statement will not be admissible under section 120(1),(3) (though it appears that nothing in section 123 will prevent the use of the document for memory refreshing purposes in such circumstances). It also appears, however, that, in consequence of the operation of section 121(1)(a) of the 2003 Act, which is considered at 2.7.1 below, the fact that a statement in a memory refreshing document itself contains or is based upon a

---

328 See "*Evidence in Criminal Proceedings: Hearsay and Related Topics*", Law Com No 245, at paragraph 10.82.

329 See 2.2.5.2.1 above.

hearsay statement will not prevent the admission of the former statement under section 120(1),(3) to prove that the latter statement was made (though, presumably, the latter statement will only be admissible if it, also, falls within the ambit of an exception to the rule against hearsay which the 2003 Act will create, retain or preserve).

Where a statement in a memory refreshing document does fall within the ambit of the hearsay exception created by section 120(1),(3), it must not be forgotten, however, that its admissibility will still be subject to the exercise of the court's exclusionary discretion.[330]

Section 120(3) will only apply to a document which is used by a witness to refresh his memory whilst he is giving evidence. Thus, it is submitted, it is unclear whether section 120(3) will apply where a witness reads through a document prior to going into the witness box but does not use the document for memory refreshing purposes whilst testifying, another party inspects the document, cross-examines the witness in relation to it and the document thus becomes admissible under common law principles which the 2003 Act will not abolish.[331] Since, in such circumstances, the witness will not use the document to refresh his memory whilst he is giving evidence, it is submitted that the answer appears to be that the section 120(3) hearsay exception will not apply, and that the statement in the document will not be admitted as evidence of matters stated unless it is admissible under some other exception to the hearsay rule which the 2003 Act creates, retains or preserves.

It should be noted that if circumstances arise in which the hearsay exception created by section 120(1),(3) does not apply to a memory refreshing document, the document may, even so, be admissible under one or more of the other hearsay exceptions which the 2003 Act will create, preserve or retain.

Finally, it should be noted that where a documentary statement is admitted under section 120 of the 2003 Act and the document or a copy thereof is exhibited (which will be the case where a memory refreshing document is put in evidence), the effect of section 122 of the 2003 Act will be that the jury cannot take the document with them when they retire unless either the court considers this appropriate or all the parties agree that the jury should take it with them.

---

330 *Perhaps at common law or under section 78 of the Police and Criminal Evidence Act 1984 (see section 126(2) of the Criminal Justice Act 2003) or under section 126(1) of the 2003 Act (see, generally, 2.7.5 below).*

2.2.6 Previous statements made by witnesses who cannot reasonably be expected to remember the matters to which they relate well enough to give oral evidence thereof

Section 120(1),(4),(6) of the 2003 Act will create a new hearsay exception concerning previous statements made by persons who are called to give oral evidence in criminal proceedings. In recommending the creation of the hearsay exception which is now embodied in section 120(1),(4),(6), the Law Commission[332] recognised in relation to memory refreshing at common law that where the witness' memory is not refreshed, memory refreshing becomes a legal fiction; the statement relied upon for memory refreshing becomes, in effect, a hearsay statement and may, in reality, be the best evidence. Further, the Law Commission[333] recognised that where the essential common-law prerequisites of memory refreshing are not satisfied, the result may be that the statement contained in the memory refreshing document is never put before the jury unless, anomalously, it either concerns identification evidence[334] or falls within the ambit of an exception to the hearsay rule. Moreover, the Law Commission[335] recognised the absurdity of the fact (considered at 2.2.5.1 above) that, at common law, a witness can read a non-contemporaneous document outside of the witness box but, subject to the court's discretion, cannot take it into the witness box with him.[336] Thus, whilst (as was seen at 2.2.5.2.2 above) the Law Commission did not recommend the abolition of memory refreshing, they did recommend the creation of the hearsay exception which now manifests itself in the form of section 120(1),(4),(6) of the 2003 Act, those provisions providing as follows.

"(1) This section applies where a person (the witness) is called to give evidence in criminal proceedings....

(4) A previous statement by the witness is admissible as evidence of any matter stated of which oral evidence by him would be admissible, if–

(a) any of the following three conditions is satisfied, and

(b) while giving evidence the witness indicates that to the best of his belief he made the statement, and that to the best of his belief it states the truth...

(6) The second condition is that the statement was made by the witness when the matters stated were fresh in his memory but he does not remember them, and cannot reasonably be expected to remember them, well enough to give oral evidence of them in the proceedings."

---

331 *See Owen v Edwards (1983) 77 Cr App R 191.*

332 *See "Evidence in Criminal Proceedings: Hearsay and Related Topics", Law Com No 245, at paragraph 10.66.*

333 *See "Evidence in Criminal Proceedings: Hearsay and Related Topics", Law Com No 245, at paragraphs 10.67-10.68.*

334 *See 2.2.4.3.2 above.*

335 *See "Evidence in Criminal Proceedings: Hearsay and Related Topics", Law Com No 245, at paragraph 10.69.*

336 *Note that, as was seen at 2.2.5 above, the common law prerequisites of memory refreshing are, in Line with Lord Justice Auld's report, to replaced with a new and more generous statutory test.*

Thus, it appears that the hearsay exception created by section 120(1),(4),(6) will apply so as to render a previous statement made by a witness who is called to give oral evidence admissible as evidence of a matter stated therein provided that the statement was made contemporaneously with the occurrence of the relevant matter, the witness does not remember the relevant matter, the witness cannot reasonably be expected to remember the relevant matter well enough to give oral evidence thereof, the witness indicates that to the best of belief he both made the statement and it is true and the witness' oral evidence of the relevant matter would be admissible.

Presumably where the witness remembers some of the matters to which the statement relates but not others, the statement may be admitted under the section 120(1),(4),(6) hearsay exception to fill in the missing details[337] (though the wording of section 120(6), in requiring that "the statement was made by the witness when the matters stated were fresh in his memory but he does not remember them" does not make clear whether the hearsay exception may be relied upon when the witness does remember some of the matters stated).

In determining whether the witness can reasonably be expected to remember the matters stated well enough to give oral evidence thereof, the court will presumably be entitled (and indeed required) to take into account factors such as the witness' personal characteristics (e.g. age, state of health etc) and the nature of the information (e.g. was it the sort of information (such as a car number plate) that the witness would be unlikely to remember in the long term).

The section does not make clear whether, in determining whether the witness can reasonably be expected to remember the relevant maters sufficiently well, the court should take into account (where this is so) either the fact that the witness had the opportunity to read a memory refreshing document prior to going into the witness box and/or the fact that he has a memory refreshing document with him in the witness box.

Conversely, it does appear to be clear that the requirements of section 120(6) will not be satisfied if the effect of reading through a memory refreshing document either before going into the witness box or whilst in the witness box is that the witness' memory actually is refreshed because, in such circumstances, the witness will now remember the matters stated. Whilst this appears to be so, whether the court, as a matter of practice, will normally give the witness the opportunity to memory refresh prior to determining whether the section 120(6) condition requirements are satisfied remains to be seen.

Moreover, where the witness testifies that he does remember the relevant matter but the court, having heard his evidence (perhaps having heard the witness give evidence of a car number plate which is inconsistent with his police statement),

---

337 See *"Evidence in Criminal Proceedings: Hearsay and Related Topics"*, *Law Com No 245*, *at paragraph* 10.73.

---

decides that the witness does not remember the relevant matter, will the section 120(6) requirement be satisfied?

It should be noted that, even where the technical requirements of section 120(6) are not satisfied, a hearsay statement may be admissible under one or more of the other hearsay exceptions which the 2003 Act will create, preserve or retain.

In relation to the requirement that the witness' oral evidence would be admissible in relation to the relevant matter, it is submitted that the hearsay exception created by section 120(1),(4),(6) will not apply where for example, the evidence is irrelevant, amounts to inadmissible evidence of opinion or to inadmissible evidence of bad character. Similarly, where the maker of the statement did not have the "required capability" to make it (i.e. was not competent to make it) at the time when he made it, the effect of section 123 of the 2003 Act (considered at 2.7.2, below) will be that the statement will not be admissible under section 120 as evidence of matters stated. It also appears, however, that, in consequence of the operation of section 121(1)(a) of the 2003 Act, which is considered at 2.7.1 below, the fact that the statement itself contains or is based upon a hearsay statement will not prevent the admission of the statement under section 120(1),(4),(6) to prove that the latter statement was made (though, presumably, the latter statement will only be admissible if it, also, falls within the ambit of an exception to the rule against hearsay). Equally, it appears that, again in consequence of the operation of section 121(1)(a) of the 2003 Act, a statement which is admissible under section 120 may be proved by a hearsay statement which is admissible under some other exception to the rule against hearsay.

Where a consistent statement does fall within the ambit of the hearsay exception created by section 120(1),(4),(6), it must not be forgotten that its admissibility will still be subject to the exercise of the court's exclusionary discretion.[338]

In the Law Commission's consultation paper the Law Commission[339] had been of the view that the option which eventually resulted in the hearsay exception created by section 120(1),(4),(6):

"...would ensure that evidence which is of sufficient importance to be worthy of consideration by the fact-finders would be admissible. It would also recognise the difficulty that witnesses have in remembering detailed evidence."

---

338 *Perhaps at common law or under section 78 of the Police and Criminal Evidence Act 1984 (see section 126(2) of the Criminal Justice Act 2003) or under section 126(1) of the 2003 Act (see, generally, 2.7.5 below).*

339 *See "Evidence in Criminal Proceedings: Hearsay and Related Topics", Law Com No 245, at paragraphs 10.70.*

The Law Commission[340] recognised that:

> 10.71 If such statements were admissible, the witness could of course be cross-examined on the truth of the contents of the earlier statement and the circumstances in which it was made, and contradictory evidence could be led about the matters dealt with in the statement. Any objection could be taken, to the statement or any part of it, and any question put to the witness, which could properly have been taken or put if the witness had given the evidence in chief in the ordinary way."

In relation to the nature of those circumstances in which the Law Commission envisaged that hearsay evidence may be admissible under this hearsay exception and the means by which they envisaged that such a statement may be proved, their report provides the following guidance. [Note: in the following extract from the Law Commission's report, references to the "unavailability exception" refers to what is now section 116 of the 2003 Act.]

> "10.73 In our view the rules applicable in this situation should be as follows. First, the fact that the witness (W) has to rely on another person (X),[89] or a document, or both, to fill in details which she can no longer recall, should go to the weight of the evidence of those details but should not in itself make it inadmissible.[90] This is so whether W recorded the details in person, or X recorded what W said they were, or X gives evidence of what W said they were.
>
> 10.74 However, in order to exclude previous statements of inadequate reliability, W's previous statement should not be admissible unless
>
> (1) she made it when the details were fresh in her memory;
>
> (2) he does not, and cannot reasonably be expected to, remember them well enough to give oral evidence of them; and
>
> (3) she adopts it, in the course of her evidence, as her statement. In other words she must indicate that, to the best of her belief, she made the statement and it is true.[91]
>
> 10.75 If these requirements are satisfied, we believe that the statement should be admissible. This means it would be possible to prove what W then stated the now-forgotten details to be. The terms of the previous statement could be proved in various ways. Where W made the statement in a document, for example (which includes verifying and acknowledging a document in which X had recorded the terms of W's oral statement), it could be proved by producing the document, or a copy of it. Where the statement was neither

---

340 See *"Evidence in Criminal Proceedings: Hearsay and Related Topics", Law Com No 245,* at paragraphs 10.71.

made in a document nor recorded, it could be proved by calling a witness who heard it and remembers it.

10.76   Where the statement was oral and was recorded in a document by X, but W did not verify and acknowledge it, we believe it should be possible to rely on the document as proof of what she said. Under our draft Bill this result would be achieved by treating X's record as a statement by X, and therefore admissible subject to the conditions set out in paragraph 10.74 above. In other words X must have made the record when W's statement was fresh in his memory; it must not be reasonable to expect him to remember it well enough to give oral evidence of it; and he must confirm that, to the best of his belief, the document is an accurate record of what W said.

10.77   If X fell within the unavailability exception his statement would be automatically admissible, without having to prove that it was made when W's statement was fresh in X's memory.[92] Although his statement is multiple hearsay (being evidence of W's hearsay statement), and in general we do not believe that multiple hearsay should be admissible merely because the declarant is unavailable to testify,[93] the fact that W is available for cross-examination seems to us to justify admitting X's statement of what W said.[94]

10.78   In the great majority of cases there will be a document of some sort in which W or X has recorded what W observed. This is because, if the fact in question is the sort of fact that W cannot reasonably be expected to remember without the help of a document, it is unlikely that another person will be able, without such help, to remember what W stated that fact to be. But this is not inconceivable, because different people find different facts memorable. Suppose that W reads the model name of a car and tells X what it was. W may then forget it, because she knows nothing about cars and to her it is just a meaningless word; but X may remember it because he has an encyclopaedic knowledge of the motor industry and, to him, the name summons up a mental image of the model in question. In such a case we see no reason why X should not fill the gap in W's recollection. The rule that we recommend is therefore not confined to cases where the statement is recorded in a document, but applies also where X gives oral evidence that he remembers what W said.

10.79   We acknowledge that it would be possible for witnesses to collude so that evidence could be admitted under this exception; but they can be cross-examined. W might be asked about visibility at the time, and X about how clearly he heard what W said, whether he checked it and so on. It is one of the main functions of cross-examination to alert the fact-finders to the danger that evidence has been fabricated, and we do not see why this should not be possible in such a case.

89 W is for convenience assumed to be female, and X male.

90 Following the lead of the Court of Appeal in Osbourne and Virtue [1973] QB 678, 690, per Lawton LJ: "One asks oneself as a matter of commonsense why, when a witness has forgotten what she did, evidence should not be given by another witness with a better memory to establish what, in fact, she did when the events were fresh in her mind".

91 Obviously W need not remember what she said: that would be tantamount to a requirement that she remember the details she stated. It is sufficient if W says "what I told X was true" and X says "this is truly what W told me".

92 See paras 8.34 – 8.43 above, and cls 3 and 5 of the draft Bill.

93 See paras 8.15 – 8.17 above.

94 Clause 10(2) of the draft Bill would not exclude X's statement because W's statement is admissible under cl 8(4), ie otherwise than under cl 3 or a rule preserved by cl 6. See para 8.21 above."

One matter which the Law Commission did not and could not have considered in the above extract is the nature of the relationship between the hearsay exception now embodied in section 120(1),(4),(6) of the 2003 Act and the new test for determining whether a witness may memory refresh which will be created by section 139(1) of that Act (considered at 2.2.5.2.1 above). The Law Commission could not have considered the nature of this relationship because reform of the latter test did not form one of the Law Commission's recommendations and section 139(1) does not reflect any provision of their draft Bill.[341] Thus, so far as the Law Commission would have been concerned, what is now section 120(6) would be applicable where, *inter alia*, the matters stated were fresh in the witness' memory when he made the statement and memory refreshing would be permissible where, *inter alia*, the memory refreshing document was a contemporaneous document. Consequently, so far as the Law Commission was concerned, both the operation of what is now section 120(6) and the availability of memory refreshing would (subject to the exercise of the courts' discretion to permit memory refreshing from a non-contemporaneous document) have effectively been dependant upon the practical application of the concept of contemporaneity.

Under the 2003 Act, however, whilst the operation of section 120(6) will still effectively depend upon the practical application of that concept, the concept of contemporaneity will no longer regulate the use of a document for memory

---

341 *Rather, it stems from one of Lord Justice Auld's proposals (see 2.2.5.2.1 above).*

refreshing purposes. Consequently, it appears that there may be circumstances in which a witness will be permitted to memory refresh in the witness box under section 139(1) from a documentary statement which is not admissible under the hearsay exception created by section 120(1),(4),(6). Equally, it appears that there may be circumstances in which a memory refreshing document which would not admissible under the hearsay exception created by section 120(1),(4),(6) is admitted in evidence under the hearsay exception created by section 120(1),(3)

Where neither the hearsay exception created by section 120(1),(3) nor the hearsay exception created by section 120(1),(4),(6) apply to a statement, the statement may, of course, be potentially admissible under one or more of the other hearsay exceptions which the 2003 Act will create, preserve or retain.

Finally, it should be noted that where a documentary statement is admitted under section 120 of the 2003 Act and the document or a copy thereof is exhibited, the effect of section 122 of the 2003 Act will be that the jury cannot take the document with them when they retire unless either the court considers this appropriate or all the parties agree that the jury should take it with them.

2.2.7 Confessions as evidence for co-defendants

Section 128 of the Criminal Justice Act 2003 will insert a new section 76A into the Police and Criminal Evidence Act 1984 concerning the admissibility of a confession made by a defendant as evidence for his co-defendant.

2.2.7.1 The position prior to the 2003 Act

Whilst the position is not absolutely clear, it is submitted that in circumstances in which the accused's confession has been excluded under section 76(2) of the Police and Criminal Evidence Act 1984[342] (or would have been so excluded if it had been tendered by the prosecution), the best view of the current legal position (i.e. the legal position before the new section 76A comes into force) is that the confession, as well as being inadmissible for the prosecution, is not admissible as evidence of the truth of the matters stated on behalf of a co-defendant.[343] Should the accused testify and give evidence which incriminates his co-defendant, however, then, provided that the accused's excluded confession is inconsistent with the accused's testimony and that such cross-examination is relevant to the co-

---

342 *The nature and effect of section 76(2) are considered at 2.4.2.9.2 below.*
343 *R v Myers [1998] AC 124 (see, also, R v Corelli [2001] Crim LR 914). The issue did not form part of the ratio of their Lordships' decision in Myers and their Lordships speeches, whilst appearing to suggest that a confession is inadmissible for a co-accused in such*

circumstances as evidence of the truth of the facts stated, do not provide absolute clarity in relation to this issue. In R v Rigot LTL 18/2/2000, however, the Court of Appeal appears to have accepted that, post Myers, a confession which is inadmissible under section 76 will not be admissible for a co-defendant as evidence of the truth of the facts stated.

accused's defence, the co-defendant may[344] cross-examine the accused on the confession in order to discredit the accused's testimony.[345] In such circumstances the trial judge should direct the jury to the effect that the confession does not form part of the prosecution's case against the accused.[346] Moreover, in such circumstances, the prosecution cannot cross-examine the accused on the confession.[347]

The position appears to be different where the accused's confession has only been excluded in the exercise of the trial judge's exclusionary discretion[348], or where it would have been so excluded had it been tendered by the prosecution, in circumstances in which the confession is not rendered inadmissible by virtue of the operation of section 76(2) of the 1984 Act. In this situation, the best view of the current legal position (i.e. the legal position before the new section 76A comes into force) appears to be that the confession is admissible as evidence of the truth of the matters stated on behalf of the co-defendant provided that the confession is relevant either to support the co-defendant's defence or to undermine the prosecution's case against the co-defendant.[349] It appears, however, that in such circumstances, the trial judge should direct the jury to the effect that the confession does not form part of the prosecution's case against the accused.[350] Moreover, circumstances may be encountered in which, regardless of how a jury are directed in relation to the admission of an excluded confession as defence evidence, its admission will almost certainly result in the accused's conviction. In

---

344 *Subject to the relevant provisions of the Criminal Procedure Act 1865 (considered at 2.2.3.1.2 above). Cross-examining counsel will not be permitted to challenge the accused's assertion that his confession was either obtained by oppression or in consequence of something said or done which was likely to have rendered any confession the accused might have made in the circumstances unreliable, but, subject to the relevant provisions of the 1865 Act, he will be able to adduce evidence to prove that the accused made the confession should he deny this (R v Corelli [2001] Crim LR 914). In contrast, where the confession was admissible under section 76 of the 1984 Act but was merely excluded under section 78 and the purpose of cross-examination of the accused by the co-accused is to prove that his confession is true, it appears that the question of whether the confession was obtained by oppression or in consequence of something said or done which was likely to have rendered any confession the accused might have made in the circumstances unreliable is one which may be re-opened before the jury (R v Corelli [2001] Crim LR 914). The admissibility of evidence of the accused's excluded confession for a co-accused where the confession was merely excluded under section 78 of the 1984 Act is considered in the following paragraph.*

345 *See: R v Rowson [1986] QB 174; Lui Mei Lin v R [1989] AC 288; R v Corelli [2001] Crim LR 914.*

346 *Lui Mei Lin v R [1989] AC 288; R v Corelli [2001] Crim LR 914.*

347 *R v Treacy [1944] 2 All ER 229.*

348 *I.e. either under section 78(1) of the 1984 Act or in the exercise of the court's common law exclusionary discretion, which is preserved by section 78(2). Section 78(1),(2) are considered at 2.7.5.2 below.*

349 *R v Myers [1998] AC 124. It is submitted that the speeches of their Lordships in Myers do not make clear the basis of the hearsay exception under which such evidence is admitted. Moreover, Myers appears to provide some authority for the proposition that a trial judge may possess discretion to exclude a confession tendered by a co-defendant in such circumstances (see R v Rigot LTL 18/2/2000). If this is indeed so then this appears to be a new development of the common law which, it is submitted, formerly did not recognise the existence of discretion to exclude defence evidence.*

350 *R v Rigot LTL 18/2/2000. As a general rule, however, evidence adduced by the accused may be relied upon by the prosecution (R v Rigot LTL 18/2/2000; Murdoch v Taylor [1965] AC 574).*

such circumstances it may be that the judge, upon application for severance of the indictment, should order separate trials.[351]

Finally, there may be circumstances in which the co-defendant relies in his defence upon a confession made by the accused which was not tendered by the prosecution in circumstances in which the confession would not have been excluded either under section 76 or under section 78 of the Police and Criminal Evidence Act 1984. In such circumstances, the current legal position (i.e. the legal position before the new section 76A comes into force) appears to be that the confession, if relevant either to support the co-defendant's defence or to undermine the prosecution's case against the co-defendant, is admissible as evidence of the truth of the facts stated.[352] Moreover, it appears that, in such circumstances, the jury may rely upon the accused's confession as part of the prosecution's case against the accused; the general rule being that evidence adduced by the accused may be relied upon by the prosecution.[353]

2.2.7.2 The position under the 2003 Act

The Law Commission's recommendation and the clause of their draft Bill which resulted in section 128 of the 2003 Act and in section 76A of the 1984 Act were, respectively, made and drafted prior to the decision of the House of Lords in *R v Myers*[354] and the subsequent case law, the effect of which was considered at 2.2.7.1 above. It is submitted that, viewed in the context of the hearsay reforms of the 2003 Act as a whole, the new provisions do not adequately deal with all of the issues to which the case law including and following the decision of their Lordships in *Myers* has given rise.

Section 128 of the 2003 Act provides as follows.

"(1) In the Police and Criminal Evidence Act 1984 (c. 60) the following section is inserted after section 76–

"76A Confessions may be given in evidence for co-accused

(1) In any proceedings a confession made by an accused person may be given in evidence for another person charged in the same proceedings (a co-accused) in so far as it is relevant to any matter in issue in the proceedings and is not excluded by the court in pursuance of this section.

(2) If, in any proceedings where a co-accused proposes to give in evidence a confession made by an accused person, it is represented to the court that the confession was or may have been obtained–

---

351 See *R v Rigot* LTL 18/2/2000; *R v O'Boyle* (1991) 92 Cr App R 202.
352 See *R v Rigot* LTL 18/2/2000; *R v Myers* [1998] AC 124.

353 *R v Rigot* LTL 18/2/2000; *Murdoch v Taylor* [1965] AC 574.
354 [1998] AC 124.

(a) by oppression of the person who made it; or

(b) in consequence of anything said or done which was likely, in the circumstances existing at the time, to render unreliable any confession which might be made by him in consequence thereof, the court shall not allow the confession to be given in evidence for the co-accused except in so far as it is proved to the court on the balance of probabilities that the confession (notwithstanding that it may be true) was not so obtained.

(3) Before allowing a confession made by an accused person to be given in evidence for a co-accused in any proceedings, the court may of its own motion require the fact that the confession was not obtained as mentioned in subsection (2) above to be proved in the proceedings on the balance of probabilities.

(4) The fact that a confession is wholly or partly excluded in pursuance of this section shall not affect the admissibility in evidence–

(a) of any facts discovered as a result of the confession; or

(b) where the confession is relevant as showing that the accused speaks, writes or expresses himself in a particular way, of so much of the confession as is necessary to show that he does so.

(5) Evidence that a fact to which this subsection applies was discovered as a result of a statement made by an accused person shall not be admissible unless evidence of how it was discovered is given by him or on his behalf.

(6) Subsection (5) above applies–

(a) to any fact discovered as a result of a confession which is wholly excluded in pursuance of this section; and

(b) to any fact discovered as a result of a confession which is partly so excluded, if the fact is discovered as a result of the excluded part of the confession.

(7) In this section "oppression" includes torture, inhuman or degrading treatment, and the use or threat of violence (whether or not amounting to torture)."

(2) Subject to subsection (1), nothing in this Chapter makes a confession by a defendant admissible if it would not be admissible under section 76 of the Police and Criminal Evidence Act 1984 (c. 60).

(3) In subsection (2) "confession" has the meaning given by section 82 of that Act."

The effect of section 76A(1)–(3) appears to be that the accused's confession will be admissible as evidence of the matters stated (i.e. under an exception to the hearsay rule) for his co-accused if it is relevant to an issue in the proceedings unless either another party (i.e. the accused) represents to the court that the confession was or may have been obtained either in the way specified by section 76A(2)(a) or in the way specified by section 76A(2)(b) or the court itself raises the issue of whether the confession was or may have been so obtained. Where the issue of the confession's admissibility is raised, it appears that the confession will not be admissible as evidence of the matters stated for the co-accused unless the co-accused proves on the balance of probabilities that the confession was not obtained in the relevant way(s).[355]

Section 76A(1)–(3)) effectively reprise section 76(1)–(2) of the 1984 Act (which deal with the admissibility of confessions for the prosecution), other than in that, first, the new provisions relate to the admissibility of the confession in evidence for a co-accused rather than for the prosecution (and, consequently, it is submitted that the accused's confession will only be relevant to an issue in the proceedings within the meaning of section 76A(1) if it is relevant either to support the co-accused's defence or to undermine the case against him[356]), secondly, it appears that the burden of proof is borne by the co-defendant tendering the confession, not by the prosecution, and, thirdly, the requisite standard of proof is not the criminal standard but, rather, is proof on the balance of probabilities. Thus, it is submitted that when interpreting these provisions (and, in particular, when interpreting section 76A(2)(a) and (b)), the approach of the courts is likely to equate with their approach to the equivalent provisions of section 76 (which is considered at 2.4.2.7, below).

In relation to the differing standards of proof imposed, respectively, by section 76(2) and section 76A(2), it is submitted that a potential consequence of these differing standards will be that a confession which is inadmissible for the prosecution (because the prosecution fail to prove beyond reasonable doubt that the confession was not obtained in either of the ways specified by section 76(2)), may still be admissible as evidence of the matters stated for a co-accused if the co-accused proves on the balance of probabilities that the confession was not so obtained. This, it appears, might be the case where, for example, the accused asserts that he was beaten by the police prior to confessing, the prosecution fail to persuade the judge to the criminal standard of proof that the accused was not beaten by the police but the defence persuade the judge that the accused was probably not beaten by the police. Presumably, in such circumstances, the jury

---

355 *Whilst the section does not expressly state that the burden or proof is borne by the co-defendant who tenders the relevant evidence, that this is so is in line with the general principle of the law of evidence that the burden of proving the admissibility of evidence is borne by the party* tendering the relevant evidence (see, for example, R v Mattey and Queeley [1995] 2 Cr App R 409, (a case concerning section 23 of the Criminal Justice Act 1988).

356 *Support for this proposition may, it is submitted, be derived from R v Myers [1998] AC 124*

would be directed to the effect that the confession could not be relied upon as evidence of its maker's guilt.

In relation to the remaining provisions of section 76A, (i.e. section 76A(4)–(7), it is submitted that these provisions merely reprise the equivalent provisions of section 76 of the 1984 Act and, consequently, that the courts are likely to construe the former provisions in line with the latter. The effect of the relevant provisions of section 76 is considered at 2.4.2.7, below.

Having considered the effect of section 76A of the 1984 Act in isolation from the regime of hearsay exceptions created by the Criminal Justice Act 2003, it is now necessary to consider the significance of section 76A (and that of section 128 of the 2003 Act as a whole) in the context of that regime. It is submitted that the authorities considered at 2.2.7.1 demonstrate that there are three main situations in which the admissibility of a confession made by co-accused A as evidence for co-accused B may come into issue. First, where A's confession (whether or not tendered by the prosecution) is inadmissible for the prosecution due to the operation of section 76(2) of the 1984 Act. Secondly, where A's confession (whether or not tendered by the prosecution) is not rendered inadmissible for the prosecution by section 76(2) but is (or would, if tendered by the prosecution, be) excluded by the court under section 78 of the 1984 Act. Thirdly, where A's confession would be admissible for the prosecution but has not been relied on thereby.

In relation to the first of these three situations, it is submitted that the effect of section 76A will be that co-accused A's confession will be admissible for co-accused B (but not for the prosecution) as evidence of the matters stated if it is relevant to a matter in issue and B proves on the balance of probabilities that the confession was not obtained in the ways specified by section 76A(2)(a)–(b). If, B fails to discharge this burden of proof, however, then, it appears, the confession will not be admissible for B as evidence of the matters stated.

In the context of circumstances in which A's confession is neither admissible for the prosecution nor for B as evidence of the matters stated, what section 76A does not make clear, however, is whether, should A testify and give evidence inconsistent with his confession which implicates B, B will be entitled to have A cross-examined on the confession for the purposes of discrediting A's testimony if such cross-examination is relevant to B's defence. As was seen at 2.2.7.1 above, the current position (i.e. the position before section 128 of the 2003 Act comes into force) appears to be that cross-examination is permissible in such circumstances. Section 76A(2) expressly provides, however, that where B fails to discharge the burden of proof which that provision imposes upon him, "the court shall not allow the confession to be given in evidence for the co-accused". Conversely, section 118 (1) 5 of the 2003 Act, which is considered at 2.3.2.8 below, will preserves "Any rule of law relating to the admissibility of confessions or mixed statements in criminal proceedings".

If it is assumed that a confession will not be "given in evidence" within the meaning of section 76A(2) in circumstances in which it is merely relied upon as an inconsistent statement for the purpose of cross-examination of its maker as to his credibility, then it is submitted that section 76A(2) will not prevent cross-examination of co-accused A for this limited purpose. If such cross-examination will be permissible when section 76A of the 1984 Act is in force, however, this raises a further problem. Under section 119 of the 2003 Act (as was seen at 2.2.3.2 above) where a witness admits making a previous inconsistent statement or a previous inconsistent statement is proved under sections 3–5 of the Criminal Procedure Act 1865, the previous inconsistent statement will be admitted as evidence of the matters stated provided that the witness could have given oral evidence of the relevant matter. Section 128(2) provides, however, that

> "Subject to subsection (1), nothing in this Chapter makes a confession by a defendant admissible if it would not be admissible under section 76 of the Police and Criminal Evidence Act 1984 (c. 60)."

Thus, it is submitted, in circumstances in which A's confession is not admissible under section 76A of the 1984 Act but B, relying upon the confession as a previous inconsistent statement made by A, is permitted to cross-examine A in relation to it and the confession is either admitted by A or is proved under the 1865 Act, the effect of section 128 of the 2003 Act will be that the confession will not be admissible under section 119 as evidence of the matters stated.

In relation to the second and third of the three situations identified above, in which the admissibility of co-accused A's confession as evidence for co-accused B may come into issue (i.e. that in which A's confession is not rendered inadmissible by section 76(1) of the 1984 Act but is excluded as prosecution evidence by the court under section 78 of PACE and that in which A's confession is admissible for the prosecution but is not tendered thereby), it is submitted that, provided that A's confession is relevant to B's defence, the confession will, when that provision is in force, be admissible for B under section 76A(1) of the 1984 Act. Thus, in such circumstances, it is submitted that B could potentially adduce evidence of A's confession via cross-examination of A, via examination in chief or cross-examination of other witness or by adducing documentary evidence of the confession, the confession, in any of these situations, being admitted as evidence of the matters stated.

2.2.8 Statements upon which expert evidence is based

Essentially, section 127 of the Criminal Justice Act 2003 concerns both the admissibility of hearsay evidence upon which expert opinion evidence is based and the admissibility of expert opinion evidence which is based upon hearsay evidence. Before considering the nature and significance of section 127 and the position of such evidence within the regime of hearsay exceptions which the 2003 Act will create, it is first necessary to consider the current (i.e. pre 2003 Act) status of such evidence; i.e. the principles of the law of evidence which the hearsay provisions of the 2003 Act will modify.

2.2.8.1 The position prior to the 2003 Act

It is not necessary for an expert to have personal knowledge of the primary facts upon which his expert opinion is based as long as those facts are proved by admissible evidence.[357] Where an expert witness does not have personal knowledge of the primary facts upon which his opinion is based, however, inadmissible hearsay evidence cannot be relied upon to prove the relevant facts.[358] In such circumstances, admissible evidence will be required to fill the "evidential gap".[359]

Thus, where the opinion evidence of an expert witness is based upon hearsay evidence, the expert evidence will not be admissible unless an exception to the hearsay rule is applicable.[360] For example, a doctor might, in the context of criminal proceedings, be permitted to repeat a hearsay statement made by a patient concerning the patient's contemporaneous physical sensations as evidence of the existence of those sensations because such a statement forms part of the res gestae.[361]. Equally, hearsay evidence which forms the basis of expert evidence might, for example, be admissible under a statutory exception to the hearsay rule such as 23 or section 24 of the Criminal Justice Act 1988.[362] It should be noted, however, that whilst section 30 of the Criminal Justice Act 1988[363] renders expert reports admissible in criminal proceedings as evidence of any fact or opinion of which their maker could have given oral evidence, section 30 does not render hearsay evidence of primary facts which the expert did not personally perceive admissible, because the expert could not have given oral evidence of such facts.

Where an expert repeats a statement which was made to him out of court but the statement is not relied upon as evidence of the truth of the facts stated then the hearsay rule is not infringed. Thus, for example, a doctor may refer to hearsay statements made by a patient concerning the patient's symptoms in order to explain how the doctor reached his diagnosis without infringing the hearsay rule, but the statements will fall within the ambit of the hearsay rule if relied upon to prove that the patient did, in fact, possess the relevant symptoms at the relevant

357 *See, for example, R v Jackson [1996] 2 Cr App R 420.*

358 *See, for example, Chester-Nash v Crown Prosecution Service LTL 18/4/2000. It should be noted that in the context of civil proceedings, now that section 1 of the Civil Evidence Act 1995 is in force, the hearsay basis of expert evidence no longer presents a problem of admissibility, though the weight of the relevant evidence may be limited (see, for example, G Newman (H.M. Inspector of Taxes) v FDL Hatt [2002] 04 EG 175).*

359 *See Chester-Nash v Crown Prosecution Service LTL 18/4/2000;*

360 *Chester-Nash v Crown Prosecution Service LTL 18/4/2000; R v Edwards [2001] EWCA Crim 2185.*

361 *See Amys v Barton [1912] 1 KB 40. This preserved common law exception to the hearsay rule is considered at 2.3.2.7.3 below.*

362 *See, for example, Khatibi v DPP [2004] EWHC 83 (Admin). As was seen at 2.2.1-2.2.2 above, sections 23 and 24 of the 1988 Act are effectively to be replaced by sections 116 and 117 of the 2003 Act.*

363 *Considered at 2.4.2.2 below.*

time.[364] In practice, such hearsay statements would be admissible in the context of criminal proceedings under a common law exception to the hearsay rule if they concerned the patient's contemporaneous physical sensations and, thus, formed part of the *res gestae*[365], but not if the statements concerned non-contemporaneous symptoms.[366]

The decision of the Court of Appeal in *R v Golizadeh*[367] provides authority for the proposition that, in the context of criminal proceedings, an expert may be entitled to rely upon data provided by a machine even though the machine's printout was not adduced in evidence. Whilst this does not appear in the reasoning of the Court of Appeal in *Golizadeh*, it is submitted that the decision may best be justified upon the basis that the printout was not hearsay evidence (because the machine had not processed data which had first passed through a human mind) but, rather, was real evidence.[368]

Where a printout on which expert opinion evidence is based is hearsay evidence (because the machine which produced the printout processed data which had first passed through a human mind[369]), it is submitted that, in the context of criminal proceedings, the evidence will only be admissible if an appropriate exception to the hearsay rule (such as section 24 of the Criminal Justice Act 1988) is applicable thereto.[370]

2.2.8.2 The position under the 2003 Act

Section 127 of the 2003 Act provides as follows.

"(1) This section applies if–

(a) a statement has been prepared for the purposes of criminal proceedings,

(b) the person who prepared the statement had or may reasonably be supposed to have had personal knowledge of the matters stated,

(c) notice is given under the appropriate rules that another person (the expert) will in evidence given in the proceedings orally or under section 9 of the Criminal Justice Act 1967 (c. 80) base an opinion or inference on the statement, and

(d) the notice gives the name of the person who prepared the statement and the nature of the matters stated.

---

364 *R v Bradshaw [1986] 82 Cr App R 79.*
365 *See Amys v Barton [1912] 1 KB 40. The relevant common law hearsay exception is considered at 2.3.2.7.3 below.*
366 *R v Bradshaw [1986] 82 Cr App R 79.*
367 *[1995] Crim LR 232.*

368 *See 1.9.1 above.*
369 *See R v Spiby (1990) 91 Cr App R 186 (considered at 2.2.1 above).*
370 *As was seen at 2.2.2 above, section 24 of the 1988 is effectively to be repealed by section 117 of the 2003 Act.*

(2) In evidence given in the proceedings the expert may base an opinion or inference on the statement.

(3) If evidence based on the statement is given under subsection (2) the statement is to be treated as evidence of what it states.

(4) This section does not apply if the court, on an application by a party to the proceedings, orders that it is not in the interests of justice that it should apply.

(5) The matters to be considered by the court in deciding whether to make an order under subsection (4) include—

(a) the expense of calling as a witness the person who prepared the statement;

(b) whether relevant evidence could be given by that person which could not be given by the expert;

(c) whether that person can reasonably be expected to remember the matters stated well enough to give oral evidence of them.

(6) Subsections (1) to (5) apply to a statement prepared for the purposes of a criminal investigation as they apply to a statement prepared for the purposes of criminal proceedings, and in such a case references to the proceedings are to criminal proceedings arising from the investigation.

(7) The appropriate rules are rules made—

(a) under section 81 of the Police and Criminal Evidence Act 1984 (c. 60) (advance notice of expert evidence in Crown Court), or

(b) under section 144 of the Magistrates' Courts Act 1980 (c. 43) by virtue of section 20(3) of the Criminal Procedure and Investigations Act 1996 (c. 25) (advance notice of expert evidence in magistrates' courts)."

It appears that the effects of section 127 will be that, when its requirements are satisfied in relation to a hearsay statement, an expert witness will be able to base his opinion or an inference upon the hearsay statement and, if the expert does so, the statement itself will also become admissible in evidence. The section will only apply, however, to a statement which was prepared either for the purposes of criminal proceedings or for those of a criminal investigation by a person who had or may reasonably be supposed to have had personal knowledge of the matters stated. Moreover, the section will only apply if, in accordance with rules of court, notice is given[371] that the expert will, either in the course of oral evidence or in

---

371 *Either under Crown Court rules made under section 81 of the Police and Criminal Evidence Act 1984 or under Magistrates Courts' Rules made under section 20(3) of the Criminal Procedure and Investigations Act 1996.*

evidence given under section 9 of the Criminal Justice Act 1967[372], base an opinion or inference on the statement and the notice both names the person who prepared the statement and indicates the nature of the matters stated. Further, it should be noted that section 127 does not appear to apply where an expert's report is admitted in his absence under section 30 of the Criminal Justice Act 1988 (which is considered at 2.4.2.3 below).

Section 127 will not apply if, upon application by a party, the court orders that it is not in the interests of justice for the section to apply. Section 127(5) provides a non-exhaustive list of matters which the court is to consider when determining whether the making of such an order under section 127(4) is in the interests of justice. Presumably, in the context of exercising this discretion, another matter which the court should take into account is whether the admission of the relevant hearsay evidence might give rise to a violation of Article 6 of the European Convention on Human Rights.[373] Moreover, it should be noted that apart from the operation of the exclusionary discretion conferred on the court by section 127(4), the admissibility of evidence under section 127 appears to be potentially subject to the court's exclusionary discretion as created and preserved by section 126 of the 2003 Act (which is considered at 2.7.5 below).

Section 127 is not expressly limited in its application to statements which were either made in or are in documents, and, indeed, the definition of "statement" in section 115 is clearly wide enough to encompass an oral statement. Section 127 will, however, only apply to a statement which has been "prepared" by a person for the purposes of criminal proceedings. Whether there may be circumstances in which the courts will regard an oral statement as one which has been "prepared" for the purposes of criminal proceedings, or whether they will regard section 127 as applicable only to documentary hearsay, remains to be seen.

If the latter, narrower, interpretation of the section, as only encompassing documentary statements, is adopted by the courts, presumably a tape recorded or video recorded statement made by the relevant person could still fall within the ambit of the section. What, however, of an answer phone message left thereby? If the former, wider, interpretation of section 127, as potentially encompassing oral statements, is adopted by the courts, presumably the way in which the statement was "prepared" is a matter which the court might take into account in the exercise of its exclusionary discretion under section 127(4).

Section 127 will clearly not provide a blanket hearsay exception which renders admissible any expert opinion evidence based on hearsay statement regardless of its source. Where the requirements of section 127 are not satisfied, however, the relevant evidence (both the underlying hearsay statement and the expert opinion evidence which is based upon it) may still be admissible if some other applicable

---

372 *Section 9 of the 1967 Act is considered at 2.4.2.1 below.*

373 *The significance of Article 6 is the hearsay context is considered at 2.8 below.*

exception to the hearsay rule which the 2003 Act creates, retains or preserves can be identified.

Section 127 makes clear that the matters stated in a statement to which the section applies must be matters of which the person who prepared the statement had or may reasonably be supposed to have had personal knowledge. It appears that one of the effects of this requirement will be to prevent the admissibility of multiple hearsay under section 127.[374] Thus, for example, it appears that section 127 will not apply to a hearsay statement made by X on the basis of which expert Y forms his opinion if X did not have personal knowledge of the primary fact but, rather, was told about them by Z.

It is submitted, however, that whilst the person who prepared the statement must at least be reasonably supposed to have had personal knowledge of the relevant facts, this does not mean that the statement could not itself be proved for the purposes of section 127 by another hearsay statement admissible under another hearsay exception which the 2003 Act will create, retain or preserve, provided that the requirements of section 121 of the 2003 Act (which are considered at 2.7.1 below) are satisfied. Thus, for example, if X prepared a statement which satisfied the requirements of section 127, Z read that statement but then lost it, Z told expert Y what he had read and Y based his opinion upon it, it is submitted that X's statement might be proved under section 117 (or section 114(1)(d)) of the 2003 Act via Z's oral secondary evidence and that Y's expert evidence might, accordingly, be admissible under section 127(2).

The Law Commission[375], with reference to the hearsay exception which now exists in the form of section 127, regarded the exception as only encompassing matters in relation to which the person who prepared the statement could have given oral evidence.

> "9.27 The exception we propose would be confined to matters of which the assistant could have given direct oral evidence. It follows that it would not extend to matters of opinion, or to facts which only a person with the necessary expertise could establish (such as the scientific analysis of samples), if the assistant in question did not have the necessary expertise to give admissible evidence of those matters. In the somewhat unlikely event of there being a real issue as to whether the assistant was qualified to supply the information in question, it would clearly be a case for a direction that the assistant must give evidence. The admissibility of the assistant's evidence would then be

---

374 See *"Evidence in Criminal Proceedings: Hearsay and Related Topics"*, Law Com No 245, at paragraph 9.25, footnote 40.

375 See *"Evidence in Criminal Proceedings: Hearsay and Related Topics"*, Law Com No 245, at paragraph 9.27.

determined in the ordinary way, on a *voir dire*,[41] and the expert could rely on the assistant's information only to the extent that the assistant was permitted to, and did, give evidence of it.

[41] See Silverlock [1894] 2 QB 766; Bonython (1984) 38 SASR 45."

It is submitted, however, that section 127 does not expressly require that the matters stated be matters of which the person who prepared the statement could have given oral evidence had he been called. Moreover, section 123 (which concerns the "required capability (i.e. competence to testify in criminal proceedings) of the maker of a hearsay statement to make the statement and is considered at 2.7.2 below) does not appear to apply to the hearsay exception created by section 127. Further, section 127 does not impose any express requirement concerning the competence of the person who prepared the statement to give expert evidence. Thus, it is submitted that where the matters to which the statement relate are matters of which the person who prepared the statement may reasonably be supposed to have had personal knowledge but of which he could not have given oral evidence (because, for example, he is not competent to testify in criminal proceedings at all or is not competent to testify as an expert), the admissibility of the relevant evidence will be dependant either upon the operation of other rules of evidence (such as the common law rules concerning the competence of a witness to give expert evidence and the admissibility thereof) or will fall to be dealt with in the exercise of the court's exclusionary discretion under section 127(4). Presumably, if circumstances arise in which a statement made by a person whose competence, or competence to give expert evidence, is dubious is admitted in evidence under section 127, the party who opposed its opposition will be entitled to attack the credibility of its maker under section 124 of the 2003 Act.[376]

Finally, it is submitted that where the person who prepared a statement relied, in preparing it, upon printouts or other readings produced by machines which did not depend for their accuracy upon information supplied by a person[377], the person's reliance upon the relevant data will not affect the admissibility of the relevant evidence under section 127, other than to the extent to which it may be a matter which the court finds it necessary to consider in the exercise of its exclusionary discretion under section 127(4). In contrast, where the person who prepared the statement relied, in preparing it, upon printouts or other readings produced by machines which did depend for their accuracy upon information supplied by a person[378], it is submitted (without anything approaching absolute confidence) that the admissibility of the statement (or the relevant parts thereof) and thus of the expert's opinion (or of the relevant parts thereof) will depend upon the party tendering the relevant evidence proving, as required by section 129(1) of the 2003 Act[379], that the relevant information was accurate.

---

376 *Section 124 is considered at 2.7.3 below.*
377 *See 1.9.2.1 above.*

378 *See 1.9.2.2 above.*
379 *Section 129(1) was considered at 1.9.2.2 above.*

2.2.9 Witness' video recorded contemporaneous accounts of events witnessed thereby

Sections 137 and 138 of the Criminal Justice Act 2003 concern the admissibility of a witness' video recorded contemporaneous account of events witnessed thereby, both in criminal proceedings for offences triable on indictment only and in criminal proceedings for certain either way offences. Sections 137 and 138 are not contained in Chapter 2 of Part 11 of the 2003 Act (which concerns hearsay evidence) but, rather, are contained in Chapter 3 of Part 11 (Miscellaneous and Supplemental). The provisions are dealt with in this book, however, because, it is submitted, their effect will be to create a new statutory exception to the hearsay rule.

It should be noted that the operation of section 137 of the 2003 Act will not prejudice the admissibility of a video recording which would be admissible in evidence other than under that section.[380] Thus, for example, the video recorded evidence in chief of an eligible witness may be admissible under the special measures regime created by Part II of the Youth Justice and Criminal Evidence Act 1999 (see 2.4.2.6 below). Equally, a video recording may be admissible in evidence under some other exception to the hearsay rule which the 2003 Act will create, retain or preserve, for example, under section 116 or 117 of the 2003 Act (see, respectively, 2.2.1 and 2.2.2 above) or, (perhaps if it forms part of the res gestae, under section 118 thereof (see 2.3.2.7 below).

Sections 137 and 138 of the 2003 Act provide as follows.

> "137 Evidence by video recording
>
> (1)   This section applies where–
>
>> (a)   a person is called as a witness in proceedings for an offence triable only on indictment, or for a prescribed offence triable either way,
>>
>> (b)   the person claims to have witnessed (whether visually or in any other way)–
>>
>>> (i)   events alleged by the prosecution to include conduct constituting the offence or part of the offence, or
>>>
>>> (ii)   events closely connected with such events,
>>
>> (c)   he has previously given an account of the events in question (whether in response to questions asked or otherwise),

---

380 *See section 138(5).*

(d) the account was given at a time when those events were fresh in the person's memory (or would have been, assuming the truth of the claim mentioned in paragraph (b)),

(e) a video recording was made of the account,

(f) the court has made a direction that the recording should be admitted as evidence in chief of the witness, and the direction has not been rescinded, and

(g) the recording is played in the proceedings in accordance with the direction.

(2) If, or to the extent that, the witness in his oral evidence in the proceedings asserts the truth of the statements made by him in the recorded account, they shall be treated as if made by him in that evidence.

(3) A direction under subsection (1)(f)–

   (a) may not be made in relation to a recorded account given by the defendant;

   (b) may be made only if it appears to the court that–

      (i) the witness's recollection of the events in question is likely to have been significantly better when he gave the recorded account than it will be when he gives oral evidence in the proceedings, and

      (ii) it is in the interests of justice for the recording to be admitted, having regard in particular to the matters mentioned in subsection (4).

(4) Those matters are–

   (a) the interval between the time of the events in question and the time when the recorded account was made;

   (b) any other factors that might affect the reliability of what the witness said in that account;

   (c) the quality of the recording;

   (d) any views of the witness as to whether his evidence in chief should be given orally or by means of the recording.

(5) For the purposes of subsection (2) it does not matter if the statements in the recorded account were not made on oath.

(6) In this section "prescribed" means of a description specified in an order made by the Secretary of State.

138 Video evidence: further provisions

(1) Where a video recording is admitted under section 137, the witness may not give evidence in chief otherwise than by means of the recording as to any matter which, in the opinion of the court, has been dealt with adequately in the recorded account.

(2) The reference in subsection (1)(f) of section 137 to the admission of a recording includes a reference to the admission of part of the recording; and references in that section and this one to the video recording or to the witness's recorded account shall, where appropriate, be read accordingly.

(3) In considering whether any part of a recording should be not admitted under section 137, the court must consider—

   (a) whether admitting that part would carry a risk of prejudice to the defendant, and

   (b) if so, whether the interests of justice nevertheless require it to be admitted in view of the desirability of showing the whole, or substantially the whole, of the recorded interview.

(4) A court may not make a direction under section 137(1)(f) in relation to any proceedings unless—

   (a) the Secretary of State has notified the court that arrangements can be made, in the area in which it appears to the court that the proceedings will take place, for implementing directions under that section, and

   (b) the notice has not been withdrawn.

(5) Nothing in section 137 affects the admissibility of any video recording which would be admissible apart from that section."

The rationale underlying what is now section 137 of the 2003 Act (and was then clause 121 of the Criminal Justice Bill) was expressed in Standing Committee B by Mr Michael Wills, the Parliamentary Under-Secretary of State for the Home Department, as follows.[381]

> "We want to rebalance the system in the interests of victims and witnesses, and the provisions are key to helping witnesses give the best evidence. It is crucial to ensure that rules of evidence do not artificially prevent the true and full story from being presented in court, and the provisions in chapter 3 will make it much easier for witnesses to give their evidence.

---

381 *Hansard (Commons) 28 January 2003, Column 672.*

Clause 121 will allow a video-recorded statement to stand in place of the witness's main evidence in important cases... The main objectives of the reforms are to improve the position of witnesses giving evidence and to ensure that courts have the best evidence available to them and that rules of evidence assist in providing full and accurate accounts."

Section 137 will apply in the context of criminal proceedings either in respect of an offence triable only on indictment or in respect of an either way offence which has been prescribed by the Home Secretary.[382] Essentially, the section will empower the court to direct[383] that a video recording[384] (or a part of a video recording[385]) of a contemporaneous account given by a person other than the defendant[386] who is called as a witness in the proceedings and who claims (whether visually or otherwise) either to have witnessed events which allegedly include conduct which constitutes the relevant offence (or constitutes part of the relevant offence) or to have witnessed events closely connected to such events, be admitted as the witness' evidence in chief.[387] Where such a recording is played in the proceedings in accordance with the court's direction then, to the extent to which the witness asserts the truth of the video recorded statements whilst giving oral evidence in the proceedings, the effect of section 137(2) will be that the video recorded statements (whether or not they were made on oath[388]) will be treated as if they were made by the witness in the course of his oral evidence. Where such a recording is admitted in evidence under section 137, the witness will not be permitted to give evidence in chief other than via the video recording in relation to any matter which, in the court's opinion, has been adequately dealt with in the video recorded account.[389]

The court will only be entitled to direct that such a video recording (or part thereof[390]) be admitted as a witness' evidence in chief if it appears both that the witness' recollection of the relevant events is likely to have been significantly better when he gave the video recorded account than it will be when he testifies and that the admission in evidence of the video recording is in the interests of justice.[391]

In relation to the issue of whether the witness' recollection of the events is likely to have been substantially better on the former occasion, Mr Michael Wills, the Parliamentary Under-Secretary of State for the Home Department, had this to say.[392]

---

382 See section 137(1)(a), (6).

383 *The court may not so direct unless the Home Secretary has notified the court that arrangements can be made for implementing such directions in the area in which it appears that the proceedings will take place (section 138(4)(a)).*

384 *"video recording" being defined, for this purpose (by section 140), as:*
"...any recording, on any medium, from which a moving image may by any means be produced, and includes the accompanying soundtrack."

385 See section 138(2).

386 *Section 137(3)(a). The defendant, for this purpose, is a person who is charged with an offence in the proceedings (see section 140).*

387 See section 137(1)(b)-(f).

388 See section 137(5).

389 *Section 138(1).*

390 See section 138(2).

391 *Section 137(3).*

392 *Hansard (Commons) 28 January 2003, Column 672.*

"Upon clause 121(3), a video recording of an interview with a witness can replace the witness's main evidence if it appears to the court that his recollection of events is likely to have been better when the recording was made than by the time of the trial. That is intended to be no more than a common-sense-test—one that the vast majority of witnesses would meet, unless there were particularly traumatic or unusual circumstances surrounding the recording of the statement."

In determining whether the admission in evidence of the video recording (or of part thereof[393]) is in the interests of justice, section 137(3)(b)(ii) will require the court to have particular regard to:

"(a) the interval between the time of the events in question and the time when the recorded account was made;

(b) any other factors that might affect the reliability of what the witness said in that account;

(c) the quality of the recording;

(d) any views of the witness as to whether his evidence in chief should be given orally or by means of the recording."[394]

Finally, it should be noted that when the court is considering whether part of a video recording should not be admitted, section 138(3) will require the court to consider:

"(a) whether admitting that part would carry a risk of prejudice to the defendant, and

(b) if so, whether the interests of justice nevertheless require it to be admitted in view of the desirability of showing the whole, or substantially the whole, of the recorded interview."

Mr Michael Wills, the Parliamentary Under-Secretary of State for the Home Department, explained the position as follows.[395]

"Consider the following scenario: admitting part of a statement might result in a slight or marginal risk of prejudicing the defendant; however, that may be substantially outweighed in the interests of justice by showing the video recorded evidence in full. If one part was excluded it might be harder for the jury to understand other parts of the recording. There are a great many circumstances in which that might happen. It may be important in understanding how a witness id developing the evidence. There are times when that slight risk of prejudice is substantially outweighed."

---

393 *See section 138(2).*
394 *These matters are mentioned in section 137(4).*

395 *Hansard (Commons) 28 January 2003, Column 680.*

2.3 Common law exceptions to the hearsay rule which will be preserved by the 2003 Act

The Criminal Justice Act 2003 will not abolish all of the common law exceptions to the hearsay rule which exist at the time when it comes into force. Rather, whilst section 118(2) of the 2003 Act will abolish some common law hearsay exceptions, section 118(1) will preserve a number of others.

In relation to those common law hearsay exceptions which do not fall within the ambit of section 118(1), section 118(2) provides that:

> "(2) With the exception of the rules preserved by this section, the common law rules governing the admissibility of hearsay evidence in criminal proceedings are abolished."

Where a hearsay statement falls outside the ambit of the common law hearsay exceptions which section 118(1) will preserve, the statement may still be admissible under one or more of the statutory exceptions to the hearsay rule which the 2003 Act will create or retain. For example, where a statement does not form part of the res gestae because at the time of its making its maker's mind would not have been dominated by an exciting event, the statement may, for example, still be admissible under section 116 of the 2003 Act (which was considered at 2.2.1 above) or under the "safety valve" inclusionary discretion provided by section 114(1)(d) (considered at 2.6 below).

Of the common law exceptions to the hearsay rule which will not be preserved (i.e. which will be abolished) by the 2003 Act, the most famous is undoubtedly the "dying declaration" (essentially encompassing statements made by homicide victims before their death concerning the cause thereof).[396] The other common law exceptions to the hearsay rule which will be abolished in the context of criminal proceedings when the relevant provisions of the 2003 Act come into force appear to include those relating to: statements which were against their now deceased maker's pecuniary or proprietary interest at the time of their making[397]; statements which were made by their now deceased maker in compliance with his duty to record or report his conduct; statements made by persons now deceased concerning the contents of their wills[398]; and statements made by witnesses in earlier proceedings who are now either dead or too ill to attend the current proceedings.[399]

It should be noted, however, that the abolition of the abovementioned common law hearsay exceptions does not mean that the operation of the hearsay rule will now inherently exclude evidence which formerly fell within their ambit where such evidence is of relevance to an issue in criminal proceedings. Rather, evidence

---

396 *See, for example, R v Jenkins (1869) LR 1 CCR 187.*

397 *See, for example, R v Rogers [1995] 1 Cr App R 374.*

398 *See, for example, Sugden v Lord St Leonards (1876) 1 PD 154.*

399 *See, for example, R v Thompson [1982] 1 QB 647.*

which formerly fell within the ambit of an abolished common law hearsay exception will potentially be admissible in criminal proceedings under one or more of the statutory exceptions to the hearsay rule which will be created or retained by the 2003 Act. Thus, for example, a dying declaration might in future be admissible under section 116 of the 2003 Act (which was considered at 2.2.1 above), under section 117 of that Act (which was considered at 2.2.2 above), or under the "safety valve" inclusionary discretion provided by section 114(1)(d) (considered at 2.6 below).

Finally, it should be noted that several of the common law hearsay exceptions which will be preserved by the 2003 Act in the context of criminal proceedings (such as, for example, the hearsay exceptions relating to statements which form part of the res gestae) have already been abolished in the civil context. The remaining common law hearsay exceptions in the civil context are those which are preserved by section 7 of the Civil Evidence Act 1995. In practice, in relation to the admissibility of hearsay evidence in civil proceedings, evidence which would have fallen within a common law hearsay exception which has been abolished in the civil context will either fall within the ambit of hearsay exception created by section 1 of the 1995 Act or, where applicable, will fall within the ambit of a hearsay exception created by some other statutory provision.

2.3.1 Other provisions of the 2003 Act which apply to preserved common law hearsay exceptions

Apart from section 118(1) of the 2003 Act itself (the provision by virtue of the operation of which the remaining common law exceptions will be preserved, which is examined below), several other provisions of the 2003 Act will, inter alia, affect the future operation of the common law hearsay exceptions which section 118(1) will preserve.

First, it is submitted that the definitions of "statement" and of "matter stated" in section 115 of the 2003 Act appear to be applicable in the context of the hearsay exceptions preserved by section 118(1) 4 (*res gestae*), 118(1) 6 (admissions by agents etc) and 118(1) 7 (common enterprise), as all three of these provisions contain both of these terms. To the extent (if at all) that the application of the section 115 definitions is arguably capable of altering the nature of the respective common law hearsay exceptions, it should be noted that section 118 of the 2003 Act (unlike section 7 of the Civil Evidence Act 1995[400]) does not contain a provision to the effect that the words used to describe the preserved common law hearsay exceptions are only intended to describe the relevant rules and are not intended to alter them.

It is submitted that the potential effect of the section 115(2) definition of "statement" in this context will merely be to make clear (if, indeed, that was not

---

400 *See Civil Evidence Act 1995, section 7(4).*

already the case at common law) that a statement may fall within the ambit of any of the relevant preserved common law exceptions regardless of the means by which the relevant representation of fact was made. In relation to the potential significance of the section 115(3) definition of "matter stated" in this context, it is submitted that a statement which was not made either for the purpose of causing a person to believe the relevant matter or for that of causing a person to act or a machine to operate on the basis that the relevant matter was as stated will not be capable of falling within the ambit of any of the relevant preserved common law hearsay exceptions. Since, once the hearsay provisions of the 2003 Act are in force, such a statement will not fall within the ambit of the hearsay rule itself, however, the fact that it does not fall within the ambit of a hearsay exception does not appear to be a matter which is of any practical significance.

Secondly, it appears that, when Chapter 2 of Part 11 of the 2003 Act is in force, a hearsay statement which falls within the ambit of a preserved common law exception to the hearsay rule may prove or be proved by another hearsay statement, provided that the requirements of section 121 of the 2003 Act, which relate to the admissibility of multiple hearsay (and which are considered at 2.7.1 below) are satisfied.

Thirdly, it appears that section 124 of the 2003 Act, which concerns the credibility of the maker of a hearsay statement who is not called to give oral evidence in criminal proceedings in relation to its subject matter, will be applicable where hearsay evidence is admitted under a common law exception to the hearsay rule which section 118(1) preserves. The nature and effect of section 124 is considered at 2.7.3 below.

Fourthly, it appears that, when Chapter 2 of Part 11 of the 2003 Act is in force, the court's obligations under section 125 of the 2003 Act ("stopping the case where evidence is unconvincing") may arise where hearsay evidence is admitted in criminal proceedings under a preserved common law exception to the hearsay rule. The nature and effect of section 125 is considered at 2.7.4 below.

Finally, it seems that the courts discretion, created or preserved by section 126 of the 2003 Act, to exclude hearsay evidence which is otherwise admissible in criminal proceedings, is applicable to hearsay evidence which is tendered under a preserved common law exception to the hearsay rule. The nature and effect of section 126 is considered at 2.7.5 below.

2.3.2 The common law exceptions which the Act will preserve

As was seen at 2.3 above, whilst section 118(2) of the 2003 Act will abolish some of those exceptions to the hearsay rule which are currently recognised by the common law, section 118(1) of that Act will preserve a number of others. Section 118 of the 2003 Act provides as follows.

"(1) The following rules of law are preserved.

Public information etc

1   Any rule of law under which in criminal proceedings–

    (a)   published works dealing with matters of a public nature (such as histories, scientific works, dictionaries and maps) are admissible as evidence of facts of a public nature stated in them,

    (b)   public documents (such as public registers, and returns made under public authority with respect to matters of public interest) are admissible as evidence of facts stated in them,

    (c)   records (such as the records of certain courts, treaties, Crown grants, pardons and commissions) are admissible as evidence of facts stated in them, or

    (d)   evidence relating to a person's age or date or place of birth may be given by a person without personal knowledge of the matter.

Reputation as to character

2   Any rule of law under which in criminal proceedings evidence of a person's reputation is admissible for the purpose of proving his good or bad character.

Note

The rule is preserved only so far as it allows the court to treat such evidence as proving the matter concerned.

Reputation or family tradition

3   Any rule of law under which in criminal proceedings evidence of reputation or family tradition is admissible for the purpose of proving or disproving–

    (a)   pedigree or the existence of a marriage,

    (b)   the existence of any public or general right, or

    (c)   the identity of any person or thing.

Note

The rule is preserved only so far as it allows the court to treat such evidence as proving or disproving the matter concerned.

Res gestae

4   Any rule of law under which in criminal proceedings a statement is admissible as evidence of any matter stated if—

    (a)   the statement was made by a person so emotionally overpowered by an event that the possibility of concoction or distortion can be disregarded,

(b)   the statement accompanied an act which can be properly evaluated as evidence only if considered in conjunction with the statement, or

(c)   the statement relates to a physical sensation or a mental state (such as intention or emotion).

Confessions etc

5   Any rule of law relating to the admissibility of confessions or mixed statements in criminal proceedings.

Admissions by agents etc

6   Any rule of law under which in criminal proceedings—

(a)   an admission made by an agent of a defendant is admissible against the defendant as evidence of any matter stated, or

(b)   a statement made by a person to whom a defendant refers a person for information is admissible against the defendant as evidence of any matter stated.

Common enterprise

7   Any rule of law under which in criminal proceedings a statement made by a party to a common enterprise is admissible against another party to the enterprise as evidence of any matter stated.

Expert evidence

8   Any rule of law under which in criminal proceedings an expert witness may draw on the body of expertise relevant to his field.

(2)   With the exception of the rules preserved by this section, the common law rules governing the admissibility of hearsay evidence in criminal proceedings are abolished."

The nature of those common law exceptions to the hearsay rule which section 118(1) will preserve will now be considered.

2.3.2.1 Published works dealing with matters of a public nature

Section 118(1) 1 (a) will preserve:

"1   Any rule of law under which in criminal proceedings—

(a)   published works dealing with matters of a public nature (such as histories, scientific works, dictionaries and maps) are admissible as evidence of facts of a public nature stated in them..."

The Law Commission[401] recommended the preservation of this common law exception to the hearsay rule because it fulfils a useful function and, apparently, does not cause any difficulties. Thus, for example, when the court is required to determine a fact of a public nature it is, and will remain, entitled, where appropriate, to refer to an historical work.[402]

It should be noted that this common law exception to the hearsay rule is preserved in the context of civil proceedings by section 7(2)(a) of the Civil Evidence Act 1995.

2.3.2.2 Public documents

Section 118(1) 1 (b) will preserve:

> "1 Any rule of law under which in criminal proceedings
>
>   (b) public documents (such as public registers, and returns made under public authority with respect to matters of public interest) are admissible as evidence of facts stated in them..."

The Law Commission[403] recommended the preservation of this common law exception to the hearsay rule because it fulfils a useful function and, apparently, does not cause any difficulties.

Essentially, under this common law hearsay exception, statements contained in public documents (i.e. documents made and preserved for public use and to which the public have access, such as company returns[404]) are admissible if the statements were recorded by a public official (such as an officer of a company or an official in the Companies Registry[405]) acting under a duty to enquire and record.[406] The exception is applicable even though one official (for example. an official of a company) has the duty to enquire and record and a different official (for example an official of the Registry of Companies) has the duty to preserve the document for public inspection.[407] In order to be admissible, the entry need not be made contemporaneously with the occurrence of the events which it records, though lack of contemporaneity may affect the weight of the hearsay evidence.[408] The exception does not apply, however, to documents which are not intended to be preserved indefinitely but, rather, are merely of temporary effect.[409]

It should be noted that a variety of statutory provisions provide for the proof of public documents. Examination of these provisions falls outside the scope of the

---

401 See *"Evidence in Criminal Proceedings: Hearsay and Related Topics"*, Law Com No 245, at paragraph 8.132.
402 See, for example, *Read v Bishop of Lincoln* [1892] AC 644.
403 See *"Evidence in Criminal Proceedings: Hearsay and Related Topics"*, Law Com No 245, at paragraph 8.132.

404 See *R v Halpin* [1975] QB 907; *Sturla v Freccia* (1880) 5 App Cas 623.
405 See *R v Halpin* [1975] QB 907.
406 *R v Halpin* [1975] QB 907.
407 *R v Halpin* [1975] QB 907.
408 *R v Halpin* [1975] QB 907.
409 *White v Taylor* [1969] 1 Ch 150.

present work. For consideration of examples thereof see May, Criminal Evidence, 4th Ed, Sweet and Maxwell 1999 at 3-21-3-23.

It should also be noted that this common law exception to the hearsay rule is preserved in the context of civil proceedings by section 7(2)(b) of the Civil Evidence Act 1995.

2.3.2.3 Records

Section 118(1) 1 (c) will preserve:

> "1 Any rule of law under which in criminal proceedings—...
>
> (c) records (such as the records of certain courts, treaties, Crown grants, pardons and commissions) are admissible as evidence of facts stated in them..."

The Law Commission[410] recommended the preservation of this common law exception to the hearsay rule because it fulfils a useful function and, apparently, does not cause any difficulties. For consideration of related statutory provisions, examination of which falls outside the scope of the present work, see Phipson on Evidence, 15th ed, Sweet and Maxwell, 2000 at 41–42 (and see, also, 41–39).

It should be noted that this common law exception to the hearsay rule is preserved in the context of civil proceedings by section 7(2)(c) of the Civil Evidence Act 1995.

2.3.2.4 Age, date or place of birth

Section 118(1) 1 (d) will preserve:

> "1 Any rule of law under which in criminal proceedings—...
>
> (d) evidence relating to a person's age or date or place of birth may be given by a person without personal knowledge of the matter."

Whilst the Law Commission[411] recommended the preservation of this common law exception to the hearsay rule because it fulfils a useful function and, apparently, does not cause any difficulties, it is submitted that examination of the authorities does not reveal any established general principle of the law of evidence under which such evidence is admissible. Rather, authorities may be identified in support of the proposition that even a witness' evidence of his own age, date and place of birth, may be rendered inadmissible by virtue of the operation of the hearsay rule.[412]

---

410 See *"Evidence in Criminal Proceedings: Hearsay and Related Topics"*, *Law Com No 245*, at paragraph 8.132.

411 See *"Evidence in Criminal Proceedings: Hearsay and Related Topics"*, *Law Com No 245*, at

paragraph 8.132.

412 *See, for example, R v Inhabitants of Erith (1807) 8 East 539 and R v Inhabitants of Rishworth (1842) 2 QB 476.*

Conversely, however, examination of the authorities also suggests that, in practice, the courts do appear to be prepared to admit evidence of a latently hearsay nature for the purpose of proving the identity of a person named in a birth certificate.[413] Indeed, the authors of Cross and Tapper on Evidence have previously suggested that such evidence should be classified as received under a hearsay exception.[414]

Whether or not the effect of section 118(1) 1 (d) is that such evidence will now be formally classified by the courts in the way that the authors of Cross and Tapper suggested, it is clear that evidence of a person's age, date or place of birth may, nevertheless, be admissible under one or more of the statutory exceptions to the hearsay rule which the 2003 Act will create or retain.

Finally, it should be noted that this common law exception to the hearsay rule was not preserved in the context of civil proceedings by the Civil Evidence Act 1995, nor was it previously preserved by the Civil Evidence Act 1968. In the civil context, however, the effect of section 1 of the Civil Evidence Act 1995 is that the operation of the hearsay rule would not prevent the admission of such evidence.

2.3.2.5 Reputation as evidence of good or bad character

Section 118(1) 2 of the 2003 Act will preserve:

> "2   Any rule of law under which in criminal proceedings evidence of a
> person's reputation is admissible for the purpose of proving his good or
> bad character.
>
> *Note*
>
> The rule is preserved only so far as it allows the court to treat such
> evidence as proving the matter concerned."

The Law Commission in their report "Evidence in Criminal Proceedings: Hearsay and Related Topics"[415] recommended the preservation of this common law exception to the hearsay rule because it fulfils a useful function and, apparently, does not cause any difficulties. Conversely, in their subsequent report "Evidence of Bad Character in Criminal Proceedings[416], the Law Commission, suggesting that the former justification for its retention was at most weakly applicable to this exception and, doubting that the exception was much relied on in practice, recommended its abolition to the extent to which it renders evidence of bad character admissible in criminal proceedings. Section 99 of the 2003 Act provides, however, that:

> "(1)   The common law rules governing the admissibility of evidence of bad
> character in criminal proceedings are abolished.

---

413 *See, for example, R v Weaver (1873) LR 2 CCR
    85 and R v Bellis (1911) 6 Cr App R 283.*
414 *9th ed, Butterworhhs ,1999 at p. 597.*

415 *Law Com No 245, at paragraph 8.132.*
416 *Law Com No 273, at paragraphs 4.79 and 4.84.*

(2) Subsection (1) is subject to section 118(1) in so far as it preserves the rule under which in criminal proceedings a person's reputation is admissible for the purposes of proving his bad character."

Thus, it is the recommendation of the earlier of the two Law Commission reports, namely that the common law hearsay exception be preserved in its entirety, which will in fact be implemented by the 2003 Act. It should be noted that this common law exception to the hearsay rule is also preserved in the context of civil proceedings by section 7(3)(a) of the Civil Evidence Act 1995.

Whilst this common law rule will be preserved by the 2003 Act, section 118(1) 2 makes clear that "The rule is preserved only so far as it allows the court to treat such evidence as proving the matter concerned." The Explanatory Notes to the Criminal Justice Bill[417] provide the following guidance in relation to the significance of this preserved common law rule in the context of the Bad Character provisions of Chapter 1 of Part 11 of that Act.

"This common law rule is preserved as a category of admissible hearsay in section 118(1). However the admissibility of a person's bad character, in circumstances where it was being proved by reputation, would fall to be determined under this part of the Act."

Thus, whilst evidence of reputation will continue to be admissible for the purpose of proving the accused's good or bad character when Part 11 of the 2003 Act is in force[418], the nature of those circumstances in which evidence of the accused's bad character will be admissible in criminal proceedings once Part 11 is in force will be governed by the provisions of Chapter 1 of Part 11 (which fall outside the scope of this book).

Evidence of the accused's good character will, presumably, continue to be admissible in criminal proceedings under the common law principles which have long governed its admissibility[419] (and which also fall outside the scope of this book).

2.3.2.6 Reputation or family tradition as evidence of pedigree etc

Section 118(1) 3 of the 2003 Act will preserve:

"3 Any rule of law under which in criminal proceedings evidence of reputation or family tradition is admissible for the purpose of proving or disproving–

(a) pedigree or the existence of a marriage,

(b) the existence of any public or general right, or

---

417 *See paragraph 358.*
418 *See R v Rowton (1865) Le & CA 520; R v Redgrave (1981) 74 Cr App R 10.*

419 *See: R v Rowton (1865) Le & CA 520; R v Redgrave (1981) 74 Cr App R 10.*

(c) the identity of any person or thing.

Note

The rule is preserved only so far as it allows the court to treat such evidence as proving or disproving the matter concerned."

The Law Commission[420] recommended the preservation of the common law exceptions to the hearsay rule which section 118(1) 3 concerns because they fulfil useful functions and, apparently, do not cause any difficulties. The relevant hearsay exceptions are preserved in the context of civil proceedings by section 7(3)(b) of the Civil Evidence Act 1995.

In relation to evidence of pedigree, the position is, essentially. that where questions of pedigree (such as the legitimacy of a child[421]) are in issue[422], statements made by blood relatives[423] or their spouses[424], since deceased, before the relevant question became disputed[425] are admissible as evidence of pedigree.[426] This, it appears, is so even if the person who made the statement did not have personal knowledge of the facts which he stated.[427]

Where the existence of a public right (for example, a public highway[428]) or that of a general right (for example, the boundaries or customs of a district[429]) is in issue, the position, essentially, is that a statement concerning the right's existence[430] which was made by a person since deceased before the existence of the right became disputed[431] is admissible as evidence of the existence of the right. The exception does not apply to statements concerning the existence of private rights[432] unless either the private and public rights equate[433] or the question before the court is whether the relevant right is public or private.[434] Moreover, a statement is only admissible as evidence of the existence of a general right if its maker had an appropriate connection with the relevant locality.[435]

Finally, an example of the admission of evidence of reputation to identify a person as the subject of a libel is provided by the admission of evidence of statements

---

420 See "Evidence in Criminal Proceedings: Hearsay and Related Topics", Law Com No 245, at paragraph 8.132.
421 See, for example, Re Turner (1885) 29 Ch D 985.
422 Such statements are not admissible under this exception where pedigree is not at issue in the proceedings (see Haines v Guthrie (1884) 13 QBD 818).
423 See: Re Jenion, Jenion v Wynne [1952] CH 454; Johnson v Lawson (1824) 2 Bing 86..
424 See Vowles v Young (1806) 13 Ves 140.
425 Butler v Mountgarret (1859) 7 HL Cas 633.
426 Sturla v Freccia (1880) 5 App Cas 623.
427 See Doe d. Banning v Griffin (1812) 15 East 293.
428 See Crease v Barrett (1835) 1 CM & R 919.

429 See Crease v Barrett (1835) 1 CM & R 919; Nicholls v Parker (1805) 14 East 331n.
430 If the statement does not concern the right's reputed existence , it will not be admissible under this exception (see Attorney-General v Horner (No 2) [1913] 2 Ch 140) and this will be so even though the statement provides evidence of facts from which the existence or non-existence of the right might be inferred (see Mercer v Denne [1905] 2 Ch 538).
431 See Moseley v Davies (1822) 11 Price 162.
432 See White v Taylor [1969] 1 Ch 150.
433 For example, where private and public boundaries follow the same boundary lines (see Thomas v Jenkins (1837) 6 A &E 525).
434 R v Bliss (1837) 7 A & E 550.
435 See Crease v Barrett (1835) 1 CM & R 919.

made at a public meeting by persons identifying the plaintiff as the subject of the alleged libel.[436]

It should be noted in relation to the operation of the hearsay exceptions which will be preserved by section 118(1) 3 that where the common law requirements of the relevant exception are not satisfied in relation to a specific hearsay statement, hearsay evidence may still be admissible under one or more of the statutory hearsay exceptions that the 2003 Act will create or retain.

2.3.2.7 Statements which form part of the res gestae

Section 118(1) 4 of the 2003 Act will preserve:

> "*Res gestae*
>
> 4   Any rule of law under which in criminal proceedings a statement is admissible as evidence of any matter stated if—
>
> (a)   the statement was made by a person so emotionally overpowered by an event that the possibility of concoction or distortion can be disregarded,
>
> (b)   the statement accompanied an act which can be properly evaluated as evidence only if considered in conjunction with the statement, or
>
> (c)   the statement relates to a physical sensation or a mental state (such as intention or emotion)."

Section 118(1) 4 (a)–(c) will preserve four of the common law exceptions to the hearsay rule under which hearsay evidence is admissible in criminal proceedings because it forms part of the "*res gestae*".

Essentially, statements are said to form part of the "*res gestae*" if they form part of the transaction or event with which the court is concerned.[437] If such statements were not admissible in evidence, there might be circumstances in which a jury could not properly understand the events to which the evidence before them related.[438]

Where a statement which forms part of the res gestae is not tendered as evidence of the truth of a matter stated, the statement, not falling within the ambit of the hearsay rule, may be admissible as original evidence.[439] Where a statement which forms part of the res gestae is tendered as evidence of the truth of a matter stated, the statement, whilst a hearsay statement, is admissible because it falls within the ambit of a common law exception to the hearsay rule.

---

436 *Jozwiak v Sadek [1954] 1 All ER 3.*
437 *See Sir Frederick Pollock at [1931] 2 Ch 112 at p.120.*
438 *Teper v R [1952] AC 480.*
439 *In relation to the admissibility of such evidence see 1.5, above.*

It is submitted that those hearsay statements which may be admissible in evidence because they form part of the *res gestae* fall within either of two main categories.[440] First, statements made by persons who were emotionally overpowered by unusual, startling or dramatic events when they made them, namely, the hearsay exception which section 118(1) 4 (a) of the 2003 Act will preserve. Secondly, statements which relate to their makers' contemporaneous actions, contemporaneous physical sensations or contemporaneous mental states, namely, the hearsay exceptions which will be preserved by section 118(1) 4 (b)–(c).

The distinction between these two categories of hearsay exceptions is, it is submitted, that, in relation to the former category, the basis of admissibility is domination of the maker's mind by the unusual, startling or dramatic event such that the possibility of concoction or distortion of evidence can be ignored whereas, in relation to the latter category, the basis of admissibility is the contemporaneity of the making of the statement to, respectively, the existence of the relevant physical state or state of mind or the performance of the relevant acts.

In *R v Callender*[441], the Court of Appeal treated remoteness of possibility of concoction or distortion of evidence as forming the general test of admissibility to be applied in determining whether hearsay evidence was admissible under the *res gestae* doctrine. As is demonstrated at 2.3.2.7.1 to 2.3.2.7.3, below, however, examination of the authorities does not support this conclusion. Rather, it is submitted that the application of the remoteness of possibility of concoction or distortion test should properly be regarded as restricted to the context of determining the admissibility of statements under the hearsay exception which section 118(1) 4 (a) will preserve.

It should be noted that to the extent to which a hearsay statement does not satisfy the requirements of any of the hearsay exceptions which section 118(1) 4 of the 2003 Act will preserve, the statement may, nevertheless, be admissible under one or more of the statutory exceptions to the hearsay rule which the 2003 Act will create or retain. Conversely, where a hearsay statement is admissible in criminal proceedings under one or more of the common law hearsay exceptions which section 118(1) 4 will preserve, its admissibility will still be subject to the exercise of the exclusionary discretion which section 126 of the 2003 Act creates and preserves.[442]

The common law hearsay exceptions which section 118(1) 4 preserves in the criminal context have not been preserved in the context of civil proceedings, but statement which fall within their ambit are admissible in the civil context under the hearsay exception created by section 1 of the Civil Evidence Act 1995.

---

440 *There may be a further category, namely statements in furtherance of a common purpose, see 2.3.2.10 below.*

441 *[1998] Crim LR 337.*
442 *Section 126 is considered at 2.7.5 below.*

2.3.2.7.1 Statements made by persons emotionally overpowered by events

Section 118(1) 4 of the 2003 Act will preserve:

> "Any rule of law under which in criminal proceedings a statement is admissible as evidence of any matter stated if–
>
> (a) the statement was made by a person so emotionally overpowered by an event that the possibility of concoction or distortion can be disregarded..."

The Law Commission[443] were concerned that where the identity of the maker of a statement which falls within the ambit of this common law hearsay exception is not known he cannot be discredited by the party against whom the hearsay evidence is tendered. Following consultation, however, the Law Commission[444] appear to have accepted that in circumstances in which there is no possibility that the hearsay evidence was concocted or distorted (which, essentially, are the circumstances in which this hearsay exception operates), this concern is one which is of relatively little significance. The Law Commission[445] did recognise the possibility that the hearsay evidence of a person who made a statement which is admissible under this exception may have been mistaken, but believed that this possibility could be dealt with in closing speeches and summing up and that it would be strange if relevant evidence falling within the ambit of this common law hearsay exception was excluded. Thus, the Law Commission[446] recommended the preservation of this common law exception to the hearsay rule, which section 118(1) 4 (a) will preserve.

Essentially, a hearsay statement falls within the ambit of the hearsay exception which will be preserved by section 118(1) 4 (a) of the 2003 Act if it was made in close association with an unusual, startling or dramatic event (such as a violent attack) by a person whose thoughts were so dominated by the event that the trial judge can disregard the possibility that the person had concocted the statement or had deliberately distorted the facts.[447] The fact that the maker of a hearsay statement which falls within the ambit of this common law exception to the hearsay rule is available to be called as a witness does not render the hearsay evidence inadmissible.[448] Where the maker of the hearsay statement is available, however, the court may well find it necessary to exclude evidence which falls within the ambit of this hearsay exception in the exercise of its exclusionary discretion under section 78 of the Police and Criminal Evidence Act 1984 because,

---

443 See *"Evidence in Criminal Proceedings: Hearsay and Related Topics"*, *Law Com No 245*, at paragraph 8.119.

444 See *"Evidence in Criminal Proceedings: Hearsay and Related Topics"*, *Law Com No 245*, at paragraph 8.119.

445 See *"Evidence in Criminal Proceedings: Hearsay and Related Topics"*, *Law Com No 245*, at

paragraph 8.120

446 See *"Evidence in Criminal Proceedings: Hearsay and Related Topics"*, *Law Com No 245*, at paragraph 8.121.

447 See *R v Andrews* [1987] AC 281.

448 *Attorney General's Reference (No 1 of 2003)* [2003] 2 Cr App R 453.

otherwise, the defence would be deprived of the opportunity of cross-examining the maker of the hearsay statement.[449]

In determining whether the possibility that the maker of the statement concocted the statement or deliberately distorted the facts can be disregarded, the judge must consider both whether the event was sufficiently unusual, startling or dramatic to dominate the thoughts of the maker and whether, at the time when the statement was made, the maker's thoughts were still dominated by the event.[450] In particular, if, upon the facts of the case, there is evidence which gives rise to the possibility of deliberate concoction or distortion (such as evidence of bias against the accused on the part of the maker of the statement), the trial judge must consider whether, taking into account this evidence, he can still disregard the possibility that the maker had concocted the statement or had deliberately distorted the facts.[451] Similarly, if, upon the facts of the case, there is evidence which gives rise to the possibility of error on the part of the maker of the statement (such as the fact that he was drunk or had poor eyesight), the trial judge must consider whether, taking into account this evidence, he can disregard the possibility that the statement was erroneous.[452] Moreover, if the trial judge admits the hearsay evidence, he must, where appropriate, direct the jury to consider the possibility of error, concoction, distortion or exaggeration.[453]

If the trial judge admits the hearsay evidence he must direct the jury to the effect that: they must decide what was said and must be sure that the witnesses whose evidence is relied upon to prove the statement were not mistaken about what was said; they must be satisfied that the maker of the statement did not concoct the statement either to his advantage or to the accused's disadvantage(and, where there is evidence to raise the issue of malice or ill will, that the maker of the statement was not motivated thereby); and they must, where there are special features which relate to the possibility that a mistake was made, pay attention to those special features.[454] It appears, however, that the giving of a warning concerning the possibility of concoction or distortion by the maker of the statement will not be necessary in circumstances in which there is no realistic possibility of concoction or distortion.[455]

The fact that the unusual, startling or dramatic event took place cannot be proved merely by the content of the statement itself.[456] It appears, however, that the content of the statement may, in the context of other evidence to the same effect,

---

449 *Attorney General's Reference (No 1 of 2003) [2003] 2 Cr App R 453. Their Lordship's recognised that the fact that the maker of the hearsay statement could be called by the defence in such circumstances would not adequately compensate the defence for the lost opportunity to cross-examine the maker of the hearsay statement.*
450 *See R v Andrews [1987] AC 281.*
451 *See R v Andrews [1987] AC 281.*
452 *See R v Andrews [1987] AC 281.*
453 *R v Andrews [1987] AC 281; R v Nelson LTL 16/2/2000.*
454 *R v Andrews [1987] AC 281; R v Nelson LTL 16/2/2000.*
455 *Brown v The State [2003] UKPC 10.*
456 *Ratten v R [1972] AC 378.*

be taken into account when determining whether the unusual, startling or dramatic event did take place.[457]

Whilst the maker of the statement is often the victim of the relevant offence[458], it may be made by a third party who witnesses the exciting event[459] or even by the accused himself.[460] Moreover, whilst the unusual, startling or dramatic event may well be the commission of the offence itself, it appears that a statement made prior to the commission of the offence may still be admissible if made in circumstances in which its maker's mind was dominated by an unusual, startling or dramatic event.[461] If, however, an unusual, startling or dramatic event was not taking place at the time when the statement was made, the fact that one subsequently occurred will not render the statement admissible.[462]

Finally, it should be noted that where a hearsay statement fails to satisfy the requirements of the common law hearsay exception which will be preserved by section 118(1) 4 (a) of the 2003 Act, the statement may, nevertheless, be admissible under one or more of the statutory exceptions to the hearsay rule which the 2003 Act will create or retain.

2.3.2.7.2: Statements accompanying acts

Section 118(1) 4 (b) of the 2003 Act will preserve

> "Any rule of law under which in criminal proceedings a statement is admissible as evidence of any matter stated if...
>
> > (b) the statement accompanied an act which can be properly evaluated as evidence only if considered in conjunction with the statement...""

The Law Commission[463] recommended the preservation of this common law exception to the hearsay rule because:

> "We believe that there might be occasions when this exception is justified, and we are not aware of any injustice being caused by it. On balance we think it worth retaining."

Essentially, the effect of the common law exception to the hearsay rule which section 118(1) 4 (b) of the 2003 Act will preserve appears to be that that where a person performed an act, a contemporaneous statement made by that person explaining why he performed the act (for example, a statement whereby the person who makes it explains why he is giving money to another person at the time when

---

457 *Ratten v R [1972] AC 378.*

458 *As in R v Nye and Loan (1977) 66 Cr App R 252, R v Andrews [1987] AC 281 and R v Carnall [1995] Crim LR 944, all examined at 5.1.1 above.*

459 *See R v Fowkes Times, March 8th*

460 *R v Glover [1991] Crim LR 48.*

461 *See Ratten v R [1972] AC 378.*

462 *R v Newport [1998] Crim LR 581.*

463 *See "Evidence in Criminal Proceedings: Hearsay and Related Topics", Law Com No 245, at paragraph 8.124.*

he does so[464]), may, as an exception to the hearsay rule, be admissible to prove why the person so acted.[465] The statement will not be admissible, however, if the person who made it was not the person who performed the relevant act.[466] Moreover, in order for the statement to be admissible, the act must be relevant to a fact in issue.[467]

In relation to the requirement that the statement must be explanatory of the relevant act[468], it appears to be sufficient in practice to establish that the statement was so mixed up with the relevant act that it became part of the res gestae[469], to establish that that the statement reflects light upon the relevant act[470], to establish that the statement qualifies the relevant act[471] or at least to establish that the statement had a connection with the relevant act[472].

Finally, in relation to the requirement of contemporaneity, whilst statements explaining their maker's actions are only admissible if the making of the statement is contemporaneous with the performance of the act[473], whether statement and act are sufficiently contemporaneous is a question of fact and degree the determination of which in relation to the facts of a particular case will depend upon the relationship between the statement and the act; precise contemporaneity not being an essential prerequisite of the admissibility of hearsay evidence under this hearsay exception.[474] Indeed, it appears that statements made at various times during the continuance of a continuing act which lasts for weeks, months or years could potentially all be contemporaneous with the continuing act.[475]

2.3.2.7.3 Statements relating to physical sensations or to mental states

Section 118(1) 4 (c) of the 2003 Act will preserve:

> "Any rule of law under which in criminal proceedings a statement is admissible as evidence of any matter stated if...
>
> > (c) the statement relates to a physical sensation or a mental state (such as intention or emotion)."

Thus, section 118(1) 4 (c) will preserve two common law hearsay exceptions to the hearsay rule, namely that which renders admissible statements relating to their

---

464 See "Evidence in Criminal Proceedings: Hearsay and Related Topics", Law Com No 245, at paragraph 8.123.

465 See, for example: Rouch v Great Western Railway Co (1841) 1 QB 5; R v McCay [1990] 1 WLR 645.

466 See Howe v Malkin (1878) 40 LT 196.

467 See R v Bliss (1837) 7 A&E 550; R v Kearley [1992] 2 AC 228.

468 See Patterson J in R v Bliss (1837) 7 A&E 550 at p.556 and see, also, Lord Oliver of Aylmerton in R v Kearley [1992] 2 AC 228 at p. 272.

469 See Grove J in Howe v Malkin (1878) 40 LT 196 at p. 196 and see, also, R v McCay [1990] 1 WLR 645.

470 See Coltman J in Wright v Doe d. Tatham (1837) 7 Ad & E 313.

471 See Coltman J in Wright v Doe d. Tatham (1837) 7 Ad & E 313.

472 See Williams J in R v Bliss (1837) 7 A&E 550 at p.556.

473 See Peacock v. Harris (1836) 5 Ad & El 449.

474 See, for example, Rouch v Great Western Railway Co (1841) 1 QB 51.

475 See, for example, Rouch v Great Western Railway Co (1841) 1 QB 51.

makers' contemporaneous physical sensations and that which renders admissible statements relating to their makers' contemporaneous mental states.

The Law Commission[476], recognising that such evidence may be the best or even the only evidence of the declarant's physical sensations, recommended the retention of the former of these two common law exceptions to the hearsay rule because:

> "We believe that this exception serves a useful purpose and succeeds in giving part of the overall picture.[180]
>
> > 180 Thus in Conde (1867) 10 Cox CC 547, where the accused were charged with murdering a child by starving it, the prosecution was able to produce evidence concerning the child's complaints of hunger."

The Law Commission[477] recommended the retention of the latter of these two common law exceptions to the hearsay rule both in recognition of the impossibility[478] of proving the declarant's state of mind in any other way and because, unless the declarant has a motive to misrepresent the facts, statements which fall within the ambit of this hearsay exception are more likely to be true than to be false. In particular, the Law Commission[479] recognised that:

> "This exception has contemporary significance because it is often the only way in which a party can prove that a witness is too frightened to attend court – for example, by calling a police officer to say that the witness said that he or she was afraid."

In relation to the first of the two hearsay exceptions which section 118(1) 4 (c) will preserve, it should be noted that whilst a statement concerning its maker's physical sensations (for example of his hunger or of the pain in his head) may admitted under this common law hearsay exception as evidence of the sensations experienced thereby[480], such a statement is not admissible under this hearsay exception as evidence of the cause of the relevant sensations.[481]

Similarly, in relation to the second of the two hearsay exceptions which section 118(1) 4 (c) will preserve, whilst a statement concerning its maker's contemporaneous state of mind (for example of his knowledge, belief, intention or fear) may be admitted under this common law hearsay exception as evidence of

---

476 See "Evidence in Criminal Proceedings: Hearsay and Related Topics", Law Com No 245, at paragraphs 8.127 to 8.129.

477 See "Evidence in Criminal Proceedings: Hearsay and Related Topics", Law Com No 245, at paragraphs 8.125 to 8.126.

478 Whilst it is clearly not inherently impossible to prove the existence of a person's mental state at a particular in the absence of contemporaneous statements made by that person in relation thereto, there clearly may be circumstances in which it is difficult to do so and, moreover, there clearly may be circumstances in which such statements provide the best evidence thereof.

479 See "Evidence in Criminal Proceedings: Hearsay and Related Topics", Law Com No 245, at paragraph 8.126.

480 See Gilbey v Great Western Railway (1910) 102 LT 202; Amys v Barton [1912] 1 KB 40; R v Conde (1867) 10 Cox CC 547.

481 See Gilbey v Great Western Railway (1910) 102 LT 202; Amys v Barton [1912] 1 KB 40.

the existence of the relevant state of mind[482], such a statement is only admissible under this hearsay exception as evidence of the existence of the relevant state of mind and is not admissible under this hearsay exception as evidence of the truth of the matters which its maker knew or believed to be true.[483] There is, however, authority both for[484] and against[485] the proposition that a statement of intention to perform an act may be admissible not merely to prove its maker's state of mind but also to prove that its maker actually performed the intended act. The position remains unclear, but it is submitted that the view that such statements are admissible at common law merely as evidence of their maker's state of mind is to be preferred.

Whilst the common law requires that, in order to fall within the ambit of the hearsay exceptions which will be preserved by section 118(1) 4 (c) of the 2003 Act, the making of the hearsay statement concerning its maker's physical sensations or mental state must be contemporaneous with, respectively, the existence of the relevant physical sensation or that of the relevant mental state[486], in practice, the law does not appear to require precise contemporaneity between the making of the statement and the existence of the physical sensation or mental state[487] and, moreover, the question of contemporaneity is a question of fact and degree.[488] Thus, whilst statements concerning their maker's physical sensations are not admissible if the making of the statement and the experiencing of the sensations are not contemporaneous, it appears that, in practice, statements concerning sensations experienced hours or even days earlier may be admitted in appropriate circumstances.[489] Similarly, whilst statements concerning their maker's state of mind are not admissible where the making of the statement and the maker's possession of the relevant state of mind are not contemporaneous, it appears that, in practice, whether the making of the statement and the possession of the state of mind by the maker of the statement are held to be sufficiently contemporaneous will depend upon the specific facts of the particular case before the court.[490]

Finally, it should be noted that, in appropriate circumstances, a statement may be admissible as evidence of a person's state of mind not because it falls within the ambit of an exception to the hearsay rule but, rather, because it does not fall within the ambit of the hearsay rule at all. This may be so, for example, in circumstances in which a statement made by A in the presence of B is tendered as evidence of B's

---

482 *See: Neill v North Antrim Magistrates' Court [1992] 1 WLR 1228; Thomas v. Connell (1838) 4 M&W 267; R v Moghal (1977) 65 Cr App R 56.*

483 *See Thomas v. Connell (1838) 4 M&W 267.*

484 *See R v Buckley (1873) 13 Cox CC 293 and see also, R v Moghal (1977) 65 Cr App R 56.*

485 *See: R v Wainwright (1875) 13 Cox CC 171; R v Thomson [1912] 3 KB 19.*

486 *See, for example, R v Gloster (1888) 16 Cox 471.*

487 *See, for example: Aveson v Lord Kinnaird (1805) 6 East 188; R v Black (1922) 16 Cr App R 118.*

488 *See R v Moghal (1977) 65 Cr App R 56.*

489 *See Aveson v Lord Kinnaird (1805) 6 East 188 and see R v Black (1922) 16 Cr App R 118.*

490 *See, for example, R v Moghal (1977) 65 Cr App R 56 and R v Gilfoyle, [1996] 1 Cr App R 302.*

state of mind and the issue before the court is not whether the facts were as stated by A but, rather, is whether B believed that what A had said was true.[491]

2.3.2.8 Confessions and mixed statements

Section 118(1) 5 of the 2003 Act will preserve:

> "5   Any rule of law relating to the admissibility of confessions or mixed statements in criminal proceedings."

When the provisions of Chapter 2 of Part 11 of the 2003 Act are in force the admissibility of confessions and mixed statements in criminal proceedings will continue to be governed primarily by section 76 of the Police and Criminal Evidence Act 1984 (considered at 2.4.2.9 below) and will continue to be subject both to the exclusionary discretion conferred by section 78 of the 1984 Act and to the exclusionary discretion preserved by section 82(3) of that Act (which will both be preserved by section 126(2)(b) of the 2003 Act and which are both considered at 2.7.5.2 below). It should be noted, however, that whilst the statutory regime which the 1984 Act introduced superseded some of the common law rules which governed or concerned the admission and exclusion of confessions in criminal proceedings, other common law principles do continue to govern some aspects of the law related to the admission and exclusion thereof. The rules of law which regulate the admissibility of confessions and mixed statements in criminal proceedings, both at present and when the hearsay provisions of the 2003 Act are in force, are considered at 2.2.7 above and at 2.3.2.9 and 2.4.2.7, below. [The position in relation to wholly exculpatory statements was considered at 2.2.4.3, above.]

As has already been demonstrated, at 2.2.7 above, section 128 of the 2003 Act will replace the existing rules concerning the admissibility of a confession made by the accused as evidence for his co-accused but, otherwise, it appears that the provisions of the 2003 Act will not modify the existing regime concerning the admissibility of confessions. It is presumed that the purpose of section 118(1) 5 of the 2003 Act is to prevent the possibility that other provisions of the 2003 Act may be treated by the courts as having abolished various common law principles related to the admission or exclusion of confessions, the abolition of which was neither desired by the Law Commission nor intended by Parliament. Moreover, as was seen at 2.2.1.1. above, the affect of section 128(2) of the 2003 Act appears to be that a confession made by a defendant which is not admissible under section 76 of the 1984 Act will not be admissible under any of the other exceptions to the hearsay rule which the 2003 Act will create, preserve or retain except, potentially, under section 76A of the 1984 Act.

---

491 *See, for example, Subramaniam v Public Prosecutor [1956] 1 WLR 965, concerning the admissibility of statements made to the accused as evidence of his state of mind, the facts of which were considered at 1.5.1 above.*

Finally, it should be noted that, in the context of civil proceedings, section 7(1) of the Civil Evidence Act 1995 expressly abolished the common law hearsay exception relating to informal admissions, informal admissions now being admissible in civil proceedings under the general hearsay exception created by section 1 of the 1995 Act.

2.3.2.9 Admissions made by agents

Section 118(1) 6 of the 2003 Act will preserve:

> "6   Any rule of law under which in criminal proceedings–
>
> (a)   an admission made by an agent of a defendant is admissible against the defendant as evidence of any matter stated, or
>
> (b)   a statement made by a person to whom a defendant refers a person for information is admissible against the defendant as evidence of any matter stated."

The Law Commission in their report "Evidence in Criminal Proceedings: Hearsay and Related Topics"[492] recommended the preservation of the common law hearsay exception relating to informal admissions made by agents because it fulfils a useful function and, apparently, does not cause any difficulties.

In relation to the admissibility in criminal proceedings of admissions made by the accused's agent, the position at common law is, essentially, that if a party to criminal proceedings wishes to adduce such an admission in evidence, the party must prove that the agent made the admission whilst acting within the scope of his authority.[493] In the case of an admission made by the accused's counsel on behalf of his client, it appears that the court will assume that counsel was authorised to make the relevant admission.[494] In the case of an admission made in a letter by the accused's solicitor on behalf of the accused, however, it appears that the admission will only be admissible if the party who wishes to adduce the admission in evidence shows that it was written upon the client's instructions.[495]

An example of the admission at common law of a statement of the type referred to by section 118(1) 6 (b) is provided by the facts of *R v Mallory*.[496] In *Mallory* the Court for Consideration of Crown Cases Reserved held that a list itemising goods which the accused (who was charged with receiving stolen goods) had bought from the thief together with the prices that he had paid for the goods had properly been admitted in evidence. The list had been made out by the accused's wife acting under the accused's instructions and had been handed by her to the police in the

---

492 See "*Evidence in Criminal Proceedings: Hearsay and Related Topics*", Law Com No 245, at paragraph 8.132.

493 *R v Turner (1975) 61 Cr App R 67; R v Downer (1880) 14 Cox CC 486.*

494 *R v Turner (1975) 61 Cr App R 67.*

495 *R v Downer (1880) 14 Cox CC 486.*

496 *(1884) 13 QBD 33.*

accused's presence, the accused having previously told the police in answer to their questions that his wife would make out such a list.

It should be noted that where an admission made by the accused's agent does not fall within the ambit of the common law hearsay exception which section 118(1) 6 of the 2003 Act preserves it may be that the admission will still be admissible under one or more of the statutory exceptions to the hearsay rule which the 2003 Act will create or retain. Whilst the effect of section 128(2) of the Criminal Justice Act 2003 appears to be that a confession made by a defendant which is not admissible under section 76 of the Police and Criminal Evidence Act 1984[497] will not be admissible under any of the hearsay exceptions which the 2003 Act will create, preserve or retain except, potentially under section 76A of the 1984 Act[498], it is submitted that an admission which falls within the ambit of section 118(1) 6 will not fall within the ambit of section 128(2) for two reasons. First, because such an admission is not (adopting the words of section 128(2)) made "by a defendant" but, rather (adopting the words of section 118(1) 6 (a)), is "made by an agent". Secondly, because such an admission, not being "adverse to the person who made it" (i.e. not being adverse to the agent), is not a confession either for the purposes of section 128(2) of the 2003 Act or for those of section 76 of the 1984 Act.[499]

If these submissions are correct, it appears that there is no conflict between section 128(2) of the 2003 Act and the preservation of the common law rule preserved by section 118(1) 6 of that Act. Presumably, if circumstances arise in which it is alleged that a defendant gave his agent authority to make an admission on the defendant's behalf in consequence of oppression or something said or done to the defendant which was likely in the circumstances to have rendered any confession that the defendant might have made in consequence of the thing said or done unreliable, the court will deal with the admissibility of the admission in the exercise of its exclusionary discretion under section 78 of the 1984 Act.[500]

Finally, it should be noted that this common law hearsay exception was not preserved by the Civil Evidence Act 1995, but evidence which would formally have fallen within its ambit will now be admissible in the context of civil proceedings under the hearsay exception created by section 1 of the 1995 Act.

2.3.2.10 Statements made by parties to a common enterprise

Section 118(1) 7 of the 2003 Act will preserve:

> "7   Any rule of law under which in criminal proceedings a statement made by a party to a common enterprise is admissible against another party to the enterprise as evidence of any matter stated."

---

497 *Section 76 of the 1984 Act is considered at 2.2.4.9.2 below.*

498 *Section 76A was considered at 2.2.7.2 above.*

499 *See section 128(3) of the 2003 Act and section 82 (1) of the 1984 Act and see, also, Andrews and*

Hirst on Criminal Evidence, 4th Ed, Jordans, 2001 at p. 602.

500 *The nature of this discretion is considered at 2.7.5.2 below.*

The Law Commission recommended the retention of this common law exception to the hearsay rule.

> "8.131 The exception can be justified as a pragmatic one, as it might be hard to prove a conspiracy without it, and we would not seek to change the law about how a conspiracy may be proved; and so it is our view that the exception should be retained."

The basis of the exception to the hearsay rule[501] which section 118(1) 7 will preserve is, essentially, that statements made or acts performed by a person in furtherance of a common purpose (i.e. a conspiracy) may be admissible against all of the alleged conspirators as evidence of matters stated[502], and this is so even where the alleged conspirator who made the relevant statement or performed the relevant act is not charged in the proceedings.[503] Indeed, evidence of such statements or acts may be admitted under this rule even where the defendant(s) is/are not charged with conspiracy, provided that the offence(s) with which he/they is/are charged were committed in pursuance of the common purpose.[504]

It appears, however, that statements which were not made in furtherance of the common purpose but which, rather, merely amount to a narrative of past events which have already taken place, are not admissible under the abovementioned rule.[505] The same appears to be true of statements which were not made in furtherance of the common purpose but which, rather, were made for some other purpose, such as that of covering up an earlier mistake or irregularity.[506] Moreover, where one of the alleged conspirators was not initially a party to the conspiracy but joined it at a later date, statements or acts of other alleged conspirators prior to that date are admissible against the conspirator who joined late as evidence of the existence of the conspiracy but are not admissible against him as evidence that he was a party to the conspiracy.[507]

---

501 *Some writers regard hearsay statements which are admitted under this exception to the hearsay rule as admissible in evidence because they form part of the res gestae (see, for example, Andrews and Hirst on Criminal Evidence, 4th ed, 2001, Jordans at 20.26). Others regard the basis of this hearsay exception as being the admission of vicarious admission which, when made by an agent, may be admissible at common law against his principal (see, for example, Cross and Tapper on Evidence, 9th ed, Butterworths, 2000 at pp. 559–562 and see 2.3.2.9, above). Yet others regard such statements as admissible because they do not fall within the ambit of the hearsay rule (see, for example, Murphy on Evidence, 8th ed, Blackstone Press, 2003 at p. 263). For examples of the judicial treatment of the rule as a hearsay exception, see R v Murray [1997] 2 Cr App R 136, R v Jenkins [2003] Crim LR 107 and R v*
Williams [2002] EWCA Crim 2208. For apparent judicial recognition of the relationship between the rule and the res gestae doctrine see R v Jones [1997] 2 Cr App R 119.

502 *See, for example: R v Gray [1995] 2 Cr App R 100; R v Murray [1997] 2 Cr App R 136; R v Devenport [1996] 1 Cr App R 221.*

503 *See, for example, R v Jones [1997] 2 Cr App R 119.*

504 *See, for example, R v Murray [1997] 2 Cr App R 136 and R v Williams [2002] EWCA Crim 2208.*

505 *See R v Blake (1844) 6 QB 126, R v Devenport [1996] 1 Cr App R 221, R v Jones [1997] 2 Cr App R 119 and R v Ilyas [1996] Crim LR 810.*

506 *See R v Jenkins [2003] Crim LR 107.*

507 *See R v Governor of Pentonville Prison, ex parte Osman [1990] 1 WLR 277.*

Evidence of such a statement or act is not admissible against the other conspirators under the abovementioned rule unless there is independent evidence (i.e. evidence other than the statements or acts themselves) both of the existence of the conspiracy/common purpose and of the fact that the other alleged conspirator(s) was/were party to it.[508] Thus, if evidence of such statements or acts is admitted but no independent evidence of the existence of the conspiracy and of the fact that the other alleged conspirator(s) was/were party to it is adduced, it will be necessary to direct the jury to the effect that the evidence of the statements or acts is not evidence against the other alleged conspirators. Where evidence of such a statement or such an act is admitted and independent evidence of the existence of the conspiracy and of the fact that the other alleged conspirator(s) was/were party to it is adduced, it may still be necessary for the judge, in circumstances in which there is a danger that the jury might disbelieve the independent evidence, to warn the jury not to conclude that the defendant(s) is/are guilty purely upon the basis of the hearsay evidence.[509]

Finally, it should be noted that whilst evidence of statements or acts made or performed by A in pursuance of a common purpose is not admissible against B unless there is independent evidence that B was a party to the common purpose, it is not necessary for the independent evidence to prove all of the terms of the agreement between A and B. Thus, for example, where B was charged with conspiracy to supply cocaine, independent evidence of B's involvement in a conspiracy to supply cocaine was not required, independent evidence that B had been a party to a conspiracy with A to supply drugs including cannabis resin sufficing.[510]

Where the requirements of the common law exception to the hearsay rule which section 118(1) 7 of the 2003 Act will preserve are not satisfied, it is submitted that the relevant hearsay evidence may still be admissible under one or more of the statutory exceptions to the hearsay rule which the 2003 Act will create or retain.

2.3.2.11 Expert witnesses and the body of expertise relevant to their field

Section 118(1) 8 of the Criminal Justice Act 2003 will preserve:

"8   Any rule of law under which in criminal proceedings an expert witness may draw on the body of expertise relevant to his field."

The Law Commission[511] regarded the rule to which section 118(1) 8 refers as encompassing two common law hearsay exceptions, one relating to knowledge which forms part of an expert's professional expertise and the second relating to

---

508 *See, for example, R v Donat (1985) 82 Cr App R 173 and see, also, R v Murray [1997] 2 Cr App R 136 and R v Williams [2002] EWCA Crim 2208.*

509 *R v Jones [1997] 2 Cr App R 119; R v Williams [2002] EWCA Crim 2208*

510 *R v Smart [2002] EWCA Crim 772.*

511 *See "Evidence in Criminal Proceedings: Hearsay and Related Topics", Law Com No 245, at paragraphs 9.4-9.5.*

technical information which is widely used by members of the expert's profession and which is regarded as being reliable. Believing the two hearsay exceptions to which they referred to be "readily justifiable", the Law Commission[512] recommended their retention.

The authorities relied upon by the Law Commission in support of the existence of the former of the two hearsay exceptions referred to immediately above were Australian and American.[513] It is submitted that examination of the English case law does not suggest the division of the common law rule referred to by section 118(1) 8 into two distinct hearsay exceptions. What the English authorities do make clear, however, is that an expert is, in forming his opinion, entitled to make use of research carried out by others providing that the primary facts have been proved by admissible evidence.[514] Such information might, for example, include textbooks, articles, tables of statistics, unpublished material and even, it appears, discussions with colleagues.[515] The operation of the hearsay rule does not prevent the expert from relying upon such information in order to assist him to form his expert opinion[516], though the expert should make clear upon what information he has relied in order that the weight of his evidence may properly be determined.[517] Indeed, it appear that an expert may be entitled to rely upon research carried out by others even where the research falls outside the ambit of his own expertise though, again, this may reduce the weight of his evidence.[518] Similarly, where an expert primarily relies upon the research of others rather than his own experience, this may also reduce the weight of his evidence.[519] The effect of section 118(1) 8 of the 2003 Act is, it is submitted, that the principles outlined in this paragraph will continue to govern the use of such material by expert witnesses in the context of criminal proceedings when the hearsay provisions of the 2003 Act are in force.

The common law exception to the hearsay rule which will be preserved by section 118(1) 8 of the 2003 Act in the criminal context has not been preserved by the Civil Evidence Act 1995 and was not preserved by its predecessor, the Civil Evidence Act 1968. If reliance upon material of the type to which section 118(1) 8 relates by an expert witness does, in fact, infringe the hearsay rule then such evidence will now admissible in civil proceedings under the general hearsay exception created by section 1 of the Civil Evidence Act 1995. It may be, however, that the true basis upon which the courts permit an expert to rely upon such

512 See *"Evidence in Criminal Proceedings: Hearsay and Related Topics"*, Law Com No 245, at paragraphs 9.8.
513 See *"Evidence in Criminal Proceedings: Hearsay and Related Topics"*, Law Com No 245, at paragraph 9.4 at notes 4 and 5.
514 *R v Abadom [1983] 1 WLR 126.*
515 *R v Abadom [1983] 1 WLR 126; English Exporters (London) Ltd v Eldonwall Ltd [1973] Ch 415.*
516 *R v Abadom [1983] 1 WLR 126; English Exporters (London) Ltd v Eldonwall Ltd [1973] Ch 415.*
517 *R v Abadom [1983] 1 WLR 126.*
518 See *R v Somers [1963] 1 WLR 1306.*
519 *Huxley v Elvicta Wood Engineering Ltd LTL 19/4/2000.*

material in forming his opinion is, in fact, that the admission of expert opinion formed upon the basis of such reliance does not infringe the hearsay rule at all provided that the primary facts have been proved by admissible evidence.[520] If this is indeed the true basis upon which such evidence is admitted then it may be that recourse to, or preservation of, a hearsay exception in this context is, in reality, unnecessary.

2.4 Statutory exceptions to the hearsay rule created by statutory provisions other than the 2003 Act

Prior to the enactment of the Criminal Justice Act 2003, earlier statutes had created a variety of hearsay exceptions, the vast majority of which will remain in force when the hearsay provisions of the 2003 Act are brought into force. Examination of all of the miscellaneous statutory exceptions to the hearsay rule which will continue in force after this date falls outside the scope of the present book. Indeed, the Government have themselves recognised both the difficulty and the potential danger of attempting to produce an exhaustive list of the existing statutory exceptions to the hearsay rule.[521] Rather, the purposes of the present section of this book are, first, to identify those statutory exceptions to the hearsay rule which the 2003 Act will repeal, replace or modify and, secondly, to consider the nature and effect of the major pre-existing statutory exceptions to the hearsay rule which will remain in force under the new hearsay regime which the 2003 Act will create.

2.4.1 Pre-existing statutory exceptions to the hearsay rule which the 2003 Act will repeal, replace or modify

The repeal[522], and replacement by two related but by no means identical statutory hearsay exceptions[523], of two major statutory exceptions to the hearsay rule, namely, sections 23 and 24 of the Criminal Justice Act 1988, and their related provisions[524], has already been considered above.[525] Other than sections 23 and 24 of the 1988 Act, the 2003 Act will also repeal sections 5A, 5B, 5C 5D, 5E and 5F of the Magistrates' Courts Act 1980[526], section 68 of and Schedule 2 to the

---

520 See *English Exporters (London) Ltd v Eldonwall Ltd* [1973] Ch 415.

521 See *Hansard (Lords) 28 September 2003 Columns 603-605. For a non-exhaustive list of some of the more obscure statutory exceptions to the hearsay rule which will be retained when the hearsay provisions of the 2003 Act come into force see Appendix C to the Law Commission's Consultation Paper No. 138.*

522 See *sections 136 and 332 of and Part 6 of Schedule 37 to the 2003 Act.*

523 *Namely, by the hearsay exceptions created by sections 116 and 117 of the 2003 Act.*

524 *Contained in Part II of the 1988 Act and in Schedule 2 and Paragraphs 2 to 5 of Schedule 13 to the 1988 Act.*

525 *At 2.2.1 and 2.2.2 above.*

526 See *section 41 and Part 2 of Schedule 3 to the 2003 Act and section 332 and Part 4 of Schedule 37 to the same Act. Note, also, that paragraph 3 of Schedule 1 to the Criminal Procedure and Investigations Act 1996, which inserted sections 5A to 5E into the 1980 Act, will be repealed by section 332 and Part 4 of Schedule 37 to the 2003 Act.*

Criminal Procedure and Investigations Act 1996[527] and paragraph 5(4) of Schedule 3 to the Crime and Disorder Act 1998[528], and will substitute a new provision for paragraphs 1 and 1A of Schedule 2 to the Criminal Appeal Act 1968.[529] The 2003 Act will also repeal a number of other miscellaneous provisions, the repeal of which will not in itself result in the abolition of any pre-existing hearsay exceptions and which it is, thus, unnecessary to consider further in the context of the present work.[530]

2.4.1.1 Magistrates' Courts Act 1980, sections 5A to 5F

These provisions concern both the admissibility of evidence and the proof of statements in committal proceedings. They will be repealed as part of the raft of amendments and repeals concerning the allocation of cases triable either way and the sending of cases to the Crown Court which will come into effect when the relevant provisions of the 2003 Act are brought into force.[531]

2.4.1.2 Criminal Procedure and Investigations Act 1996, section 68 and Schedule 2.

Schedule 2 to the Criminal Procedure and Investigations Act 1996 was brought into effect by section 68 of that Act.

Essentially, where paragraph 1 of Schedule 2 applies, a written statement which was admitted in evidence in committal proceedings may be read as evidence at the accused's trial without further proof.

Essentially, where paragraph 2 of Schedule 2 applies, a deposition which was admitted in evidence in committal proceedings may be read as evidence at the accused's trial without further proof.

Section 68 and Schedule 2 will be repealed by the 2003 Act as part of the raft of amendments and repeals concerning the allocation of cases triable either way and the sending of cases to the Crown Court which will come into effect when the relevant provisions of the 2003 Act are brought into force.[532]

---

527 *See section 332 of and Part 4 of Schedule 37 to the 2003 Act. Note that Part 4 of Schedule 37 (which is concerned with repeals concerning allocation and sending of offences) is not reproduced in the appendix to this book.*

528 *See sections 130 and 332 of and Part 6 of Schedule 37 to the 2003 Act.*

529 *See section 131 of the 2003 Act.*

530 *For the provisions so affected see Part 6 of Schedule 37 to the 2003 Act, which is reproduced in the appendix to this book and to which effect is given by section 332 of the 2003 Act.*

531 *Other than section 332 the provisions of the 2003 which concern these matters, namely section 41 and Part 2 of Schedule 3 and section 332 and Part 4 of Schedule 37, fall outside the scope of this book and are thus not reproduced in its appendix.*

532 *Other than section 332 the provisions of the 2003 which concern these matters, namely, Part 6, Schedule 3 and Part 4 of Schedule 37, fall outside the scope of this book and are thus not reproduced in its appendix.*

2.4.1.3 Crime and Disorder Act 1998, paragraph 5(4) of Schedule 3.

Paragraph 5 of Schedule 3 to the 1998 Act applies when a deposition has been taken under paragraph 4 of schedule 3, i.e. in the context of an offence in relation to which a person has been sent for trial under section 51 of the 1998 Act. The effect of the repeal of paragraph 5(4) of Schedule 3[533] will be that where a party objects to a deposition being read as evidence under paragraph 5 of Schedule 3, the court will no longer possess the power to overrule the objection. Consequently, in the context of such an objection it appears that, once paragraph 5(4) is repealed, such a deposition will only be admissible if one of the other exceptions to the hearsay rule which the 2003 Act creates, preserves or retains is applicable thereto.

2.4.1.4 Criminal Appeal Act 1968, paragraphs 1 and 1A of Schedule 2.

In substituting new provisions for the existing paragraphs 1 and 1A of Schedule 2 to the Criminal Appeal Act 1968[534], section 131 of the 2003 Act provides as follows.

"For paragraphs 1 and 1A of Schedule 2 to the Criminal Appeal Act 1968 (c. 19) (oral evidence and use of transcripts etc at retrials under that Act) there is substituted–

"*Evidence*

1   (1)   Evidence given at a retrial must be given orally if it was given orally at the original trial, unless–

   (a)   all the parties to the retrial agree otherwise;

   (b)   section 116 of the Criminal Justice Act 2003 applies (admissibility of hearsay evidence where a witness is unavailable); or

   (c)   the witness is unavailable to give evidence, otherwise than as mentioned in subsection (2) of that section, and section 114(1)(d) of that Act applies (admission of hearsay evidence under residual discretion).

   (2)   Paragraph 5 of Schedule 3 to the Crime and Disorder Act 1998 (use of depositions) does not apply at a retrial to a deposition read as evidence at the original trial.""

Paragraph 1 (1) of this provision will, it appears[535], replace both the common law hearsay exception (referred to at 2.4.1 above) which concerns the admissibility of statements made by witnesses during earlier legal proceedings who are dead or unfit to attend by the time of a subsequent trial (which the 2003 Act will abolish)

---

533 *See sections 130 and 332 of and Part 6 of*
     Schedule 37 to the 2003 Act.
534 *See*

535 *See "Evidence in Criminal Proceedings: Hearsay*
     and Related Topics", Law Com No 245, at
     paragraphs 8.105 to 8.107.

and paragraphs 1 and 1A of Schedule 2 to the Criminal Appeal Act 1968, which concern the use of written statements and depositions at a retrial (which the 2003 Act will repeal).

The effect of paragraph 1 (1) will be that, unless all the parties to the retrial agree otherwise, where evidence was given orally at the original trial it must, other than in either of two exceptional situations, be given orally at a retrial. The first of the two exceptional situations in which oral evidence was given at the trial but is not required at the retrial will exist when the requirements of section 116 of the 2003 Act (considered at 2.2.1 above) are satisfied. The second of these two exceptional situations will exist when section 116 does not apply because the requirements of section 116(2) (concerning the unavailability of the maker of the hearsay statement) are not satisfied, but the relevant witness is unavailable for some other reason and the court admits the hearsay evidence in the exercise of its "safety valve" inclusionary discretion under section 114(1)(d) of the 2003 Act.[536]

2.4.2 Major examples of pre-existing statutory exceptions to the hearsay rule which the 2003 Act will retain

As was indicated at 2.4 above, to attempt to examine all of the miscellaneous pre-existing statutory exceptions to the hearsay rule which will continue to exist in the context of criminal proceedings when the hearsay provisions of the 2003 Act are in force is a task which falls outside the scope of the present book. The considerably less ambitious purpose of the present section of this book is merely to consider the nature and effect of some of the more significant or better known examples of pre-existing statutory hearsay exceptions which the 2003 Act will retain.

It should be noted that where a pre-existing statutory hearsay exception continues to exist when the hearsay provisions of the 2003 Act are in force, sections 124 (credibility), 125 (stopping the case) and 126 (exclusionary discretion) of the 2003 Act will all be potentially applicable in the context of the retained statutory hearsay exception's operation. Sections 124–126 are, respectively, considered at 2.7.3, 2.7.4 and 2.7.5, below.

2.4.2.1 Statements admitted upon service of notice or by agreement under section 9 of the Criminal Justice Act 1967

The Law Commission's provisional view that the statutory hearsay exception created by section 9 of the Criminal Justice Act 1967 Act should be retained was accepted on consultation.[537] Indeed, as is seen at 2.7.7 below, the Law Commission envisaged that section 9 of the 1967 Act would have a significant role to play in the context of their proposed new hearsay regime.

---

536 *The nature and significance of the section 114(1)(d) discretion are considered at 2.6 below.*

537 *See "Evidence in Criminal Proceedings: Hearsay and Related Topics", Law Com No 245, at paragraphs 8.100 and 8.102.*

The effect of section 9 of the 1967 Act is that, where the conditions which the section lays down are satisfied, a written statement made by a person is admissible in evidence in criminal proceedings (other than committal proceedings[538]) to the same extent as its maker's oral evidence would be admissible.[539] Essentially, in order for a hearsay statement to be admissible under section 9, the following four requirements must be satisfied. First, the statement must purport to be signed by its maker.[540] Secondly, the statement must contain a declaration by its maker,

> "...to the effect that it is true to the best of his knowledge and belief and that he made the statement knowing that, if it were tendered in evidence, he could be liable to prosecution if he wilfully stated in it anything in it that he knew to be false or did not believe to be true..."[541];

Thirdly, before the hearing at which the statement is tendered a copy of the statement must have been served[542] on all other parties to the proceedings.[543] Finally, none of the other parties to the proceedings must, within 7 days of receiving the notice, have served notice on the party proposing to tender the statement in evidence objecting to its being tendered under section 9.[544] It is, however, unnecessary to satisfy the latter two of these requirements if, either before or during the hearing, the parties agree that the statement shall be tendered in evidence under section 9.[545]

Where a party has served a copy of a statement on the other parties in accordance with section 9, this does not prevent that party from subsequently calling the maker of the statement to give evidence.[546] Further, either of its own motion or upon the application of a party, the court may require the maker of the statement to give evidence.[547]

Where a statement is admitted in evidence under section 9, the statement is read aloud at the hearing unless the court directs otherwise.[548] An oral account is given

---

538 *The reference in section 9(1) of the 1967 Act to committal proceedings will be removed by paragraph 43(2) of Schedule 3 to the Criminal Justice Act 2003 as part of the raft of amendments and repeals concerning the allocation of cases triable either way and the sending of cases to the Crown Court which will come into effect when the relevant provisions of the 2003 Act are brought into force. Other than section 332 the provisions of the 2003 which concern these matters, namely, Part 6, Schedule 3 and Part 4 of Schedule 37, fall outside the scope of this book and are thus not reproduced in its appendix.*

539 *Section 9(1).*

540 *Section 9(2)(a), and see also section 9 (3)(b) concerning statements made by persons who cannot read.*

541 *Section 9(2)(b). The wording of the declaration is slightly different where the statement was made by*

a person who was under 14 years of age when he made it (section 9(3A). Further, the statement must give its maker's age, if he is under 18 years of age(section 9(3)(a)). See, also, section 9 (3)(b) concerning statements made by persons who cannot read.

542 *Provision concerning the service of documents for the purposes of section 9 is made by section 9(8).*

543 *Section 9(2)(c).*

544 *Section 9(2)(d). When a copy is served on another party, it must be accompanied either by a copy of any other document referred to therein as an exhibit or by information enabling the party to inspect the relevant exhibit or a copy thereof (section 9(3)(c)).*

545 *Section 9(2).*

546 *Section 9(4)(a).*

547 *Section 9(4)(b),(5).*

548 *Section 9(6).*

of any part of the statement which the court directs should not be read aloud.[549] Where the statement refers to and identifies an exhibit, the exhibit is treated as though the maker of the statement had produced and identified it in court.[550]

Where a statement is admitted in evidence under section 9, the statement is not conclusive evidence of the facts which it concerns.[551] Thus, the fact that a statement is admitted in evidence does not prevent another party who has not served notice objecting to the statement being tendered in evidence from challenging the hearsay evidence in the course of the trial though, in such circumstances, the party who adduced the hearsay evidence may well wish to apply for an adjournment in order to call its maker to give evidence.[552]

2.4.2.2 Expert reports admitted under section 30 of the Criminal Justice Act 1988.

The Law Commission[553] regarded the hearsay exception created by section 30 of the Criminal Justice Act 1988 as "readily justifiable" and thus did not recommend any modification of section 30.

Section 30 of the 1988 Act renders an expert report[554] admissible in criminal proceedings as evidence of any fact or opinion of which the expert could have given oral evidence.[555] Section 30 renders an expert report admissible whether or not the expert is to attend court to give oral evidence. If the expert is not to attend court to give oral evidence, however, then the expert report is only admissible under section 30 with the leave of the court.[556] Section 30(3) provides that:

"For the purpose of determining whether to give leave the court shall have regard—

(a) to the contents of the report;

(b) to the reasons why it is proposed that the person making the report shall not give oral evidence;

(c) to any risk, having regard in particular to whether it likely to be possible to controvert statements in the report if the person making it does not attend to give oral evidence in the proceedings, that its admission or exclusion will result in unfairness to the accused or, if there is more than one, to any one of them; and

(d) to any other circumstances that appear to the court to be relevant."

---

549 *Section 9(6).*
550 *Section 9(7).*
551 *Lister v Quaife (1982) 75 Cr App R 313.*
552 *Lister v Quaife (1982) 75 Cr App R 313.*
553 *See "Evidence in Criminal Proceedings: Hearsay and Related Topics", Law Com No 245, at paragraph 9.8.*

554 *Defined by section 30(5) as "...a written report by a person dealing wholly or mainly with matters on which he is (or would if living be) qualified to give expert evidence."*
555 *Section 30(1),(4).*
556 *Section 30(2). The requirement of leave does not apply in the context of committal proceedings (section 30(4)(A)).*

Expert reports may, alternatively, be admissible under section 9 of the Criminal Justice Act 1967 (considered at 2.4.2.1 above), but admissibility under section 30 of the 1988 Act, as opposed to admissibility under section 9 of the 1967 Act, is not dependent upon none of the other parties having an objection to the admission of the relevant evidence. In practice, however, in relation to the giving of leave under section 30(2), the Law Commission[557] regarded it as:

> "...extremely unlikely that the courts would allow an expert report to be adduced without calling the maker if the opposing party had a genuine wish to cross-examine on it."

Thus, where an expert is not being called to give oral evidence in criminal proceedings and a party to the proceedings objects to the admission of his report in evidence, it appears unlikely that the report will be admitted. It is submitted that the admission of such evidence in such circumstances must be particularly unlikely when it is the defence who wish to cross-examine a prosecution expert whose report is tendered under section 30.

2.4.2.3 Depositions of child victims admitted under Section 43 of the Children and Young Persons Act 1933

Essentially, section 43 of the Children and Young Persons Act 1933 provides that, in the context of criminal proceedings for an offence specified by Schedule 1 to the 1933 Act[558], the deposition[559] of a child[560] or young person[561] who is the alleged victim of the relevant offence is admissible in evidence either for the prosecution or for the defence if attending court would involve serious danger to the child's life or health.[562] The deposition is not admissible against the accused unless reasonable notice of the intention to take the deposition was served on him and the defence had the opportunity to attend to cross-examine the deponent.

2.4.2.4 Copies of entries in bankers' books admitted under section 3 of the Bankers' Books Evidence Act 1879.

Where the requirements of sections 4 of the Bankers' Books Evidence Act 1879 (concerning proof that the relevant book is a bankers' book) and 5 of that Act (concerning proof that the copy has been verified by comparison with the original) are satisfied, section 3 (which applies in the contexts of criminal and civil proceedings) renders copies of entries in bankers' books admissible as evidence both of the relevant entries and as evidence of the matters, transactions and accounts which they record. Section 9(2) of the 1879 Act provides that:

---

557 See *"Evidence in Criminal Proceedings: Hearsay and Related Topics"*, Law Com No 245, at paragraph 9.7.

558 For example, common assault or battery, incest or indecent assault.

559 Taken either under Part III of the 1933 Act or under the Indictable Offences Act 1848.

560 I.e. a person under the age of 14 (section 107).

561 I.e. a person under the age of 18 but who is at least 14 years old (section 107).

562 The court must be satisfied that this is so on the evidence of a medical practitioner.

"...bankers' books include ledgers, day books, cash books, account books and other records used in the ordinary business of the bank, whether those records are in written form or are kept on microfilm, magnetic tape or any other form of mechanical or electronic data retrieval mechanism."

Bankers' books do not, however, include paid cheques or paying in slips[563] or records of conversations between employees and customers.[564]

Section 3 of the 1879 Act only renders copies of entries in bankers' books admissible rather then the originals. The Law Commission[565] believed, however, that originals would be potentially admissible in criminal proceedings under what is now section 117 of the 2003 Act and recognised that originals are admissible in civil proceedings under section 1 of the Civil Evidence Act 1995. Equally, whilst "copy" is not defined by the 1879 Act, the Law Commission[566] believed that, in the light of the section 9(2) definition of "bankers' books" (reproduced above), the courts would regard computer printouts of bankers' records as copies thereof.

2.4.2.5 Statutory declarations admitted under section 27(4) of the Theft Act 1968.

Section 27(4) of the Theft Act 1968 applies in the context of criminal proceedings for :

"...the theft of anything in the course of transmission (whether by post or otherwise), or for handling stolen goods from such a theft..."

Essentially, the subsection renders a statutory declaration by a person to the effect that he dispatched, received or failed to receive the relevant goods, or received them in a particular state or condition, admissible as evidence of the facts stated. The statutory declaration is only so admissible, however, if, or to the extent to which, oral evidence to the same effect would have been admissible[567] and, moreover, is only admissible if the accused, having been given a copy of the declaration at least seven days before the hearing, did not, at least three days before the hearing[568], give the prosecutor written notice requiring the attendance of the declarant.[569]

---

563 *Williams v Williams [1988] QB 161.*
564 *Re Howglen Ltd [2001] 1 All ER 376.*
565 *See "Evidence in Criminal Proceedings: Hearsay and Related Topics", Law Com No 245, at paragraph 8.103 and see note 138.*
566 *See "Evidence in Criminal Proceedings: Hearsay and Related Topics", Law Com No 245, at paragraph 8.104.*

567 *Section 27(4)(a). The requirement that oral evidence to the same effect would have been admissible does not apply in the context of committal proceedings (section 27(4A)).*
568 *Though, in special circumstances, the court may allow the accused further time to give such notice (section 27(4)(b)).*
569 *Section 27(4)(b). These notice requirements do not apply in the context of committal proceedings (section 27(4A)).*

2.4.2.6 Video recorded evidence in chief, cross-examination and re-examination admissible under Part II of Youth Justice and Criminal Evidence Act 1999.

Under the special measures regime, created by Part II of the Youth Justice and Criminal Evidence Act 1999, the video recorded evidence in chief, cross-examination and re-examination of eligible witnesses may be admissible in criminal proceedings. In relation to the admission of a witness' video recorded statement under a special measures direction, the effect of section 31(2)(a) of the 1999 Act is that the statement is to be treated as though the witness had made it whilst giving direct oral testimony in court and, accordingly, is admissible as evidence of facts of which the witness' direct oral testimony would be admissible.[570] The witness' video recorded statement cannot, however, corroborate other evidence which he has given.[571]

An examination of the nature of those circumstances in which a criminal court may direct that special measures (such as video recording) apply to the evidence of an eligible witness falls outside the scope of the present book.

2.4.2.7 Confessions

When the hearsay provisions of the Criminal Justice Act 2003 come into force, the principles of the law of evidence which govern the admissibility in criminal proceedings of confessions made by the accused will be relatively little altered. Indeed, section 128(2) of the 2003 Act[572] provides that, other than section 128(1), nothing in Chapter 2 of Part 11 of the 2003 Act makes a defendant's confession admissible if it would not be admissible under section 76 of the Police and Criminal Evidence Act 1984 and section 118(1) 5 of the 2003 Act[573] preserves "Any rule of law relating to the admissibility of confessions or mixed statements in criminal proceedings."

Whilst the principles of the law of evidence which govern the admissibility of confessions in criminal proceedings will not be substantially altered by the provisions of the 2003 Act, that is not to say that the 2003 Act will not produce some changes of significance in this context. In particular, the new section 76A of the 1984 Act (inserted into the 1984 Act by section 128(1) of the 2003 Act and considered at 2.2.7.2 above) will impose a new statutory regime in relation to the admissibility for the accused of a confession made by his co-accused. Further, it is

---

570 *Moreover, the effect of section 31(3) of the 1999 Act in conjunction with section 31(2) thereof appears to be that where a witness would have been competent to give sworn testimony had he testified in court, the fact that his video recorded evidence in chief, cross-examination or re-examination is not made under oath does not render it inadmissible.*

571 *See section 31(2)(b) of the 1999 Act. Presumably, whilst the section does not expressly state this, such evidence could, similarly, not act as supporting evidence in the context of a direction under R v Turnbull [1977] QB 224 or R v Makanjuola [1995] 1 WLR 1348 (see, also, R v Islam [1999] 1 Cr App R 22).*

572 *Already referred to at 2.2.1.1, 2.2.2.1, 2.2.3.2, 2.2.7.2 and 2.3.2.9, above.*

573 *Which was considered at 2.3.2.8 above.*

submitted that section 121 of the 2003 Act[574], which concerns the admissibility of multiple hearsay in criminal proceedings, may be of significance in the context of confessions. Moreover (as is seen at 2.4.2.7.9 below), the Law Commission believed that confessions made by third parties might fall within the ambit of their proposed regime of statutory hearsay exceptions which, essentially, will come into existence in the guise of Chapter 2 of Part 11 of the 2003 Act. Finally, it is submitted that section 125 of the 2003 Act, concerning the court's duty to stop the case where it is based wholly or partly on unconvincing evidence contained in a statement[575] and the new discretion, conferred by section 126(1), to exclude hearsay statements the admission of which would result in undue waste of time[576] may both potentially be applicable in the context of confessions.

The sections of this book which concern confessions seek to consider those principles under which confessions will be admitted or excluded when Chapter 2 of Part 11 of the 2003 Act is in force. Since much of the existing law will remain unchanged, many of the principles of the law of evidence considered in these sections may well already be familiar to the reader, but, to the extent to which there are any, the implications of the 2003 Act as regards the law relating to the admission and exclusion of confessions are considered in context.

2.4.2.7.1 The nature of a confession

Section 82(1) of the 1984 Act defines a confession as including:

> "...any statement wholly or partly adverse to the person who made it, whether made to a person in authority or not and whether made in words or otherwise..."

A confession may be made orally, in writing or by conduct (for example, by video-re-enactment) and may be made expressly or by implication.[577] A statement which is neither wholly nor partly adverse to its maker (i.e. a statement which is totally in its maker's favour and is thus wholly exculpatory) is not, however, a confession.[578]

There is established authority for the proposition that a statement which was not wholly or partly adverse to its maker at the time when it was made is not a confession, even if by the time of his trial it can be shown to be false or to be inconsistent with his evidence in court.[579] Most recently, however, in *R v Z*[580], the Court of Appeal has held that a statement which was neither wholly nor partly

---

574 *See 2.4.2.7.7 and 2.7.1, below.*

575 *For a potential example of the operation of section 125 in the context of confessions see 2.4.2.7.15, below. For more general consideration of its operation see 2.7.4 below.*

576 *See 2.4.2.7.5 and 2.7.5.1 below.*

577 *See Police and Criminal Evidence Act 1984, s. 82(1) and see Li Shi-Ling v R [1989] AC 270.*

578 *R v Aziz [1996] AC 41. The admissibility of wholly exculpatory statements made by the accused in criminal proceedings was considered at 2.2.4.2.3 and 2.2.4.3 above.*

579 *See, R v Sat-Bhambra (1988) 88 Cr App R 55 and see, for example, R v Park (1994) 99 Cr App R 270.*

580 *[2003] 1 WLR 1489.*

adverse to its maker at the time when it was made, but which by the time when it is tendered in evidence has become wholly or partly adverse thereto (because, for example, it is inconsistent with his testimony in court), is a confession within the meaning of section 82(1). In *R v Z*, Their Lordships regarded themselves as bound to reconsider this issue (by virtue of the operation of section 3(1) of the Human Rights Act 1998) in consequence of the jurisprudence of the European Court of Human Rights concerning the right not to incriminate oneself under Article 6 of the Convention. Under this jurisprudence, the Article 6 right is not restricted to directly incriminating statements obtained under compulsion but also encompasses exculpatory statements obtained under compulsion which are subsequently used by the prosecution to support their case (for example to contradict the accused's testimony), the fundamental issue being the use to which the statements are put at the trial.[581] Thus, in *R v Z*, their Lordships held that when determining whether or not a statement is a confession, the court must consider whether the statement is adverse at the time when it is tendered in evidence, not whether it was adverse at the time when it was made.

Finally, it should be noted that the wording of section 82(1) makes clear that a statement which was wholly or partly adverse to its maker but which was not made to the police or to some other "person in authority" is still a confession within the meaning of section 82(1).

2.4.2.7.2 The admissibility of a confession as evidence for the prosecution

Section 76(1) of the Police and Criminal Evidence Act 1984 provides that:

> "In any proceedings a confession made by an accused person may be given in evidence against him in so far as it is relevant to any matter in issue in the proceedings and is not excluded by the court in pursuance of this section."

Thus, whilst a confession falls within the ambit of the hearsay rule, it is potentially admissible in evidence if it also falls within the ambit of the hearsay exception contained in section 76(1) of the 1984 Act (i.e. if it is relevant to an issue in the proceedings). The potential admissibility of a confession under section 76(1) is, however, subject to the fact that section 76(2) may require the court to exclude it. Section 76(2) provides that:

> "If, in any proceedings where the prosecution proposes to give in evidence a confession made by an accused person, it is represented to the court that the confession was or may have been obtained–
>
> (a) by oppression of the person who made it; or
>
> (b) in consequence of anything said or done which was likely, in the circumstances existing at the time, to render unreliable any confession which might be made by him in consequence thereof,

---

581 See *Saunders v The United Kingdom* (1997) 23 EHRR 313.

the court shall not allow the confession to be given in evidence against him except in so far as the prosecution proves to the court beyond reasonable doubt that the confession (notwithstanding that it may be true) was not obtained as aforesaid."

Section 76(2) expressly states that the burden of proving that a confession was not obtained in either of the two ways specified by the subsection is borne by the prosecution.[582] Moreover, where the defence do not raise the issue of the admissibility of a confession under section 76(2), the court may, of its own motion, require the prosecution to prove that the confession was not so obtained.[583]

It should be noted that section 76(2) concerns the admissibility of a confession in criminal proceedings in which the maker of the confession is a defendant and thus it appears that the operation of section 76(2) does not prevent a witness for the prosecution from giving "Queen's evidence" against his accomplices in line with his confession.[584] Thus, it appears that where one of several co-accused makes a confession which also implicates his accomplices but subsequently pleads guilty and testifies for the prosecution against them, the fact that, due to the operation of section 76(2), the confession would not have been admissible against him had he pleaded not guilty, does not mean that his evidence will be inadmissible.[585]

Further, it should also be noted that, where a confession is admissible, it is the accused's entire statement that is normally admitted and, as is seen at 2.4.2.7.11 below, the prosecution are not permitted to rely upon those parts of a mixed statement which are in their favour whilst excluding those parts which are not. There are, however, two situations where editing may take place. First, as is seen at 2.4.2.7.10 below, editing may take place in order to protect a co-accused who is implicated by the accused's confession. Secondly, editing may take place in order to remove matters detrimental to the accused of which the jury should not hear, such as statements concerning his previous convictions.[586]

Finally, in relation to the significance of section 76(1),(2) of the 1984 Act once the hearsay provisions of the Criminal Justice Act 2003 are in force, it is important to note that the effect of section 128(2) of the 2003 Act appears to be that a confession made by a defendant which would not be admissible under section 76 of the 1984 Act (i.e. which would not be admissible because it was or may have been obtained by oppression or in consequence of something said or done etc) will not be rendered admissible by any of the other hearsay exceptions which the 2003 Act will create, preserve, or retain.

582 *See, for example, R v Taylor LTL 5/6/2000; R v Allen [2001] EWCA Crim 1607.*
583 *Police and Criminal Evidence Act 1984, section 76(3).*
584 *R v Jamieson [2003] EWCA Crim 193*
585 *R v Jamieson [2003] EWCA Crim 193.*
586 *See Turner v Underwood [1948] 2 KB 286; R v Weaver [1968] ! QB 805; R v Knight (1946) 36 Cr App R 52.*

2.4.2.7.3 Oppression

Essentially, where the court is required to consider the admissibility of a confession under section 76(2)(a) of the Police and Criminal Evidence Act 1984, the confession will be inadmissible unless the prosecution prove beyond reasonable doubt that it was not obtained by oppression. Thus, it is submitted that when applying section 76(2)(a) in the course of determining the admissibility of a confession, the court is required to consider the following matters. First, whether the accused was subjected to oppression. Secondly, if the accused was subjected to oppression, whether the confession was obtained in consequence of the oppression.

Section 76(8) of the 1984 Act partially defines oppression as including:

> "...torture, inhuman or degrading treatment, and the use or threat of violence (whether or not amounting to torture).[587]

Further, in *R v Fulling*[588], the Court of Appeal (without reference to section 76(8)), held that "oppression" is to be given its ordinary dictionary definition (encompassing the burdensome, harsh or wrongful exercise of power, unjust or cruel treatment and the imposition of burdens which are unreasonable or unjust), their Lordships finding it difficult to imagine circumstances in which oppression would not involve improper conduct on the part of those interviewing the accused. Thus, it appears that conduct only amounts to oppression for the purposes of section 76(2)(a) if, taking into account section 76(8), it would, in ordinary language, be regarded as oppression.[589] In particular, it should be noted that the word "wrongful", in the context of the definition of oppression, must be construed in the context of the terms "burdensome", "harsh", "unjust", "cruel", etc.[590] Examples of conduct which, it appears, is capable of constituting oppression include heavy handed questioning (such as shouting and persistent repetition of allegations contrary to the accused's repeated denials)[591], the use of tricks (such as the invention of evidence or the deliberate distortion of the weight of evidence against the accused)[592] and the denial of access to a solicitor (in breach of section 58 of the Police and Criminal Evidence Act 1984).[593] Breaches of requirements of the Police and Criminal Evidence Act 1984, of the Codes of

---

587 *Article 3 of the European Convention on Human Rights (which is set out in Schedule 1 to the Human Rights Act 1998) provides that: "No one shall be subjected to torture or to inhuman or degrading treatment or punishment." Section 76(2)(a) and section 76(8) of the Police and Criminal Evidence Act 1984 make clear that a confession obtained in violation of Article 3 is inadmissible in English Law.*

588 *[1987] Q.B. 426.*

589 *R v Mason, Wood, McClelland and Tierney [2002] 2 Cr App R 38.*

590 *See: R v Parker [1995] Crim LR 233; Re Proulx*

[2001] 1 All ER 57.

591 *R v Miller, R v Parris, R v Abdullahi (1993) 97 Cr App R 99.*

592 *See R v Beales [1991] Crim LR 118.*

593 *See R v Samuel (1988) 87 Cr App R 232, in which the Court of Appeal recognised that such denial could amount to oppression or could form part of an oppressive course of conduct. In reality, it is likely that such denial would, without more, generally be dealt with under section 76(2)(b) (unreliability, see 3.3.3 below) or under section 78 (exclusionary discretion, see 3.4.2 below). In Samuel itself it was dealt with under section 78.*

Practice made thereunder or of other similar requirements are not, however, automatically oppressive.[594]

The mere fact that the accused was subjected to oppression will not render his confession inadmissible if there is no causal link between the oppression and the confession (i.e. if the confession was not obtained by oppression).[595] It is, however, for the prosecution to disprove the existence of such a causal link beyond reasonable doubt.[596] If the prosecution prove beyond reasonable doubt that the accused did not confess in consequence of the oppression, the mere fact that oppression of the accused took place will not render the confession inadmissible because, in such circumstances, the confession was not "obtained" by oppression.

It appears that the individual characteristics of the accused are of relevance in determining whether his confession was "obtained" by oppression.[597] This is so because oppressive conduct which might induce one person to confess might not have the same effect on another (tougher, more intelligent or more experienced) person.

The wording of section 76(2) makes clear that when a trial judge is determining the admissibility of a confession under section 76(2)(a), the truth or falsehood of the confession is irrelevant. Thus, where the prosecution fail to prove that the accused's confession was not obtained by oppression, the confession is inadmissible, even if it is true.

Finally, it should be noted that where a confession is excluded on the basis of oppression but the accused confessed again in the course of a subsequent interview which was conducted properly, it may be that, in consequence of the earlier oppression, the subsequent confession should also be excluded.[598]

2.4.2.7.4 Unreliability

Essentially, where the court is required to consider the admissibility of a confession under section 76(2)(b) of the Police and Criminal Evidence Act 1984, the confession will be inadmissible unless the prosecution prove beyond reasonable doubt that it was not obtained in consequence of something said or done which was likely in the circumstances existing at the time to have rendered unreliable any confession which the accused might have made in consequence thereof. Thus, it appears that when applying section 76(2)(b) in the course of determining the admissibility of a confession, the judge is required to consider the following matters.[599] First, the nature of that which was said or done. Secondly, the nature of the circumstances that existed at the time when the accused confessed. Thirdly,

594 See, for example, R v Parker [1995] Crim LR 233.
595 R v Parker [1995] Crim LR 233.
596 See section 76(2) at 3.3 above.
597 See R v Seelig [1992] 1 WLR. 148 and R v Miller, R v Parris, R v Abdullahi (1993) 97 Cr App R 99.
598 R v Ismail [1990] Crim LR 109.
599 See Re Proulx [2001] 1 All ER 57; R v Barry (1992) 95 Cr App R 384.

whether the thing that was said or done was something which was likely, in the circumstances that existed at the time when the accused confessed, to have rendered unreliable any confession which the accused might have made in consequence of the thing said or done. Finally, whether the accused's confession was (or may have been) obtained in consequence of the thing said or done.

Perhaps unsurprisingly, it appears that an unreliable confession is a confession the truthfulness of which cannot be relied upon.[600]

Examples of things said or done which have been held in appropriate circumstances to give rise to the inadmissibility of confessions under section 76(2)(b) include breaches of requirements of the Police and Criminal Evidence Act 1984 and of the Codes of Practice made thereunder, such as unlawful refusal of access to legal advice[601], breaches of requirements relating to rest periods[602], interviewing a person of low IQ in the absence of an independent adult[603] and interviewing the accused immediately following his arrest and prior to his arrival at the police station without cautioning him and without giving him an opportunity to check the accuracy of the interview record.[604] Other examples of things said or done which have been held in appropriate circumstances to give rise to the inadmissibility of confessions under section 76(2)(b) include inducements to confess (such as, inducements relating to the increased likelihood of bail if the suspect co-operates[605]) and a suggestion that psychiatric treatment would be more appropriate in the accused's case than the imposition of a criminal sanction.[606]

The thing said or done need not be something said or done by the police.[607] Indeed, it may even be something said or done by the accused's solicitor.[608] It appears, however, that advice given to a client by his solicitor concerning the advantages of confessing will not normally result in the exclusion of the confession under section 76(2)(b), though it may do so if the client's personal characteristics make him particularly vulnerable.[609]

It appears that a confession may be excluded under section 76(2)(b) even though there is no suggestion of impropriety on the part of those interviewing the accused.[610] It also appears, however, that, for the purposes of section 76(2)(b), the thing said or done must be said or done by someone other than the maker of the confession and cannot merely consist either of the maker's own mental or physical state[611] or of things said or done by the maker or on his instructions if his decision to say or do the thing or to give the instruction was not influenced by anything said or done by another.[612] Equally, the fact that the accused's motive

---

600 See *Re Proulx [2001] 1 All ER 57; R v Crampton (1991) 92 Cr App R 369.*
601 See *R v McGovern (1991) 92 Cr App R 228.*
602 *R v Trussler [1988] Crim LR 446.*
603 *R v Everett [1988] Crim LR 826.*
604 *R v Allen [2001] EWCA Crim 1607.*
605 *R v Barry (1992) 95 Cr App R 384.*
606 *R v Delaney (1989) 89 Cr App R 338.*

607 *R v Wahab [2003] 1 Cr App R 15.*
608 *R v Sidney 12 June 2000.*
609 *R v Wahab [2003] 1 Cr App R 15.*
610 See: *R v Fulling [1987] QB 426; R v Harvey [1988] Crim LR 241.*
611 *R v Goldenberg (1988) 88 Cr App R 285.*
612 *R v Wahab [2003] 1 Cr App R 15.*

for confessing was that he would be released or would obtain a lesser sentence will not affect the admissibility of his confession unless it affects the reliability of the confession.[613]

The mere fact that something was said or done which was likely in the circumstances existing at the time to have rendered unreliable any confession which the accused might have made in consequence thereof will not render the accused's confession inadmissible if there is no causal link between the thing said or done and the confession.[614] In other words if the prosecution can prove to the criminal standard of proof that the confession was not obtained in consequence of the thing said or done, the mere fact that the thing was said or done will not render the confession inadmissible. Moreover, the mere fact that something was said or done will not render the accused's confession inadmissible if the prosecution can prove beyond reasonable doubt that the thing said or done was not likely in the circumstances to have rendered unreliable any confession which he might have made in consequence thereof.[615] In practice, however, factors such as, for example, the failure of the police to permit the accused to see the record of an interview which took place after arrest but before the accused was taken to the police station or their failure to mention the confession which the accused made during the former interview when he was subsequently interviewed at the police station in the presence of his solicitor may make it difficult or impossible for the prosecution to persuade the judge to the criminal standard of proof that confession was not obtained in consequence of something said or done which was likely in the circumstances to have rendered unreliable any confession which he might have made in consequence thereof.[616]

In determining whether a confession should be excluded under section 76(2)(b), it is necessary to take into account the circumstances existing at the time when the confession was made, such as, for example, the personal characteristics of the accused.[617] This is patently necessary in determining whether the thing said or done was likely in the circumstances existing at the time to have rendered unreliable any confession which the accused might have made in consequence thereof.[618] Thus, the issue of reliability cannot be determined by analogy to the facts of earlier cases but, rather, depends on the specific circumstances of the case before the court and, in particular, on the characteristics of the specific defendant the admissibility of whose confession is under consideration.[619] Equally, when considering whether the confession was obtained in consequence of the thing said or done, it appears to be necessary to take the surrounding circumstances into account.[620]

---

613 *R v Wahab [2003] 1 Cr App R 15.*
614 *R v Barry (1992) 95 Cr Ap R 384.*
615 *See R v Barry (1992) 95 Cr App R 384 and section 76(2).*
616 *R v Allen [2001] EWCA Crim 1607.*
617 *See, for example, R v Everett [1988] Crim LR 826 and see, also, R v Wahab [2003] 1 Cr App R 15.*

618 *See the express wording of section 76(2) (at 2.4.2.7.2 above) and see, for example, R v Barry (1992) 95 Cr App R 384.*
619 *R v Wahab [2003] 1 Cr App R 15.*
620 *See R v Barry (1992) 95 Cr App R 384.*

In determining whether a confession should be excluded under section 76(2)(b), the wording of section 76(2) expressly makes clear that the court is not concerned with the truth or falsehood (i.e. the reliability or unreliability) of the specific confession before it.[621] Rather, the issue is whether "any confession" which the accused might have made in the relevant circumstances in consequence of the thing said or done is likely to have been rendered unreliable.[622] Thus, it is perfectly possible that a judge, correctly applying section 76(2)(b), may be required to rule that a confession which is true is inadmissible.[623] It seems, however, that "any confession" does not mean any hypothetical confession that the accused might have made but, rather, means such a confession as was made by the accused, the crucial point being that the court is not required to consider the accuracy or truthfulness of the accused's confession but, rather, is concerned with the likelihood that such a confession as the accused made would be rendered unreliable in the circumstances in consequence of the thing said or done.[624]

Where a confession is excluded under section 76(2)(b), for example, in consequence of breaches of requirements of the Police and Criminal Evidence Act 1984, but the accused confessed again in the course of a subsequent interview which was conducted properly, it may well be that the second confession should also be excluded in consequence of the earlier breaches.[625] In particular, the fact that the accused confessed during the course of the first interview may well have affected the accused's conduct during the second interview.[626]

2.4.2.7.5 The discretionary exclusion of confessions tendered by the prosecution

Where a confession is admissible under section 76 of the Police and Criminal Evidence Act 1984, it may still be excluded in the exercise of the court's exclusionary discretion. The court possesses discretion to exclude evidence tendered by the prosecution both at common law and under section 78 of the Police and criminal Evidence Act 1984.

Essentially, at common law the court possesses discretion to exclude a confession either upon the basis that its probative value is outweighed by its prejudicial effect or where it was unfairly or improperly obtained from the accused.[627] In practice, it appears that resort is now rarely had to the common law exclusionary discretion in this context and that the discretionary exclusion of confessions is normally achieved by the exercise of the section 78 discretion.

---

621 *R v Crampton (1991) 92 Cr App R 369.*
622 *See: R v Barry (1992) 95 Cr App R 384; R v Taylor LTL 5/6/2000.*
623 *See R v McGovern (1991) 92 Cr App R 228*

624 *See Re Proulx [2001] 1 All ER 57.*
625 *R v McGovern (1991) 92 Cr App R 228.*
626 *R v McGovern (1991) 92 Cr App R 228.*
627 *See R v Sang [1980] AC 425.*

Section 78(1) of the 1984 Act provides as follows.

"(1) In any proceedings the court may refuse to allow evidence on which the prosecution proposes to rely to be given if it appears to the court that, having regard to all the circumstances, including the circumstances in which the evidence was obtained, the admission of the evidence would have such an adverse effect on the fairness of the proceedings that the court ought not to admit it."

Factors which may be of relevance when the court is considering the exercise of its exclusionary discretion in the context of a confession may include the reliability of the confession, the privilege against self-incrimination and the importance that the police behave properly towards the accused whilst he is in their custody, unreliability not being the sole basis upon which the court may exclude a confession in the exercise of its exclusionary discretion.[628]

Significant and substantial breaches of requirements of the Police and Criminal Evidence Act 1984 or of the Codes of Practice made thereunder are likely to persuade a judge to exclude a confession in the exercise of his section 78 discretion, though it appears that the judge should only do so if, in the circumstances, admitting the confession would such an adverse affect on the fairness of the proceedings that it should not be admitted.[629] The personal characteristics of the accused may be relevant in determining whether the court should exercise its discretion so as to exclude a confession in the context of the breach of such a requirement.[630]

Examples of substantial breaches of the Codes of Practice include failure to caution the accused prior to interviewing him and failure to permit the accused to read the interview record in order to check its accuracy.[631] Examples of factors which could make these substantial breaches of Code C even more significant include the fact that the accused's confession, made in the course of the abovementioned interview, formed a fundamental part of the prosecution case against him and the fact that if his confession was admitted the accused would effectively be required to challenge the evidence of the interviewing officers with the consequence that he would lose his "shield" under section 1(3)(ii) of the Criminal Evidence Act 1898 and could thus be cross-examined in relation to his previous convictions.[632]

---

628 *See Re Proulx [2001] 1 All Erv 57; Lam Chi-ming v R [1991] 3 All ER 172.*

629 *R v Walsh (1989) 91 Cr App R 161; R v Allen [2001] EWCA Crim 1607.*

630 *See, for example, R v Alladice (1988) 87 Cr App R 380 and R v Sansui [1992] Crim LR 43.*

631 *R v Allen [2001] EWCA Crim 1607.*

632 *R v Allen [2001] EWCA Crim 1607. Section 1(3) of the 1898 Act will be repealed by the Criminal Justice Act 2003 as part of the reforms concerning evidence of Character which for the subject matter of Chapter 1 of Part 11 of the 2003 Act (see section 332 and Part 5 of Schedule 37). Chapter 1 of Part 11 falls outside the scope of the present book.*

Minor breaches of requirements of the 1984 Act or of the Codes of Practice are unlikely to result in the exclusion of a confession[633] though it appears that bad faith on the part of the police may render significant and substantial a breach which would not otherwise have been so classified.[634] Good faith will not, however, justify the admission of a confession where there has been a significant or substantial breach.[635]

Where there has been no breach of requirements of the 1984 Act or the Codes of Practice, improper conduct (such as lying to the accused and his legal advisor[636]) may still justify the exclusion of a confession under section 78. Equally, it appears that where a solicitor advises his client to confess for an improper purpose which is not in the interests of the client (e.g. because the solicitor has another client who will benefit if the former client confesses or because the solicitor is in league with the police), the court may decide to exclude the confession in the exercise of its discretion regardless of the fact that the confession is clearly reliable.[637]

Where a confession is excluded under section 78 in consequence of breaches of the 1984 Act or of the Codes of Practice, it may be that confessions obtained in subsequent, properly conducted, interviews should also be excluded under that section[638], though this will not necessarily be so.[639]

Further, it should be noted that where the accused makes a confession to a probation officer who is interviewing him in order to prepare a pre-sentence report or to a doctor who is interviewing him in order to report into his mental state for sentencing purposes, the confession will not be inherently inadmissible but the judge will need to consider whether the confession should be excluded in the exercise of his exclusionary discretion.[640] In such circumstances, factors which the court should take into account in the exercise of its discretion include the fact that if offenders cannot speak freely to probation officers (or doctors) in such circumstances this could prevent the probation officers (or the doctors) from properly performing their duties, the fact (where this is so) that there is no reliable record of the conversation between the accused and the probation officer (or doctor), the fact that the offender was not cautioned and the fact that he did not have a legal representative present.[641]

Finally, it is suggested that the new discretion, conferred by section 126(1) of the 2003 Act[642], to exclude a hearsay statement upon the basis that admitting it would result in undue waste of time will be potentially applicable in the context of confessions. It is submitted that this exclusionary discretion may be potentially

---

633 *R v Matthews (1989) 91 Cr App R 43; R v Blackwell [1995] 2 Cr App R 625.*

634 *See R v Walsh (1989) 91 Cr App R 161; R v Alladice (1988) 87 Cr App R 380.*

635 *R v Walsh (1989) 91 Cr App R 161.*

636 *See R v Mason [1987] 3 All ER 481.*

637 *R v Wahab [2003] 1 Cr App R 15.*

638 *See R v Canale (1990) 91 Cr App R 1; R v Webster LTL 12/1/2001.*

639 *See R v Gillard and Barrett (1991) 92 Cr App R 61.*

640 *See R v Elleray [2003] 2 Cr App R 165; R v McDonald (CA 23:7:90).*

641 *R v Elleray Elleray [2003] 2 Cr App R 165.*

642 *And considered at 2.7.5.1 below.*

applicable to a confession which is tendered by the prosecution in circumstances in which the confession is admissible under section 76 of the Police and Criminal Evidence Act 1984 but possesses very little probative value (perhaps, for example, because it was made by someone whose mental illness made his statements particularly unreliable). In practice, of course the judge could already exclude such a confession in the exercise of his section 78 or preserved common law discretion[643] upon the basis that its probative value outweighed its prejudicial effect.

What, however, if the confession is tendered not by the prosecution but by a co-accused in circumstances in which it is admissible under section 76A(2) of the 2003 Act?[644] In such circumstances, neither the section 78 nor the preserved common law exclusionary discretion will be applicable as the exercise of both is restricted to the context of prosecution evidence. The exercise of the section 126(1) discretion will not be restricted to the ambit of prosecution evidence, however, and, consequently, it is suggested that the section 126(1) discretion might be deployed in such circumstances so as to exclude the accused's confession when tendered by a co-accused. Whilst the exclusion of a confession in this way does appear to be a technical possibility, it is not suggested, however, that the author regards the exercise of the section 126(1) discretion so as to exclude defence evidence of a co-accused's confession as a practice which is necessarily likely to find judicial favour.

2.4.2.7.6 The admissibility of a confession as evidence for a co-defendant

The nature of the existing law concerning the admissibility of a confession made by a defendant as evidence for a co-defendant and the nature of the law in this context as it will exist when section 128 of the Criminal Justice Act 2003 is in force was considered at 2.2.7 above.

2.4.2.7.7 Confessions made by persons whose knowledge is derived from a hearsay source

A confession is not admissible as evidence of matters stated by its maker (though it may be admissible as evidence of its maker's state of mind) if the knowledge on the part of its maker which forms its basis is derived from a hearsay source.[645] When the hearsay provisions of the 2003 Act are in force, it is submitted that a confession may be admissible to prove (or may be proved by[646]) a hearsay statement, provided that the hearsay statement also falls within the ambit of an exception to the hearsay rule and that the requirements of section 121 of the 2003 Act[647],

---

643 See, for example, R v Miller [1986] 3 All ER 119.

644 Section 76A was considered at 2.2.7.2, above.

645 See: R. v. Hulbert (1979) 69 Cr App R 243; Comptroller of Customs v Western Lectric Co Ltd [1966] AC 367.

646 An example of the proof of admissions made to

the author of a documentary statement by that statement admitted under an exception to the hearsay rule is provided by The Ymnos [1981] 1 Lloyd's Rep 550, a case concerning section 2 of the Civil Evidence Act 1968 (a provision which has since been repealed).

647 Which are considered at 2.7.1 below.

concerning the admissibility of multiple hearsay, are satisfied. Thus, for example, it is submitted that, when the hearsay provisions of the 2003 Act are in force, if A, being suspected of handling stolen goods, confesses that he bought the goods from B, who had told him that he (B) had stolen the goods, the court, applying section 76 of the 1984 Act and sections 114(1)(d) and 126(1)(c) of the 2003 Act, will, if the requirements of those sections are all satisfied, be entitled to admit the confession not merely as evidence of A's state of mind but also, in proving B's statement, as evidence that the goods were stolen.

2.4.2.7.8 Confessions and evidence of opinion

Where a confession takes the form of a statement of opinion, it may be evidentially valueless (and thus inadmissible) if its maker does not possess sufficient knowledge or expertise to make it of some value.[648] This might be the case, for example, where the prosecution seek to rely upon the confession of A that the substance found in his possession was a controlled drug as evidence that the substance was a controlled drug in circumstances in which A had no knowledge or experience of drugs at the time when he made the confession.

2.4.2.7.9 Confessions made by third parties

In relation to confessions made by third parties to criminal proceedings (i.e. the situation in which someone other than the accused confessed to the offence with which the accused is charged), the Law Commission[649] recognised that whilst such confessions are inadmissible at common law in consequence of the operation of the hearsay rule[650], third party confessions might, potentially, fall within the ambit of their proposed regime of new statutory hearsay exceptions (namely, either within that of the hearsay exception which will be created by section 116 of the 2003 Act (considered at 2.2.1 above) or within that of the hearsay exception which will be created by section 114(1)(d) thereof (considered at 2.6 below)).[651] The problem which the Law Commission[652] also identified was, however, that, following the restrictive approach to the concept of relevance adopted by the House of Lords in this context in *R v Blastland*[653], the nature of those circumstances in which a third party confession will be relevant (and thus will be admissible if the third party confession is not excluded by virtue of the operation of the hearsay rule) would appear to be limited to those circumstances in which:

---

648 *See: R v Chatwood [1980] 1 All ER 467; Bird v Adams [1972] Crim LR 224.*

649 *See "Evidence in Criminal Proceedings: Hearsay and Related Topics", Law Com No 245, at paragraph 8.97.*

650 *See R v Turner (1975) 61 Cr App R 67; R v Blastland [1986] AC 41; R v Parsons LTL 17/12/99.*

651 *Indeed, the Law Commission's example of evidence potentially admissible under section 116*

of the 2003 Act which was considered at 2.2.1.2.2 above, appears to concern a third party confession.

652 *See "Evidence in Criminal Proceedings: Hearsay and Related Topics", Law Com No 245, at paragraph 8.97.*

653 *[1986] AC 41.*

"...the inescapable conclusion is that only the third party could have committed the crime...".[654]

Whilst the Law Commission was of the view that third party confessions are logically relevant, the Law Commission accepted that whether evidence is or is not relevant is an issue for the court to determine upon the facts of the case before it. Thus, if the Law Commission's view of the effect of the decision of the House of Lords in *Blastland* in relation to the relevance of third party confessions is correct, it appears that, whilst third party confessions will potentially fall within the ambit of hearsay exceptions created by the 2003 Act, such confessions will largely be treated as irrelevant and, consequently, as inadmissible in criminal proceedings.

It is submitted, however, that, contrary to the Law Commission's view, *Blastland* is not authority for the proposition stated immediately above. Rather, it is submitted that where a third party confession falls within the ambit of a hearsay exception which the 2003 Act will create, retain or preserve, the decision of the House of Lords in *Blastland* will not prevent a criminal court from treating such a confession as relevant to an issue in the proceedings even though the fact that only the third party could have committed the crime is not an inescapable conclusion. The basis of this submission is, first, that the ratio of the decision of the House of Lords in *Blastland* did not concern the admissibility of a third party confession (because, in *Blastland*, leave to appeal to the House of Lords was not granted in relation to the admissibility of third party confessions) and, secondly, that that their Lordships in *Blastland* did not, in any event, regard the third party confession which the Court of Appeal had held to be inadmissible as being inadmissible because it was irrelevant but, rather, regarded it as inadmissible because it fell within the ambit of the hearsay rule but did not fall within the ambit of one of the rule's exceptions.

Thus, it is submitted, that once the new hearsay exceptions which the Criminal Justice Act 2003 will create are in force, it will be open to a criminal court to admit a third party confession in evidence in circumstances in which one or more of the hearsay exceptions which that Act will create is/are applicable. Indeed, there is already authority for the proposition that, in appropriate circumstances, evidence of a third party confession may be admissible under one or other of the statutory exceptions to the hearsay rule created by sections 23 and 24 of the Criminal Justice Act 1988[655], these being hearsay exceptions which (as was seen at 2.2.1 and 2.2.2 above) provisions of the Criminal Justice Act 2003 will effectively replace.

Finally, whilst the effect of section 128(2) of the Criminal Justice Act 2003 appears to be that a confession made by a defendant which is not admissible under section 76 of the Police and Criminal Evidence Act 1984[656] will not be admissible under

---

654 See "*Evidence in Criminal Proceedings: Hearsay and Related Topics*", *Law Com No 245*, at paragraph 8.97 (quoting from paragraph 7.37, note 72. of their consultation paper).

655 *That this may possibly be so was accepted by the Court of Appeal in R v Rigot LTL 18/2/2000 and see also R v Murray (CA) 28/1/2000.*

656 *Section 76 of the 1984 Act is considered at 2.4.2.9.2 below.*

any of the hearsay exceptions which the 2003 Act will create, preserve or retain except, potentially under section 76A of the 1984 Act[657], it is submitted that the operation of section 128(2) will not prevent the admission of a third party confession under a hearsay exception other than that created by section 76 of the 1984 Act because a third party confession is not made "by a defendant" and thus does not fall within the ambit of section 128(2).

2.4.2.7.10 Confessions which implicate co-defendants

In general, a confession which implicates not only the defendant who made it but also implicates his co-defendant is not admissible in evidence against the co-defendant.[658] [Indeed, the hearsay exception created by section 76(1) of the Police and Criminal Evidence 1984[659] (which is considered at 2.4.2.7.2 below) makes the accused's confession admissible against him.] Thus, where the accused's confession implicates his co-accused and separate trials have not been ordered[660], editing of the confession and/or the rehearsing of witnesses to remove references to the co-accused or (where editing the confession or rehearsing witnesses is not practicable[661]) an appropriate direction to the jury to the effect that the accused's confession is not evidence against the co-accused will normally be required.[662]

It appears, however, that there is one situation in which a confession made by one person may be admissible in evidence against another.[663] This, it appears, may be the case where the latter person has, expressly or by implication, adopted the former person's confession as his own (for example, where the former person makes a confession in the presence of the latter person which implicates both the former person and the latter person and the latter person expressly or implicitly admits that the confession is true). In this situation, it is submitted that the latter person has confessed that the former person's confession is true and has thus made a confession which may be admissible under section 76 of the 1984 Act.[664] This is one aspect of the more general principle that, in appropriate circumstances, the court may be entitled to infer from the accused's response to an allegation that he has accepted the truth of the allegation.[665]

What of the operation of hearsay exceptions other than section 76(1) of the 2003 Act in this context? Essentially, section 128(2) of the Criminal Justice Act 2003 provides that nothing in Chapter 2 of Part 11 of the 2003 Act (which regulates the admissibility of hearsay evidence in criminal proceedings) makes a confession

---

657 *Section 76A was considered at 2.2.7.2 above.*

658 *See, for example, R v Gunewadene [1951] 2 KB 600*

659 *Which is considered at 3.3 below.*

660 *It would appear to be exceptional for the court to order separate trials for this purpose (see R v Lake (1976) 64 Cr App R 172).*

661 *For example, it would not be practicable to edit the accused's confession or permit a witness to be rehearsed to avoid reference to a co-accused if this*

would result in the removal of exculpatory material which would favour the accused (see R v Gunewadene [1951] 2 KB 600).

662 *R v Gunewadene [1951] 2 KB 600; R v Allen LTL 13/2/2001.*

663 *For the admissibility of an admission made by an agent against his principal see 2.3.2.9 above.*

664 *See R v Christie [1914] AC 545.*

665 *See R v Christie [1914] AC 545.*

made by a co-defendant admissible if the confession would not be admissible under section 76 or section 76A of the 1984 Act. Moreover, section 118(1) 5 of the 2003 Act preserves any rule of law relating to the admisibility of confessions in criminal proceedings. It is submitted that the combined effect of these provisions in the present context is that none of the exceptions to the hearsay rule which the 2003 Act creates, preserves or retains (other than section 76(1) of the1984 Act) are capable of making a confession made by the accused admissible for the prosecution against his co-accused. Moreover, as was recognised above, it appears that section 76(1) itself will only make the accused's confession admissible against his co-accused in circumstances in which the latter co-accused adopted the former co-accused's confession.

Further, it should be noted that where the guilt of one co-defendant is dependant upon the guilt of another, whilst admissions made by the latter co-defendant are not admissible against the former, if the jury are satisfied beyond reasonable doubt that the latter co-defendant is guilty they may rely upon their conclusion to this effect when determining whether the former co-defendant is guilty.[666]

2.4.2.7.11 Mixed statements

As was seen at 2.3.2.8 above, section 118(1) 5 of the 2003 Act preserves, *inter alia*, "any rule of law relating to the admissibility of...mixed statements in criminal proceedings."

Where a confession which is not wholly inculpatory but which, rather, is partly adverse to its maker and is partly in his favour is admitted in evidence, it appears that the tribunal of fact may rely, as evidence of the truth of matters stated, not just on those parts of the "mixed statement" which are adverse to their maker but also on those parts which are in his favour.[667] The court will not permit the prosecution to rely upon the inculpatory parts of the statement whilst excluding its exculpatory parts as to permit this would be to permit the prosecution to mislead the jury.[668]

Where a mixed statement is admitted in evidence, the trial judge may find it necessary to suggest to the jury that those parts of the mixed statement which are inculpatory are more likely to be deserving of weight than those which are exculpatory.[669]

It appears that, at present, where, the prosecution do not adduce the accused's mixed statement in evidence, the statement is not admissible in evidence in his defence.[670] It is submitted, however, that (whilst section 128(2) of the 2003 Act effectively provides that the hearsay provisions of that Act will not render a

---

666 *R v Hayter [2003] 1 WLR 1910.*
667 *See R v Sharp [1988] 1 WLR 7; R v Aziz [1996] AC 41.*
668 *See R v Pearce (1979) 69 Cr App R 365.*

669 *See R v Sharp [1988] 1 WLR 7; R v Aziz [1996] AC 41.*
670 *R v Aziz [1996] AC 41.*

---

confession made by a defendant admissible in evidence, other than under section 76A of the Police and Criminal Evidence Act 1984[671], if the confession would not be admissible in evidence under section 76 of the 1984 Act[672]) if the prosecution choose not to adduce a mixed statement in evidence in circumstances in which it would be admissible under section 76 of the 1984 Act, it may be possible for the defendant, once the relevant provisions of the 2003 Act are in force, to adduce the mixed statement in evidence under one or more of the exceptions to the hearsay rule which the 2003 Act will create, preserve or retain, for example, under section 114(1)(d), which is considered at 2.6 below.

2.4.2.7.12 The voir dire

In the context of trial on indictment, the admissibility of a confession is determined by the judge. Normally, the judge determines the admissibility of a confession in the absence of the jury, during a "trial within a trial" known as a "*voir dire*". Exceptionally, however, it appears that the defence may decide to permit the jury to hear the accused's confession and to subsequently challenge its admissibility or weight.[673] In this latter situation, it appears that any challenge to the admissibility of the confession could not be made under section 76 or section 78 of the Police and Criminal Evidence Act 1984, because both sections only relate to evidence which the prosecution proposes to adduce, and, consequently, in order to have the confession excluded, the defence would need to persuade the judge to exercise his common law exclusionary discretion.[674]

In a magistrates' court, the admissibility of a confession is determined by the magistrates. It appears that the admissibility of a confession in the magistrates' court is now also normally determined on the voir dire. It seems that where the admissibility of a confession is objected to under section 76(2) of the Police and Criminal Evidence Act 1984 before the close of the prosecution case, the magistrates must hold a voir dire by the end of the prosecution case.[675] Alternatively, however, the defence may choose to attack the confession as part of the defence case.[676] Moreover, where the admissibility of a confession is objected to solely under section 78 of the 1984 Act, it appears that the magistrates are not required to hold a voir dire, though they may decide to do so.[677]

It appears that during a voir dire, the accused should not be asked during cross-examination whether his confession is true, because the purpose of the voir dire is not to determine whether the confession is true but whether it is admissible.[678]

---

671 *Which was considered at 2.2.7.2 above.*

672 *And whilst section 118(1) 5 of the 2003 Act preserves any rule of law concerning the admissibility of mixed statements in criminal proceedings.*

673 *R v Liverpool Juvenile Court, ex parte R [1988] QB 1.*

674 *See R v Sat Bhambra (1988) 88 Cr App R 55 and see section 82(3) of the Police and Criminal*

Evidence Act 1984.

675 *R v Liverpool Juvenile Court, ex parte R [1988] QB 1.*

676 *R v Liverpool Juvenile Court, ex parte R [1988] QB 1.*

677 *See Halawa v Federation Against Copyright Theft [1995] 1 Cr App R 21.*

678 *See Wong Kam-Ming v R [1980] AC 247; R v Cox [1991] Crim LR 276; section 76(2).*

Moreover, it appears that, following the voir dire, the evidence which the accused gave on the voir dire is normally not admissible against him.[679] If, however, the accused's evidence on the voir dire was irrelevant to the admissibility of the confession, it appears that the evidence may be admissible against him.[680] Further, if the accused's confession is admitted and the accused testifies, it appears that, for the purpose of discrediting him, he can be cross-examined in relation to statements which he made on the voir dire which are inconsistent with his testimony.[681]

Where the accused's confession is admitted, the jury are still entitled to decide that the confession is not true. The jury are not concerned with the admissibility of the confession but the defence may raise before the jury the same matters (e.g. cross-examine the same prosecution witnesses) that they raised on the voir dire when disputing the admissibility of the confession and these matters may influence the jury's view as to the confession's evidential weight.[682] The trial judge should not, however, reveal to the jury his decision on the voir dire to admit the confession.[683] This is so because revealing the judge's decision on the voir dire might prejudice the jury in favour of the credibility of the prosecution witnesses and against the credibility of the accused.[684]

Finally, where the accused denies that he made the confession, the issue is one for the jury, not for the judge.[685] Thus, if the defence do not dispute the admissibility of a confession but assert that the accused did not make it, it appears that a voir dire will not be required.

2.4.2.7.13 Facts discovered in consequence of the making of an excluded confession

Section 76(4)(a) of the Police and Criminal Evidence Act 1984 provides that:

> "The fact that a confession is excluded wholly or partly in pursuance of this section shall not affect the admissibility in evidence—
>
> (a)   of any facts discovered as a result of the confession;…"

Thus, where a fact (such as, for example, a murder weapon) is discovered in consequence of the making of a confession which was excluded under section 76(2) of the 1984 Act, the inadmissibility of the confession under section 76(2) does not render evidence of the relevant fact inadmissible.

---

679 *See Wong Kam-Ming v R [1980] AC 247; R v Brophy [1982] AC 476.*
680 *See R v Brophy [1982] AC 476.*
681 *Wong Kam-Ming v R [1980] AC 247.*
682 *See R v Murray [1951] 1 KB 391; R v Burgess [1968] 2 QB 112; Prasad v R (1981) 72 Cr App R 218.*

683 *Mitchell v R [1998] AC 695; Thompson v R [1998] AC 811; R v Adams and Lawrence [2002] UKPC 14.*
684 *Mitchell v R [1998] AC 695.*
685 *Ajodha v The State [1982] AC 204.*

Section 76(5),(6) of the 1984 Act provide, however, that:

> "(5) Evidence that a fact to which this subsection applies was discovered as a result of a statement made by an accused person shall not be admissible unless evidence of how it was discovered is given by him or on his behalf.
>
> (6) Subsection (5) above applies–
>
> (a) to any fact discovered as a result of a confession which is wholly excluded in pursuance of this section; and
>
> (b) to any fact discovered as a result of a confession which is partly so excluded, if the fact is discovered as a result of the excluded part of the confession."

Consequently, whilst the exclusion of a confession under section 76(2) does not render evidence of a fact discovered in consequence of the confession inadmissible, neither the prosecution nor a co-accused may give evidence to the effect that the fact was discovered in consequence of the confession unless evidence concerning the discovery of the relevant fact was given in the accused's defence.

Where a confession is not excluded under section 76(2) of the 1984 Act but, rather, is excluded in the exercise of the Court's exclusionary discretion, whether under section 78 of the 1984 Act or at common law, section 76(4)–(6) do not apply and the position is, thus, governed by the common law. The common law position appears to equate with the position under section 76(4)(a), namely, that the exclusion of the confession does not render evidence of facts discovered in consequence of the making of the confession inadmissible.[686] Whether, in such circumstances, the court is entitled to admit evidence concerning how the relevant facts were discovered if the accused does not first raise the issue remains unclear, though there is authority at common law for the proposition that the part of the excluded confession in which the accused referred to the discovery of the relevant evidence is admissible.[687] Presumably, however, if such evidence is admissible at common law, the court could exclude the evidence in the exercise of its exclusionary discretion under section 78 of the Police and Criminal Evidence Act 1984.

---

[686] *See R v Warwickshall (1783) 1 Leach 263.*   [687] *See, for example, R v Gould (1840) 9 C&P 364.*

2.4.2.7.14 Excluded confessions and evidence of the accused's mode of speech, writing or expression

Section 76(4)(b) of the Police and Criminal Evidence Act 1984 provides that:

"The fact that a confession is excluded wholly or partly in pursuance of this section shall not affect the admissibility in evidence–

(b) where the confession is relevant as showing that the accused speaks, writes or expresses himself in a particular way, of so much of the confession as is necessary to show that he does so."

Thus, where a confession is excluded under section 76(2) of the 1984 Act, part of the confession may be admissible to prove that the accused adopts a particular mode of speech, writing or expression.[688]

Section 76(4)(b) does not apply where a confession is not excluded under section 76(2) of the 1984 Act but, rather, is excluded in the exercise of the Court's exclusionary discretion, whether under section 78 of the 1984 Act or at common law. In such circumstances, the admissibility of the relevant parts of the excluded confession is governed by the common law. The position is not clear, but it may be that at common law the prosecution are not entitled to use part of an excluded confession as evidence of the accused's mode of speech, writing or expression. The evidence would not fall within the ambit of the hearsay rule when tendered for this purpose but the proposition that inadmissible statements made by the accused whilst under arrest should not be referred to in court by the prosecution is derived from *R v Treacy*[689], in which the Court of Appeal held that the prosecution cannot cross-examine the accused on such a statement.[690] Consequently, where a confession is not inadmissible under section 76(2) but is excluded in the exercise of the court's exclusionary discretion, it may be that no part of it can be used by the prosecution to prove that the accused speaks, writes or expresses himself in a particular way (but, as was indicated above, the position remains unclear).

2.4.2.7.15 Confessions made by mentally handicapped persons and section 77 of the Police and Criminal Evidence Act 1984

Section 77 of the 1984 Act does not regulate the admissibility of confessions but, rather, merely imposes a warning requirement in circumstances in which a confession made by a mentally handicapped defendant in the absence of an independent person is admitted in evidence.

---

688 *Section 76(4). An example of the admission of evidence for this purpose, though not forming part of an inadmissible confession, is provided by R v Voisin [1918] 1 KB 531.*

689 *[1944] 2 All ER 229.*

690 *A co-accused may cross-examine the accused on his excluded confession (see R v Myers [1998] AC 124).*

Section 77(1),(2) of the 1984 Act provide that:

"(1) Without prejudice to the general duty of the court at a trial on indictment to direct the jury on any matter on which it appears to the court appropriate to do so, where at such a trial—

 (a) the case against the accused depends wholly or substantially on a confession by him; and

 (b) the court is satisfied—

  (i) that he is mentally handicapped; and

  (ii) that the confession was not made in the presence of an independent person,

 the court shall warn the jury that there is a special need for caution before convicting the accused in reliance on the confession, and shall explain that the need arises because of the circumstances mentioned in paragraphs (a) and (b) above.

(2) In any case where at the summary trial of a person for an offence it appears to the court that a warning under subsection (1) above would be required if the trial were on indictment, the court shall treat the case as one in which there is a special need for caution before convicting the accused on his confession."

A "mentally handicapped" person is defined by section 77(3) as a person

"...in a state of arrested or incomplete development of mind which includes significant impairment of intelligence and social functioning..."

A police officer, police employee or person engaged on police purposes is not an independent person (see section 77(3)) and neither is any person (including a member of the public) to whom a confession is made.[691]

For the purposes of section 77, the case against the accused depends substantially upon his confession if the prosecution case would be substantially less strong in the absence of the confession.[692]

Where section 77 applies, the section does not render confessions made by a mentally handicapped defendant in the absence of an independent person inadmissible. Rather, where the section applies, it merely imposes a mandatory warning requirement upon the Crown Court and a similar requirement upon a magistrates' court.

In circumstances in which section 77 is potentially applicable, it may well be that, in practice, the confession will often either be inadmissible by virtue of the operation of section 76(2) of the 1984 Act or will be excluded, in the exercise of the

---

691 *See R v Bailey [1995] 2 Cr App R 262.*   692 *R v Bailey [1995] 2 Cr App R 262.*

court's exclusionary discretion, under section 78 of the 1984 Act.[693] Alternatively, where unconvincing confessions to which section 77 applies are admitted and form the only evidence against the accused, the judge may find it necessary to withdraw the case from the jury under the principles stated by the Court of Appeal in *R v MacKenzie*[694] concerning unconvincing confessions made by mentally handicapped defendants.[695] Again, in such circumstances, it might be that, when Chapter 2 of Part 11 of the 2003 Act is in force, the court will now be required to stop the case under section 125 of the 2003 Act (which will applies where the case against the accused is wholly or partly based on a statement which was not made in oral evidence in the proceedings and the evidence in the statement is so unconvincing that, in the context of its importance to the case against the accused, it would be unsafe to convict him).[696] In any of these three situations, the section 77 warning will, of course, be otiose.

2.4.2.7.16 The exclusion of confessions and the European Convention on Human Rights

Where a confession is obtained illegally, improperly or unfairly, its admission in evidence may give rise to a violation of Article 6 of the Convention.[697] As a general rule, however, it is for the domestic courts to determine whether evidence is admissible and the European Court of Human Rights will not, in general, substitute its view for that of the domestic court unless either the domestic court's decision was arbitrary or capricious or the safeguards which applied in assessing the reliability of the accused's confession were manifestly inadequate.[698]

It is submitted that the safeguards imposed by the English Law (for example, the tape recording of police station interviews, the existence of section 76(2) and section 78 of the Police and Criminal Evidence Act 1984 and the fact that the admissibility of confessions is determined on the voir dire) should normally ensure that confessions are only admitted in circumstances in which their admission will not give rise to a violation of Article 6.[699] It is clear, however, that the admission of a confession which is obtained in circumstances in which there has been a failure to comply with provisions of Article 6 (for example, where the suspect has been denied access to a solicitor, has been deprived of outside contact, has been detained in austere conditions, has been cautioned as to the potential consequences of silence and has been subjected to extensive questioning) may give

---

693 *R v Moss (1990) 91 Cr App R 371.*

694 *(1993) 96 Cr App R 98.*

695 *In R v MacKenzie (1993) 96 Cr App R 98, the Court of Appeal indicated that where the prosecution case is entirely based upon a confession, the accused has a significant mental handicap and the confession is so unconvincing that no properly directed jury could convict on it then the judge should withdraw the case from the jury.*

696 *Section 125 is considered at 2.7.4, below.*

697 *Austria v Italy (1963) 6 YB 740.*

698 *Brennan v The United Kingdom (2002) 34 EHRR 18.*

699 *See G v the United Kingdom (1983) 35 DR 75; Brennan v The United Kingdom (2002) 34 EHRR 18.*

rise to a violation of Article 6.[700] This, it appears, may be the case even though there have been no breaches of requirements of the 1984 Act or the Codes of Practice and even though the confession is not inadmissible under section 76(2) of the 1984 Act.[701] It is submitted, however, that if, like the Court of Appeal in *R v Z*[702] (which was considered at 2.4.2.7.1 above), the courts comply with their duty (under section 3(1) of the Human Rights Act 1998) to read and give effect to the relevant provisions of the 1984 Act in a Convention compatible way, this should ensure that circumstances in which the admission of a confession in criminal proceedings gives rise to a violation of Article 6 are encountered extremely rarely.

2.4.2.7.17 Admissions made by agents

The admissibility in evidence in criminal proceedings of admissions made by the accused's agent was considered at 2.3.2.9 above.

2.5 The admissibility of hearsay evidence by agreement of the parties

At paragraph 8.150 of its report[703], the Law Commission considered whether hearsay evidence should be admissible in criminal proceedings by agreement of the parties.

> "At present, uncontested evidence can be given in the form of written statements or depositions: they can be read out in court, thereby avoiding the inconvenience or expense that would otherwise be incurred in summoning the witness to testify in person. Written statements may also be tendered if certain conditions are satisfied: these conditions include service of the statement by the party proposing to tender it upon the other parties to the proceedings, and none of those other parties serving a counter-notice objecting to its being tendered in evidence.[215] **We recommend that hearsay evidence should be admissible if all parties to the proceedings agree to it being admissible.**[216] **(Recommendation 31)**
>
> [215] Criminal Justice Act 1967, s 9.
> [216] See cl 1(1)(c) of the draft Bill."

---

701 *In Magee v The United Kingdom (2001) 31 EHRR 35 the European Court of Human Rights held that there had been a violation of Article 6 even though the suspect had not been ill treated, denial of access to a solicitor was authorised by domestic law and the suspect's confession had been voluntary. Equally, the admission of statements made under compulsion by the accused in Saunders v the United Kingdom (1997) 23 EHRR 313 resulted in a violation of Article 6 even though the statements were properly admitted by the trial judge under domestic law (see*

R v Lyons, Parnes, Ronson and Saunders [2001] EWCA Crim 2860). Again, in Allan v The United Kingdom The Times November 12 2002 the admission of a confession in evidence was held to have resulted in a violation of Article 6 of the Convention in circumstances in which the trial judge had admitted the relevant evidence and the Court of Appeal had refused the defendant leave to appeal.
702 *[2003] WLR 1489.*
703 *"Evidence in Criminal Proceedings: Hearsay and Related Topics", Law Com No 245.*

Section 114(1)(c) of the 2003 Act provides that:

> "(1) In criminal proceedings a statement not made in oral evidence in the proceedings is admissible as evidence of any matter stated if, but only if—...
>
> (c) all parties to the proceedings agree to it being admissible...".

Moreover, section 132 of the 2003 Act provides for the making of rules of court (i.e. Crown Court Rules, Criminal Appeal Rules and Magistrates' Courts Rules). Section 132(4) provides that:

> "(4) The rules may provide that the evidence is to be treated as admissible by agreement of the parties if—
>
> (a) a notice has been served in accordance with provision made under subsection (3), and
>
> (b) no counter-notice in the prescribed form objecting to the admission of the evidence has been served by a party."

The operation of section 132 and the potential significance of the failure of a party who proposes to tender a statement under a provision of Chapter 2 of Part 11 of the 2003 Act to comply with a requirement prescribed by rules of court is considered at 2.7.7 below. No such rules of court have yet been made at the time of writing.

It should be noted that whilst, when the provisions of the 2003 Act are in force, hearsay evidence may be admissible under section 114(1)(c) of that Act by agreement of the parties, the 2003 Act will not repeal section 9 of the Criminal Justice Act 1967[704], to which the Law Commission referred, and, moreover depositions will remain potentially admissible under retained statutory exceptions to the hearsay rule.[705] Indeed, as is seen at 2.7.7. below, the Law Commission[706] envisaged that the normal way for a party to give notice of his intention to rely on hearsay evidence would be via section 9 of the 1967 Act.

Finally, it should also be noted that under section 121(1)(b) of the 2003 Act, which concerns multiple hearsay, a hearsay statement may, with the agreement of the parties, be admissible to prove that an earlier hearsay statement was made. Section 121(1)(b) is considered at 2.7.1 below.

---

704 *Considered at 2.4.2.1 above.*

705 *See, in particular, paragraph 5 of Schedule 3 to the Crime and Disorder Act 1998, which is considered at 2.4.1.3 above.*

706 *"Evidence in Criminal Proceedings: Hearsay and Related Topics", Law Com No 245, at paragraph 11.7.*

2.6 The admissibility of hearsay evidence under section 114(1)(d) of the 2003 Act

As was seen at 2.1 above, when the hearsay provisions of the Criminal Justice Act 2003 are in force hearsay evidence will, essentially, be admissible in criminal proceedings in any of four situations, namely, when it is admissible under a statutory exception to the hearsay rule other than that created by section 114(1)(d) of the 2003 Act, when it is admissible under a preserved common law exception to the hearsay rule, when the parties agree to its admission and when it is admissible under section 114(1)(d) of the 2003 Act. Section 114(1)(d),(2) provide as follows.

"(1) In criminal proceedings a statement not made in oral evidence in the proceedings is admissible as evidence of any matter stated if, but only if–...

    (d) the court is satisfied that it is in the interests of justice for it to be admissible.

"(2) In deciding whether a statement not made in oral evidence should be admitted under subsection (1)(d), the court must have regard to the following factors (and to any others it considers relevant)–

    (a) how much probative value the statement has (assuming it to be true) in relation to a matter in issue in the proceedings, or how valuable it is for the understanding of other evidence in the case;

    (b) what other evidence has been, or can be, given on the matter or evidence mentioned in paragraph (a);

    (c) how important the matter or evidence mentioned in paragraph (a) is in the context of the case as a whole;

    (d) the circumstances in which the statement was made;

    (e) how reliable the maker of the statement appears to be;

    (f) how reliable the evidence of the making of the statement appears to be;

    (g) whether oral evidence of the matter stated can be given and, if not, why it cannot;

    (h) the amount of difficulty involved in challenging the statement;

    (i) the extent to which that difficulty would be likely to prejudice the party facing it."

The version of what is now section 114(1)(d) which appeared as clause 98(1)(d) of the Criminal Justice Bill as originally introduced in the House of Commons differed from section 114(1)(d) of the 2003 Act in that clause 98(1)(d) provided that:

> "(1) In criminal proceedings a statement not made in oral evidence in the proceedings is admissible as evidence of any matter stated if, but only if–...
>
> (d) the court is satisfied that, despite the difficulties there may be in challenging the statement, it would not be contrary to the interests of justice for it to be admissible."

What is now section 114(1)(d) is the result of amendments to the Criminal Justice Bill in both Houses of Parliament which culminated in the House of Lords agreeing to the House of Common's amendment which resulted in section 114(1)(d) of the 2003 Act.[707] Whereas a hearsay statement would have been admissible under clause 98(1)(d) of the original version of the Criminal Justice Bill provided that this was not contrary to the interests of justice, a hearsay statement will only be admissible under section 114(1)(d) of the 2003 Act if the court is satisfied that its admission in evidence is in the interests of justice. Prior to moving the Commons amendment that resulted in section 114(1)(d), the Government had:

> "...listened very carefully to concerns that have been expressed that subsection (1)(d) was insufficiently focused."[708]

The Government asserted that:

> "The proposed amendment would tighten up the language used in the discretion to ensure that this evidence can be given only where it is in the interests of justice to do so."[709]

In the form in which it was enacted, section 114(1)(d) of the 2003 Act appears to be more closely related to clause 9 of the Law Commission's draft Bill than was clause 98(1)(d) of the Criminal Justice Bill as originally introduced in the House of Commons. Clause 9 of the Law Commission's draft Bill provided that:

> "9. In criminal proceedings a statement not made in oral evidence in the hearsay. proceedings is admissible as evidence of any matter stated if the court is satisfied that, despite the difficulties there may be in challenging the statement, its probative value is such that the interests of justice require it to be admissible."

---

707 *See Hansard (Lords) 19 November 2003 Column 2005.*

708 *Baroness Scotland of Asthal (Hansard (Lords) 19 November 2003 Column 2005).*

709 *See Hansard (Lords) 19 November 2003 Column 2005.*

Indeed, the origin of section 114(1)(d) of the 2003 Act appears to be the Law Commission's[710] recommendation for the creation of:

"...a limited inclusionary discretion (a "safety-valve") to admit hearsay where the court is satisfied that, despite the difficulties in challenging the statement, its probative value is such that the interests of justice require it to be admissible."

The Law Commission[711] regarded the function of this "safety valve" limited inclusionary discretion, which took the form of clause 9 of their draft Bill, as being:

"...to admit hearsay which falls within no other exception. Its purpose would be to prevent potential injustice which could arise through the exclusion of hearsay evidence. We envisage that it would only be used exceptionally."

The Law Commission[712] had recommended that the new inclusionary discretion to admit hearsay evidence:

"(1) should extend to oral as well as documentary hearsay, and to multiple as well as first-hand hearsay; and

(2) should be available if the court is satisfied that, despite the difficulties there may be in challenging the statement, its probative value is such that the interests of justice require it to be admissible."

Section 114(1)(d) of the 2003 Act essentially appears to implement the former of these two recommendations though (as is seen at 2.7.1 below), it appears that the operation of section 114(1)(d) to multiple hearsay (unlike that of clause 9 of the Law Commission's draft Bill) will be subject to the requirements of the Act's multiple hearsay provision, namely, section 121. In relation to the latter recommendation, section 114(1)(d) (unlike clause 9 of the draft Bill) does not require that the probative value of the hearsay evidence be such that the interests of justice require its admission. Rather, section 114(1)(d) of the 2003 Act merely requires that the admission of the hearsay evidence is in the interests of justice. The Law Commission's intention in including the phrase "probative value" in their recommendations was as follows.[713]

"The phrase "probative value" is designed to encourage the court to consider, amongst other features, the degree of relevance of the statement, the circumstances in which it was made, the extent to which it appears to supply evidence which would not otherwise be available, and the creditworthiness of the declarant. In considering the interests of justice the court would take into

---

710 See *"Evidence in Criminal Proceedings: Hearsay and Related Topics"*, *Law Com No 245*, at paragraph 1.39.

711 See *"Evidence in Criminal Proceedings: Hearsay and Related Topics"*, *Law Com No 245*, at paragraph 8.133.

712 See *"Evidence in Criminal Proceedings: Hearsay and Related Topics"*, *Law Com No 245*, at paragraph 8.141.

713 See *"Evidence in Criminal Proceedings: Hearsay and Related Topics"*, *Law Com No 245*, at paragraph 8.142.

account the reason the declarant cannot give oral evidence, the extent to which the accused can controvert the statement, and the risk of unfairness to the accused."

It appears that, in the context of the section 114(1)(d) test, it is sought to achieve the abovementioned objectives by means of the section 114(2) requirement that in determining whether it is in the interests of justice to admit the hearsay evidence the court must, *inter alia*, have regard to the factors specified by section 114(2)(a)-(i), factors which appear to more than encompass those which the Law Commission intended the court to consider when exercising its recommended inclusionary discretion. Paragraphs 397–398 of the Explanatory Notes to the Criminal Justice Act provide some guidance as to the rationale of what is now section 114(2).

> "327. Subsection (2) sets out some of the factors that the court must consider when deciding whether to grant leave under the discretion in Subsection (1)(d). Some of these factors are:
>
> 1   the degree of relevance of the statement in proving a matter in issue in the trial (assuming the statement to be true);
>
> 1   the circumstances in which it was made (if indeed it was made at all);
>
> 1   the extent to which it supplies evidence which would not otherwise be available;
>
> 1   the creditworthiness of the maker of the statement;
>
> 1   the reason why oral evidence cannot be given;
>
> 1   the extent to which the other party can challenge the statement, and the risk of unfairness.
>
> 328. The list is intended to focus attention on whether the circumstances surrounding the making of the out of court statement indicate that it can be treated as reliable enough to admit it as evidence, despite the fact that it will not be subject to cross-examination."

It is submitted that in circumstances in which the admission of hearsay evidence in criminal proceedings would result in a violation of Article 6 of the European Convention on Human Rights, the effect of section 3(1) of the Human Rights Act 1998 is that the court should not regard the admission of hearsay evidence under section 114(1)(d) as being in the interests of justice.[714]

---

714 *The extent to which the admission or exclusion of hearsay evidence in criminal proceedings has the potential to result in a violation of Article 6 of the convention is considered at 2.8 below.*

The Law Commission[715] was of the view that the "safety valve" which their recommended inclusionary discretion would create would operate in practice in the following way.

> "A party would only need to turn to the safety-valve where none of the other exceptions could be used. By definition, therefore, the declarant must be unavailable for some reason other than death, illness, fear, disappearance, or being outside the United Kingdom. The declarant need not have been competent at the time the statement was made. The declarant need not even be identified. We do not anticipate that there would be a large number of applications to admit evidence via the safety-valve. The Crown Prosecution Service was concerned that there would be a large number of unmeritorious applications, particularly in the magistrates' courts. Our view is that all courts would regard the safety-valve as an exception to be used in very limited circumstances, and if it is too freely used, the Court of Appeal or Divisional Court will give guidance."

It is submitted, however, that even the wording of clause 9 of the Law Commission's draft Bill did not expressly limit the operation of the safety valve to those circumstances in which no other hearsay exception was available. Thus, it may be that given that the section 114(1)(d) hearsay exception is not fettered by the miscellaneous technical requirements which limit the ambit of the various statutory and common law hearsay exceptions, is applicable to multiple hearsay (if, it seems, subject to the requirements of section 121, which are considered at 2.7.1 below) and may potentially render admissible the hearsay evidence of a person who was not competent to give evidence at the time when he made the hearsay statement, applications to admit hearsay evidence under section 114(1)(d) may, in practice, be more numerous that the Law Commission had envisaged.

Finally, it is submitted that whether section 114(1)(d) (or clause 9 of the Law Commission's draft Bill) should technically be regarded as creating a "discretion" is arguable. Certainly, in support of the Law Commission's classification of its recommended "safety valve" as an inclusionary discretion, the Explanatory Notes to the Criminal Justice Act[716] treat the process which the court will undertake when required to determine the admissibility of hearsay evidence under the section 114(1)(d) hearsay exception as being that of determining whether to grant leave in the exercise of its discretion. Moreover, the Government, on a number of occasions during its progression through both Houses of Parliament, clearly regarded what is now section 114(1)(d) of the 2003 Act as creating an inclusionary discretion.[717] It should be noted, however, that section 114(1)(d) of the 2003 Act (like clause 9 of the draft Bill), does not provide that the court "may" admit hearsay

---

715 See "Evidence in Criminal Proceedings: Hearsay and Related Topics", Law Com No 245, at paragraph 8.143.

716 See paragraphs 395 to 398.

717 See, for example, Hansard (Commons) 28 January 2003 Column 608 and Hansard (Lords) 19 November 2003 Column 2005.

evidence when the requirement imposed by the provision are satisfied but, rather, provides that where the relevant requirement is satisfied the evidence "is" admissible. Thus, it is arguable that where "...the court is satisfied that it is in the interests of justice for it to be admissible", the effect of section 114(1)(d) is, at least technically, not to give the court discretion to admit the relevant hearsay evidence but, rather, is to require the court, subject to the exercise of the court's exclusionary discretion, derived from other statutory provisions or from the common law[718], to admit it. The Law Commission[719] was, however, of the view that the exercise of the exclusionary discretion would, in practice, be otiose in the context of evidence admissible under their recommended "safety valve" inclusionary discretion.

> "In theory, both section 78(1) of PACE and the common law discretion to exclude prosecution evidence will apply. In practice, these discretions will add nothing, as they are both concerned with fairness to the accused, and it would be illogical for a judge to decide that it was in the interests of justice to admit evidence, but that to do so would have such an adverse effect on the fairness of the proceedings that that same evidence ought to be excluded. Similarly it is inconceivable that evidence which would otherwise have been admitted under the safety-valve might be excluded under our recommended discretion to exclude evidence which would result in undue waste of time.206 If evidence is sufficiently reliable to justify invoking the safety-valve, it cannot be the kind of evidence that would result in undue waste of time.
>
> 206 See paras 11.16 – 11.18 below."

It is submitted that, in practice, the Law Commission's view as to the limited significance of exclusionary discretion in the context of what is now the section 114(1)(d) hearsay exception is likely to be valid and that the Courts are likely to treat section 114(1)(d) of the 2003 Act as creating an inclusionary discretion. Indeed, it should be noted that whereas the exclusionary discretion created by section 78 of the Police and Criminal Evidence Act 1984 and the common law exclusionary discretion preserved by section 82(3) of the 1984 Act (considered at 2.7.5.2 below) are only applicable to prosecution evidence, the "inclusionary discretion" created by section 114(1)(d) of the 2003 Act (like the exclusionary discretion created by section 126(1) of the 2003 Act[720]) is applicable to hearsay evidence whether tendered by prosecution or defence.

2.7 Other provisions contained in Chapter 2 of Part 11 of the 2003 Act

Sections 121 to 126 of the Criminal Justice Act 2003 comprise a number of supplementary provisions concerning the admissibility of hearsay evidence in criminal proceedings and related matters, section 133 of the 2003 Act concerns the proof of statements made in documents in criminal proceedings and section 132

---

718 *The nature of the court's exclusionary discretion is considered at 2.7.5 below.*

719 *See "Evidence in Criminal Proceedings: Hearsay*

and Related Topics", Law Com No 245, at paragraph 8.145.

720 *Which is considered at 2.7.5.1 below.*

of the 2003 Act concerns the court's rule-making powers. Whilst the effect of section 122 of the 2003 Act (concerning the use of documents produced as exhibits where a statement made in a document is admitted under section 119 or 120) has already been considered[721], the remainder of these provisions (whilst many of them have already been referred to on more than one occasion in Part Two of this book) still require further consideration.

2.7.1 Multiple hearsay

Section 121 of the Criminal Justice Act 2003 concerns the admissibility of multiple hearsay in criminal proceedings. Section 121 provides as follows.

"121   Additional requirement for admissibility of multiple hearsay

(1)   A hearsay statement is not admissible to prove the fact that an earlier hearsay statement was made unless–

(a)   either of the statements is admissible under section 117, 119 or 120,

(b)   all parties to the proceedings so agree, or

(c)   the court is satisfied that the value of the evidence in question, taking into account how reliable the statements appear to be, is so high that the interests of justice require the later statement to be admissible for that purpose.

(2)   In this section "hearsay statement" means a statement, not made in oral evidence, that is relied on as evidence of a matter stated in it."

Originally, within the Criminal Justice Bill as introduced in the House of Commons, the issue of multiple hearsay was dealt with by clause 105. Clause 105, which was based upon clause 10 of the Law Commission's draft Bill[722], was a somewhat unusual provision to which section 121 of the 2003 Act bears little resemblance.[723]

The Government recognised that clause 105 was one of the more complex clauses of the Criminal Justice Bill[724] and accepted that the clause (by this stage in the

---

721 At 2.2.3.2, 2.2.4.3, 2.2.5.2.2 and 2.2.6, above.

722 See "Evidence in Criminal Proceedings: Hearsay and Related Topics", Law Com No 245.

723 Clause 105 provided as follows (note that the clauses to which it refers were eventually enacted in the guise of sections 117, 119 and 120 of the 2003 Act):

"(1) If there is a series of statements not made in oral evidence (such as "A said that B said that C shot the deceased") sections 107 and 109 to 114 apply as follows.

(2) If a statement–

(a) is relied on as evidence of a matter stated in it, and

(b) is admissible for that purpose only under section 109 or a rule preserved by section 111, the fact that the statement was made must be proved by evidence admissible otherwise than under section 109.

(3) Otherwise–

(a) sections 107 and 109 to 114 apply to the admissibility of each statement, and

(b) different statements may be admissible under different sections (or different provisions of the same section)."

724 See Hansard (Commons) 28 January 2003 Column 651.

legislative process re-numbered as clause 104) was both difficult to understand and did not expressly state the circumstances in which multiple hearsay is sufficiently reliable to be admissible.[725] Consequently, the Government decided to insert a revised clause at the Bill's Third Reading in the Lords, the Government's intention being that:

> "This revised clause will make clear that Clause 99, which allows evidence to be admitted where a witness is unavailable for good reason, will not operate to allow a chain of such statements to be admissible. However, where the hearsay is admissible in a reliable form, such as in a business document or in a previous statement of a witness who is in court to give evidence and can therefore be questioned on the statement, we consider that the evidence should be admissible."[726]

A new clause, clause 93, was thus inserted into the Criminal Justice Bill by amendment at the Bill's Third Reading in the Lords, the original multiple hearsay clause being left out.[727] It is this new provision, rather than the original clause 105, which has now been enacted as section 121 of the 2003 Act.

Baroness Scotland of Asthal (the Minister of State for the Criminal Justice System and Law Reform) explained the purpose and intended operation of the new clause in the following way.[728] (It should be noted that the clauses 89, 91 and 92 to which her Ladyship refers have now been enacted in the guise of sections 117, 119 and 120 of the 2003 Act, respectively).

> "The new clause proposed in the amendment seeks to set out clearly the circumstances where multiple hearsay can be admitted. Its subsection (1)(a) provides for multiple hearsay to be admissible where one of the statements is admissible under Clauses 89, 91 or 92. That is where it includes a business statement and is therefore inherently reliable, and where it includes a previous statement of a witness who is giving evidence in court and can therefore be questioned about the statement. Subsection 1(b) covers evidence where all parties agree that the evidence should be given. In those circumstances, there is of course no reason to think that the evidence should not properly be given.
>
> However, there may also be cases not falling within those narrow circumstances where multiple hearsay should be admitted. In those circumstances where it is important for the evidence to be given, the hearsay rules should not preclude its admission. We therefore have retained a narrow

---

725 *See Hansard (Lords) 4 November 2003 Column 760.*

726 *Baroness Scotland of Asthal (Hansard (Lords) 4 November 2003 Column 760). Clause 99 subsequently became section 116 of the 2003 Act, which was examined at 2.2.1 above.*

727 *Hansard (Lords) 17 November 2003 Column 1794.*

728 *Hansard (Lords) 17 November 2003 Columns 1791–1793.*

discretion to admit multiple hearsay evidence that falls without proposed new subsection (1)(a) and (b) but should nevertheless be admissible.

Of course, such circumstances will be exceptional, and the test in proposed new subsection (1)(c) is therefore worded to reflect that a substantial threshold should be met before such evidence can be given. The test is worded so that such evidence can be given where the court is satisfied that the value of the evidence in question, taking into account how reliable the statement appears to be, is so high that the interests of justice require the later statement to be admissible.

It may assist the House if I outline an example of a situation where it may be appropriate to use the discretion to admit multiple hearsay evidence. Let us take the case involving rape of an 80 year-old lady who suffers a serious stroke shortly afterwards and cannot tell the police what has happened to her. However, let us say that before losing consciousness she told the doctor what happened to her, and that she could not identify her attacker. The doctor immediately writes that all down, but is working abroad by the time of the trial.

One key issue in the case is identity, on which the 80 year-old's evidence can shed no light. However, the prosecution has good independent evidence to establish identity, but no medical evidence showing injuries to establish that she was attacked. Her statement is, therefore, vital to establish another key issue – that she was raped. But it is multiple hearsay, being an out-of-court statement by the doctor of what she said. In such circumstances it would be quite wrong for the rules of evidence to bar the courts from admitting that evidence.

This is not a far-fetched scenario, as the courts in New Zealand dealt with a similar situation involving an out-of-court statement in the case of Hovell. It highlights the need for some discretion to cover exceptional cases. One of the central criticisms of the hearsay rule under the current law is that it is inflexible and can in some circumstances prevent the court admitting evidence when it is clearly in the interests of justice to do so. The discretion will provide a degree of flexibility within the hearsay rules that is much needed and much called for.

In drawing up the revised clause, we have listened to concerns in the House on the subject that multiple hearsay should not generally be admissible. The revised clause will ensure that that is not the case. The proposed new clause strikes the right balance between admitting evidence where it is appropriate in exceptional cases to be given, and ensuring sufficient safeguards against the admission of unreliable evidence."

So far as the effect of section 121 is concerned, it is submitted that whilst, on its face, this provision appears to be less complex than clause 105, the courts may well find that both its interpretation and its practical application is less than straightforward.

2.7.1.1 Section 121(1)(a)

Section 121(1)(a) provides that:

> "(1) A hearsay statement is not admissible to prove the fact that an earlier hearsay statement was made unless–
>
> (a) either of the statements is admissible under section 117, 119 or 120,…"

Reference to the statements made by Baroness Scotland (reproduced at 2.7.1 above), makes clear that the rationale underlying section 121(1)(a) of the 2003 is that the admissibility of "multiple hearsay" under section 117 of the 2003 Act is justified by the reliability of "business documents" and that the admissibility of "multiple hearsay" under sections 119 and 120 of the 2003 Act is justified by the fact that where a previous inconsistent or consistent statement was made by a witness who is testifying in the proceedings, the witness can be questioned about the statement. Similarly, whilst, in relation to the rationale underlying clause 105, the Law Commission[729] regarded multiple hearsay as being, in general, too unreliable to be admitted in criminal proceedings, they regarded the presumed reliability of business documents admissible under what is now section 117 of the 2003 Act and the fact that where a witness' previous statement is admissible under what is now section 119 or section 120 of that Act, the witness will be available for cross-examination, as outweighing or compensating for the multiple hearsay nature of the relevant evidence.

Whilst it is not difficult to identify the rationale underlying section 121(1)(a) of the 2003 Act, it is suggested, however, that determining exactly how section 121(a) will operate in practice is a more difficult task. This, it is submitted, is so because whilst section 121(1)(a) will require that either the earlier or the later statement must be admissible under section 117, section 119 or section 120 of the 2003 Act, section 121(1)(a) does not expressly require that the other statement (the one which is not admissible under one of these three sections, unless, of course, both statements are admissible under one or more of these three sections) must be admissible under some other hearsay exception which the 2003 Act will create, retain or preserve. Thus, it is possible to argue that the effect of section 121(1)(a) will be that where either the earlier or the later hearsay statement falls within the ambit of section 117, section 119 or section 120, the other hearsay statement will be rendered admissible by section 121(1)(a) itself.

---

729 See *"Evidence in Criminal Proceedings: Hearsay and Related Topics"*, *Law Com No 245*, at paragraph 8.21–8.22.

Alternatively, it is possible to argue that where the earlier hearsay statement falls within the ambit of section 117, section 119 or section 120, then the effect of section 121(1)(a) will be that the later hearsay statement, regardless of whether it falls within the ambit of one of the hearsay exceptions which the 2003 Act will create, retain or preserve, will be admissible to prove the earlier statement, but that where it is the later statement which falls within the ambit of section 117, section 119 or section 120, the later statement will be admissible to prove the earlier statement but the earlier statement, in order to be admissible, must still fall within the ambit of a hearsay exception.

A third possible interpretation of section 121(1)(a) is that, in order for multiple hearsay to be admissible under section 121(1)(a), both hearsay statements must fall within the ambit of hearsay exceptions which the 2003 Act will create, retain or preserve and at least one of them must fall within the ambit of section 117, section 119 or section 120 of the 2003 Act. Certainly, under clause 105 of the Criminal Justice Bill (had that provision been enacted) as under clause 10 of the Law Commission's draft Bill, it appears that both earlier and later statements would have been required to fall within the ambit of hearsay exceptions created, preserved or retained by the 2003 Act and, moreover, that if the earlier statement was only admissible under section 116 of the 2003 Act or under a common law exception to the hearsay rule preserved by section 118, the hearsay exception under which the later statement was admissible could not have been that which will be created by section 116 of the 2003 Act.[730]

It is submitted that, having regard to the integrity of the new statutory hearsay regime which the 2003 Act will create, it is the final of the three interpretations of section 121(1)(a), which were considered above, which is to be preferred. Indeed, it is submitted that this interpretation is in line with the statutory heading (retained from clause 105) "Additional requirement for admissibility of multiple hearsay").

If this third possible interpretation of section 121(1)(a) is adopted by the courts then section 121(1)(a) will only operate where both hearsay statements fall within the ambit of hearsay exceptions created, preserved or retained by the 2003 Act, one of them falling within that of a hearsay exception created by section 117, 119 or 120 of that Act. Even if this interpretation of section 121(1)(a) is correct, however, it is submitted that the ambit of the provision is still potentially extremely wide, given the fact that the majority of documentary hearsay in the criminal context will at some stage be "received" by a person in the course of a trade, business, profession etc, and will thus potentially fall within the ambit of section 117 of the 2003 Act.[731]

---

730 See *"Evidence in Criminal Proceedings: Hearsay and Related Topics", Law Com No 245,* at paragraph 8.24.

731 See 2.2.2.2.3 above.

2.7.1.2 Section 121(1)(b)

Section 121(1)(b) provides that:

> "(1) A hearsay statement is not admissible to prove the fact that an earlier hearsay statement was made unless–...
>
> (b) all parties to the proceedings so agree,..."

Of the three paragraphs of section 121(1), the application of section 121(1)(b) appears least likely to trouble the courts. Section 114(1)(c) of the 2003 Act (which was considered at 2.5 above) will render hearsay evidence admissible by agreement in criminal proceedings. Section 132(4) (which was considered at 2.5 above) makes provision for the making of rules of court concerning the procedure to be followed where hearsay evidence is to be admitted in criminal proceedings by agreement.

2.7.1.3 Section 121(1)(c)

Section 121(1)(c) provides that:

> "(1) A hearsay statement is not admissible to prove the fact that an earlier hearsay statement was made unless–...
>
> (c) the court is satisfied that the value of the evidence in question, taking into account how reliable the statements appear to be, is so high that the interests of justice require the later statement to be admissible for that purpose."

The interpretation and practical application of the section 121(1)(c) "discretion"[732] is likely to be somewhat more troublesome than that of section 121(1)(b). First, will section 121(1)(c) only apply where the earlier and later statements both fall within the ambit of hearsay exceptions which the 2003 Act creates, retains or preserves or will section 121(1)(c) potentially render the later statement admissible to prove the earlier statement even though the later statement does not fall within the ambit of a hearsay exception which the 2003 Act creates, retains or preserves?

It seems that clause 105 of the Criminal Justice Bill, like clause 10 of the Law Commission's draft Bill, was not intended to have the latter effect. Clause 105 certainly would have had no potential application independent of the various hearsay exceptions which the 2003 Act will create, retain or preserve. Rather, the wording of clause 105 clearly indicated that the clause merely related to the operation of what are now sections 114 and 116 to 120 of the 2003 Act.

---

732 *The issue of whether this provision should technically be regarded as creating an inclusionary discretion appears to equate with that concerning the nature of section 114(1)(d) of the 2003 Act, which was considered at 2.6 above. It was, of course, described as a "discretion" by Baroness Scotland in the extract from Hanrard reproduced above. It is also so described in the Explanatory notes to the Criminal Justice Act (at paragraph 417).*

Consequently, it appears that, under clause 105, if the earlier statement did not fall within the ambit of a hearsay exception which the 2003 Act will create, retain or preserve, it would not have been admissible and could not have been proved by any other statement.[733] Similarly, even if the earlier statement did fall within the ambit of an exception to the hearsay rule which the 2003 Act will create, retain or preserve, it seems that the statement could only have been proved under clause 105 by the later statement if the later statement also fell within the ambit of a hearsay exception which the 2003 Act will create, retain or preserve.[734] Moreover, where the earlier statement only fell within the ambit of the hearsay exception which section 116 of the 2003 Act will create or within that of one of the common law hearsay exceptions which section 118 of the 2003 Act will preserve, it appears that the statement could not have been proved under clause 105 by another hearsay statement which was itself admissible only under section 116 of the 2003 Act.[735]

Unlike the wording of clause 105, however, the wording of section 121(1)(c) of the 2003 Act does not expressly relate to the operation of section 114 and sections 116 to 120 of the 2003 Act. Rather, it is submitted that a possible interpretation of section 121(1)(c) is that that the later statement may be admissible under section 121(1)(c) to prove the earlier statement, regardless of whether it satisfies the requirements of one of the other hearsay exceptions which the 2003 Act will create, retain or preserve.

Another possible interpretation of section 121(1)(c) is, however, that the earlier and later statements must both fall within the ambit of one of the other hearsay exceptions which the 2003 Act will create, retain or preserve and that, even where this is so, unless the requirements of section 121(1)(a) or (b) are satisfied, section 121(1)(c) will form an additional admissibility requirement which must be satisfied if the later statement is to be admissible to prove the former.

Having regard both to the integrity of the new statutory hearsay regime which the 2003 Act will create and to the section 121's heading (retained from clause 105) "Additional requirement for admissibility of multiple hearsay", it is submitted that the latter interpretation of section 121(1)(c) is to be preferred, If this interpretation of section 121(1)(c) is adopted by the courts, then section 121(1)(c) will only operate where both hearsay statements fall within the ambit of hearsay exceptions created, preserved or retained by the 2003 Act. Even so, unlike the position as it would have existed under clause 105 and under clause 10 of the Law Commission's draft Bill, it appears that under section 121(1)(c) it will be possible for a hearsay statement which is admissible either under section 116 of the 2003

---

733 See *"Evidence in Criminal Proceedings: Hearsay and Related Topics"*, Law Com No 245, at paragraph 8.24.

734 See *"Evidence in Criminal Proceedings: Hearsay and Related Topics"*, Law Com No 245, at paragraph 8.24.

735 See *"Evidence in Criminal Proceedings: Hearsay and Related Topics"*, Law Com No 245, at paragraph 8.24.

Act or under a common law hearsay exception which section 118 of the 2003 Act will preserve to be proved by a hearsay statement which is admissible under section 116 of the 2003 Act.

In relation to the issue of whether the earlier or later statement must fall within the ambit of another hearsay exception which the 2003 Act will create, retain or preserve, the example provided by Baroness Scotland, reproduced above, does not expressly suggest that either statement must fall within the ambit of such a hearsay exception; but neither does it say that either need not. It is submitted, however, that her ladyship's example is potentially flawed in any event in that, provided that the doctor is regarded as having created the document in the course of his profession, the hearsay evidence appears to be potentially admissible under section 117 of the 2003 act, in which case section 121(1)(a) appears to apply and consideration of section 121(1)(c) in the context of the example thus appears to be unnecessary.

A second problem which the courts will presumably face in the context of the application of section 121(1)(c) will be the practical application of the section 121(1)(c) interests of justice test. It is submitted that, in practice, determining when the value of the earlier statement is so high that, taking into account the reliability of the earlier and later statements, the interests of justice require the admission of the later statement for the purpose of proving the earlier statement, may often be a difficult task. It should be noted that in Baroness Scotland's example, she did not consider the reliability of the old lady's evidence. It is submitted, however, that, in practice, the old lady's state of mind at the time when she made the statement might be crucial. It should also be noted, however, that if, as was submitted above, the facts of Baroness Scotland's example are properly regarded as falling within the ambit of the hearsay exception created by section 117 of the 2003 Act, then the safeguard concerning the capability (i.e. the competence) of the maker of a hearsay statement to make it, created by section 123 of the 2003 Act, would be applicable thereto.

2.7.1.4 The "safety valve" inclusionary discretion and multiple hearsay

As was seen at 2.6 above, the Law Commission intended that their "safety valve" "inclusionary discretion", which now, in modified form, exists in the guise of section 114(1)(d) of the 2003 Act, would be applicable to multiple hearsay. Had it been enacted, it appears that clause 105 of the Criminal Justice Bill, like clause 10 of the Law Commission's draft Bill, would not have limited the power of the court to admit multiple hearsay under section 114(1)(d). In relation to the operation of section 121(1) of the 2003 Act, however, it is submitted that, under this provision, multiple hearsay will only be admissible in criminal proceedings if the requirements of section 121(1)(a),(b) or (c) are satisfied. Thus, it appears that unless one of the hearsay statement falls within the ambit of section 117, section 119 or section 120 or the parties agree to the admission of the multiple hearsay, multiple hearsay will only be admissible under section 114(1)(d) if the requirements of section 121(1)(c) are also satisfied.

Even if this view as to the combined effect of section 114(1)(d) and section 121(1)(c) is correct, however, it may be that in circumstances in which the court is satisfied that the admission of a hearsay statement is in the interests of justice for the purposes of the section 114(1)(d) inclusionary discretion, the court is unlikely to then rule under section 121(1)(c) that the interests of justice do not require its admission. That being said, it appears to be arguable that the section 121(1)(c) "interests of justice require" test imposes a higher threshold than the section 114(1)(d) "the court is satisfied that it is in the interests of justice" test.

2.7.1.5 Statements which do not fall within the ambit of the hearsay rule and representations made by machines

Finally, it should be noted that section 121 is only applicable to a "hearsay statement". A "hearsay statement" is defined by section 121(2) as "…a statement, not made in oral evidence, that is relied on as evidence of a matter stated in it." Thus, since, for the purposes of Chapter 2 of Part 11 of the 2003 Act, a representation of fact which was made not by a person but by a machine is not a "statement"[736], it appears that where a hearsay statement is relied upon to prove a representation made by a machine, the requirements of section 121 of the 2003 Act will not be applicable. Similarly, it appears that section 212 of the 2003 Act will not be applicable where a hearsay statement is relied upon to prove another statement if the latter statement is not relied upon as evidence of matters stated in it but, rather, is relied upon merely to prove that the relevant matters were stated.[737] Moreover, since the provisions of Chapter 2 of Part 11 of the 2003 Act do not apply to a "matter stated" where the maker of the relevant statement neither intended to cause a person to believe the relevant matter nor intended to cause a person to act or a machine to operate on the basis that the matter was as stated[738], it appears that the requirements of section 121 will not apply where a hearsay statement is relied upon to prove an implied assertion, an implied assertion not falling within the ambit of the hearsay rule in the form in which that rule will exist when the hearsay provisions of the 2003 Act are in force.[739]

2.7.2 Required capability of the maker of a statement and of those who supply or receive information or create or receive documents

Section 123 of the Criminal Justice Act 2003 concerns both the "required capability" of the maker of a hearsay statement which is tendered under sections 116, 119 or 120 of the 2003 Act and, in the context of a hearsay statement which is tendered under section 117 of the 2003 Act, the "required capability" of a person

---

736 *See section 115(3) and see 1.9.2 above.*
737 *The admissibility of such "original evidence" is considered at 1.5 above.*
738 *See section 115(3) and see 1.6.2 above.*
739 *The status of implied assertions under the 2003 Act was considered at 1.6.2, above.*

who supplied or received information or created or received a document.[740] Section 123 provides as follows.

"(1) Nothing in section 116, 119 or 120 makes a statement admissible as evidence if it was made by a person who did not have the required capability at the time when he made the statement.

(2) Nothing in section 117 makes a statement admissible as evidence if any person who, in order for the requirements of section 117(2) to be satisfied, must at any time have supplied or received the information concerned or created or received the document or part concerned—

(a) did not have the required capability at that time, or

(b) cannot be identified but cannot reasonably be assumed to have had the required capability at that time.

(3) For the purposes of this section a person has the required capability if he is capable of—

(a) understanding questions put to him about the matters stated, and

(b) giving answers to such questions which can be understood.

(4) Where by reason of this section there is an issue as to whether a person had the required capability when he made a statement—

(a) proceedings held for the determination of the issue must take place in the absence of the jury (if there is one);

(b) in determining the issue the court may receive expert evidence and evidence from any person to whom the statement in question was made;

(c) the burden of proof on the issue lies on the party seeking to adduce the statement, and the standard of proof is the balance of probabilities."

Essentially, in relation to the operation of sections 116, 119 and 120 of the 2003 Act, the effect of section 123(1) will be that if the maker of a hearsay statement tendered under one of those provisions did not have the "required capability" at the time when he made the hearsay statement, then the hearsay statement will not be rendered admissible by, as appropriate, section 116, section 119 or section 120. Similarly, in relation to the operation of section 117 of the 2003 Act, the position will, essentially, be that if the person who supplied or received the relevant information or created or received the relevant document did not have the required capability at the time when he did so (or cannot be identified but cannot reasonably be assumed to have had the required capability at the relevant time), then the hearsay evidence will not be rendered admissible by section 117.

---

740 *Sections 116, 117, 119 and 120 are considered, respectively, at 2.2.1. 2.2.2, 2.2.3 and 2.2.4 above.*

2.7.2.1 Persons who cannot be identified

For the purposes of section 123(2)(b), in determining whether a person who cannot identified may or may not reasonably be presumed to have had the required capability at the relevant time, presumably the court (as it currently may when determining for the purposes of section 24(1)(ii) of the Criminal Justice Act 1988 whether the supplier of information may reasonably be supposed to have had personal knowledge of the matters dealt with by the documentary statement which is tendered under section 24) may, in appropriate circumstances, be entitled to infer that this is so from matters such as the nature and source of the document.[741]

2.7.2.2 "Required Capability"

The section 123(3) test of "required capability" essentially equates with the competence requirement which was imposed in the context of criminal proceedings by section 53(3) of the Youth Justice and Criminal Evidence Act 1999. It should be noted, however, that section 53(3) of the 1999 Act concerns a person's ability to understand and give understandable answers to "questions put to him as a witness" whereas section 123(3) of the 2003 Act concerns a person's capability to understand and give understandable answers to "questions put to him about the matters stated." It may well be that this is a distinction without any practical significance, though, it is submitted, it is at least theoretically possible that a person who, perhaps due to his youth, mental illness, low I.Q. or limited communication skills, would not be able to answer questions generally as a witness (and who would thus fail the section 53(3) test of competence) might be able to answer questions about a specific matter (and thus could potentially satisfy the section 123(3) test in relation to a hearsay statement which he had made concerning the specific matter).

What of the position of a person who had the "required capability" when he made a hearsay statement but, perhaps in consequence of an accident, is not competent to give evidence by the time of the trial? In such circumstances it appears that the operation of section 53(3) of the 1999 Act will prevent the person from giving oral evidence in the proceedings but section 123(3) of the 2003 Act will not prevent the admission of his hearsay statement under any of sections 116, 117, 119 or 120 of the 2003 Act.

2.7.2.3 Section 123(4)

Section 123(4) provides that proceedings for the determination of the issue of whether a person had the required capability at the time when he made a statement should take place in the absence of the jury, that the court may, in determining this issue, receive both expert evidence and evidence from a person to

---

741 *See R v Foxley [1995] 2 Cr App R 523, R v Ilyas [1996] Crim LR 810 and Vehicle and Operator Services Agency v George Jenkins Transport Ltd The Times December 5 2003, all cases concerning section 24 of the 1988 Act.*

whom the statement was made, that the burden of proof in relation to this issue is borne by the party who tenders the hearsay evidence and that the requisite standard of proof is proof on the balance of probabilities.

In relation to the incidence of the burden of proof, the imposition of the burden of proving that the maker of the statement had the required capability at the relevant time upon the party tendering the hearsay evidence is consistent both with the general principle that the burden of establishing the admissibility of evidence is borne by the party who tenders the relevant evidence[742] and with the position encountered under section 54(2) of the Youth Justice and Criminal Evidence Act 1999 concerning the incidence of the burden of proving that a witness is competent to give evidence in criminal proceedings

In relation to the standard of proof, section 123(4)(c), merely requires the party tendering the hearsay evidence, in order to discharge the burden of proof imposed upon him, to satisfy the court on the balance of probabilities that the person who made the hearsay statement had the required capability at the relevant time. The requisite standard of proof is proof on the balance of probabilities, and this is so whether the hearsay evidence is tendered by the defence or by the prosecution, Thus, whilst section 123(4) is consistent with the position encountered under section 54(2) of the Youth Justice and Criminal Evidence Act 1999 concerning the discharge of the burden of proving that a witness is competent to give evidence in criminal proceedings, it should be noted that neither of these provisions are consistent with the general principle that where the prosecution bear the burden of establishing the admissibility of evidence, this burden must be discharged to the criminal standard of proof.[743]

2.7.2.4 The ambit of section 123

The "required capability" requirement imposed by section 123 of the 2003 Act will not apply to hearsay evidence tendered under a hearsay exception other than those created by sections 116, 117, 119 and 120 of the 2003 Act. Thus, for example, the Law Commission[744] expressly recognised that the "safety valve" inclusionary discretion, which will be created by section 114(1)(d) of the 2003 Act (and was considered at 2.6 above), may be applicable to a hearsay statement the maker of which would not have been competent at the time when he made it.[745] Equally, it

---

742 *See, for example, R v Jenkins (1869) LR 1 CCR 187). The imposition of the burden of proof on the party tendering the hearsay evidence is not, however, consistent with the position in civil proceedings, in which context it is for the party who asserts that the maker of a hearsay statement was not competent at the time when he made it to prove that this was not so (see Civil Evidence Act 1995, section 5(1) and see C v C [2001] EWCA Civ 1625).*

743 *See, for example, R v Jenkins (1869) LR 1 CCR 187).*

744 *See "Evidence in Criminal Proceedings: Hearsay and Related Topics", Law Com No 245, at paragraph 8.143.*

745 *Though, it is submitted, this must be likely to substantially affect the court's view reliability of the maker for the purposes of section 114(2)(e) and must, consequently, substantially increase the likelihood that the court will regard the hearsay as inadmissible under section 114(1)(d).*

appears that section 123 will not apply where hearsay evidence is tendered under any other hearsay exception which the 2003 Act creates, under a common law exception to the hearsay rule which the 2003 Act preserves or under a pre-existing statutory exception to the hearsay rule which the 2003 Act retains. This being said, it is submitted that where hearsay evidence is tendered under a hearsay exception to which section 123 of the 2003 Act does not apply and it is established that the maker of the hearsay statement would not have been a competent witness at the time when it was made, the court is likely to exclude the relevant evidence.

Thus, for example, if such evidence was tendered under section 127 of the 2003 Act (considered at 2.2.8.2 above), it is submitted that the court would be likely to decide, under section 127(4), that it was not in the interests of justice for the section to apply. Similarly, if a statement made by a person whose mind was dominated by an unusual, startling or dramatic event was tendered as forming part of the res gestae (see 2.3.2.7 above), it is submitted that the court would be likely to decide that the evidence should not be admitted in consequence of the possibility of error.[746]

Fundamentally, where the admission in evidence for the prosecution of a hearsay statement made by a person who was not competent to give evidence at the time when he made it would adversely affect the fairness of the proceedings (and thus, potentially, might result in a violation of Article 6 of the European Convention of Human Rights[747]), the court will, of course, be able (and perhaps be required by virtue of the operation of section 3(1) of the Human Rights Act 1998) to exclude it under section 78 of the Police and Criminal Evidence Act 1984.[748]

2.7.3 Credibility of the maker of a hearsay statement and those who supply or receive information or create or receive documents

Section 124 of the Criminal Justice Act 2003 concerns both the credibility of the maker of a hearsay statement which is admitted in evidence in criminal proceedings and, in the context of the admission of a hearsay statement under section 117 of the 2003 Act, the credibility of a person who supplied or received information or created or received a document.[749]

It appears that section 124 will apply not just where hearsay evidence is admitted under a hearsay exception which the 2003 Act will create but will also apply where hearsay evidence is admitted under a common law hearsay exception which the

---

746 *See R v Andrews [1987] AC 281. At common law it has been long recognised that the lack of competence of the maker of a hearsay statement at the time when he made it may result in the exclusion of the relevant evidence (see, for example, R v Pike (1829) 3 C & P 598, concerning the admissibility at common law of a "dying declaration" under a hearsay exception which section 118 of the 2003 Act will abolish).*

747 *The extent to which the admission of hearsay evidence in criminal proceedings is likely to give rise to a violation of Article 6 is considered at 2.8 below.*

748 *See R v D [2002] EWCA Crim 990.*

749 *Section 117 is considered at 2.2.2 above.*

2003 Act will preserve[750] or under a pre-existing statutory exception to the hearsay rule which the 2003 Act will retain.[751] Section 124 will only apply, however, where the maker of the hearsay statement (or, in the context of the hearsay exception created by section 117 of the 2003 Act, the person who supplied or received the relevant information or created or received the relevant document) does not give oral evidence in the proceedings in connection with the statement's subject matter.[752] Thus, it appears that section 124 will be inapplicable where hearsay evidence is admitted under sections 119 of the 2003 Act and will be of limited application when it is admitted under section 120.[753] This, it is submitted, will be so because both sections119 and section 120 only apply when the maker of the hearsay statement gives oral evidence in the proceedings, though it appears that there may be circumstances in which evidence is admitted under section 120 (for example, under section 120(6)), even though the witness does not give oral evdience about the matter stated.

Section 124 provides as follows.

"(1) This section applies if in criminal proceedings–

    (a) a statement not made in oral evidence in the proceedings is admitted as evidence of a matter stated, and

    (b) the maker of the statement does not give oral evidence in connection with the subject matter of the statement.

(2) In such a case–

    (a) any evidence which (if he had given such evidence) would have been admissible as relevant to his credibility as a witness is so admissible in the proceedings;

    (b) evidence may with the court's leave be given of any matter which (if he had given such evidence) could have been put to him in cross-examination as relevant to his credibility as a witness but of which evidence could not have been adduced by the cross-examining party;

    (c) evidence tending to prove that he made (at whatever time) any other statement inconsistent with the statement admitted as evidence is admissible for the purpose of showing that he contradicted himself.

---

750 *The common law exceptions to the hearsay rule which the 2003 Act preserves were considered at 2.3 above.*

751 *The extent to which the 2003 Act retains pre-existing statutory exceptions to the hearsay rule was considered at 2.4.2 above.*

752 *Section 124(1)(b), (4).*

753 *Section 119 of the 2003 Act was considered at 2.2.3 above. Section 120 of the 2003 Act was considered at 2.2.4 above.*

(3)   If as a result of evidence admitted under this section an allegation is made against the maker of a statement, the court may permit a party to lead additional evidence of such description as the court may specify for the purposes of denying or answering the allegation.

(4)   In the case of a statement in a document which is admitted as evidence under section 117 each person who, in order for the statement to be admissible, must have supplied or received the information concerned or created or received the document or part concerned is to be treated as the maker of the statement for the purposes of subsections (1) to (3) above."

Where the hearsay evidence of a person who is not called to give evidence in criminal proceedings is admitted in criminal proceedings under a hearsay exception other than that created by section 117 of the 2003 Act, the operation of section 124 will, essentially, have four potential consequences.

First, evidence relating to the person's credibility which would have been admissible had he been called as a witness will be admissible.[754] This, presumably, will include evidence relating to collateral matters in relation to which evidence in rebuttal of the person's answers during cross-examination would have been admissible (had he been called as a witness) under an exception to the rule that a witness' answers to questions put to him during cross-examination concerning collateral matters are final.[755]

Secondly, but only with the leave of the court, evidence may be given of collateral matters in respect of which the person could have been cross-examined had he been called as a witness but in relation to which, in consequence of the operation of the rule that a witness' answers to questions concerning collateral matters are final, the cross-examining party could not have adduced evidence in rebuttal of the witness' answers.[756]

---

754 *Section 124(2)(a).*

755 *I.e. evidence of the witness' bias or partiality (see, for example, R v Mendy (1976) 64 Cr App R 4) , evidence of the witness' previous convictions (see section 6 of the Criminal Procedure Act 1865), evidence of physical or mental problems which may affect the reliability of the witness' evidence (see Toohey v Metropolitan Police Commissioner [1965] AC 595) and evidence of the witness' general reputation for untruthfulness (See R v Richardson; R v Longman [1969] 1 QB 299; R v Colwill [2002] EWCA Crim 1320). In relation to evidence falling within the latter of these four categories it is submitted (though without absolute confidence) that this exception to the rule that answers to questions concerning collateral matters are final will be abolished by section 99(1) of the Criminal Justice Act 2003 (one of the provisions of Chapter 1 of Part 11 of*

the 2003 Act, concerning evidence of character, detailed consideration of which falls outside the scope of the present book). If this view is correct then, it is submitted, such evidence, in relation to the maker of a hearsay statement, will not be rendered admissible by the operation of section 124 of the 2003 Act.

756 *See: R v Hitchcock (1847) 16 LJ Exch 259; R v Somers [1999] Crim LR 744. Under paragraph 1 of Schedule 2 to the Criminal Justice Act 1988, which will be repealed by the Criminal Justice Act 2003, such evidence is admissible, again only with the leave of the court, in the context of hearsay evidence admitted under section 23 or section 24 of the 1988 Act. In contrast, in the context of civil proceedings, section 5(2) of the Civil Evidence Act 1995 essentially provides that such evidence is not admissible for the purpose of discrediting the maker of a hearsay statement.*

Thirdly, evidence of the person's inconsistent statement(s) (whether made prior or subsequent to the hearsay statement) will also be admissible.[757] Whilst section 124(2)(c) states that evidence of inconsistent statements is admitted for the purpose of showing that the witness contradicted himself, section 119(2)[758] makes clear that where evidence is admitted under section 124(2)(c), the evidence will be admitted as evidence of any matter stated of which the person's oral evidence would be admissible.

Finally, where an allegation is made against the maker of a hearsay statement in consequence of evidence admitted under section 124, the court may, in the exercise of its discretion, permit a party to adduce additional evidence (of a type specified by the court) in rebuttal thereof.[759] Presumably such evidence will normally be adduced by the party who tendered the hearsay evidence, but the provision appears to be sufficiently wide to encompass the admission of such evidence on behalf another party (for example, on behalf of a co-accused to whose defence the hearsay evidence is also of relevance).

2.7.3.1 Statements admitted under section 117

Section 124(4) of the 2003 Act makes specific provision for the application of section 124 in the context of the hearsay exception which section 117 of the 2003 Act will create. The effect of section 124(4) appears to be that where hearsay evidence is admitted under section 117, the provisions of section 124 will apply to the person or persons who supplied or received the relevant information or created or received the relevant document. As was seen at 2.7.3 above, section 124 will only be applicable if the relevant person does not give oral evidence in the proceedings in connection with the hearsay statement's subject matter.[760]

2.7.3.2 Statements which do not fall within the ambit of the hearsay rule

Section 124 is only applicable where "…a statement not made in oral evidence in the proceedings is admitted as evidence of a matter stated…". Thus, since the provisions of Chapter 2 of Part 11 of the 2003 Act will not apply to a "matter stated" where the maker of the relevant statement neither intended to cause a person to believe the relevant matter nor intended to cause a person to act or a machine to operate on the basis that the matter was as stated[761], it appears that section 124 will not be applicable in relation to the maker of an implied assertion, as implied assertions will not fall within the ambit of the hearsay rule in the form in which that rule will exist when the hearsay provisions of the 2003 Act are in force.[762] Equally, it appears that section 124 will not apply to a statement which is not tendered as evidence of matters stated but which is merely tendered to prove

---

757 *Section 124(2)(c).*
758 *Which was considered at 2.2.3.2 above.*
759 *Section 124(3).*
760 *Section 124(1)(b),(4).*

761 *See section 115(3) and see 1.6.2 above.*
762 *The status of implied assertions under the 2003 Act was considered at 1.6.2 above.*

---

that the relevant matters were stated.[763] Again, since, for the purposes of Chapter 2 of Part 11 of the 2003 Act, a representation of fact which was made not by a person but by a machine is not a "statement"[764], it appears that section 124 will not apply to a representation made by a machine (i.e. it is submitted that section 124 will not be applicable in relation to the credibility of a person who fed data into the machine). In this latter context it is submitted, however, that the reliability of the relevant person may be a factor which the court should take into consideration when determining the admissibility of the machine produced representation under section 129(1) of the 2003 Act and (if the representation is admitted) which the jury should take into account when determining its evidential weight.

2.7.4 Prosecution cases based on unconvincing evidence

It appears that section 125 of the Criminal Justice Act 2003, which will only apply in the context of trial on indictment, will create an exception to the rule in *R v Galbraith*[765] (the rule in *Galbraith* concerning the nature of those circumstances in which the judge should stop the case and direct an acquittal in the context of a submission of no case to answer).[766] Section 125 of the 2003 Act provides as follows.

"(1) If on a defendant's trial before a judge and jury for an offence the court is satisfied at any time after the close of the case for the prosecution that—

(a) the case against the defendant is based wholly or partly on a statement not made in oral evidence in the proceedings, and

(b) the evidence provided by the statement is so unconvincing that, considering its importance to the case against the defendant, his conviction of the offence would be unsafe,

the court must either direct the jury to acquit the defendant of the offence or, if it considers that there ought to be a retrial, discharge the jury.

(2) Where—

(a) a jury is directed under subsection (1) to acquit a defendant of an offence, and

(b) the circumstances are such that, apart from this subsection, the defendant could if acquitted of that offence be found guilty of another offence,

the defendant may not be found guilty of that other offence if the court is satisfied as mentioned in subsection (1) in respect of it.

---

763 *The status of such original evidence was considered at 1.5 above.*
764 *See section 115(3) and see 1.9.2 above.*
765 *[1981] 1 WLR 1039.*

766 *See "Evidence in Criminal Proceedings: Hearsay and Related Topics", Law Com No 245, at paragraphs 11.26-11.32. .*

(3) If–

    (a   a jury is required to determine under section 4A(2) of the Criminal Procedure (Insanity) Act 1964 (c. 84) whether a person charged on an indictment with an offence did the act or made the omission charged, and

    (b) the court is satisfied as mentioned in subsection (1) above at any time after the close of the case for the prosecution that–

        (i) the case against the defendant is based wholly or partly on a statement not made in oral evidence in the proceedings, and

        (ii) the evidence provided by the statement is so unconvincing that, considering its importance to the case against the person, a finding that he did the act or made the omission would be unsafe,

the court must either direct the jury to acquit the defendant of the offence or, if it considers that there ought to be a rehearing, discharge the jury.

(4) This section does not prejudice any other power a court may have to direct a jury to acquit a person of an offence or to discharge a jury."

Where section 125(1) of the 2003 Act applies, the court will be required either to direct the jury to acquit the accused of an offence with which he is charged or (where a retrial is considered to be appropriate) to discharge the jury. Essentially, section 125(1) will apply (only in the context of trial on indictment) in circumstances in which, at any time following the close of the prosecution case, the judge is satisfied both that the case against the accused is wholly or partly based on a statement which was not made in oral evidence in the proceedings and that the evidence which the statement provides is so unconvincing that, in the context of its importance to the case against the accused, the accused's conviction of the relevant offence would be unsafe.

Further, it appears that the effect of section 125(2) will be that where, under section 125(1), the judge directs the jury to acquit the accused of an offence with which he is charged in the indictment, the accused cannot be convicted of another offence with which he was not charged in the indictment but of which he could have been convicted if acquitted of the offence with which he was charged, if the judge is satisfied that the requirements of section 125(1) are satisfied in relation to the other offence.[767]

Finally, in relation to an accused who is unfit to plead, section 125(3) makes effectively equivalent provision to section 125(1) concerning those circumstances in which a jury is required to determine whether the accused did the act or made the omission charged for the purposes of section 4A(2) of the Criminal Procedure (Insanity) Act 1964.

---

767 *See paragraph 423 of the Explanatory Notes to the Criminal Justice Act.*

With regard to the relationship between section 125 and the rule laid down by the Court of Appeal in *R v Galbraith*, (the basis of the rule in *Galbraith* being that the resolution of questions of fact is a matter for the jury and not one for the judge[768]), it appears that the Law Commission[769] regarded clause 14 of their draft Bill (i.e. the provision which now exists in the form of section 125 of the 2003 Act), like the principles laid down by the Court of Appeal in *R v Turnbull*[770] (concerning identification evidence) and the principles laid down by the Court of Appeal in *R v MacKenzie*[771] (concerning confessions made by mentally handicapped defendants), as amounting to a derogation from the *Galbraith* rule. The Law Commission[772] believed that the derogation from *Galbraith* which section 125 now embodies was justified for the following reasons.

> "11.31 The justifications for creating exceptions to the rule in *Galbraith* is that the risk that the jury may act upon evidence which is not to be relied upon "may well be seen as serious enough to outweigh the general principle that the functions of the judge and jury must be kept apart".[58] Experience has shown that identification evidence, and confessions, can be unreliable. The same can be said of hearsay. It seems to us that a derogation from *Galbraith* may be justified in the case of hearsay evidence on the same basis: even though the (absent) declarant may be honest, his or her evidence, being hearsay, may be so poor that a conviction would be unsafe.[59]
>
> [58] *Daley v R* [1994] 1 AC 117, 129D, per Lord Mustill. In that case the Judicial Committee of the Privy Council examined the relationship between *Galbraith and Turnbull* [1977] QB 224. Their Lordships justified the approach adopted in the identification cases on the ground that "the case is withdrawn from the jury not because the judge considers that the witness is lying, but because the evidence even if taken to be honest has a base which is so slender that it is unreliable and therefore not sufficient to found a conviction": p 129F.
>
> [59] It is possible, for example, to envisage a case in which the defendant is charged with assault, and the evidence against him consists of the statement from the alleged victim (who is unavailable to testify at the trial) and medical evidence. The defence is self-defence. The medical evidence is consistent with both the

---

768 *It should be noted that, as the Privy Council recognised in Daley v R [1994] 1 AC 117 (at pp. 675-676), there are well established exceptions to the principle that questions of law are determined by the judge and that questions of fact are determined by the jury, such as the role of the judge in determining the admissibility of a confession under section 76(2) of the Police and Criminal Evidence Act 1984.*

769 *See "Evidence in Criminal Proceedings: Hearsay and Related Topics", Law Com No 245, at paragraphs 11.26-11.32.*

770 *[1977] QB 224.*

771 *(1993) 96 Cr App R 98.*

772 *See "Evidence in Criminal Proceedings: Hearsay and Related Topics", Law Com No 245, at paragraph 11.31.*

prosecution and the defence version of events. At the trial, the defence adduces evidence that the alleged victim was so drunk at the time of the assault that it is likely that his perception of events at the time, and his recollection of them, were inaccurate. In such circumstances, the court would be likely to conclude that the alleged victim's statement is not to be relied upon, and that a conviction would be unsafe."

It should be noted, however, that, in *Daley v R*[773], the Privy Council, on the basis of the justification quoted by the Law Commission themselves at their foot note 58 (which was reproduced immediately above), did not regard *Turnbull* as amounting to an exception to *Galbraith* but, rather, regarded *Turnbull and Galbraith* as consistent. Equally, in *R v MacKenzie*[774], the Court of Appeal, regarded themselves as applying the rule in *R v Galbraith* rather than derogating from that rule.

The view that the Law Commission did indeed intend clause 14 of their draft Bill (i.e. the provision which now exists as section 125 of the 2003 Act) to amount to a derogation from the *Galbraith* rule appears to be supported by the use of the word "unsafe" in clause 14 of their draft Bill (that word also appearing in section 125(1)(b)). In *Galbraith*, the Court of Appeal had made clear that the use of this word in the context of a submission of no case to answer is dangerous because it is capable of being used either to mean that there is no evidence upon which a properly directed jury could convict or to mean that in the view of the judge it would be unsafe for the jury to convict the accused. If, indeed, the Law Commission did intend the word "unsafe" to be understood in this latter sense, then, it is submitted, they clearly did intend what is now section 125 of the 2003 Act to amount to a derogation from *Galbraith*.

It is submitted that the example given by the Law Commission at their footnote 59 (which was reproduced above) demonstrates that, in determining whether a conviction would be unsafe for the purposes of what is now section 125 of the 2003 Act, the Law Commission did intend that the reliability of the maker of the hearsay statement at the time when he made it would fall within the province of the judge. Thus, it is submitted, it appears that the Law Commission did intend, by virtue of what is now section 125 of the 2003 Act, to achieve a true derogation from *Galbraith*.

Mr Michael Wills (the Parliamentary Under-Secretary of State for the Home Department explained the relationship between what is now section 125 and the power of the court to direct an acquittal where there is no case to answer.[775]

"This clause...builds on the court's existing powers to direct an acquittal where there is no case to answer, but these powers are discretionary. It ensures that, where unconvincing hearsay evidence has been adduced and admitted,

---

773 *[1994] 1 AC 117.*
774 *(1993) 96 Cr App R 98.*

775 *Hansard (Commons) 28 January 2003 Column 654.*

and the safety of the conviction has been affected, the court must stop the trial. It does not prejudice existing powers; rather, it clarifies and tightens them up in relation to unconvincing hearsay evidence."

[It is submitted, that, to the extent to which this extract from Hansard suggests that the court possesses a discretion, as opposed to being under a duty, in the context of a submission of no case to answer, it is misleading, the rule in *Galbraith* clearly being stated in mandatory rather than in discretionary terms.[776]]

Mr Wills went on to consider the nature of those circumstances in which a judge might, rather than directing an acquittal, find it appropriate to order a retrial under section 125.[777]

"…the clause does not require the whole case to be based on an out of court statement. Rather, it makes provision for situations in which only part of the case is based on a hearsay statement and where other evidence may be sufficiently compelling that it would allow the prosecution case to be properly mounted. In such instances, it would not be proper to continue with the existing jury, because it would already have heard the unconvincing out of court statement, and the judge would conclude that any conviction based on it would be unsafe. However, in exceptional cases, it may be proper to order a retrial. The compelling evidence could then be heard and considered without the defendant's right to a fair trial being endangered."

2.7.4.1 Statements which do not fall within the ambit of the hearsay rule

The Law Commission intended the provision which now takes the form of section 125 of the 2003 Act to apply to unconvincing hearsay evidence. This also appears to have been the Government's intention.[778]

It is submitted, however, that the wording of section 125(1)(a), in requiring that the statement to which section 125(1) relates must be "a statement not made in oral evidence in the proceedings", does not expressly restrict the operation of section 125(1) merely to unconvincing "hearsay" evidence. Rather, at least on a literal interpretation, it appears that section 125(1) (and section 125(2)-(3)) will also potentially encompass unconvincing evidence provided by statements which were not made in oral evidence in the proceedings and which were admitted in evidence not because they fell within the ambit of an exception to the rule against hearsay but, rather, because they did not fall within the ambit of the hearsay rule at all. Thus, for example, whilst (in consequence of the operation of section 115(3) of the 2003 Act[779]) an implied assertion will not fall within the ambit of the hearsay rule in the form in which that rule will exist when the hearsay provisions of the 2003 Act are in force[780], it is submitted that an implied assertion will still fall within the ambit of section 125(1)(a).

---

776 *[1981] 1 WLR 1039 at p.1042.*

777 *Hansard (Commons) 28 January 2003 Column 654.*

778 *See Hansard (Commons) 28 January 2003 Columns 652-659.*

779 *Which was considered, in the context of implied assertions, at 1.6.2, above.*

780 *The evidential status of implied assertions under the 2003 Act was considered at 1.6.2, above.*

It may be, however that, even upon the assumption that section 125 of the 2003 Act is construed so as to encompass both hearsay and non-hearsay statements, the nature of those circumstances in which the importance of a non-hearsay statement in the context of a criminal case will be sufficiently great to bring section 125(1) of the 2003 Act into play will, in practice, be extremely limited.

2.7.4.2 Representations made by machines

Finally, it appears that, in consequence of the limited definition of "statement" in section 115(2) of the 2003 Act (limiting a statement for the purposes of Chapter 2 of Part 11 of the 2003 Act to a representation made by a person), the ambit of section 125(1) of that Act will not be broad enough to encompass representations made not by persons but, rather, made by machines. Thus, it is submitted, in the context of a representation of fact made by a machine, the court's power to stop the case will continue to depend upon the rule laid down by the Court of Appeal in *R v Galbraith*. [781] The admissibility of representations of fact made by machines under the 2003 Act was considered at 1.9.2, above.

2.7.5 Exclusionary discretion

As was noted at 2.1 and 2.2 above, the Criminal Justice Act 2003, as well as repealing sections 23 and 24 of the Criminal Justice Act 1988 (and thus abolishing the hearsay exceptions which those sections created [782]) will also repeal both the exclusionary discretion and the leave requirement relating to the admission of hearsay evidence under section 23 or 24 which were, respectively, conferred and imposed by sections 25 and 26 of the 1988 Act.[783] Whilst sections 23 and 24 of the 1988 Act will, effectively, be replaced by sections 116 and 117 of the 2003 Act[784], the 2003 Act does not contain provisions which will directly replace sections 25 and 26 of the 1988 Act. As was seen also above, however, section 116(2)(e),(4) of the 2003 Act will impose a leave requirement in the context of section 116(2)(e)[785] which will also be applicable in the context of section 117(5)(a)[786] and, moreover, section 117(6) and (7) will confer upon the court discretion to exclude evidence tendered under section 117.[787]

Whilst the Criminal Justice Act 2003 will not provide direct replacements for sections 25 and 26 of the 1988 Act, section 126(1) of the 2003 Act will create a new statutory exclusionary discretion which, it appears, will encompass hearsay evidence whether tendered by the prosecution or by the defence and, it seems, will encompass such evidence whether the evidence is admissible under a statutory exception to the hearsay rule which the 2003 Act will create, under a pre-existing statutory exception to the hearsay rule which the 2003 Act will retain or under a common law exception to the hearsay rule which the 2003 Act will preserve.

---

781 *[1981] 1 WLR 1039.*
782 *See 2.4.1 above.*
783 *See 2.2.1 and 2.2.2 above.*
784 *See, respectively, 2.2.1 and 2.2.2 above.*

785 *See 2.2.1.2.8 above.*
786 *See 2.2.2.2.4 above.*
787 *See 2.2.2.2.5 above.*

Moreover, section 126(2) of the 2003 Act will, respectively, retain and preserve the court's pre-existing statutory and common law discretion to exclude prosecution evidence.

Section 126 of the 2003 Act provides as follows.

"(1) In criminal proceedings the court may refuse to admit a statement as evidence of a matter stated if–

  (a) the statement was made otherwise than in oral evidence in the proceedings, and

  (b) the court is satisfied that the case for excluding the statement, taking account of the danger that to admit it would result in undue waste of time, substantially outweighs the case for admitting it, taking account of the value of the evidence.

(2) Nothing in this Chapter prejudices–

  (a) any power of a court to exclude evidence under section 78 of the Police and Criminal Evidence Act 1984 (c. 60) (exclusion of unfair evidence), or

  (b) any other power of a court to exclude evidence at its discretion (whether by preventing questions from being put or otherwise)."

2.7.5.1 The new statutory exclusionary discretion

Essentially, section 126(1) of the 2003 Act will confer upon the criminal courts discretion to exclude hearsay evidence if the case for excluding the hearsay evidence, taking account of the danger that its admission would result in undue waste of time, substantially outweighs the case for admitting the hearsay evidence, taking into account the value of the hearsay evidence. Clause 15(1)(b) of the Law Commission's draft Bill[788] was worded differently to section 126(1)(b) of the 2003 Act, clause 15(1)(b) providing that:

"(b) the court is satisfied that the statement's probative value is substantially outweighed by the danger that to admit it would result in undue waste of time."

Essentially, the Law Commission[789] believed that this new exclusionary discretion was necessary because the existing statutory and common law exclusionary discretion (which will be retained/preserved by section 126(2)) of the 2003 Act, and which is considered at 2.7.5.2 below) does not empower the court to exclude superfluous evidence the admission of which would not make a trial unfair and, moreover, do not empower the court to restrict the quantity of defence evidence.

---

788 *Contained in "Evidence in Criminal Proceedings: Hearsay and Related Topics", Law Com No 245.*

789 *See "Evidence in Criminal Proceedings: Hearsay and Related Topics", Law Com No 245 at paragraph 11.17.*

In relation to the nature and operation of this new exclusionary discretion, the Law Commission[790] indicated that:

> "The new power to exclude superfluous hearsay would be available in relation to all hearsay evidence which would otherwise be admissible under our recommended scheme. We envisage that exercise of this power will be appropriate only in exceptional cases, where the probative value of the evidence is so slight that almost nothing is gained by admitting it. This power will help the opposing party and also ensure that the court's time is not wasted, thereby meeting the point which concerned some respondents, that the admission of hearsay would lead to a lot of barely relevant evidence being adduced."

Further, paragraph 424 of the Explanatory Notes to the Criminal Justice Act provides the following guidance concerning the operation of section 126(1) of the 2003 Act.

> "This section provides a further discretion to exclude superfluous out of court statements if the court is satisfied that the value of the evidence is substantially outweighed by the undue waste of time which its admission would cause."

Moreover, during the Criminal Justice Bill's Committee Stage in the House of Lords[791], Baroness Scotland of Asthal (the Minister of State for the Criminal Justice System and Law Reform), with reference to the then clauses 119 and 103 of the Criminal Justice Bill (now, respectively, sections 126 and 114 of the 2003 Act) stated that:

> "Clause 119 indeed provides the court with a general discretion to exclude an out of court statement, if it is satisfied that the statement's probative value is substantially outweighed by the danger that admitting it would result in undue waste of time. It will enable the court to exclude superfluous hearsay evidence.

> The Law Commission took the view that it was important to provide the courts with some power to control the quantity and quality of out of court statements that are adduced. Evidence that is wholly irrelevant is not admissible at all—nor should it be—but out of court statements that have marginal relevance to the issues will be prima facie admissible, providing they meet the criteria in Clause 103. The commission was concerned that in some cases that evidence will be superfluous to the issues and highlighted the risk that the parties might seek to use every conceivable piece of evidence, no matter how marginal its value, to bolster their case. We agree with the commission's conclusion that an exclusionary discretion is necessary to

---

790 *See "Evidence in Criminal Proceedings: Hearsay and Related Topics", Law Com No 245 at paragraph 11.18.*

791 *Hansard (Lords) 18 September 2003 Columns 1134–1135.*

ensure that court time is not wasted and to address concerns that the greater admission of hearsay will lead to barely relevant evidence being adduced. Of course, the evidence that the prosecution seeks to adduce may still be excluded by the court in the exercise of its discretion at common law or under Section 78(1) of PACE. However, that would not provide a means of controlling the quantity and quality of evidence that would be used by the defence.

Clause 119(1)(b) will therefore enable the court to exclude superfluous hearsay statements from any party if it is satisfied that the value of the evidence is substantially outweighed by the undue waste of time that its admission would cause."

Thus, whilst the wording of section 126(1)(b) of the 2003 Act is not identical to that of clause 15(1)(b) of the Law Commission's draft Bill, it appears that the purpose of the section equates with that of the clause and that the Law Commission's view as to the nature of those circumstances in which their recommended exclusionary discretion is likely to be exercised is equally applicable to the operation of the new statutory discretion which will be created by section 126(1).

In relation to the operation of the section 126(1) exclusionary discretion, it should be noted that the subsection will empower the court to "refuse to admit a statement as evidence of a matter stated". Thus, where a statement is tendered other than as evidence of a matter stated, for example, where the statement is tendered merely to prove that the relevant matters were stated but not as evidence of the matters stated[792] or if the statement is an implied assertion (since, as was seen above, such assertions do not fall within the ambit of section 115(3) of the 2003 Act[793]), it appears that the section 126(1) discretion will not be applicable to it. Equally, where the relevant evidence does not amount to a statement within the meaning of section 115(2) of the 2003 Act (for example, where it takes the form of a representation of fact which was made by a machine rather than by a person[794]) it appears that the section 126(1) discretion will not be applicable thereto. Moreover, where evidence of a statement made by a witness who gives oral evidence in the proceedings (for example, evidence of the witness' previous consistent or inconsistent statement) is tendered primarily for the purpose, respectively, of enhancing or attacking the credibility of the relevant witness, it is submitted that the 2003 Act does not make clear whether the exercise of the section 126(1) exclusionary discretion is capable of preventing the admission of the relevant statement for any purpose or whether the exercise of that discretion is merely capable of preventing the admission of the relevant evidence as evidence of the matter stated.

---

792 *The evidential status of such "original evidence" was considered at 1.5 above.*
793 *Which was considered at 1.6.2 above.*
794 *For consideration of the admissibility of such evidence under the 2003 Act see 1.9.2 above.*

2.7.5.2 Pre-existing statutory and preserved common law exclusionary discretion

Section 126(2)(a) of the Criminal Justice Act 2003 makes clear that when Chapter 2 of Part 11 of the 2003 Act is in force, the court will continue to possess the discretion conferred upon it by section 78 of the Police and Criminal Evidence Act 1984 to exclude evidence tendered by the prosecution the admission of which would have such an adverse effect on the fairness of the proceedings that it should not be admitted. Similarly, section 126(2)(b) of the 2003 Act appears to preserve the court's common law discretion to exclude evidence tendered by the prosecution the probative value is outweighed by its prejudicial effect[795] or which was unfairly or improperly obtained from the accused after the offence with which he is charged was committed.[796] Thus, in circumstances in which hearsay evidence which is tendered by the prosecution will be admissible either under a statutory exception to the hearsay rule which the 2003 Act will create or retain or under a common law exception to the hearsay rule which the 2003 Act will preserve, the

---

795 *That what is now section 126(2)(b) would in fact preserve the common law discretion to exclude prosecution evidence the probative value of which was outweighed by its prejudicial effect was doubted both in the Commons and the Lords but, in both Houses, the Government provided assurances that this was in fact the case (see Hansard (Commons) 28 January 2003 Column 666 and Hansard (Lords) 18 September 2003 Column 1135).*

796 *In relation to the nature of this second limb of the common law exclusionary discretion see R v Sang [1980] AC 425. It should be noted that other than in making clear that it does include admissions and confessions, the speeches of their Lordships in Sang do not make clear the precise nature of that other evidence which, having being obtained from the accused following the commission of the offence, may be excluded at common law on the basis that it was unfairly or improperly obtained. Thus, whether such evidence should properly be regarded as restricted to evidence tantamount to a confession, whether, for example, it extends to evidence produced by an illegal search of the accused's person or premises or whether, indeed, the ambit of the common law discretion is more extensive, remains unclear. Indeed, neither the Law Commission's Report (see "Evidence in Criminal Proceedings: Hearsay and Related Topics", Law Com No 245 at paragraph 11.15) nor the Explanatory Notes to the Criminal Justice Act (see paragraph 424) mention this second limb of the common law exclusionary discretion in this context, both referring only, in the context of what is now section 126(2), to the court's common law discretion to exclude evidence* tendered by the prosecution the probative value of which is outweighed by its prejudicial effect. It is submitted, however, that the effect of section 126(2) of the Act is to preserve both limbs of the common law discretion, the existence of the latter limb remaining of potential significance in circumstances in which the statutory discretion conferred by section 78 of the 1984 Act is inapplicable, namely, where the relevant evidence has already been adduced and the defence subsequently submit that it should be excluded (see R v Sat-Bhambra (1988) 88 Cr App R 55). Other than in this situation, however, it appears that the circumstances in which evidence tendered by the prosecution may be excluded at common law are encompassed by the ambit of the section 78 discretion (see Matto v Wolverhampton Crown Court [1987] RTR 337) and, moreover, it appears that the ambit of the section 78 discretion, unlike that of the second limb of the common law discretion, extends to encompass the discretionary exclusion of prosecution evidence even though the evidence was not obtained from the accused following the commission of the offence and its probative value is not outweighed by its prejudicial effect (see, for example, R v Nathaniel [1995] 2 Cr App R 565 and R v Smurthwaite [1994] 1 All ER 898). Indeed, following the decision of the House of Lords in R v Loosely [2001] 1 WLR 2066, it appears that even where evidence is of substantial probative value and its admission would not affect the procedural fairness of the trial itself, the court may still exclude the evidence in the exercise of its section 78 discretion in circumstances in which the court would have been prepared to grant a stay of proceedings.*

admissibility of the hearsay evidence will be subject to the exercise of the section 78 and common law exclusionary discretions which section 126(2), will, respectively, retain and preserve.

As regards the potential overlap between the section 78 and common law exclusionary discretions and the new section 126(1) exclusionary discretion (which was considered at 2.7.5.1 above), the ambit of the section 78 discretion and that of the common law discretion clearly both exceed that of the section 126(1) exclusionary discretion in that the section 78 and common law exclusionary discretions, unlike the section 126(1) exclusionary discretion, both appear to enable the court to exclude evidence which possesses more than the slight probative value which (as was seen as 2.7.5.1) the Law Commission envisaged that evidence excluded under section 126(1) would possess.[797] Conversely, however, the section 78 and common law exclusionary discretions are clearly both more limited in ambit than the section 126(1) discretion in that neither of the former two exclusionary discretions empower the court to exclude evidence tendered by the defence and neither of them appear to encompass the discretionary exclusion of relevant evidence of limited probative value, the admission of which would neither be unfair or prejudicial to the accused.

In relation to the exercise of exclusionary discretion in the context of the operation of the hearsay exceptions which sections 116 and 117 of the 2003 Act will create, it is submitted that there will clearly be a degree of overlap between the ambit of the section 78 and common law exclusionary discretions and that of the leave requirement which section 116(2)(e),(4) of the 2003 Act will impose (both in the context of the operation of section 116(2)(e)[798] and in the context of the operation of section 117(5)(a)[799]). It should be noted, however, that the ambit of the section 116(2)(e) leave requirement, unlike that of the section 78 and common law exclusionary discretions, is not restricted to the context of evidence tendered by the prosecution.

Similarly, it is submitted that there will clearly be a degree of overlap between the ambit of the section 78 and common law exclusionary discretions and that of the exclusionary discretion which section 117(6),(7) of the 2003 Act[800] will confer upon the criminal courts in the context of the operation of section 117 of that Act. It should again be noted, however, that the ambit of the section 117(6),(7) discretion is not restricted to the exclusion of evidence tendered by the prosecution.

Again, it is submitted that the exercise of the section 78 or common law exclusionary discretions may technically be encountered in the context of the

---

797 *For examples of the exclusion at common law and under section 78 of the 1988 Act of evidence of more than slight probative value see, respectively, R v Payne [1963] 1 WLR 637 and R v O'Connor (1986) 85 Cr App R 298.*

798 *In relation to the operation of the section 116(2)(e),(4) discretion in the context of section*

116(2)(e) see 2.2.1.2.8, above.

799 *In relation to the operation of the section 116(2)(e),(4) discretion in the context of section 117(5)(a) see 2.2.2.2.4, above.*

800 *Provisions which were considered at 2.2.2.2.5 above.*

court's discretion to admit multiple hearsay under section 121(1)(c) of the 2003 Act. It is submitted, however, that in circumstances in which the court, under section 121(1)(c), finds that the interests of justice require the admission of the relevant evidence, the court is unlikely to then exclude the relevant evidence in the exercise of its exclusionary discretion.

Finally, whilst both the section 78 and common law exclusionary discretions will be potentially applicable when the court is considering whether to admit hearsay evidence tendered by the prosecution under the "safety valve" inclusionary discretion which section 114(1)(d) of the 2003 Act will create[801], it appears to be unlikely that where the court has decided in the exercise of the section 114(1)(d) inclusionary discretion that hearsay evidence should be admitted, it will subsequently decide to exclude the relevant evidence in the exercise of its exclusionary discretion. Thus, it is submitted that the nature of the relationship between the section 114(1)(d) inclusionary discretion and the section 78 and common law exclusionary discretions may well, in practice, be similar to that which presently exists between the leave requirement imposed by section 26 of the Criminal Justice Act 1988 and the exclusionary discretion conferred by section 25 of that Act.[802]

2.7.6 Proof of statements in documents

Section 133 of the Criminal Justice Act 2003 concerns the proof of statements in documents in criminal proceedings. Section 133 of the 2003 Act provides as follows.

> "Where a statement in a document is admissible as evidence in criminal proceedings, the statement may be proved by producing either–
>
> (a   the document, or
>
> (b)   (whether or not the document exists) a copy of the document or of the material part of it,
>
> authenticated in whatever way the court may approve."

Section 133 of the Criminal Justice Act 2003 will replace section 27 of the Criminal Justice Act 1988, which the 2003 Act will repeal. The wording of section 27 of the 1988 Act is effectively identical to that of section 8 of the Civil Evidence Act 1995; the latter section applying in the context of civil proceedings. The wording of section 133 of the 2003 Act is not identical to that of section 27 of the

---

801 *And which was considered at 2.6 above.*

802 *The nature of the relationship between the section 26 leave requirement and the section 25 exclusionary discretion (both of which will cease to exist when the hearsay provisions of the 1988 Act are in force) appears to be that whilst, where section 26 applies, the court should technically exercise its section 26 and section 25 discretions* separately *(see R v Lockley [1995] 2 Cr App R 554), it should not normally be necessary, in practice, for the court, having decided to give or refuse leave to admit or exclude a hearsay statement under section 26, to separately consider the exercise of the section 25 exclusionary discretion (see R v Grafton [1995] Crim LR 61).*

1988 Act. The only difference of any apparent significance between section 27 of the 1988 and section 133 of the 2003 Act is, however, that section 27(2), unlike section 133, provides that:

> "...it is immaterial for the purposes of this subsection how many removes there are between a copy and the original."

It should be noted, however, that section 134(1) of the 2003 Act provides that:

> ""copy", in relation to a document, means anything on to which information recorded in the document has been copied, by whatever means and whether directly or indirectly;... "document" means anything in which information of any description is recorded;..."

Thus, it may be that, reading section 133 of the 2003 Act in the context of the section 134(1) definition of "copy" (which encompasses both a copy made directly and one made indirectly), the courts will regard section 133, like section 27 of the 1988 Act, as being applicable regardless of the number of removes which exist between an original and a copy.[803] It should be noted, however, that the definition of "copy", both for the purposes of section 27 of the 1988 Act[804] and for the purposes of section 8 of the Civil Evidence Act 1995[805] (the Act which inserted the relevant definition into the 1988 Act[806]), equates with that contained in section 134(1) of the 2003 Act. Thus, if the effect of the section 134(1) definition of copy is indeed that section 133 is applicable regardless of the number of removes which exist between an original and a copy, then the express wording of section 27(2) of the 1988 Act, and that of the equivalent section 8(2) of the 1995 Act to this effect, appears to be superfluous.

Upon the assumption that section 133 of the 2003 Act will apply where there are several removes between copy and original document, it appears that section 133 of the 2003 Act and section 27 of the 1988, which section 133 will replace, are of equivalent effect. In relation to the effect of section 27 of the 1988 Act and that of section 133 of the 2003 Act, it is submitted that the better view is that section 27 of the 1988 Act is applicable, and that section 133 of the 2003 Act will be applicable, to statements in documents whether the relevant documentary evidence is tendered under a hearsay exception or whether, for the purpose for which it is tendered, the relevant evidence does not fall within the ambit of the hearsay rule at all. There has not yet been any judicial guidance as to the ambit of section 27, however, and there is a divergence of academic opinion in relation to the issue.[807] It is submitted that, adopting a literal interpretation of their wording, neither the wording of section 27 nor that of section 133 appear to justify the view that the ambit of either section is restricted to the context of hearsay evidence. If the view

---

803 *See Cross and Tapper on Evidence, 9th ed, Butterworths at p 641.*
804 *Criminal Justice Act 1988, Schedule 2, paragraph 5(1).*
805 *Civil Evidence Act 1995, section 13.*
806 *Civil Evidence Act 1995, section 15(1); Schedule 1, paragraph 12.*

that section 27 of the 1988 Act does, and that section 133 of the 2003 Act will, extend to encompass non-hearsay documentary evidence is incorrect, however, then the admissibility of copies of documents which do not contain hearsay statements will be governed by the common law principles which are considered at 2.7.6.1, below.

The wording of section 27 of the 1988 Act, and that of section 133 of the 2003 Act, makes clear that section 27 does not, and section 133 will not, authorise the use of the oral evidence of a witness who read a document to prove its contents. Thus, where it is sought to prove the contents of a document via the oral evidence of a witness rather than via a copy, the admissibility of such secondary evidence will be governed by the common law principles which are examined at 2.7.6.1, below.

Moreover, where a document does not contain a "statement" within the meaning of section 115(2) of the 2003 Act (i.e. where the document does not contain a "representation of fact or opinion made by a person"), it appears that section 133 of the 2003 Act, which applies to a "statement in a document", will not be applicable. Thus, it is submitted that, in consequence of the section 115(2) definition of "statement", a document produced by a machine which does not contain a representation of fact or opinion made by a person will not fall within the ambit of section 133 of the 2003 Act whereas such a document would, in consequence of the wider definition of "statement" in the 1988 Act[808], fall within the ambit of section 27 of the 1988 Act.[809] Consequently. whilst it is submitted that this is unlikely to have been the intention of the draftsman, it appears that a consequence of the narrower definition of statement which will be encountered in the context of section 133 of the 2003 Act will be that where a document does not contain a "representation of fact or opinion made by a person", the contents of the document must be proved at common law (under the principles which are considered at see 2.7.6.1, below).

In relation to the requirement, which section 27 of the 1988 Act imposes and which section 133 of the 2003 Act will impose, that the statement be proved by "producing" the original document or a copy thereof, it is submitted that "producing", both for the purposes of section 27 of the 1988 Act and for those of section 133 of the 2003 Act[810], essentially appears to mean a witness who is

---

807 Thus, for example, in *The Modern Law of Evidence*, 5th ed, Butterworths, at p. 228, in *Cross and Tapper on Evidence*, 9th ed, Butterworths, 1999, at p.641, and in *Andrews and Hirst on Criminal Evidence*, 4th ed, Jordans, 2001 at pp.313-314, Keane, Tapper and Hirst are, respectively, of the view that section 27 applies to hearsay and non-hearsay evidence. In contrast, in *Murphy on Evidence*, 8th ed, Blackstone Press, 2003, at page 654 and in *Criminal Evidence*, 4th ed, Sweet and Maxwell, 1999, at paragraph 3.12, Murphy and May are, respectively, of the view that section 27 only applies to hearsay evidence.

808 See paragraph 5(1) of Schedule 2 to the 1988 Act. The position in civil proceedings, under section 8 of the Civil Evidence Act 1995, equates with the position under section 27 of the 1988 Act in that the definition of statement in section 13 of the 1995 Act is not restricted to statements made by persons.

809 The admissibility of evidence produced by machines under Chapter 2 of Part 11 of the 2003 Act was considered at 1.9.2 above.

810 And for those of section 8 of the Civil Evidence Act 1995.

qualified to do so producing the document and saying what it is.[811] Where this is not possible, however, it appears that the statement may be proved by any lawful means, for example, by using another admissible hearsay statement for this purpose.[812]

Finally, it should be noted that consideration of the miscellaneous collection of statutory provisions which make provision both for the proof of the contents of public documents and for the proof of certain categories of private documents, such as Banker's Books, falls outside the scope of the present book, the relevant provisions not being considered herein. The reader who wishes to consider these provisions further is directed to paragraphs F8.7-8.27 of Blackstone's Criminal Practice 2003, published by Oxford University Press.

2.7.6.1 The admissibility of secondary evidence of the contents of documents at common law

In circumstances in which section 133 of the Criminal Justice Act 2003 is inapplicable (perhaps because neither the original document nor a copy thereof are available or perhaps because the document does not contain a "statement" within the meaning of section 115(2) of the 2003 Act), proof of the contents of a document will (in the absence of some other applicable statutory provision) be governed by the common law. Indeed, it is submitted that even in relation to a statutory exception to the hearsay rule (such as section 117 of the Criminal Justice Act 2003) which only applies to hearsay evidence which is contained in a document, if the contents of the relevant document cannot (perhaps for the reasons stated above) be proved under section 133 of the 2003 Act, secondary evidence of the document's contents in the form of the oral evidence of a witness who read it may, in appropriate circumstances, be admitted at common law.[813]

At common law, secondary evidence of the contents of a document, either in the form of a copy[814] of the document or in the form of the evidence of a witness who read the document, may be admissible. Whether secondary evidence is admissible appears to depend upon the weight of the relevant evidence.[815] Thus, if the party

811 See *Ventouris v Mountain [1992] 3 All ER 414* (an authority under the Civil Evidence Act 1968, since repealed).

812 See *Ventouris v Mountain [1992] 3 All ER 414* (an authority under the Civil Evidence Act 1968, since repealed).

813 See *R v Nazeer [1998] Crim LR 750*, an authority concerning the admission of oral secondary evidence in the context of the operation of section 24 of the Criminal Justice Act 1988.

814 There are no degrees of secondary evidence at common law (see *R v Nazeer [1998] Crim LR 750*) and, thus, the copy need not be a direct copy of the original but, rather, may be a copy of a copy.

815 *Masquerade Music Ltd v Springsteen [2001] EMLR 654*. The admissibility of such evidence at common law was long said to be governed by the best evidence rule, an old rule of evidence, long obsolescent, which the decision of the Court of Appeal in Springsteen now appears to have rendered obsolete. For consideration of the common law rule of exclusion and its exceptions (in case the decision of the Court of Appeal in the Masquerade Music case has not finally laid it to rest) see paragraph F8.1 of Blackstone's Criminal Practice 2003, published by Oxford University Press.

who tenders the secondary evidence could readily produce the original document, it appears that the court, acting upon the assumption that a party who has the original document readily available but chooses to tender secondary evidence of its contents has some improper purpose in mind, will, in the absence of special circumstances, regard the secondary evidence as worthless and will thus exclude the evidence upon, it appears, the basis that it is irrelevant.[816] Conversely, where the party who tenders the secondary evidence genuinely cannot produce the original document, it appears that the court will, in the absence of special circumstances (such, it appears, as allegations of forgery, bad faith or impropriety), admit the secondary evidence and ascribe to it such weight as is appropriate in the circumstances.[817] Again, where the party who tenders the secondary evidence could produce the original document but could not do so readily, it will be for the court, when determining the admissibility of the secondary evidence, to determine whether, in the circumstances, any weight can be ascribed to it.[818]

Thus, in general, it appears that secondary evidence of the contents of a document will be admissible at common law unless the party tendering the secondary evidence either has the original in court or could produce it without difficulty.[819] Where secondary evidence is admitted, however, the weight of the evidence may still be significantly reduced in consequence of factors such as the failure of the party relying upon the secondary evidence to take proper care of the original documents.[820]

2.7.7 Rules of Court

Section 132 of the Criminal Justice Act 2003 makes provision for the making of Crown Court Rules, Criminal Appeal Rules and Magistrates' Courts Rules for the purposes of Chapter 2 of Part 11 of the 2003 Act. Section 132 of the 2003 Act provides as follows.

> "(1) Rules of court may make such provision as appears to the appropriate authority to be necessary or expedient for the purposes of this Chapter; and the appropriate authority is the authority entitled to make the rules.
>
> (2) The rules may make provision about the procedure to be followed and other conditions to be fulfilled by a party proposing to tender a statement in evidence under any provision of this Chapter.

---

816 *Masquerade Music Ltd v Springsteen [2001] EMLR 654.*

817 *Masquerade Music Ltd v Springsteen [2001] EMLR 654. In the context of jury trial it is submitted that it will be for the judge to determine the admissibility of the secondary evidence but if it is admitted it will be for the jury to determine what weight should be ascribed to it.*

818 *Masquerade Music Ltd v Springsteen [2001] EMLR 654.*

819 *See: R v Governor of Pentonville Prison, ex parte Osman. [1990] 1 WLR 277; Masquerade Music Ltd v Springsteen [2001] EMLR 654; Kajala v Noble (1982) 75 Cr App R 149.*

820 *See, for example, Post Office Counters Ltd v Tarla Mahida The Times October 31 2003.*

(3)   The rules may require a party proposing to tender the evidence to serve on each party to the proceedings such notice, and such particulars of or relating to the evidence, as may be prescribed.

(4)   The rules may provide that the evidence is to be treated as admissible by agreement of the parties if–

  (a)   a notice has been served in accordance with provision made under subsection (3), and

  (b)   no counter-notice in the prescribed form objecting to the admission of the evidence has been served by a party.

(5)   If a party proposing to tender evidence fails to comply with a prescribed requirement applicable to it–

  (a)   the evidence is not admissible except with the court's leave;

  (b)   where leave is given the court or jury may draw such inferences from the failure as appear proper;

  (c)   the failure may be taken into account by the court in considering the exercise of its powers with respect to costs.

(6)   In considering whether or how to exercise any of its powers under subsection (5) the court shall have regard to whether there is any justification for the failure to comply with the requirement.

(7)   A person shall not be convicted of an offence solely on an inference drawn under subsection (5)(b).

(8)   Rules under this section may–

  (a)   limit the application of any provision of the rules to prescribed circumstances;

  (b)   subject any provision of the rules to prescribed exceptions;

  (c)   make different provision for different cases or circumstances.

(9)   Nothing in this section prejudices the generality of any enactment conferring power to make rules of court; and no particular provision of this section prejudices any general provision of it.

(10) In this section–

"prescribed" means prescribed by rules of court;

"rules of court" means–

  (a)   Crown Court Rules;

  (b)   Criminal Appeal Rules;

  (c)   rules under section 144 of the Magistrates' Courts Act 1980 (c. 43)."

In relation to the making of rules of court concerning the admission of hearsay evidence by agreement of the parties, the position was considered at 2.5 above. Section 132 also makes provision for the making of rules of court imposing procedures and conditions which a party proposing to tender a statement in evidence under a provision of Chapter 2 of Part 11 of the 2003 Act must follow or fulfil[821] and requiring such a party to serve prescribed notice and particulars of or relating to the relevant evidence on the other parties.[822] The Law Commission[823] envisaged that the giving of notice would be required where a party knew prior to the trial that he would seek to adduce hearsay evidence and envisaged, in relation to the operation of the notice requirements, that:

> "The normal way of giving notice would be by serving the statement of the witness who it is proposed should give evidence of the hearsay statement, or should produce a document containing it, under section 9 of the Criminal Justice Act 1967. In the absence of a challenge by any other party, the evidence would then be admissible."

It is submitted that where hearsay evidence is tendered under one or more of the hearsay exceptions which the 2003 Act creates it will clearly tendered *"under any provision"* of Chapter 2 of Part 11 of the 2003 Act and, consequently, that section 132(2),(3) will clearly be applicable to such evidence. This is, of course, to assume that the courts will construe section 132(3) in the context of section 132(2) and thus regard *"the evidence"* to which section 132(3) relates as meaning a statement which a party proposes to tender in evidence under any provision of Chapter 2 of Part 11 of the 2003 Act.

Whether section 132(2),(3) will be applicable to hearsay evidence which is tendered under a pre-existing statutory exception to the hearsay rule which the 2003 Act will retain or under a common law exception to the hearsay rule which the 2003 Act will preserve, however, does not appear to be absolutely clear. Arguably, once the hearsay provisions of the 2003 Act are in force, whenever hearsay evidence is tendered in criminal proceedings it will be tendered *"under any provision"* of the 2003 Act (i.e.: if it is tendered under a hearsay exception created by the 2003 Act, other than the "safety valve" inclusionary discretion, or under a retained pre-existing statutory hearsay exception it will be tendered under section 114(1)(a) of the 2003 Act; if it is tendered under a preserved common law hearsay exception it will be tendered under section 114(1)(b) of the 2003 Act, if it is tendered by agreement of the parties it will be tendered under section 114(1)(c) of the 2003 Act; if it is tendered under the "safety valve" inclusionary discretion it will be tendered under section 114(1)(d) of the 2003 Act). If this view is correct, then section 132(2),(3) will apply to all hearsay evidence. Certainly, the Law Commission appear to have envisaged that the notice requirements imposed by rules of court

---

821 *Section 132(2).*
822 *Section 132(3).*

823 *See "Evidence in Criminal Proceedings: Hearsay and Related Topics", Law Com No 245 at paragraph 11.7.*

would extend to all hearsay evidence.824 This is also the interpretation of section 132(2),(3) which is favoured by the present author.

It could, conversely, be argued, however, that where evidence falls within the ambit of a retained pre-existing statutory hearsay exception or under a preserved common law hearsay exception it will not be tendered *"under any provision"* of Chapter 2 of Part 11 of the 2003 Act but, rather, will be tendered under the retained pre-existing statutory hearsay exception or under the preserved common law hearsay exception. If this is indeed the proper interpretation of sections 132(2) and 114(1) in combination, then, it appears that section 132(2),(3) will not apply to such evidence. Even if this is so, however, section 132(9) provides that:

> "Nothing in this section prejudices the generality of any enactment conferring power to make rules of court; and no particular provision of this section prejudices any general provision of it."

Thus, even if section 132(2),(3) will not encompass hearsay evidence which is admitted either under a retained pre-existing statutory hearsay exception or under a preserved common-law hearsay exception it is submitted that the effect of section 132(9) will be that the authority entitled to make the rules will, if it regards this as *"necessary and expedient"*, be entitled, under section 132(1), "for the purposes of this chapter", to make rules relating to such hearsay evidence which equate with those which it will be entitled to make in relation to hearsay evidence which is tendered under a provision of Chapter 2 of Part 11 of the 2003 Act.

As regards implied assertions (which, as was seen above, will not fall within the ambit of the hearsay rule when Chapter 2 of Part 11 of the 2003 Act is in force[825]) and statements which are tendered not as evidence of matters stated but, merely, to prove that the relevant matters were stated[826], it is submitted that such statements, not falling within the ambit of the hearsay rule, will not be tendered *"under any provision"* of Chapter 2 of Part 11, and consequently, that section 132(2) will not be applicable thereto. Moreover, if, construing section 132(3) in the context of section 132(2), *"the evidence"* to which section 132(3) relates does mean a statement which a party proposes to tender in evidence under any provision of Chapter 2 of Part 11 of the 2003 Act, then it appears that section 132(3) will also be inapplicable to such evidence. Presumably, however, if the authority entitled to make the rules regards this as *"necessary or expedient"*, (which, it is submitted, is unlikely), such statements may be brought within the ambit of the notice regime by having recourse to the section 132(1) rulemaking power.[827]

The ambit of section 132(2) does not appear to encompass representations made by machines[828] as, under section 115(2), such representations will not amount to

---

824 See *"Evidence in Criminal Proceedings: Hearsay and Related Topics", Law Com No 245 at* paragraph 11.6.

825 *Which were considered at 1.6.2 above.*

826 *The admissibility of such evidence was considered at 1,5 above.*

827 *See, also, section 132(9), considered above.*

828 *The admissibility of which was considered at 1.9.2 above.*

"statements" for the purposes of Chapter 2 of Part 11 of the 2003 Act. Moreover, if, construing section 132(3) in the context of section 132(2), "the evidence" to which section 132(3) relates does mean a *"statement"* which a party proposes to tender in evidence under any provision of Chapter 2 of Part 11 of the 2003 Act, then it appears that section 132(3) will also be inapplicable to such representations. It is submitted, however, that, in relation to such representations, appropriate rules of court, imposing notice may, if the authority entitled to make the rules regards this as *"necessary or expedient"*, be made "for the purposes of this Chapter" under section 132(1).[829]

2.7.7.1 Failure to comply with prescribed requirements

It appears that section 132(5), when read in conjunction with section 132(2), will only applicable where hearsay evidence is tendered under a provision of Chapter 2 of Part 11 of the 2003 Act, though this is upon the assumption that *"evidence"* for the purposes of section 132(5) means a *"statement"* which a party proposes to tender in evidence under any provision of Chapter 2 of Part 11 of the 2003 Act. If this interpretation of section 132(2),(5) is correct, then the effects of section 132(5) of the 2003 Act[830] appears to be that: where a party who proposes to tender evidence under a provision of Chapter 2 of part 11 of the 2003 Act fails to comply with an applicable requirement prescribed by rules of court, the relevant evidence will only be admissible with the leave of the court; where the court gives leave the court or the jury will be entitled to draw appropriate inferences from the failure to comply with the requirement; and the court will be entitled to take the failure to comply with the requirement into account in the exercise of its powers concerning costs. In determining how to exercise the powers conferred upon it by section 132(5), the court will be required to consider whether there is any justification for the failure.[831]

Thus, it appears that both when the judge is considering whether there is a case to answer and when the jury are determining the guilt or innocence of the accused, the failure of a party tendering evidence under a provision of Chapter 2 of Part 11 of the 2003 Act to comply with requirements imposed by rules of court, such as notice requirements, may be a factor which will influence the court when evaluating hearsay evidence. Section 132(7) makes clear, however, that the accused may not be convicted solely on the basis of an inference drawn by the court under section 132(5). Moreover, it should be noted that rule 132(8), inter alia, appears to permit the authority entitled to make the relevant rules to limit the application of section 132(5) to prescribed circumstances and subject its operation to prescribed exceptions.

Developing an argument raised above in relation to the ambit of section 132(2),(3), it is arguable that where hearsay evidence is tendered under a pre-existing statutory

---

829 *See, also, section 132(9), considered above.*
830 *And see, also, section 132(10) for the meaning of "prescribed".*
831 *Section 132(6).*

exception to the hearsay rule which the 2003 Act retains or under a common law exception to the hearsay rule which the 2003 Act preserves, the evidence will not be tendered under a provision of Chapter 2 of Part 11. If this argument is correct (and the author does not suggest that it is), it appears that section 132(5)-(7) will not be applicable to such evidence. Even if this is so, however, it is submitted that the effect of section 132(1) and section 132(9) in combination will be that the authority entitled to make the rules will, "for the purposes of this chapter", be entitled, under section 132(1)[832], to make rules relating to such evidence the effect of which is identical to that of sections 132(5)-(7). It may be, of course, that, as was suggested above, where hearsay evidence is tendered under a pre-existing statutory exception to the hearsay rule which the 2003 Act retains or under a common law exception to the hearsay rule which the 2003 Act preserves, such evidence should, in fact, be properly regarded as tendered under section 114(1) of the 2003 Act, in which case section 132(5)-(7) will be applicable thereto.

Upon the assumption that section 132(5)-(7) of the 2003 Act are not applicable to statements which are not tendered under a provision of Chapter 2 of Part 11 of the 2003 Act, then it appears that those provisions will not apply to implied assertions (which, as was seen above, will not fall within the ambit of the hearsay rule when Chapter 2 of Part 11 of the 2003 Act is in force[833]) or to statements which are not tendered as evidence of matters stated but which are, merely, tendered to prove that the relevant words were stated.[834] Presumably, however, if the authority entitled to make the rules regards this as "necessary and expedient" (which, it is submitted, is unlikely), the making of rules of court relating to such evidence which are of equivalent effect to section 132(5)-(7) may be achieved by having recourse to the section 132(1) rulemaking power.[835]

Finally, if, construing section 132(5) in the context of section 132(2), the *"evidence"* to which section 132(5) relates is a "statement" which a party proposes to tender in evidence under any provision of Chapter 2 of Part 11 of the 2003 Act, then it appears that the ambit of section 132(5)-(7) will not encompass representations made by machines, such representations not falling within the section 115(2) definition of *"statement"*.[836] It is submitted, however, that, even if section 132(5)-(7) will not apply to such evidence, rules of court equivalent in effect to section 132(5)-(7) which relate to representations made by machines may, if the authority entitled to make the rules regards this as *"necessary or expedient"*, be made "for the purposes of this chapter" under section 132(1).[837]

---

832 *And see, also, section 132(9), considered above.*
833 *Which were considered at 1.6.2 above.*
834 *The admissibility of such "original evidence" was considered at 1.6.2 above.*
835 *See, also, section 132(9), considered above.*
836 *The admissibility of such evidence was considered at 1.9.2 above.*
837 *See, also, section 132(9), considered above.*

2.8 The Hearsay provisions of the Criminal Justice Act 2003 and the European Convention on Human Rights

It appears that both the exclusion and the admission of hearsay evidence in criminal proceedings has the potential to result in a violation of Article 6 of the European Convention on Human Rights. The first sentence of Article 6(1) of the European Convention on Human Rights[838] provides that,

> "In the determination of his civil rights and obligations or of any criminal charge against him, everyone is entitled to a fair and public hearing within a reasonable time by an independent and impartial tribunal established by law."

The admissibility of evidence is not governed by any express provisions of Article 6 and is, thus, primarily a matter to be determined by domestic law.[839] This does not mean, however, that the admission or exclusion of evidence is incapable of giving rise to a violation of Article 6. Rather, what it means is that the European Court of Human Rights is, in general, not concerned with whether a particular rule of evidence is fair in an abstract sense but, rather, is concerned with whether a particular defendant had a trial which, overall, was fair.[840] Thus, essentially, the question which concerns the European Court of Human rights is not whether a particular rule of evidence is inherently unfair but, rather, is whether, upon the facts of a given case, the operation of the relevant rule resulted in a violation of Article 6.

2.8.1 The exclusion of defence hearsay evidence

In relation to the hearsay rule specifically, it appears that, in principle, the exclusion of defence evidence by virtue of the operation of that rule in the context of criminal proceedings is not incompatible with Article 6(1).[841] Rather, the European Commission of Human Rights[842] has recognised that the purposes of the hearsay rule (namely, ensuring that the best evidence is before the jury and avoiding an over weight being given to the evidence of a witness who has not been cross-examined) are legitimate.

The fact that the hearsay rule is not, in principle, incompatible with Article 6(1) of the Convention does not mean, however, that the exclusion of defence evidence in consequence of its hearsay nature is incapable of giving rise to a violation of Article 6 in appropriate circumstances. Rather, the Law Commission[843] concluded in their consultation paper that:

---

838 Set out in Schedule 1 to the Human Rights Act 1998.
839 Schenk v Switzerland (1988) 13 EHRR 242.
840 Schenk v Switzerland (1988) 13 EHRR 242.
841 Blastland v the United Kingdom App No 12045/86.

842 Blastland v the United Kingdom App No 12045/86.
843 See "Evidence in Criminal Proceedings: Hearsay and Related Topics", Law Com No 245 at paragraph 5.31.

"...if a defendant were not allowed to use a cogent piece of evidence because it fell foul of the hearsay rule, he or she might be able to complain successfully that this infringed the right to a fair trial under Article 6(1); and the present operation of the rule leaves it open to this criticism.46

[46]The defendant in *Blastland v United Kingdom* 12045/86; (1988) 10 EHRR 528 (para 5.5, n 6 above) ran this argument, but the Strasbourg Commission declared his complaint inadmissible partly because, although he was not permitted to lead hearsay evidence of what the third party had said, he knew who the person was and there was (theoretically) nothing to stop him calling that person as a defence witness; and partly because he had the right to challenge the ruling, and it could not therefore be said that there was not *"equality of arms"*. This consideration weighed heavily with the Commission, and if this possibility had not existed the answer might have been different. See *Vidal v Belgium* (1992) Series A No 235-B, where the Strasbourg Court upheld the defendant's complaint that he had not received a fair trial where the Brussels Court of Appeal had refused to allow the defendant to call possibly relevant defence evidence, because they had given no reason for their refusal."

It is submitted, however, that, once the hearsay provisions of the Criminal Justice Act 2003 are in force, the "safety valve" inclusionary discretion which section 114(1)(d) of that Act will confer upon the criminal courts (which was considered at 2.6 above) combined with the court's obligation, imposed by section 3(1) of the Human Rights Act 1998, where this is possible, to read and give effect to legislation in a way which is compatible with the rights which the Convention guarantees, should ensure that, in general, defence evidence the exclusion of which would result in a violation of Article 6 of the Convention is admitted in criminal proceedings. It is submitted that problems could exceptionally arise in this context, however, in circumstances in which a hearsay statement (for example one made by an identification witness who is not available to testify) tends to exculpate one co-accused but incriminates another co-accused as, in such circumstances, the exclusion of the hearsay statement might violate the former co-accused's Article 6 rights but its admission might (if the maker of the hearsay statement is regarded as a *"witness against"* the latter co-accused for the purposes of Article 6(3)(d) of the Convention, which is considered below), violate the Article 6 rights of the latter co-accused.

In such circumstances, if appropriate editing of the hearsay statement is not viable, it may be that a violation of Article 6 in relation to one or other of the two co-accused could be avoided by severance of the indictment, though severance may not always be appropriate in circumstances in which defence evidence adduced by one co-accused is detrimental to another.[844] A more radical (though less satisfactory) alternative approach might be, however, that of admitting the hearsay evidence under section 114(1)(d) of the 2003 Act but directing the jury to the effect that they are not entitled to regard the hearsay evidence as evidence against the latter co-accused. This result could, it is submitted, be achieved by "reading down" section 114(1)(d) of the 2003 Act under section 3(1) of the 1998 Act in such a way that the effect of section 114(1)(d) in circumstances in which it would not be contrary to the interests of justice to admit hearsay evidence as defence evidence for co-accused A but it would be contrary to the interests of justice to admit the relevant evidence for the prosecution against co-accused B, is to render the hearsay evidence admissible for the former purpose but inadmissible for the latter purpose.

2.8.2 The admission of hearsay evidence for the prosecution

Whilst, as was indicated immediately above, the exclusion of defence hearsay evidence could potentially have human rights implications, it is submitted that a violation of Article 6 of the convention in the hearsay context is much more likely to result from the admission of hearsay evidence for the prosecution under an exception to the hearsay rule.

The existence of exceptions to the hearsay rule does not, in principle, appear to give rise to a violation of Article 6 of the Convention because the admissibility of evidence is not governed by any express provisions of Article 6 and, thus, is primarily a matter to be determined by domestic law.[845] This does not mean, however, that the admission of hearsay evidence is incapable of giving rise to a violation of Article 6. Rather, it appears that the admission of hearsay evidence may result in a violation of Article 6 if, by depriving the accused of the right to cross-examine witnesses against him, the admission of the relevant evidence deprives the accused of his right to a fair trial.[846] If the accused is deprived of the opportunity of cross-examining the maker of a hearsay statement, this may give rise to a violation of Article 6 because, under Article 6(3)(d) of the Convention, one aspect of the right to a fair trial is the right of the accused to *"examine or have examined witnesses against him"*.

Even though the Article 6(3)(d) right does not necessarily include the right to cross-examine the maker of a hearsay statement during the course of the trial itself[847] (and, thus, it appears that there may not be a violation of Article 6 where the accused could, if he chose to do so, call the maker of the hearsay statement as a defence witness[848]), Article 6(3)(d) may be potentially violated when hearsay evidence is admitted against the accused in criminal proceedings because it appears that a person who does not testify but whose hearsay statement is admitted in evidence may be classified as a "witness" for the purposes of Article 6(3)(d).[849] Thus, the potential for violation of Article 6 does appear to exist in circumstances in which a conviction is solely (or, it appears, decisively[850]) based upon the hearsay

---

844 *See R v Stephen Owen Sullivan The Times March 18 2003.*

845 *Schenk v Switzerland (1988) 13 EHRR 242.*

846 *See Unterpertinger v Austria (1991) 13 EHRR 175; R v M The Times May 2 2003.*

847 *Kostovski v The Netherlands (1990) 12 EHRR 574.*

848 *Blastland v The United Kingdom App No 12045/86*

849 *See Kostovski v The Netherlands (1990) 12 EHRR 574; Trivedi v The United Kingdom (1997) 89 D & R 136.*

850 *See Luca v Italy [2001] Crim LR 747.*

---

evidence of a witness whom the accused has had no opportunity to examine.[851] Even in such circumstances, however, it appears that the admission of hearsay evidence for the prosecution will not inherently violate Article 6 of the Convention; whether or not this is so will depend upon the specific circumstances of the case before the court.[852]

Thus, whilst the admission of hearsay evidence for the prosecution is capable of giving rise to a violation of Article 6, it appears that the admission of such evidence will not automatically have this effect. Rather, it seems that the fact that a hearsay statement made by a prosecution witness whom the defence had no opportunity to cross-examine is admitted in the course of criminal proceedings will not give rise to a violation of Article 6 if the proceedings as a whole were fair for the purposes of Article 6.[853] In determining whether the admission of hearsay evidence for the prosecution in criminal proceedings renders those proceedings unfair for the purposes of Article 6 of the Convention, it will be necessary for the court to consider matters such as whether the hearsay evidence is the only evidence relied upon by the prosecution in relation to the relevant issue, whether the defence have already had an opportunity to examine the maker of the hearsay statement on a previous occasion, whether the defence have had an opportunity to adduce evidence controverting the hearsay statement, whether the defence have had an opportunity to challenge the credibility of the maker of the hearsay statement and the nature of the direction which the judge gives to the jury concerning the weight of and, where appropriate, the danger of relying upon the hearsay evidence.[854]

Specifically, it appears that the admission of hearsay evidence for the prosecution under sections 23 or 24 of the Criminal Justice Act 1988 (which, as was seen at 2.2.1 and 2.2.2 above, will be repealed when the hearsay provisions of the Criminal Justice Act 2003 come into force) does not inherently give rise to a breach of Article 6 of the Convention.[855] Indeed, it may be that, in general, the admission of hearsay evidence under section 23 or section 24, following a proper exercise of discretion under section 25 or section 26 of the 1988 Act, is unlikely to conflict with the requirements of Article 6.[856] This, it is submitted, is so because the effect of section 3(1) of the Human Rights Act 1998 in this context is that the courts are required to exercise their section 25 and section 26 exclusionary and

---

851 See *R v M* [2003] 2 Cr App R 322.

852 See: *R v M* [2003] 2 Cr App R 322; *Vehicle and Operator Services Agency v George Jenkins Transport Ltd The Times December 5 2003*.

853 See: *Asch v Austria* (1993) 15 EHRR 597; *Trivedi v The United Kingdom* (1997) 89 D & R 136; *R v D The Times May 21 2002*. It should be noted that in *Attorney General's Reference (No 1 of 2003)* [2003] 2 Cr App R 453, the Court of Appeal distinguished *Asch v Austria* upon the basis that in the latter case (unlike the former) the witness whose hearsay statement was admitted in evidence was not a

compellable witness and the European Court of Human Rights had indicated that the right not to testify upon which the witness relied could not be permitted to "block the prosecution".

854 See: *Trivedi v The United Kingdom* (1997) 89 D & R 136; *R v Thomas* [1998] Crim LR 887; *R v M* [2003] 2 Cr App R 322.

855 See: *Trivedi v The United Kingdom* (1997) 89 D & R 136; *R v Gokal* [1997] 2 Cr App R 266; *R v Thomas* [1998] Crim LR 887.

856 *R v Gokal* [1997] 2 Cr App R 266; *R v D* [2002] The Times May 21 2002.

inclusionary discretions so as to exclude or refuse to admit hearsay evidence admissible under section 23 or section 24 in circumstances in which its admission would deprive the accused of a fair trial within the meaning of Article 6.[857] The admission of hearsay evidence under sections 23 or 24 will, of course, give rise to a breach of Article 6 if it prevents the accused from having a fair trial within the meaning of Article 6.[858].

In relation to the admission of hearsay evidence under any of the exceptions to the hearsay rule which the Criminal Justice Act 2003 will create, retain or preserve, it submitted that as currently appears to be the case in relation to the operation of sections 23 and 24 of the 1988 Act, this will not inherently give rise to a breach of Article 6 of the Convention. The hearsay exceptions which the 2003 Act will create, retain or preserve may, of course, be distinguished from the section 23 and 24 exceptions in that the former, unlike the latter, are not subject to the operation of the section 25 and 26 discretions. The Law Commission[859] were, however, of the view that where hearsay evidence was admitted for the prosecution in criminal proceedings, the accused would be given adequate protection by the safeguards which they proposed as part of their scheme. The Law Commission[860] summarised these safeguards (the first three of which have already been encountered in the course of this work[861]) as follows.

> "First, the nature of our exceptions means that there is built-in protection: hearsay would not be permitted where the declarant's oral evidence was *available*, or where the declarant was *unidentified*, except in the case of business documents, res gestae, and evidence admitted under the safety-valve.

Our recommendations include the following further safeguards.

(1) Where possible, advance notice would be given that hearsay evidence is to be adduced.[78]

(2) A party against whom hearsay evidence is admitted would be allowed to adduce evidence challenging the credibility of the absent declarant as if the declarant were present.[79]

---

857 *See R v M [2003] 2 Cr App R 322.*

858 *See R v M [2003] 2 Cr App R 322. The Court of Appeal in R v Radak [1999] 1 Cr App R 187 appears to have taken this view of the trial judge's decision to admit the hearsay evidence. Equally, in Trivedi v The United Kingdom (1997) 89 D & R 136 and R v Thomas The Times July 24 1988, the Commission and the Court of Appeal, in determining whether the admission of evidence under section 23 had given rise to a breach of Article 6, both appear to have regarded the crucial question as being whether, on the facts of the case, the accused had been given a fair trial.*

859 *See "Evidence in Criminal Proceedings: Hearsay and Related Topics", Law Com No 245 at paragraphs 5.40-5.41.*

860 *See "Evidence in Criminal Proceedings: Hearsay and Related Topics", Law Com No 245 at paragraphs 1.48-1.49.*

861 *In relation to safeguards (1)-(3) see 2.7.7, 2.7.3 and 2.7.4 above.*

(3) The judge would have a duty to direct the jury to acquit, and the magistrates would have a duty to dismiss an information, if the case against the accused depends wholly or partly on hearsay evidence which is so unconvincing that, considering its importance to the case, a conviction would be unsafe.[80]

(4) In a trial on indictment the jury would be warned in the summing-up of the weaknesses of the hearsay evidence.81

[78] See paras 11.6 – 11.7 below.

[79] See paras 11.19 – 11.22 below. Where the declarant's credibility is attacked, the judge or magistrates would have power to permit a party to adduce additional evidence for the purpose of denying or answering the allegation made: see paras 11.24 – 11.25 below.

[80] In effect, reversing *Galbraith* [1981] 1 WLR 1039 in cases where hearsay evidence forms part of the prosecution case. The Royal Commission recommended the reversal of *Galbraith* with regard to all cases: ch 4, paras 41 and 42. See further paras 11.26 – 11.32 below.

[81] There is a specimen direction issued by the Judicial Studies Board which deals with this. See para 3.23 below."

The Law Commission[862] particularly regarded the third of these safeguards (which, as was seen at 2.7.4 above, exists in the context of the 2003 Act in the form of section 125 thereof), as providing protection for the accused in this context. It is submitted that further protection of the accused's Article 6 rights, when the issue of the admissibility of hearsay evidence in criminal proceedings under one of the hearsay exceptions which the 2003 Act will create, retain or preserve arises will, potentially, be provided by another of the safeguards which the Law Commission considered in Part XI of their report[863], namely, the court's discretion (both under section 78 of the Police and Criminal Evidence Act 1984 and at common law[864]), to exclude evidence tendered by the prosecution. Indeed, it is submitted that where the admission of hearsay evidence for the prosecution would result in a violation of Article 6 of the Convention, the effect of section 3(1) of the Human Rights Act 1998 in this context will be that the court will be required to exercise its section 78 discretion so as to exclude the relevant evidence.[865] Moreover, it is submitted that this will equally be the case where the court is exercising any of the powers which the 2003 Act confers upon it concerning the admission or exclusion

862 See "Evidence in Criminal Proceedings: Hearsay and Related Topics", Law Com No 245 at paragraphs 5.40-5.41.

863 See "Evidence in Criminal Proceedings: Hearsay and Related Topics", Law Com No 245 at paragraph 11.15.

864 The nature of both of these exclusionary discretions was considered at 2.7.5 above.

865 Moreover, it is submitted that to the extent to which the court's common law discretion to exclude prosecution evidence may be applicable when the section 78 discretion is not, the court would effectively be under a duty to exclude hearsay evidence the admission of which would result in a violation of Article 6 in consequence of the operation of section 6(1) of the Human Rights Act 1998 (which makes it unlawful for a public authority to act in a way which is incompatible with a convention right).

of hearsay evidence (i.e. the leave requirement imposed by section 116(2)(e), the exclusionary discretion conferred by section 117(6),(7), the "safety valve" inclusionary discretion created by section 114(1)(d) and the section 121(1)(c) discretion to admit multiple hearsay, which were considered, respectively at 2.2.1.2.8, 2.2.2.2.5, 2.6 and 2.7.1, above).

APPENDIX

Text of those provisions of the Criminal Justice Act 2003 which are considered in this book.

Readers please note that:

- (other than section 99), Chapter 1 (Evidence of Bad Character) of Part 11 of the 2003 Act is not reproduced in this appendix because it is not considered in this book;

- the following provisions of Part 14, namely, sections 334 ("Provision for Northern Ireland"), 335 ("Expenses"), 337 ("Extent") and 338 ("Channel Islands and Isle of Man"), are not reproduced in this appendix because they are not considered in this book;

- Schedule 7 ("Hearsay Evidence: Armed Forces) and Part 5 ("Evidence") of Schedule 36 ("Further Minor and Consequential Amendments), which contains several references to Schedule 7, are not reproduced in this appendix because they are not considered in this book;

- only Part 6 of Schedule 37 is reproduced, it being the only Part of Schedule 37 that is considered herein.

PART II

EVIDENCE

CHAPTER I

EVIDENCE OF BAD CHARACTER

Introductory

99 Abolition of common law rules

(1) The common law rules governing the admissibility of evidence of bad character in criminal proceedings are abolished.

(2) Subsection (1) is subject to section 118(1) in so far as it preserves the rule under which in criminal proceedings a person's reputation is admissible for the purposes of proving his bad character.

CHAPTER 2

HEARSAY EVIDENCE

Hearsay: main provisions

114 Admissibility of hearsay evidence

(1) In criminal proceedings a statement not made in oral evidence in the proceedings is admissible as evidence of any matter stated if, but only if—

    (a) any provision of this Chapter or any other statutory provision makes it admissible,

    (b) any rule of law preserved by section 118 makes it admissible,

    (c) all parties to the proceedings agree to it being admissible, or

    (d) the court is satisfied that it is in the interests of justice for it to be admissible.

(2) In deciding whether a statement not made in oral evidence should be admitted under subsection (1)(d), the court must have regard to the following factors (and to any others it considers relevant)—

(a) how much probative value the statement has (assuming it to be true) in relation to a matter in issue in the proceedings, or how valuable it is for the understanding of other evidence in the case;

(b) what other evidence has been, or can be, given on the matter or evidence mentioned in paragraph (a);

(c) how important the matter or evidence mentioned in paragraph (a) is in the context of the case as a whole;

(d the circumstances in which the statement was made;

(e) how reliable the maker of the statement appears to be;

(f) how reliable the evidence of the making of the statement appears to be;

(g) whether oral evidence of the matter stated can be given and, if not, why it cannot;

(h the amount of difficulty involved in challenging the statement;

(i) the extent to which that difficulty would be likely to prejudice the party facing it.

(3) Nothing in this Chapter affects the exclusion of evidence of a statement on grounds other than the fact that it is a statement not made in oral evidence in the proceedings.

115 Statements and matters stated

(1) In this Chapter references to a statement or to a matter stated are to be read as follows.

(2) A statement is any representation of fact or opinion made by a person by whatever means; and it includes a representation made in a sketch, photofit or other pictorial form.

(3) A matter stated is one to which this Chapter applies if (and only if) the purpose, or one of the purposes, of the person making the statement appears to the court to have been–

(a) to cause another person to believe the matter, or

(b) to cause another person to act or a machine to operate on the basis that the matter is as stated.

Principal categories of admissibility

116 Cases where a witness is unavailable

(1) In criminal proceedings a statement not made in oral evidence in the proceedings is admissible as evidence of any matter stated if–

    (a) oral evidence given in the proceedings by the person who made the statement would be admissible as evidence of that matter,

    (b) the person who made the statement (the relevant person) is identified to the court's satisfaction, and

    (c) any of the five conditions mentioned in subsection (2) is satisfied.

(2) The conditions are–

    (a) that the relevant person is dead;

    (b) that the relevant person is unfit to be a witness because of his bodily or mental condition;

    (c) that the relevant person is outside the United Kingdom and it is not reasonably practicable to secure his attendance;

    (d) that the relevant person cannot be found although such steps as it is reasonably practicable to take to find him have been taken;

    (e) that through fear the relevant person does not give (or does not continue to give) oral evidence in the proceedings, either at all or in connection with the subject matter of the statement, and the court gives leave for the statement to be given in evidence.

(3) For the purposes of subsection (2)(e) "fear" is to be widely construed and (for example) includes fear of the death or injury of another person or of financial loss.

(4) Leave may be given under subsection (2)(e) only if the court considers that the statement ought to be admitted in the interests of justice, having regard–

    (a) to the statement's contents,

    (b) to any risk that its admission or exclusion will result in unfairness to any party to the proceedings (and in particular to how difficult it will be to challenge the statement if the relevant person does not give oral evidence),

    (c) in appropriate cases, to the fact that a direction under section 19 of the Youth Justice and Criminal Evidence Act 1999 (c. 23) (special measures for the giving of evidence by fearful witnesses etc) could be made in relation to the relevant person, and

(d)   to any other relevant circumstances.

(5)   A condition set out in any paragraph of subsection (2) which is in fact satisfied is to be treated as not satisfied if it is shown that the circumstances described in that paragraph are caused–

 (a)   by the person in support of whose case it is sought to give the statement in evidence, or

 (b   by a person acting on his behalf,

in order to prevent the relevant person giving oral evidence in the proceedings (whether at all or in connection with the subject matter of the statement).

117 Business and other documents

(1)   In criminal proceedings a statement contained in a document is admissible as evidence of any matter stated if–

 (a)   oral evidence given in the proceedings would be admissible as evidence of that matter,

 (b)   the requirements of subsection (2) are satisfied, and

 (c)   the requirements of subsection (5) are satisfied, in a case where subsection (4) requires them to be.

(2)   The requirements of this subsection are satisfied if–

 (a)   the document or the part containing the statement was created or received by a person in the course of a trade, business, profession or other occupation, or as the holder of a paid or unpaid office,

 (b)   the person who supplied the information contained in the statement (the relevant person) had or may reasonably be supposed to have had personal knowledge of the matters dealt with, and

 (c)   each person (if any) through whom the information was supplied from the relevant person to the person mentioned in paragraph (a) received the information in the course of a trade, business, profession or other occupation, or as the holder of a paid or unpaid office.

(3)   The persons mentioned in paragraphs (a) and (b) of subsection (2) may be the same person.

(4)   The additional requirements of subsection (5) must be satisfied if the statement–

 (a)   was prepared for the purposes of pending or contemplated criminal proceedings, or for a criminal investigation, but

(b)   was not obtained pursuant to a request under section 7 of the Crime (International Co-operation) Act 2003 (c. 32) or an order under paragraph 6 of Schedule 13 to the Criminal Justice Act 1988 (c. 33) (which relate to overseas evidence).

(5)   The requirements of this subsection are satisfied if–

(a)   any of the five conditions mentioned in section 116(2) is satisfied (absence of relevant person etc), or

(b)   the relevant person cannot reasonably be expected to have any recollection of the matters dealt with in the statement (having regard to the length of time since he supplied the information and all other circumstances).

(6   A statement is not admissible under this section if the court makes a direction to that effect under subsection (7).

(7)   The court may make a direction under this subsection if satisfied that the statement's reliability as evidence for the purpose for which it is tendered is doubtful in view of–

(a)   its contents,

(b)   the source of the information contained in it,

(c)   the way in which or the circumstances in which the information was supplied or received, or

(d)   the way in which or the circumstances in which the document concerned was created or received.

118 Preservation of certain common law categories of admissibility

(1) The following rules of law are preserved.

Public information etc

1   Any rule of law under which in criminal proceedings–

(a)   published works dealing with matters of a public nature (such as histories, scientific works, dictionaries and maps) are admissible as evidence of facts of a public nature stated in them,

(b)   public documents (such as public registers, and returns made under public authority with respect to matters of public interest) are admissible as evidence of facts stated in them,

(c)   records (such as the records of certain courts, treaties, Crown grants, pardons and commissions) are admissible as evidence of facts stated in them, or

(d)   evidence relating to a person's age or date or place of birth may be given by a person without personal knowledge of the matter.

Reputation as to character

2   Any rule of law under which in criminal proceedings evidence of a person's reputation is admissible for the purpose of proving his good or bad character.

Note

The rule is preserved only so far as it allows the court to treat such evidence as proving the matter concerned.

Reputation or family tradition

3   Any rule of law under which in criminal proceedings evidence of reputation or family tradition is admissible for the purpose of proving or disproving—

(a   pedigree or the existence of a marriage,

(b)   the existence of any public or general right, or

(c)   the identity of any person or thing.

Note

The rule is preserved only so far as it allows the court to treat such evidence as proving or disproving the matter concerned.

Res gestae

4   Any rule of law under which in criminal proceedings a statement is admissible as evidence of any matter stated if—

(a)   the statement was made by a person so emotionally overpowered by an event that the possibility of concoction or distortion can be disregarded,

(b)   the statement accompanied an act which can be properly evaluated as evidence only if considered in conjunction with the statement, or

(c)   the statement relates to a physical sensation or a mental state (such as intention or emotion).

Confessions etc

5   Any rule of law relating to the admissibility of confessions or mixed statements in criminal proceedings.

Admissions by agents etc

6   Any rule of law under which in criminal proceedings—

(a   an admission made by an agent of a defendant is admissible against the defendant as evidence of any matter stated, or

(b) a statement made by a person to whom a defendant refers a person for information is admissible against the defendant as evidence of any matter stated.

Common enterprise

7   Any rule of law under which in criminal proceedings a statement made by a party to a common enterprise is admissible against another party to the enterprise as evidence of any matter stated.

Expert evidence

8   Any rule of law under which in criminal proceedings an expert witness may draw on the body of expertise relevant to his field.

(2) With the exception of the rules preserved by this section, the common law rules governing the admissibility of hearsay evidence in criminal proceedings are abolished.

119 Inconsistent statements

(1) If in criminal proceedings a person gives oral evidence and–

(a) he admits making a previous inconsistent statement, or

(b) a previous inconsistent statement made by him is proved by virtue of section 3, 4 or 5 of the Criminal Procedure Act 1865 (c. 18),

the statement is admissible as evidence of any matter stated of which oral evidence by him would be admissible.

(2) If in criminal proceedings evidence of an inconsistent statement by any person is given under section 124(2)(c), the statement is admissible as evidence of any matter stated in it of which oral evidence by that person would be admissible.

120 Other previous statements of witnesses

(1) This section applies where a person (the witness) is called to give evidence in criminal proceedings.

(2) If a previous statement by the witness is admitted as evidence to rebut a suggestion that his oral evidence has been fabricated, that statement is admissible as evidence of any matter stated of which oral evidence by the witness would be admissible.

(3) A statement made by the witness in a document–

(a which is used by him to refresh his memory while giving evidence,

(b) on which he is cross-examined, and

(c) which as a consequence is received in evidence in the proceedings,

is admissible as evidence of any matter stated of which oral evidence by him would be admissible.

(4) A previous statement by the witness is admissible as evidence of any matter stated of which oral evidence by him would be admissible, if–

   (a) any of the following three conditions is satisfied, and

   (b) while giving evidence the witness indicates that to the best of his belief he made the statement, and that to the best of his belief it states the truth.

(5) The first condition is that the statement identifies or describes a person, object or place.

(6) The second condition is that the statement was made by the witness when the matters stated were fresh in his memory but he does not remember them, and cannot reasonably be expected to remember them, well enough to give oral evidence of them in the proceedings.

(7) The third condition is that–

   (a) the witness claims to be a person against whom an offence has been committed,

   (b) the offence is one to which the proceedings relate,

   (c) the statement consists of a complaint made by the witness (whether to a person in authority or not) about conduct which would, if proved, constitute the offence or part of the offence,

   (d) the complaint was made as soon as could reasonably be expected after the alleged conduct,

   (e) the complaint was not made as a result of a threat or a promise, and

   (f) before the statement is adduced the witness gives oral evidence in connection with its subject matter.

(8) For the purposes of subsection (7) the fact that the complaint was elicited (for example, by a leading question) is irrelevant unless a threat or a promise was involved.

Supplementary

121 Additional requirement for admissibility of multiple hearsay

(1) A hearsay statement is not admissible to prove the fact that an earlier hearsay statement was made unless–

    (a) either of the statements is admissible under section 117, 119 or 120,

    (b) all parties to the proceedings so agree, or

    (c) the court is satisfied that the value of the evidence in question, taking into account how reliable the statements appear to be, is so high that the interests of justice require the later statement to be admissible for that purpose.

(2) In this section "hearsay statement" means a statement, not made in oral evidence, that is relied on as evidence of a matter stated in it.

122 Documents produced as exhibits

(1) This section applies if on a trial before a judge and jury for an offence–

    (a) a statement made in a document is admitted in evidence under section 119 or 120, and

    (b) the document or a copy of it is produced as an exhibit.

(2) The exhibit must not accompany the jury when they retire to consider their verdict unless–

    (a) the court considers it appropriate, or

    (b) all the parties to the proceedings agree that it should accompany the jury.

123 Capability to make statement

(1) Nothing in section 116, 119 or 120 makes a statement admissible as evidence if it was made by a person who did not have the required capability at the time when he made the statement.

(2) Nothing in section 117 makes a statement admissible as evidence if any person who, in order for the requirements of section 117(2) to be satisfied, must at any time have supplied or received the information concerned or created or received the document or part concerned–

    (a) did not have the required capability at that time, or

    (b) cannot be identified but cannot reasonably be assumed to have had the required capability at that time.

(3) For the purposes of this section a person has the required capability if he is capable of—

    (a) understanding questions put to him about the matters stated, and

    (b) giving answers to such questions which can be understood.

(4) Where by reason of this section there is an issue as to whether a person had the required capability when he made a statement—

    (a) proceedings held for the determination of the issue must take place in the absence of the jury (if there is one);

    (b) in determining the issue the court may receive expert evidence and evidence from any person to whom the statement in question was made;

    (c) the burden of proof on the issue lies on the party seeking to adduce the statement, and the standard of proof is the balance of probabilities.

124 Credibility

(1) This section applies if in criminal proceedings—

    (a) a statement not made in oral evidence in the proceedings is admitted as evidence of a matter stated, and

    (b) the maker of the statement does not give oral evidence in connection with the subject matter of the statement.

(2) In such a case—

    (a) any evidence which (if he had given such evidence) would have been admissible as relevant to his credibility as a witness is so admissible in the proceedings;

    (b) evidence may with the court's leave be given of any matter which (if he had given such evidence) could have been put to him in cross-examination as relevant to his credibility as a witness but of which evidence could not have been adduced by the cross-examining party;

    (c) evidence tending to prove that he made (at whatever time) any other statement inconsistent with the statement admitted as evidence is admissible for the purpose of showing that he contradicted himself.

(3) If as a result of evidence admitted under this section an allegation is made against the maker of a statement, the court may permit a party to lead additional evidence of such description as the court may specify for the purposes of denying or answering the allegation.

(4)   In the case of a statement in a document which is admitted as evidence under section 117 each person who, in order for the statement to be admissible, must have supplied or received the information concerned or created or received the document or part concerned is to be treated as the maker of the statement for the purposes of subsections (1) to (3) above.

125 Stopping the case where evidence is unconvincing

(1)   If on a defendant's trial before a judge and jury for an offence the court is satisfied at any time after the close of the case for the prosecution that—

   (a)   the case against the defendant is based wholly or partly on a statement not made in oral evidence in the proceedings, and

   (b)   the evidence provided by the statement is so unconvincing that, considering its importance to the case against the defendant, his conviction of the offence would be unsafe,

the court must either direct the jury to acquit the defendant of the offence or, if it considers that there ought to be a retrial, discharge the jury.

(2)   Where—

   (a)   a jury is directed under subsection (1) to acquit a defendant of an offence, and

   (b)   the circumstances are such that, apart from this subsection, the defendant could if acquitted of that offence be found guilty of another offence,

the defendant may not be found guilty of that other offence if the court is satisfied as mentioned in subsection (1) in respect of it.

(3) If—

   (a   a jury is required to determine under section 4A(2) of the Criminal Procedure (Insanity) Act 1964 (c. 84) whether a person charged on an indictment with an offence did the act or made the omission charged, and

   (b)   the court is satisfied as mentioned in subsection (1) above at any time after the close of the case for the prosecution that—

      (i)   the case against the defendant is based wholly or partly on a statement not made in oral evidence in the proceedings, and

      (ii)   the evidence provided by the statement is so unconvincing that, considering its importance to the case against the person, a finding that he did the act or made the omission would be unsafe, the court must either direct the jury to acquit the defendant of the offence or, if it considers that there ought to be a rehearing, discharge the jury.

(4) This section does not prejudice any other power a court may have to direct a jury to acquit a person of an offence or to discharge a jury.

126 Court's general discretion to exclude evidence

(1) In criminal proceedings the court may refuse to admit a statement as evidence of a matter stated if–

(a) the statement was made otherwise than in oral evidence in the proceedings, and

(b) the court is satisfied that the case for excluding the statement, taking account of the danger that to admit it would result in undue waste of time, substantially outweighs the case for admitting it, taking account of the value of the evidence.

(2) Nothing in this Chapter prejudices–

(a) any power of a court to exclude evidence under section 78 of the Police and Criminal Evidence Act 1984 (c. 60) (exclusion of unfair evidence), or

(b) any other power of a court to exclude evidence at its discretion (whether by preventing questions from being put or otherwise).

Miscellaneous

127 Expert evidence: preparatory work

(1) This section applies if–

(a) a statement has been prepared for the purposes of criminal proceedings,

(b) the person who prepared the statement had or may reasonably be supposed to have had personal knowledge of the matters stated,

(c) notice is given under the appropriate rules that another person (the expert) will in evidence given in the proceedings orally or under section 9 of the Criminal Justice Act 1967 (c. 80) base an opinion or inference on the statement, and

(d) the notice gives the name of the person who prepared the statement and the nature of the matters stated.

(2) In evidence given in the proceedings the expert may base an opinion or inference on the statement.

(3) If evidence based on the statement is given under subsection (2) the statement is to be treated as evidence of what it states.

(4) This section does not apply if the court, on an application by a party to the proceedings, orders that it is not in the interests of justice that it should apply.

(5) The matters to be considered by the court in deciding whether to make an order under subsection (4) include–

    (a) the expense of calling as a witness the person who prepared the statement;

    (b) whether relevant evidence could be given by that person which could not be given by the expert;

    (c) whether that person can reasonably be expected to remember the matters stated well enough to give oral evidence of them.

(6) Subsections (1) to (5) apply to a statement prepared for the purposes of a criminal investigation as they apply to a statement prepared for the purposes of criminal proceedings, and in such a case references to the proceedings are to criminal proceedings arising from the investigation.

(7) The appropriate rules are rules made–

    (a) under section 81 of the Police and Criminal Evidence Act 1984 (advance notice of expert evidence in Crown Court), or

    (b) under section 144 of the Magistrates' Courts Act 1980 (c. 43) by virtue of section 20(3) of the Criminal Procedure and Investigations Act 1996 (c. 25) (advance notice of expert evidence in magistrates' courts).

128 Confessions

(1) In the Police and Criminal Evidence Act 1984 (c. 60) the following section is inserted after section 76–

"76A Confessions may be given in evidence for co-accused

(1) In any proceedings a confession made by an accused person may be given in evidence for another person charged in the same proceedings (a co-accused) in so far as it is relevant to any matter in issue in the proceedings and is not excluded by the court in pursuance of this section.

(2) If, in any proceedings where a co-accused proposes to give in evidence a confession made by an accused person, it is represented to the court that the confession was or may have been obtained—

(a) by oppression of the person who made it; or

(b) in consequence of anything said or done which was likely, in the circumstances existing at the time, to render unreliable any confession which might be made by him in consequence thereof,

the court shall not allow the confession to be given in evidence for the co-accused except in so far as it is proved to the court on the balance of probabilities that the confession (notwithstanding that it may be true) was not so obtained.

(3) Before allowing a confession made by an accused person to be given in evidence for a co-accused in any proceedings, the court may of its own motion require the fact that the confession was not obtained as mentioned in subsection (2) above to be proved in the proceedings on the balance of probabilities.

(4) The fact that a confession is wholly or partly excluded in pursuance of this section shall not affect the admissibility in evidence—

(a) of any facts discovered as a result of the confession; or

(b) where the confession is relevant as showing that the accused speaks, writes or expresses himself in a particular way, of so much of the confession as is necessary to show that he does so.

(5 Evidence that a fact to which this subsection applies was discovered as a result of a statement made by an accused person shall not be admissible unless evidence of how it was discovered is given by him or on his behalf.

(6) Subsection (5) above applies—

(a) to any fact discovered as a result of a confession which is wholly excluded in pursuance of this section; and

(b) to any fact discovered as a result of a confession which is partly so excluded, if the fact is discovered as a result of the excluded part of the confession.

(7) In this section "oppression" includes torture, inhuman or degrading treatment, and the use or threat of violence (whether or not amounting to torture)."

(2) Subject to subsection (1), nothing in this Chapter makes a confession by a defendant admissible if it would not be admissible under section 76 of the Police and Criminal Evidence Act 1984 (c. 60).

(3) In subsection (2) "confession" has the meaning given by section 82 of that Act.

129 Representations other than by a person

(1) Where a representation of any fact—

(a) is made otherwise than by a person, but

(b) depends for its accuracy on information supplied (directly or indirectly) by a person,

the representation is not admissible in criminal proceedings as evidence of the fact unless it is proved that the information was accurate.

(2) Subsection (1) does not affect the operation of the presumption that a mechanical device has been properly set or calibrated.

130 Depositions

In Schedule 3 to the Crime and Disorder Act 1998 (c. 37), sub-paragraph (4) of paragraph 5 is omitted (power of the court to overrule an objection to a deposition being read as evidence by virtue of that paragraph).

131 Evidence at retrial

For paragraphs 1 and 1A of Schedule 2 to the Criminal Appeal Act 1968 (c. 19) (oral evidence and use of transcripts etc at retrials under that Act) there is substituted—

"Evidence

1 (1) Evidence given at a retrial must be given orally if it was given orally at the original trial, unless—

(a) all the parties to the retrial agree otherwise;

(b) section 116 of the Criminal Justice Act 2003 applies (admissibility of hearsay evidence where a witness is unavailable); or

(c) the witness is unavailable to give evidence, otherwise than as mentioned in subsection (2) of that section, and section 114(1)(d) of that Act applies (admission of hearsay evidence under residual discretion).

(2) Paragraph 5 of Schedule 3 to the Crime and Disorder Act 1998 (use of depositions) does not apply at a retrial to a deposition read as evidence at the original trial."

General

132 Rules of court

(1) Rules of court may make such provision as appears to the appropriate authority to be necessary or expedient for the purposes of this Chapter; and the appropriate authority is the authority entitled to make the rules.

(2) The rules may make provision about the procedure to be followed and other conditions to be fulfilled by a party proposing to tender a statement in evidence under any provision of this Chapter.

(3) The rules may require a party proposing to tender the evidence to serve on each party to the proceedings such notice, and such particulars of or relating to the evidence, as may be prescribed.

(4) The rules may provide that the evidence is to be treated as admissible by agreement of the parties if—

(a) a notice has been served in accordance with provision made under subsection (3), and

(b) no counter-notice in the prescribed form objecting to the admission of the evidence has been served by a party.

(5) If a party proposing to tender evidence fails to comply with a prescribed requirement applicable to it—

(a) the evidence is not admissible except with the court's leave;

(b) where leave is given the court or jury may draw such inferences from the failure as appear proper;

(c) the failure may be taken into account by the court in considering the exercise of its powers with respect to costs.

(6) In considering whether or how to exercise any of its powers under subsection (5) the court shall have regard to whether there is any justification for the failure to comply with the requirement.

(7) A person shall not be convicted of an offence solely on an inference drawn under subsection (5)(b).

(8) Rules under this section may—

(a) limit the application of any provision of the rules to prescribed circumstances;

(b) subject any provision of the rules to prescribed exceptions;

(c) make different provision for different cases or circumstances.

(9) Nothing in this section prejudices the generality of any enactment

conferring power to make rules of court; and no particular provision of this section prejudices any general provision of it.

(10) In this section—

"prescribed" means prescribed by rules of court;

"rules of court" means—

(a)   Crown Court Rules;

(b)   Criminal Appeal Rules;

(c)   rules under section 144 of the Magistrates' Courts Act 1980 (c. 43).

133 Proof of statements in documents

Where a statement in a document is admissible as evidence in criminal proceedings, the statement may be proved by producing either—

(a)   the document, or

(b)   (whether or not the document exists) a copy of the document or of the material part of it,

authenticated in whatever way the court may approve.

134 Interpretation of Chapter 2

(1) In this Chapter—

"copy", in relation to a document, means anything on to which information recorded in the document has been copied, by whatever means and whether directly or indirectly;

"criminal proceedings" means criminal proceedings in relation to which the strict rules of evidence apply;

"defendant", in relation to criminal proceedings, means a person charged with an offence in those proceedings;

"document" means anything in which information of any description is recorded;

"oral evidence" includes evidence which, by reason of any disability, disorder or other impairment, a person called as a witness gives in writing or by signs or by way of any device;

"statutory provision" means any provision contained in, or in an instrument made under, this or any other Act, including any Act passed after this Act.

(2) Section 115 (statements and matters stated) contains other general interpretative provisions.

(3) Where a defendant is charged with two or more offences in the same criminal proceedings, this Chapter has effect as if each offence were charged in separate proceedings.

135 Armed forces

Schedule 7 (hearsay evidence: armed forces) has effect.

136 Repeals etc

In the Criminal Justice Act 1988 (c. 33), the following provisions (which are to some extent superseded by provisions of this Chapter) are repealed—

(a) Part 2 and Schedule 2 (which relate to documentary evidence);

(b) in Schedule 13, paragraphs 2 to 5 (which relate to documentary evidence in service courts etc).

CHAPTER 3

MISCELLANEOUS AND SUPPLEMENTAL

137 Evidence by video recording

(1) This section applies where—

(a) a person is called as a witness in proceedings for an offence triable only on indictment, or for a prescribed offence triable either way,

(b) the person claims to have witnessed (whether visually or in any other way)—

(i) events alleged by the prosecution to include conduct constituting the offence or part of the offence, or

(ii) events closely connected with such events,

(c) he has previously given an account of the events in question (whether in response to questions asked or otherwise),

(d) the account was given at a time when those events were fresh in the person's memory (or would have been, assuming the truth of the claim mentioned in paragraph (b)),

(e) a video recording was made of the account,

(f) the court has made a direction that the recording should be admitted as evidence in chief of the witness, and the direction has not been rescinded, and

(g)   the recording is played in the proceedings in accordance with the direction.

(2   If, or to the extent that, the witness in his oral evidence in the proceedings asserts the truth of the statements made by him in the recorded account, they shall be treated as if made by him in that evidence.

(3)   A direction under subsection (1)(f)–

    (a)   may not be made in relation to a recorded account given by the defendant;

    (b)   may be made only if it appears to the court that–

        (i)   the witness's recollection of the events in question is likely to have been significantly better when he gave the recorded account than it will be when he gives oral evidence in the proceedings, and

        (ii)   it is in the interests of justice for the recording to be admitted, having regard in particular to the matters mentioned in subsection (4).

(4)   Those matters are–

    (a)   the interval between the time of the events in question and the time when the recorded account was made;

    (b)   any other factors that might affect the reliability of what the witness said in that account;

    (c)   the quality of the recording;

    (d)   any views of the witness as to whether his evidence in chief should be given orally or by means of the recording.

    (5)   For the purposes of subsection (2) it does not matter if the statements in the recorded account were not made on oath.

In this section "prescribed" means of a description specified in an order made by the Secretary of State.

138 Video evidence: further provisions

(1)   Where a video recording is admitted under section 137, the witness may not give evidence in chief otherwise than by means of the recording as to any matter which, in the opinion of the court, has been dealt with adequately in the recorded account.

(2) The reference in subsection (1)(f) of section 137 to the admission of a recording includes a reference to the admission of part of the recording; and references in that section and this one to the video recording or to the witness's recorded account shall, where appropriate, be read accordingly.

(3) In considering whether any part of a recording should be not admitted under section 137, the court must consider–

   (a) whether admitting that part would carry a risk of prejudice to the defendant, and

   (b) if so, whether the interests of justice nevertheless require it to be admitted in view of the desirability of showing the whole, or substantially the whole, of the recorded interview.

(4) A court may not make a direction under section 137(1)(f) in relation to any proceedings unless–

   (a) the Secretary of State has notified the court that arrangements can be made, in the area in which it appears to the court that the proceedings will take place, for implementing directions under that section, and

   (b) the notice has not been withdrawn.

(5) Nothing in section 137 affects the admissibility of any video recording which would be admissible apart from that section.

139 Use of documents to refresh memory

(1) A person giving oral evidence in criminal proceedings about any matter may, at any stage in the course of doing so, refresh his memory of it from a document made or verified by him at an earlier time if–

   (a) he states in his oral evidence that the document records his recollection of the matter at that earlier time, and

   (b) his recollection of the matter is likely to have been significantly better at that time than it is at the time of his oral evidence.

(2) Where–

   (a) a person giving oral evidence in criminal proceedings about any matter has previously given an oral account, of which a sound recording was made, and he states in that evidence that the account represented his recollection of the matter at that time,

   (b) his recollection of the matter is likely to have been significantly better at the time of the previous account than it is at the time of his oral evidence, and

    (c)   a transcript has been made of the sound recording,

he may, at any stage in the course of giving his evidence, refresh his memory of the matter from that transcript.

140 Interpretation of Chapter 3

In this Chapter–

"criminal proceedings" means criminal proceedings in relation to which the strict rules of evidence apply;

"defendant", in relation to criminal proceedings, means a person charged with an offence in those proceedings;

"document" means anything in which information of any description is recorded, but not including any recording of sounds or moving images;

"oral evidence" includes evidence which, by reason of any disability, disorder or other impairment, a person called as a witness gives in writing or by signs or by way of any device;

"video recording" means any recording, on any medium, from which a moving image may by any means be produced, and includes the accompanying sound-track.

141 Saving

No provision of this Part has effect in relation to criminal proceedings begun before the commencement of that provision.

PART 14

GENERAL

330 Orders and rules

(1) This section applies to–

    (a) any power conferred by this Act on the Secretary of State to make an order or rules;

    (b) the power conferred by section 168 on the Lord Chancellor to make an order.

(2) The power is exercisable by statutory instrument.

(3 The power–

    (a) may be exercised so as to make different provision for different purposes or different areas, and

    (b) may be exercised either for all the purposes to which the power extends, or for those purposes subject to specified exceptions, or only for specified purposes.

(4) The power includes power to make–

    (a) any supplementary, incidental or consequential provision, and

    (b) any transitory, transitional or saving provision,

which the Minister making the instrument considers necessary or expedient.

(5 A statutory instrument containing–

    (a) an order under any of the following provisions–

section 25(5),

section 103,

section 161(7),

section 178,

section 197(3),

section 223,

section 246(5),

section 260,

section 267,

section 269(6),

section 281(2),

section 283(1),

section 291,

section 301(5),

section 325(7), and

paragraph 5 of Schedule 31,

(b)   an order under section 336(3) bringing section 43 into force,

(c)   an order making any provision by virtue of section 333(2)(b) which adds to, replaces or omits any part of the text of an Act, or

(d)   rules under section 240(4)(a),

may only be made if a draft of the statutory instrument has been laid before, and approved by a resolution of, each House of Parliament.

(6)   Any other statutory instrument made in the exercise of a power to which this section applies is subject to annulment in pursuance of a resolution of either House of Parliament.

(7)   Subsection (6) does not apply to a statutory instrument containing only an order made under one or more of the following provisions—

section 202(3)(b),

section 215(3),

section 253(5),

section 325(6)(i), and

section 336.

331 Further minor and consequential amendments

Schedule 36 (further minor and consequential amendments) shall have effect.

332 Repeals

Schedule 37 (repeals) shall have effect.

333 Supplementary and consequential provision, etc.

(1) The Secretary of State may by order make—

(a) any supplementary, incidental or consequential provision, and

(b)   any transitory, transitional or saving provision,

which he considers necessary or expedient for the purposes of, in consequence of, or for giving full effect to any provision of this Act.

(2)   An order under subsection (1) may, in particular—

  (a)   provide for any provision of this Act which comes into force before another such provision has come into force to have effect, until that other provision has come into force, with such modifications as are specified in the order, and

  (b)   amend or repeal—

    (i)   any Act passed before, or in the same Session as, this Act, and

    (ii)   subordinate legislation made before the passing of this Act.

(3)   Nothing in this section limits the power by virtue of section 330(4)(b) to include transitional or saving provision in an order under section 336.

(4)   The amendments that may be made under subsection (2)(b) are in addition to those made by or under any other provision of this Act.

(5)   In this section "subordinate legislation" has the same meaning as in the Interpretation Act 1978 (c. 30).

(6)   Schedule 38 (which contains transitory and transitional provisions and savings) shall have effect.

336 Commencement

(1)   The following provisions of this Act come into force on the passing of this Act—

  section 168(1) and (2),

  section 183(8),

  section 307(1) to (3), (5) and (6),

  section 330,

  section 333(1) to (5),

  sections 334 and 335,

  this section and sections 337, 338 and 339, and

  the repeal in Part 9 of Schedule 37 of section 81(2) and (3) of the Countryside and Rights of Way Act 2000 (c. 37) (and section 332 so far as relating to that repeal), and

  paragraphs 1 and 6 of Schedule 38 (and section 333(6) so far as relating to those paragraphs).

(2) The following provisions of this Act come into force at the end of the period of four weeks beginning with the day on which this Act is passed—

Chapter 7 of Part 12 (and Schedules 21 and 22);

section 303(b)(i) and (ii);

paragraphs 42, 43(3), 66, 83(1) to (3), 84 and 109(2), (3)(b), (4) and (5) of Schedule 32 (and section 304 so far as relating to those provisions);

Part 8 of Schedule 37 (and section 332 so far as relating to that Part of that Schedule).

(3) The remaining provisions of this Act come into force in accordance with provision made by the Secretary of State by order.

(4) Different provision may be made for different purposes and different areas.

339 Short title

This Act may be cited as the Criminal Justice Act 2003.

SCHEDULE 37

Section 332

REPEALS

PART 6

HEARSAY EVIDENCE

Short title and chapter	Extent of repeal
Registered Designs Act 1949 (c. 88)	In section 17, in subsection (8) the words "Subject to subsection (11) below," and in subsection (10) the words ", subject to subsection (11) below,".
Patents Act 1977 (c. 37)	In section 32, in subsection (9) the words "Subject to subsection (12) below," and in subsection (11) the words ", subject to subsection (12) below,".
Criminal Justice Act 1988 (c. 33)	Part 2. Schedule 2. In Schedule 13, paragraphs 2 to 5. In Schedule 15, paragraph 32. In Schedule 4, paragraph 6(2)
Finance Act 1994 (c. 9)	Section 22(2)(b). In Schedule 7, paragraph 1(6)(b).
Value Added Tax Act 1994 (c. 23)	In Schedule 11, paragraph 6(6)(b).
Criminal Justice and Public Order Act 1994 (c. 33)	In Schedule 9, paragraph 31.

Civil Evidence Act 1995 (c.38)	In Schedule 1, paragraph 12.
Finance Act 1996 (c. 8)	In Schedule 5, paragraph 2(6)(a).
Criminal Procedure and Investigations Act 1996 (c. 25)	In Schedule 1, paragraphs 28 to 31.
Crime and Disorder Act 1998 (c.37)	In Schedule 3, paragraph 5(4).
Youth Justice and Criminal Evidence Act 1999 (c.23)	In Schedule 4, paragraph 16.
Finance Act 2000 (c.17)	In Schedule 6, paragraph 126(2)(a).
Finance Act 2001 (c.9)	In Schedule 7, paragraph 3(2)(a).
Crime (International Cooperation) Act 2003 (c. 32)	In section 9(4), the words "section 25 of the Criminal Justice Act 1988 or".

Index

Admissions, agents made by, hearsay exception relating to, 2.3.2.9, 2.4.2.7.17

    exclusionary discretion and, 2.3.2.9

Age, hearsay exception relating to, 2.3.2.4

Agents, admissions made by, hearsay exception relating to see *admissions*

Agreement, admission of hearsay evidence by 2.1

    criminal proceedings, in, 2.5

    multiple hearsay, and, 2.5, 2.7.1, 2.7.1.2

    notice, giving of, and, 2.5

    retrial, at, 2.4.1.4

    rules of court, and, 2.5, 2.7.7

Aids to communication, 1.4.2

Bankers' books,

    definition of, 2.4.2.4

    hearsay exception relating to, 2.4.2.4

Birth, date or place of, hearsay exception relating to, 2.3.2.3

Burden of proof

    admissibility of evidence, 1.6.2.1, 1.7.2, 1.8.2

    burden of proving that evidence does not fall within the ambit of the hearsay rule, 1.6.2.1, 1.7.2, 1.8.2

    business documents, hearsay exception relating to (section 117) and, 2.2.2.2, 2.2.2.2.5

    competence of witnesses relating to, 2.7.2, 2.7.2.3

    confessions and, 2.2.7.2, 2.4.2.7.2, 2.4.2.7.3, 2.4.2.7.4

    exclusionary discretion and, 2.2.2.2.5

    required capability and, 2.7.2, 2.7.2.3

    unavailable witnesses, hearsay exception relating to, and, (section 116), 2.2.1.2, 2.2.1.2.7, 2.2.1.2.9

Business documents, hearsay exception relating to (section 117

    burden of proof and, see *burden of proof*

    committal proceedings and, 2.2.2.1

    confessions and, 2.2.2.1

    credibility and, 2.2.2.2.3, 2.7.3

    criminal investigations, statement prepared for purposes of, and, 2.2.2.2.4

    criminal proceedings, statement prepared for purposes of, and, 2.2.2.2.4

    custody records as, 2.2.2.2.4

    documents created in the course of a business and, 2.2.2.1, 2.2.2.2, 2.2.2.2.3

    documents, definition of for the purposes of Chapter 2 of Part 11 of the 2003 Act and, see *documents*

    documents, doubtful reliability of, 2.2.2.1, 2.2.2.2.5

    documents received in the course of a business and, 2.2.2.1, 2.2.2.2, 2.2.2.2.3

    exclusionary discretion and, 2.2.2.1, 2.2.2.2, 2.2.2.2.3, 2.2.2.2.5, 2.7.5

    expert evidence and, 2.2.8.2

    expert reports and, 2.2.2.1

    generally, 2.2.2, 2.2.2.1, 2.2.2.2, 2.2.2.2.1, 2.2.2.2.2, 2.2.2.2.3, 2.2.2.2.4, 2.2.2.2.5

    fear and, 2.2.2.1

    intermediaries and, 2.2.2.2, 2.2.2.2.1, 2.2.2.2.2, 2.2.2.2.3

letters of request, and,
2.2.2.1

memory refreshing
documents and, 2.2.2.2.4

multiple hearsay and,
2.2.2.2.2, 2.7.1.1,

opinion evidence and,
2.2.2.1, 2.2.2.2.2

person who cannot
reasonably be expected to
recollect the matters dealt
with therein, 2.2.2.2.4

person who creates or
receives, 2.2.2.1, 2.2.2.2,
2.2.2.2.1, 2.2.2.2.2,
2.2.2.2..3

required capability, maker of
hearsay statement (and
others) of, 2.2.1.1, 2.2.2.1,
2.2.2.2.2, 2.7.2, 2.7.2.1,
2.7.2.2, 2.7.2.4

retrial, evidence at, and,
2.2.2.1

standard of proof and,
2.2.2.2

statements contained in
documents, and, see
documents

stopping the case and,
2.2.2.1

statements contained in
documents, and, see
documents

supplier of information
contained in statement
and, 2.2.2.1, 2.2.2.2,
2.2.2.2.1, 2.2.2.2.2,
2.2.2.2.3

transcripts as, 2.2.2.2.4

unfitness to attend and,
2.2.1.2.5

Character, hearsay exception
relating to, 2.3.2.5

Circumstantial evidence

implied assertions as, 1.7.1

Co-accused

confessions made by, 2.2.7,
2.2.7.1, 2.2.7.2, 2.4.2.7,
2.4.2.7.6

Collateral matters

credibility and, 2.7.3

Committal proceedings,

admissibility of evidence in,
repeal of hearsay
exception relating to,
2.4.1.1

business documents, hearsay
exception relating to
(section 117) and, see
business documents

depositions admitted at,
repeal of hearsay
exception relating to,
2.4.1.2

unavailable witnesses,
hearsay exception relating
to and, 2.2.1.1

written statements admitted
at, repeal of hearsay
exception relating to,
2.4.1.2

Common enterprise, statements
made by parties, hearsay
exception relating to, 2.3.2.10

Common purpose,

statements made in
furtherance of, see
common enterprise

Competence

business documents, hearsay
exception relating to
(section 117, and, see
business documents

expert witnesses of, 2.2.8.2

required capability and,
2.7.2.2,

section 117, for purposes of,
see *business documents*

unavailable witnesses,
hearsay exception relating
to (section 116) and, see
hearsay exceptions

Computers

    hearsay, rule against, and,
      1.9.1, 1.9.2.1, 1.9.2.2

    hard disc, document as,
      2.2.2.2.1, 2.2.2.2.3

    presumption as to proper
      operation thereof, 1.9.3

    real evidence and, 1.9.1

    weight of evidence and,

Confessions

    Admissibility of, 2.2.7,
      2.2.7.1, 2.2.7.2, 2.3.2.8,
      2.4.2.7, 2.4.2.7.2, 2.4.2.7.3,
      2.4.2.7.4, 2.4.2.7.5,
      2.4.2.7.6, 2.4.2.7.7,
      2.4.2.7.8, 2.4.2.7.9,
      2.4.2.7.10, 2.4.2.7.11

    adoption by third party of,
      2.4.2.7.10

    agents, admissions made by,
      hearsay exception relating
      to, see *admissions*

    burden of proof see
      burden of proof

    business documents, hearsay
      exception relating to
      (section 117) and, see
      business documents

    co-accused, excluded
      confession made by as

    co-defendant
      adoption by, 2.4.2.7.10
      implicating, 2.4.2.7.10

    conduct, made by, 2.4.2.7.1

    defence, admissibility for,
      2.2.7, 2.2.7.1, 2.2.7.2,
      2.4.2.7, 2.4.2.7.6

    defence evidence, see *co-accused*

    definition of, 2.4.2.7.1

    editing of, 2.2.4.7.2,
      2.4.2.7.10

    excluded confessions,

    evidence of accused's mode
      of speech, writing or
      expression and, 2.4.2.7.14

    facts discovered in
      consequence thereof,
      2.4.2.7.13

    exclusionary discretion and,
      2.2.7.1, 2.2.7.2, 2.4.2.7,
      2.4.2.7.5, 2.4.2.7.5,
      2,4,2,7,13, 2.4.2.7.15

    hearsay source, confession
      based upon knowledge
      derived from, 2.4.2.7.7

    human rights and, 2.4.2.7.1,
      2.4.2.7.16

    inclusionary discretion
      (section 114(1)(d) "safety
      valve", and, 2.4.2.7.7,
      2.4.2.7.9, 2.2.4.2.7.11
      (section 121(1)(c)
      (multiple hearsay) and,
      2.4.2.7.7

    inconsistent statements as,
      2.2.3.2, 2.2.7.1, 2.2.7.2,
      2.4.2.7.1

    mentally handicapped
      persons, confessions made
      by, 2.4.2.7.15

    mixed statements,

    confessions, as, 2.4.2.7.11
      preserved common law
      hearsay exceptions relating
      to, 2.3.2.8

    multiple hearsay and, 2.4.2.7,
      2.4.2.7.7, 2.4.2.7.7

    nature of, 2.4.2.7.1

    opinion evidence and,
      2.4.2.7.8

    oppression and, 2.2.4.7.2,
      2.4.2.7.3,

    definition of, 2.4.2.7.3

    preserved common law
      hearsay exceptions relating
      to, 2.3.2.8

    prosecution, admissibility
      for, 2.3.2.8, 2.4.2.7,
      2.4.2.7.2, 2.4.2.7.3,
      2.4.2.7.4, 2.4.2.7.5,
      2.4.2.7.7, 2.4.2.7.8,
      2.4.2.7.9, 2.4.2.7.10,
      2.4.2.7.11

    relevance of, 2.4.2.7.2,
      2.4.2.7.9

    standard of proof and,
      2.2.7.2, 2.4.2.7.3, 2.4.2.7.4

stopping the case and,
2.4.2.7, 2.4.2.7.15

third parties, made by
2.4.2.7, 2.4.2.7.9

unavailable witnesses,
hearsay exception relating
to and, 2.2.1.1

unreliability of. 2.2.4.7.2,
2.4.2.7.4

voir dire, 2.4.2.7.12

common law discretion and,
2.4.2.7.12

magistrates' courts in,
2.4.2.7.12

making of confession and,
2.4.2.7.12

truth of confession and,
2.4.2.7.12

Consistent statements

corroboration as, 2.2.4.3.3

credibility and, 2.7.3

criminal proceedings,

exceptions to exclusionary
rule, 2.2.4.1, 2.2.4.2,
2.2.4.2.1, 2.2.4.2.2,
2.2.4.2.3, 2.2.4.2.4,
2.2.4.2.5, 2.2.4.2.6

exclusionary discretion,
2.2.4.3

exclusionary rule, 2.2.4.1

exculpatory statements made
to the police, 2.2.4.2.3,
2.2.4.3

exhibits, as, 2.4.2.3

generally, , 2.2.4, 2.2.4.1,
2.2.4.2, 2.2.4.2.1, 2.2.4.2.2,
2.2.4.2.3, 2.2.4.2.4,
2.2.4.2.5, 2.2.4.2.6, 2.2.4.3,
2.2.4.3.1, 2.2.4.3.2,
2.2.4.3.3

hearsay exceptions relating
to (section 120), 2.2.4,
2.2.4.3, 2.2.4.3.1, 2.2.4.3.2,
2.2.4.3.3

identification, consistent
statements concerning as,
2.2.4.2.2, 2.2.4.3, 2.2.4.3.2,
2.2.6

inclusionary discretion and,
2.2.4.3.3

incriminating articles,
persons found in
possession thereof,
2.2.4.2.6, 2.2.4.3

independent evidence,
2.2.4.2.4, 2.2.4.3.3

multiple hearsay and.
2.2.4.3, 2.7.1.1

opinion evidence and,
2.2.4.3

re-examination in relation
to, residual discretion to
permit, 2.2.4.2

recent complaints, 2.2.4.3

recent fabrication,
suggestions of during
cross-examination and,
2.2.4.2.1, 2.2.4.3, 2.2.4.3.1

recently stolen goods,
statements made by
persons found in
possession thereof,
2.2.4.2.6, 2.2.4.3

required capability of maker
and, 2.2.4.3, 2.7.2, 2.7.2.4

res gestae, statements
forming part thereof,
2.2.4.2.5, 2.2.4.3

sexual offences, voluntary
complaints made at the
first reasonable
opportunity, 2.2.4.2.4,
2.2.4.3, 2.2.4.3.3

supporting evidence and,
2.2.4.3.3

Conspiracy, statements made by
parties, hearsay exception
relating to, see *common enterprise*

Contemporaneity,

Memory refreshing and,
2.2.5.1, 2.2.5.2.1, 2.2.6

Contemporaneous actions,
hearsay exception relating to,
2.3.2.7, 2.3.2.7.2

Copy

definition of, 2.7.6

proof of contents of documents by, 2.7.6, 2.7.6.1

secondary evidence as, 2.7.6, 2.7.6.1

Corroboration

consistent statements as, see *consistent statements*

Credibility

business documents, hearsay exception relating to (section 117) and, see *business documents*

collateral matters and, see *collateral matters*

common law hearsay exceptions and, 2.3.1, 2.7.3

consistent statements and, see *consistent statements*

discretion (under section 124(3)) and, 2.7.3

exclusionary discretion and, 2.7.5.1

expert witnesses of, 2.2.8.2

human rights and, 2.8.2

implied assertions and, 2.7.3.1

inconsistent statements and, 2.7.3

maker of hearsay statement and, 2.7.3

statutory exceptions to hearsay rule not created by the 2003 Act and, 2.4.2, 2.7.3

Criminal proceedings,

definition of for the purposes of Chapter 2 of Part 11 of the 2003 Act, 1.4.1

Cross-examination

hostile witnesses of, 2.2.3.1.1

human rights and, 2.8.2

inconsistent statements in relation to, 2.2.3.1.1, 2.2.3.1.2

Death,

hearsay exceptions and, 2.2.1.2.4, 2.3

Depositions,

admissible under paragraph 5(3) of Schedule 3 to Crime and Disorder Act 1998, repeal of paragraph 5(4) by 2003 Act, 2.4.1.3

child victims, hearsay exception relating to, 2.4.2.3

repeal of hearsay exception relating to, see *committal proceedings*

Documents

computer hard disc as, see *computers*

Copies of, 2.7.6, 2.7.6.1

copy, definition of, see copy

created in the course of a business, see *business documents*

received in the course of a business, see *business documents*

definition of, for the purposes of Chapter 2 of Part 11 of the 2003 Act, 2.2.2.2.1

machines, produced by, proof of, 2.7.6

memory refreshing, 2.2.2.2.4

production of, 2.7.6

proof of contents, 2.7.6,
2.7.6.1

secondary evidence,
contents of, 2.7.6.1

statements contained in,
2.2.2.1, 2.2.2.2.1

statements made in, 2.2.1.1

video tape as, see 2.2.2.2.1

Dying declarations (hearsay exception
abolished by section 118), 2.3

E-fits

Admissibility at common
law, 1.11.1

Admissibility under the 2003
Act, 1.11.2

Editing, confessions of, see
confessions

Exclusionary discretion

agents, admissions made by,
see admissions

burden of proof and, see
burden of proof

business documents, hearsay
exception relating to
(section 117) and, see
business documents

common law discretion, 2.1,
2.2.1.1, 2.2.1.2.8, 2.2.2.1,
2.2.2.2.5, 2.4.2.7.5, 2.7.5.2

common law hearsay
exceptions and, 2.3.1

confessions and, see
confessions

consistent statements and,
see *consistent statements*

cross-examination see
cross-examination

expert evidence and, 2.2.8.2

human rights and, 2.8.2

implied assertions and,
2.7.5.1

inclusionary discretion
(section 114(1)(d) "safety
valve") and, 2.6, 2.7.5.2

inconsistent statements and,
2.2.3.2

machines, representations
made by and, 2.7.5.1

multiple hearsay and, 2.7.5.2

previous consistent
statements and, see
consistent statements

previous inconsistent
statements and, 2.2.3.2

previous statements made by
witnesses who cannot
reasonably be expected to
remember the matters to
which they relate well
enough to give oral
evidence thereof (section
120(1),(4),(6)) and, 2.2.6

res gestae, statements
forming part of, and
2.3.2.7, 2.3.2.7.1

statutory exceptions to
hearsay rule not created by
2003 Act and, 2.4.2

Criminal Justice Act 1988,
conferred by, 2.2.1.1,
2.2.1.2.8, 2.2.2.1, 2.2.2.2.5,
2.7.5, 2.7.5.2

Criminal Justice Act 2003,
conferred by, 2.2.1.1,
2.2.2.1, 2.2.2.2.3, 2.2.2.2.5,
2.2.8.2, 2.3.1, 2.4.2.7,
2.4.2.7.5, 2.4.2.7.5, 2.7.5,
2.7.5.1, 2.7.5.2

Police and Criminal
Evidence Act 1984,
conferred by, 2.2.1.1,
2.2.1.2.8, 2.2.2.1, 2.2.2.2.5,
2.3.2.10, 2.4.2.7.5,
2.4.2.7.13, 2.4.2.7.15,
2.7.5.2

unavailable witnesses,
hearsay exception relating
to (section 116) and and,
2.2.1.1, 2.2.1.2.8, 2.7.5

undue waste of time and,
2.7.5.1, 2.7.5.2

Exclusionary rule, hearsay rule as
1.1, 1.2.2

Exculpatory statements made to
the police, see *consistent
statements*

Exhibits

Consistent statements as,
2.2.4.3

inconsistent statement as,
2.2.3.2

memory refreshing
documents as, 2.2.5.2.2

previous inconsistent
statement as, 2.2.3.2

previous statements made by
witnesses who cannot
reasonably be expected to
remember the matters to
which they relate well
enough to give oral
evidence thereof (section
120(1),(4),(6)) as, 2.2.6

Expert evidence

business documents and, see
business doucments

competence and, see
competence

credibility and, 2.2.8.2

exclusionary discretion and,
see *exclusionary discretion*

expert reports, admissibility
of, 2.2.8.1, 2.2.8.2

expertise, body of, hearsay
exception relating to and,
2.3.2.11

hearsay evidence and, 2.2.8,
2.2.8.1, 2.2.8.2

hearsay exception relating to
(section 127), 2.2.8, 2.2.8.2

inclusionary discretion
(section 114(1)(d) "safety
valve" and, 2.2.8.2

machines and, 2.2.8.1

reports, admissibility of,
2.2.2.1, 2.4.2.2

required capability and,
2.2.8.2

research of others, hearsay
exception relating to and,
2.3.2.11

Expert reports

admissibility of, see
expert evidence

business documents, hearsay
exception relating
to(section 117) and, see
business documents

Expertise, body of, hearsay
exception relating to, see
expert evidence

Fear,

business documents
(hearsay exception relating
to (section 117) and, see
business documents

financial loss, of, 2.2.1.2.8

unavailable witnesses and,
2.2.1.1, 2.2.1.2.7

Films

hearsay rule and,

at common law, 1.10.1

under the 2003 Act, 1.10.2

Financial loss, fear of, see *fear*

General rights, hearsay exception
relating to existence of, 2.3.2.6

Goods etc, transmission of,
hearsay exception relating to,
2.4.2.5

Hearsay exceptions

Age, hearsay exception
relating to, see *age*

Agents, admissions made by,
hearsay exception relating
to, see *admissions*

Agreement, admission of
hearsay evidence by, see
*agreement, admission of
hearsay evidence by*

bankers' books, hearsay
exception relating to, see
bankers' books

birth, hearsay exception
relating to date of place of,
see *birth*

burden of proof and, see
burden of proof

business documents, hearsay
exception relating to
(section 117) see *business
documents*

character, hearsay exception
relating to, see *character*

child victims, depositions of,
as, see, depositions

children see *children*

civil proceedings in, 2.3,
2.3.2.1, 2.3.2.1, 2.3.2.2,
2.3.2.3, 2.3.2.4, 2.3.2.5,
2.3.2.6, 2.3.2.7, 2.3.2.8,
2.3.2.9, 2.3.2.11

committal proceedings,

admissibility of evidence in,
repeal of hearsay
exception relating to, see
committal proceedings

depositions admitted at,
repeal of hearsay
exception relating to, see,
committal proceedings

written statements admitted
at, repeal of hearsay
exception relating to, see,
committal proceedings

common enterprise,
statements made by
parties, hearsay exception
relating to, see *common
enterprise*

common law exceptions in
criminal proceedings, 2.1,
2.32.3.1, 2.3.2, 2.3.2.1,
2.3.2.2, 2.3.2.3, 2.3.2.4,
2.3.2.5, 2.3.2.6, 2.3.2.7,
2.3.2.7.1, 2.3.2.7.2,
2.3.2.7.3, 2.3.2.8, 2.3.2.9,
2.3.2.10, 2.3.2.11

credibility and, see *credibility*

exclusionary discretion and,
see *exclusionary discretion*

multiple hearsay and, 2.3.1

required capability and,
2.7.2.4

stopping the case and, 2.3.1

common purpose,
statements made by
parties, hearsay exception
relating to, see *common
enterprise*

competence of maker of hearsay of statement, see *competence*

conduct, duty to report or record, hearsay exception relating to (abolished by section 118), 2.3

confessions see *confessions*

consistent statements, relating to, see *consistent statements*

contemporaneous actions, hearsay exception relating to, 2.3.2.7, 2.3.2.7.1

copies, see *copies*

credibility of maker of hearsay statement of, see *credibility*

cross-examining maker of hearsay statement of, see *cross-examination*

death, hearsay exceptions relating to, see *death*

depositions and, see *depositions*

document, definition of, see *document*

documents, statements in see *documents*

documents, statements made in see *documents*

dying declarations see *dying declarations*

earlier proceedings, statements made in, 2.3

exclusionary discretion, see *exclusionary discretion*

expert evidence, relating to (section 127), see *expert evidence*

expert reports, admissibility of see *expert evidence*

expertise, body of, hearsay exception relating to and, see *expert evidence*

general rights, hearsay exception relating to existence of, see *general rights*

goods etc, transmission of, hearsay exception relating to, see *goods*

human rights,

identification, consistent statements concerning, see *consistent statements*

identification evidence, hearsay exception relating to, 2.2.4.3.2

inconsistent statements, hearsay exceptions relating to, 2.2.3.2

inclusionary discretion (section 114(1)(d) "safety valve")

common law exceptions to hearsay rule and, 2.3

competence and, 2.7.2.4

confessions and, see *confessions*

confessions, third parties made by, 2.4.2.7.9

consistent statements and, see *consistent statements*

exclusionary discretion and, see *exclusionary discretion*

expert evidence and, see *expert evidence*

generally, 2.1, 2.2

human rights and, 2.6, 2.8.1, 2.8.2

inconsistent statements and, 2.2.3.2

mixed statements and, 2.4.2.7.11

multiple hearsay and, 2.6, 2.7.1.4

required capability, maker of hearsay statement of, and, 2.6, 2.7.2.4

retrials and, 2.4.1.4

rules of court and, 2.7.7

unavailable witnesses, confessions made by and (section 116), 2.2.1.2.2

marriage, hearsay exception relating to existence of, 2.3.2.6

memory refreshing, hearsay exception relating to (section 120(1),(3)), 2.2.5.2.2

mental state, hearsay exception relating to, 2.3.2.7, 2.3.2.7.3

notice requirements, hearsay exceptions and, 2.7.7, 2.7.7.1

pecuniary interest, statements against, hearsay exception relating to (abolished by section 118), 2.3

pedigree, hearsay exception relating to, 2.3.2.6

person, identity of, hearsay exception relating to, 2.3.2.6

physical sensations, hearsay exception relating to, 2.3.2.7, 2.3.2.7.1

previous consistent statements, relating to, see *consistent statements*

previous inconsistent statements, hearsay exceptions relating to, 2.2.3.2

previous statements made by witnesses who cannot reasonably be expected to remember the matters to which they relate well enough to give oral evidence thereof (section 120(1),(4),(6)), 2.2.6

proprietary interest, statements against, hearsay exception relating to (abolished by section 118), 2.3

public documents, hearsay exception relating to, 2.3.2.2

public rights, hearsay exception relating to existence of, 2.3.2.6

published works, hearsay exception relating to, 2.3.2.2

recent complaints, see *consistent statements*

recent fabrication, suggestions of during cross-examination, see *consistent statements*

records, hearsay exception relating to, 2.3.2.3

res gestae, statements forming part of

contemporaneity and, 2.3.2.7, 2.3.2.7.2, 2.3.2.7.3

contemporaneous acts, hearsay exception relating to, 2.3.2.7, 2.3.2.7.2

contemporaneous physical state, hearsay exception relating to, 2.2.8.1, 2.3.2.7, 2.3.2.7.3

contemporaneous state of mind, hearsay exception relating to, 2.3.2.7, 2.3.2.7.3

exclusionary discretion and, see *exclusionary discretion*

generally, 2.3, 2.3.2.7, 2.3.2.7.1, 2.3.2.7.2, 2.3.2.7.3

intention and, 2.3.2.7..3

required capability and, 2.7.2.4

unusual, startling or dramatic events, hearsay exception relation to persons emotionally overpowered thereby, 2.3.2.7, 2.3.2.7.3

research of others, expert witnesses and, hearsay exception relating to, see *expert evidence*

retrial, admissibility of hearsay evidence at, 2.4.1.4

special measures directions and, 2.4.2.6

standard of proof and, 2.2.2.2, 2.2.7.2

state of mind, hearsay exception relating to, 2.3.2.7, 2.3.2.7.3

statutory exceptions in criminal proceedings,

created by the 2003 Act, 2.1, 2.2, 2.6

created by other statutes, 2.1, 2.4, 2.4.2, 2.4.2.1, 2.4.2.2, 2.4.2.3, 2.4.2.4, 2.4.2.5, 2.4.2.6, 2.4.2.7

repealed, replaced or modified by the 2003 Act, 2.4, 2.4.1, 2.4.1.1, 2.4.1.2, 2.4.1.3, 2.4.1.4

thing, identity of, hearsay exception relating to, 2.3.2.6

unavailable witnesses, hearsay exception relating to,

bodily condition, maker of hearsay statement of, and, 2.2.1.2.5

burden of proof and, see *burden of proof*

committal proceedings and, see *committal proceedings*

competence and, 2.2.1.2.1, 2.7.2, 2.7.2.4

confessions and, see *confessions*

death, maker of hearsay statement of, 2.2.1.2.4

exclusionary discretion and, see *exclusionary discretion*

fear, and, see *fear*

financial loss, fear of, see *fear*

generally, 2.2.1, 2.2.1.1, 2.2.1.2, 2.2.1.2.1, 2.2.1.2.2, 2.2.1.2.3, 2.2.1.2.4, 2.2.1.2.5, 2.2.1.2.6, 2.2.1.2.7

human rights and, 2.2.1.1, 2.2.1.2.8

identity of maker of hearsay statement and, 2.2.1.1, 2.2.1.2

identification evidence and, 2.2.4.3.2

inclusionary discretion (section 114(1)(d) "safety valve") and, see *hearsay exceptions*

leave, requirement of, 2.2.1.2.8

maker of hearsay statement cannot be found, 2.2.1.2.7, 2.2.1.2.9

mental condition, maker of hearsay statement of, and, 2.2.1.2.5

multiple hearsay and, 2.2.1.2.1, 2.2.1.2.2

opinion evidence and, 2.2.1.2.1

outside U.K, maker of hearsay statement, and, 2.2.1.2.6, 2.2.1.2.8

required capability of maker of hearsay statement of, 2.2.1.2.1, 2.7.2, 2.7.2.4

retrial, evidence at, and, 2.2.1.1, 2.4.1.4

special measures and, 2.2.1.2.8

standard of proof and, 2.2.1.2, 2.2.1.2.9

stopping the case and, 2.2.2.1, 2.2.1.2.7

unfitness to attend and, 2.2.1.2.5
witnesses who are dead or too ill to attend, hearsay exception relating to (abolished by section 118), 2.3

wills, contents of, hearsay exception relating to (abolished by section 118), 2.3

video recordings of witness' contemporaneous accounts, hearsay exception relating to (section 137), 2.2.9

inclusionary discretion and, 2.2.9

written statements, admissibility under Criminal Justice Act 1967, section 9, 2.4.2.1

expert reports as, 2.4.2.2

Hearsay, rule against

burden of proving that evidence does not fall within its ambit, see *burden of proof*

civil proceedings in, 1.6.2.4

E-fits and, see *e-fits*

films and, see *films*

implied assertions and
civil proceedings, in, 1.6.2.4

common law, at, 1.6.1, 1.7.1

under the 2003 Act, 1.6.2, 1.6.2.1, 1.6.2.2, 1.6.3.3, 1.6.4.4. 1.7.2

machines, evidence produced by and,

in civil proceedings, 1.9.4

at common law, 1.9.1

under the 2003 Act, 1.9.2, 1.9.2.1, 1.9.2.2

nature of at common law, 1.2.1

nature of under 2003 Act, 1.2.2

original evidence and, 1.5.1

photofits and,

at common law, 1.11.1

under the 2003 Act, 1.11.2

photographs and,

at common law, 1.10.1

under the 2003 Act, 1.10.2

records relied upon to prove
that events not recorded
did not take place and

at common law, 1.8.1

under the 2003 Act, 1.8.2

sketches and,

at common law, 1.11.1

under the 2003 Act, 1.11.2

statements made by
conduct, application to,

at common law, 1.3.1

under 2003 Act, 1.3.2

statements made during
other legal proceedings,
application to,

at common law, 1.4.1

under 2003 Act, 1.4.2

statements made in
documents, application to,

at common law, 1.3.1

under 2003 Act, 1.3.2

statements made orally,
application to,

at common law, 1.3.1

under 2003 Act, 1.3.2

tape recordings and,

at common law, 1.10.1

under the 2003 Act, 1.10.2

video recordings and,

at common law, 1.10.1

under the 2003 Act, 1.10.2

Hearsay statement

implied assertions and,
2.7.1.5

machines, statements made
by and, 2.7.1.5

multiple hearsay and, 2.7.1.5

section 121(2) definition,
2.7.1.5

Hostile witnesses,

civil proceedings,

cross-examination of, see
cross-examination

examination in chief see
examination in chief

generally, 2.2.3.1, 2.2.3.1.1,
2.2.3.2

inconsistent statements
made by, 2.2.3.1.1. 2.2.3.2

leading questions and,
2.2.3.1.1

memory refreshing and,
2.2.3.1.1

nature of, 2.2.3.1.1

previous inconsistent
statements of, 2.2.3.1.1.
2.2.3.2

re-examination,

spouse of accused as,

unfavourable witnesses,
2.2.3.1.1

Human rights

confessions and, see
confessions

credibility and, see *credibility*

defence evidence, exclusion
of, 2.8.1

examination of witnesses
and, 2.8.2

exclusionary discretion and, see *exclusionary discretion*

generally, 2.8

hearsay see *hearsay evidence*

hearsay exceptions see *hearsay exceptions*

inclusionary discretion (section 114(1)(d) "safety valve2) and, see *hearsay exceptions*

notice, giving of and, 2.7.2

prosecution evidence, admission of, 2.8.2

required capability and, 2.7.2.4

stopping the trial and, 2.8.2

tape recordings and, see

unavailable witnesses, hearsay exception relating to (section 116) and, see hearsay exceptions

Identification evidence

consistent statements and see *consistent statements*

hearsay exceptions and, see *hearsay exceptions,*

identification parades see *hearsay evidence*

implied assertions as, 1.7.1

photofits, see *hearsay*

previous consistent statements and, see *consistent statements*

previous identifications, evidence of, 2.2.4.3.2

sketches as, see *hearsay, rule against*

unavailable witnesses, hearsay exception relating to and, see hearsay exceptions

Implied assertions,

credibility and, see *credibility*

exclusionary discretion and, see exclusionary discretion

hearsay rule and, see hearsay, rule against

hearsay statements and, see *hearsay statement*

rules of court and, 2.7.7, 2.7.7.1

stopping the case and, 2.7.4.2

Inclusionary discretion,

section 114(1)(d) (safety valve) see *hearsay exceptions*

section 121(1)(c)) (multiple hearsay), 2.1, 2.7.1.3

video recordings of contemporaneous accounts, hearsay exception relating to (section 137) and, see hearsay exceptions

Inclusionary rule, hearsay rule as 1.1, 1.2.2

Inconsistent statements,

collateral matters see *collateral matters*

confessions as, see *confessions*

credibility and, see *credibility*

cross-examination in relation to, see *cross-examination*

exclusionary discretion and,
see exclusionary discretion

exhibits, as, *see exhibits*

generally, 2.2.3, 2.2.3.1,
2.2.3.1.1, 2.2.3.1.2,
2.2.3.1.3, 2.2.3.2

hearsay exceptions relating
to (section 119), see
hearsay exceptions

hostile witnesses of, see
hostile witnesses

inclusionary discretion
(section 114(1)(d)
"safety valve") and, see
hearsay exceptions

made by the makers of
hearsay statements,
2.2.3.1.3

multiple hearsay and,
2.2.3.2, 2.7.1.1

opinion evidence and,
2.2.3.2

proof of, 2.2.3.1.1, 2.2.3.1.2

required capability of maker
and, 2.2.3.2, 2.7.2, 2.7.2.4

written statements as,
2.2.3.1.2

Incriminating articles, statements
made by persons found in
possession thereof, see
consistent statements

Intention, statements of

See hearsay exceptions,
res gestae,

Intermediaries,

business doucments, heasray
exception relating to
(section 117) and, see
hearsay exceptions

Interpreters, 1.4.2

Leading questions

hostile witnesses and,
2.2.3.1.1

Leave, requirement of,

Criminal Justice Act 1988,
under, 2.2.1.1, 2.2.1.2.8,
2.7.5

unavailable witnesses,
hearsay exception relating
to (section 116) and, see
hearsay exceptions

Letters of request, business
documents, hearsay exception
relating to (section 117), see
business documents

Machines

admissibility of,
representations made by,
see *hearsay, rule against*

exclusionary discretion and
representations made by,
see *exclusionary discretion*

expert evidence and
representations made by,
see *expert evidence*

hearsay statements and
representations made by,
see *hearsay statement*

matters stated by,
1.6.2.1, 1.6.2.2, 1.6.2.3,
1.6.2.4, 1.7.2, 1.8.2

presumption as to proper
operation of, 1.9.3

real evidence and, 1.9.1

rules of court,
representations made by
and, 2.7.7, 2.7.7.1

stopping the case and
representations made by,
2.7.4.2

Marriage, hearsay exception
relating to existence of, see
hearsay exceptions

Matters stated,

machines and, see *machines*

to which Chapter 2 of Part
11 of the 2003 Act applies,
1.6.2, 1.6.2.1, 1.6.2.2,
1.6.2.3, 1.6.2.4, 1.7.2,
1.8.2, 2.3.1

Memory refreshing

admissibility of document at
common law, 2.2.5.1

at common law, 2.2.5.1

before the witness testifies,
2.2.5.1

business documents, hearsay
exception relating to
(section 117) and, see
business documents

civil proceedings,

contemporaneity,
2.2.5.1, 2.2.5.2.1

exhibits as, see *exhibits*

generally, 2.2.52.2.5.1,
2.2.5.2, 2.2.5.2.1,
2.2.5.2.2, 2.2.6

hearsay exception relating to
(section 120(1),(3)), see
hearsay exceptions

hostile witnesses and, see
hostile witnesses

multiple hearsay and,
2.2.5.2.2

opinion evidence and,
2.2.5.2.2

required capability, maker of
document of, 2.2.5.2.2

sound recordings and,
2.2.5.2.1

under the 2003 Act,
2.2.5.2, 2.2.5.2.1,

verification and 2.2.5.1

Mental state, hearsay exception
relating to, see *hearsay exceptions*

Mentally handicapped persons,
confessions made by, see
confessions

Mixed statements

confessions as, see *confessions*

inclusionary discretion
(section 114(1)(d)
"safety valve") and, see
hearsay exceptions

Multiple hearsay

agreement, admissibility of
by, 2.5, 2.7.1, 2.7.1.2

busines documents. Hearsay
exception relating to
(section 117) and, see
hearsay exceptions

common law hearsay
exceptions and, see
hearsay exceptions

confessions and, see
confessions

consistent statements and,
see *consistent statements*

exclusionary discretion and,
see *exclusionary discretion*

generally, 2.7.1

hearsay statements and, see
hearsay statement

inclusionary discretion

section 114(1)(d)
"safety valve" see hearsay
exceptions

(section 121(1)(c)) see
inclusionary discretion

inconsistent statements and,
see *inconsistent statements*

memory refreshing and, see
memory refreshing

previous consistent
statements and, see
consistent statements

previous inconsistent
statements and, see
inconsistent statements

previous statements made
by witnesses who cannot
reasonably be expected to
remember the matters to
which they relate well
enough to give oral
evidence thereof (section
120(1),(4),(6)) and, 2.2.6

unavailable witnesses,
hearsay exception relating
to and, see *hearsay
exceptions*

No case to answer, submission of,
2.7.4

Opinion Evidence

admissibility of under
hearsay exception, 2.1

business documents,
hearsay exception relating
to (section 117) and, see
business documents

confessions and, see
confessions

"evidential gap" and,
1.9.1, 2.2.8.1

consistent statements and,
see *consistent statements*

expert evidence see
expert evidence

hearsay see *hearsay evidence*

inadmissible, see 2.1, 2.2.8.1

inconsistent statements and,
see *inconsistent statements*

memory refreshing and, see
memory refreshing

previous consistent
statements and, see
consistent statements

previous inconsistent
statements and, see
inconsistent statements

previous statements made
by witnesses who cannot
reasonably be expected to
remember the matters to
which they relate well
enough to give oral
evidence thereof (section
120(1),(4),(6)) and, 2.2.6

unavailable witnesses,
hearsay exception relating
to and, see *hearsay
exceptions*

Oppression, confessions and, see
confessions

Oral evidence,

definition of for the
purposes of Chapter 2 of
Part 11 of the 2003 Act,
1.4.2, 2.2.1.2.1, 2.2.2.2.2

Original evidence, 1.5.1,

statements which form part
of res gestae as, 2.3.2.7

Pecuniary interest, statements
against, hearsay exception
relating to, see hearsay
exceptions

Pedigree, hearsay exception
relating to, see *hearsay exceptions*

Person, identity of, hearsay exception relating to, see *hearsay exceptions*

Photofits

    consistent statements, rule against, see *consistent statements*

    hearsay, rule against, see *hearsay, rule against*

    previous consistent statements, rule against, see *consistent statements*

Photographs see *hearsay, rule against*

Physical sensations, hearsay exception relating to, 2.3.2.7, 2.3.2.7.3

    Presumptions

    machines, proper operation of see *machines*

Presumptions of fact see *presumptions*

Previous consistent statements see *consistent statements*

Previous inconsistent statements see *inconsistent statements*

Previous statements made by witnesses who cannot reasonably be expected to remember the matters to which they relate well enough to give oral evidence thereof (section 120(1),(4),(6)), see hearsay exceptions

    exclusionary discretion and, see *exclusionary discretion*

    exhibits as, see *exhibits*

    multiple hearsay and, see multiple hearsay

opinion evidence and, see *opinion evidence*

required capability and, 2.2.6

Proof

    statements contained in documents of, see *documents*

Proprietary interest, statements against, hearsay exception relating to, see *hearsay exceptions*

Public documents, hearsay exception relating to, see *hearsay exceptions*

Public rights, hearsay exception relating to existence of, see *hearsay exceptions*

Published works, hearsay exception relating to, see *hearsay exceptions*

Real evidence,

    hearsay see *hearsay, rule against*

    implied assertions as, 1.7.1

    machines and, see *machines*

    photofits see *hearsay, rule against*

    photographs see *hearsay, rule against*

    sketches, see *hearsay, rule against*

    tape recordings see *hearsay, rule against*

    video recordings see *hearsay, rule against*

Recent complaints, see *consistent statements*

Recent fabrication of evidence, suggestions of during cross-examination, see *consistent statements*

Recent possession see *presumptions*

Recently stolen goods, statements made by persons found in possession thereof, see *consistent statements*

Records

    hearsay exception relating to, see *hearsay exceptions*

    relied upon to prove that events not recorded did not take place, see *hearsay, rule against*

Relevance

    confessions of, see *confessions*

consistent statements see *consistent statements*

    hearsay evidence see *hearsay evidence*

    inconsistent statements see *inconsistent statements*

Reputation

    character evidence see *character*

    hearsay evidence see *hearsay evidence*

    relevance see *relevance*

Required Capability, maker of hearsay statement (and others) of,

    burden of proof and. see *burden of proof*

    business documents, hearsay exception relating to (section 117), see *business documents*

common law hearsay exceptions and, see *hearsay exceptions*

consistent statements and, see *consistent statements*

expert witnesses of, see *expert evidence*

human rights and, see *human rights*

inclusionary discretion (section 114(1)(d) "safety valve") and, see *hearsay exceptions*

inconsistent statements and, see *inconsistent statements*

maker of memory refreshing document of, see *memory refreshing*

previous consistent statements and, see *consistent statements*

previous inconsistent statements and, see *inconsistent statements*

res gestae, statements forming part of and, see hearsay exceptions

standard of proof and, 2.7.2.3

unavailable witnesses, hearsay exception relating to (section 116), see hearsay exceptions

unusual startling or dramatic events, persons whose mindes were dominated by, and, see *hearsay exceptions*

Res gestae, statements forming part of

    consistent statements as, see *consistent statements*

    contemporaneous actions, hearsay exception relating to, see 2.3.2.7, 2.3.2.7.2

    exclusionary discretion and, see *exclusionary discretion*

    hearsay statements concerning, see *hearsay exceptions*

    identification parades and, see *hearsay exceptions*

    mental state, hearsay exception related to, see *mental state*

    original evidence as, see *original evidence*

    physical sensations, hearsay exception relating to, see *physical sensation*

    unusual, startling or dramatic events, hearsay exception relating to, 2.3.2.7, 2.3.2.7.1

Research of others, hearsay exception relating to and, see *expert evidence*

Retrial, evidence at

    Admissibility of hearsay evidence at, see *hearsay exceptions*

    unavailable witnesses, hearsay exception relating to and, see hearsay exceptions

Rules of court

    Agreement, admission of hearsay evidence by, and, see *agreement*

implied assertions and, see *implied assertions*

machines, representations made by and, see *machines*

notice requirements imposed by, 2.7.7

failure to comply, effects of, 2.7.7.1

human rights and, 2.8.2

"Safety valve" (section 114(1)(d) inclusionary discretion) see *hearsay exceptions*

"Second hand hearsay", see *multiple hearsay*

Self-serving statements see *consistent statements*

Sexual offences, voluntary complaints made at the first reasonable opportunity, see *consistent statements*

Sketches

    consistent statements, rule against and, see *consistent statements*

    hearsay, rule against and, see *hearsay, rule against*

    previous consistent statements, rule against and, see *consistent statements*

Sound recordings, memory refreshing and, see *memory refreshing*

Special measures directions, 1.4.1

    unavailable witnesses, hearsay exception relating to (section 116) and, see *hearsay exceptions*
    video recorded cross-examination, 2.4.2.6
    video recorded evidence in chief, 2.4.2.6

video-recorded
re-examination, 2.4.2.6

Standard of proof

admissibility of evidence,
1.6.2.1, 1.7.2, 1.8.2

burden of proof on defence,
1.6.2.1, 1.8.2

burden of proof on
prosecution, 1.6.2.1, 1.7.2,
1.8.2

business documents, hearsay
exception relating to
(section 117) and see
business documents

competence and, see
competence

confessions and, see
confessions

hearsay exceptions, see
hearsay exceptions

required capability and, see
required capability

unavailable witnesses,
hearsay exception relating
to and (section 116), see
hearsay exceptions

State of mind, hearsay exception
relating to, see *mental state*

Statement

contained in a document,
see *documents*

definition of for the
purposes of Chapter 2 of
Part 11 of 2003 Act, 1.3.2,
1.9.2.1, 1.10.2, 2.2.1.1,
2.2.2.1, 2.3.1, 2.7.4.2,
2.7.5.1, 2.7.6, 2.7.7, 2.7.7.1

in a document see *hearsay
exceptions*

made in a document see
hearsay exceptions

Stopping the case
(2003 Act section 125)

business documents, hearsay
exception relating to
(section 117) and, see
business documents

common law hearsay
exceptions and, see *hearsay
exceptions*

confessions and, see
confessions

generally, 2.7.4

human rights and, 2.8.2

implied assertions and, see
implied assertions

machines and, see *machines*

statutory exceptions to
hearsay rule not created by
2003 Act and, 2.4.2

unavailable witnesses,
hearsay exception relating
to (section 116), and,
2.2.1.2.7

Supporting evidence

Consistent statements as, see
consistent statements

Tape recordings

authenticity, see *authenticity*

hearsay as, see *hearsay,
rule against*

human rights and, see
human rights

proof of contents, see *proof*

Thing, identity of, hearsay
exception relating to, see
hearsay exceptions

*Turnbull guidelines see identification
evidence*

Unavailable witnesses,

>   hearsay exception relating to (section 116), see *hearsay exceptions*

Unconvincing evidence, see *stopping the case*

Undue waste of time, discretionary exclusion of hearsay evidence in context of, see *exclusionary discretion.*

>   Unfavourable witnesses see *hostile witnesses*

Unreliability, confessions of, see *confessions*

Unusual, startling or dramatic events, hearsay exception relating to persons emotionally overpowered by, see *res gestae*

Video recordings

>   authenticity, see *authenticity*
>
>   cross-examination see *cross-examination*
>
>   examination in chief see *examination in chief*
>
>   hearsay evidence as, see *hearsay, rule against*
>
>   human rights and, see *human rights*
>
>   oral evidence, proof of contents by, 2.7.6.1
>
>   real evidence as, see *real evidence*
>
>   special measures directions and, see *special measures directions*
>
>   witness' contemporaneous accounts of, hearsay exception relating to (section 137), see *hearsay exceptions*

Video tape

>   document as, see *documents*

Voir dire, see *confessions*

Witnesses

>   competence see *competence*
>
>   credibility see *credibility*
>
>   cross-examination see *cross-examination*
>
>   expert see *expert evidence*
>
>   hostile see *hostile witnesses*
>
>   human rights see *human rights*
>
>   identification see *identification*

Written statements, admissibility under Criminal Justice Act 1967, section 9, see hearsay exceptions

>   unfavourable see *unfavourable witnesses*